Copenha
Architect
Guide

Olaf Lind
Annemarie Lund

Arkitektens Forlag

1996

Copenhagen Architecture Guide
Arkitektens Forlag, Copenhagen, 1996
Authors: Olaf Lind and Annemarie Lund
Illustration editors: Kim Dirckinck-Holmfeld and Annemarie Lund
Secretary: Jacob Jessen
Translation: Martha Gaber Abrahamsen (introduction), Pete Avondoglio
Photographs: Søren Kuhn unless credited otherwise
Maps are reproduced with the permission of the National Survey and Cadastre (A 335-95) ©
and the City of Copenhagen Survey and Cadastre (reproduction permit 239/95)
Reproduction: F. Hendriksens Eftf.
Printed by Skive Bogtrykkeri
ISBN 87 7407 1629
Published with financial support from the Urban Renewal and Redevelopment Company Copenhagen,
Arbejdernes Kooperative Byggeforening (AKB), Boligselskabet KSB, Fagforeningernes Boligforening
(FB), Foreningen Socialt Boligbyggeri (FSB), KAB Bygge- og Boligadministration, and Lejerbo
Cover: Collage by Nils-Ole Lund

CONTENTS

Key

The Guide provides the category of building, year of construction, client, architect, landscape architect, and decoration, if any, together with main artist.
* denotes that the building/park is protected by law.
Map A, B, C, D, E, F, G, H and I are on a scale of 1:15.000. 1 cm is 150 m.
Map J are on scale of 1:150.000. 1 cm is 1.500 m.
Scales are given for most detail plans.

FOREWORD

This is the first guide to architecture in Copenhagen. Its publication was made possible thanks to a generous donation from the Urban Renewal and Redevelopment Company Copenhagen to the City of Copenhagen, represented by Mayor Jens Kramer Mikkelsen, The company's contribution to the celebration of Copenhagen as the Cultural Capital of Europe in 1996 is one whose benefits will last far longer than the year itself.

The more than 300 subjects were chosen as a collaborative effort by the Urban Renewal and Redevelopment Company Copenhagen; Niels Andersen, director; Freddy Avnby, architect; and Annemarie Lund and Olaf Lind, editors. Jørgen Sestoft, professor of the theory of architecture, and Lene Tranberg, architect, served as consultants when the final selection was made. Annemarie Lund was advised by Ib Asger Olsen, professor of landscape architecture, for this aspect of the guide.

The guide is divided by city quarter and period at one and the same time. The attentive reader will note that numbers jump within the various quarters, from A to J. The numbers consequently denote a chronological progression that permits the reader to judge the date of each subject. The choice of buildings was made from a rough list of about 600 subjects. Single-family houses were not included.

The authors and advisory group had a difficult time setting geographical limits, but largely confined themselves to Copenhagen and Frederiksberg Municipalities and Copenhagen County.

Various criteria served as the basis for the selection. Buildings that were considered pioneering in their day were chosen, but also typical examples of ordinary building. Special needs produce special types of buildings, and innovation in this respect was also used as a criteria, for example in the case of the "aula school." Finally, the most important parameter was architectural quality, as judged by the authors and advisory group.

The publishers would like to thank the contributors for their enthusiasm, and especially express our gratitude to the Urban Renewal and Redevelopment Company Copenhagen. We had cherished a wish to publish a guide of this type for some time, but not until it provided the necessary financial support was this made possible.

Kim Dirckinck-Holmfeld, February 1996

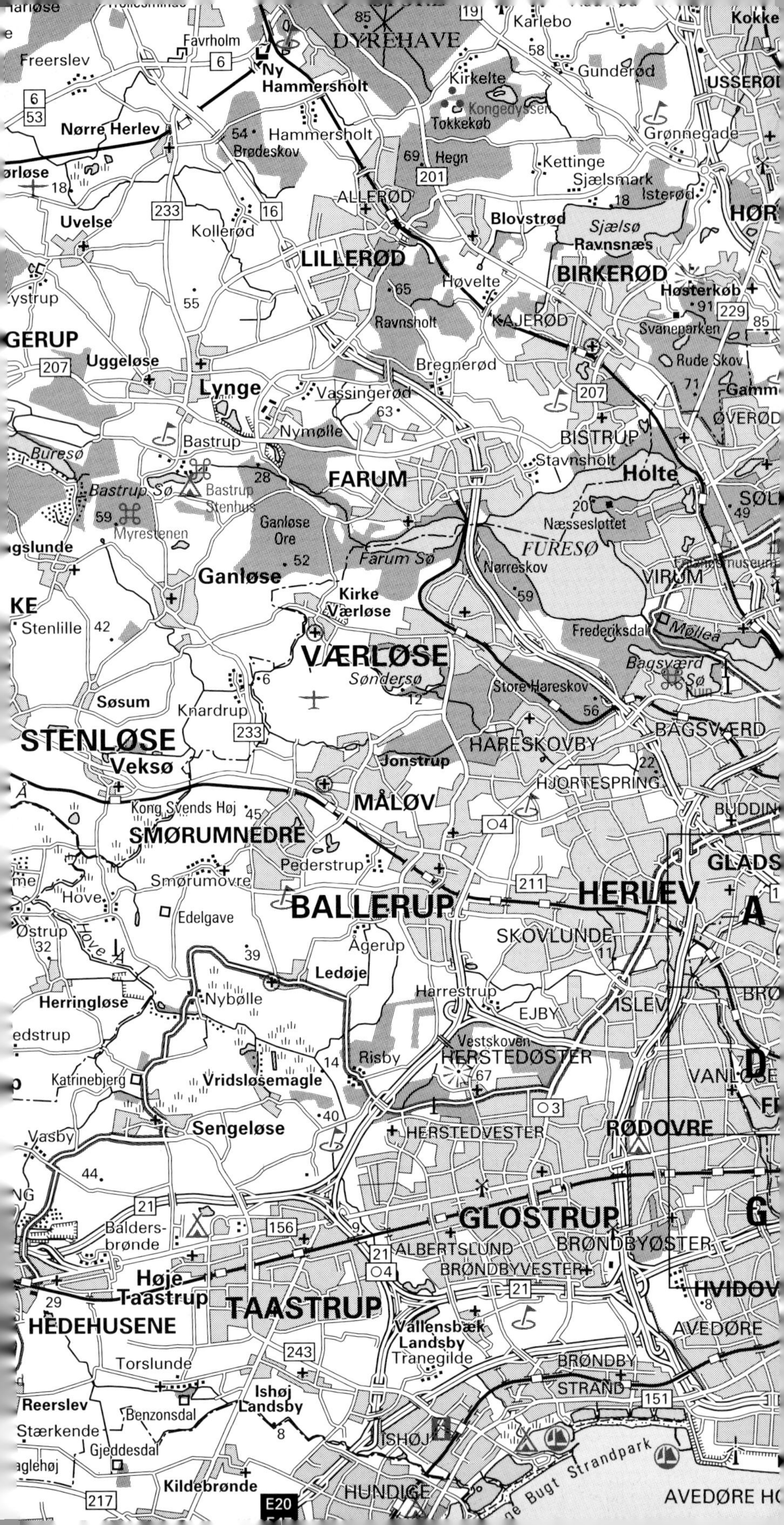

Favrholm
Freerslev
DYREHAVE
Karlebo
Kokke
Ny
Hammersholt
Kirkelte
Gunderød
USSERØD
Nørre Herlev
Hammersholt
Kongedyssen
Tokkekøb
Grønnegade
Brødeskov
Hegn
Kettinge
Sjælsmark
Isterød
ALLERØD
Blovstrød
Uvelse
Kollerød
Sjælsø
Ravnsnæs
LILLERØD
BIRKERØD
Høvelte
Høsterkøb
Ravnsholt
KAJERØD
Svaneparken
GERUP
Uggeløse
Lynge
Bregnerød
Rude Skov
Vassingerød
Nymølle
Bastrup
BISTRUP
ØVERØD
Buresø
FARUM
Stavnsholt
Holte
Bastrup Sø
Bastrup
Stenhus
Myrestenen
Ganløse
Ore
Næsseslottet
FURESØ
Farum Sø
Nørreskov
Ganløse
Kirke
Værløse
VIRUM
Stenlille
Frederiksdal
Mølleå
VÆRLØSE
Søndersø
Bagsværd
Sø
Søsum
Knardrup
Store Hareskov
STENLØSE
Veksø
HARESKOVBY
BAGSVÆRD
Jonstrup
HJORTESPRING
Kong Svends Høj
MÅLØV
SMØRUMNEDRE
Pederstrup
GLADS
Smørumovre
HERLEV
Hove
BALLERUP
Edelgave
SKOVLUNDE
Østrup
Ågerup
Ledøje
Nybølle
Harrestrup
Herringløse
EJBY
ISLEV
Vestskoven
Risby
HERSTEDØSTER
Katrinebjerg
Vridsløsemagle
VANLØSE
Sengeløse
HERSTEDVESTER
RØDOVRE
Vasby
GLOSTRUP
Balders-
brønde
ALBERTSLUND
BRØNDBYØSTER
BRØNDBYVESTER
Høje
Taastrup
TAASTRUP
HVIDOVRE
HEDEHUSENE
Vallensbæk
Landsby
Tranegilde
AVEDØRE
BRØNDBY
Torslunde
STRAND
Reerslev
Ishøj
Landsby
Benzonsdal
Stærkende
Gjeddesdal
ISHØJ
Strandpark
Kildebrønde
HUNDIGE
AVEDØRE HO
6
53
207
233
16
201
229
207
211
21
156
21
243
151
217
E20

Stjerneborg
VEN
Bäckviken
40
ØRESUND
LANDSKRONA
J
Rungsted
Rungstedlund
Smidstrup
Vedbæk
33
Jægersborg
Skodsborg
Hegn
NÆRUM
Raadvad
37
Eremitagen
Taarbæk
Jægersborg
Dyrehave
Galopbane
KLAMPENBORG
Dyrehavsbakken
BY
ORDRUP
SKOVSHOVED
Travbane
CHARLOTTENLUND
NTOFTE
Danmarks Akvarium
152
HELLERUP
19
B
C
Middelgrunds
Fort
Trekroner
Flakfort
KØBENHAVN
Refshaleøen
Kastellet
Prøvesten
E
F
CHRISTIANSHAVN
BERG
Tivoli
H
I
5
1.
SUNDBYERNE
E20
SALTHOLM
Nordre Røse
KASTRUP
Bella Center
1
2
TÅRNBY
DROGDEN
AMAGER
Tømmerup
4
-1
VESTAMAGER
E20
Store
Magleby

THAT COPENHAGEN TONE

Geological prologue

The geographic spread of the some 300 subjects in this guide reflects essential features in the history of Copenhagen. It is not surprising that most are located in the central urban area, showing that from the time the city emerged in the 12th century to the middle of the 19th, it was a clear unit, sharply separated from the world by solid fortifications. Seven centuries of building lie within this area, which also contains many of the buildings that are part of the Danish identity purely because of their historical significance.

The spread of subjects in this guide that lie outside the city ramparts – which were demolished in 1852 – is, if not surprising, then at least telling. Most are clearly located north of the city. In Trap Danmark (5th edition, 1959), Professor Axel Schou wrote about the importance of the ice age for Copenhagen's typography: "The great differences in landscape between the county's relief-rich northernmost region and the southeastern part, which is characterized by the alluvial plain that separates Copenhagen, Roskilde, and Køge, ... is explained by the curve ... in the course taken by the ice front. A seemingly minor detail in the last ice age's glacier topography here had momentous consequences for the qualitative evaluation of the present-day landscape with a view to cultivation, habitation – yes, even with regard to such small details as the choice of a destination for a Sunday outing."

This "relief-rich" northern area has for centuries attracted the people of the capital and the concept "outing" covers everything from luxurious 18th-century royal hunting

Copenhagen, 1587

lodges to a patch of contemporary grass in Dyrehaven park, where a Dane can sit with his beer. The north has been a pleasure area, in contrast to the heath west of Copenhagen and the coastal areas on Køge Bay and Amager, which have been put to more practical use. The use of the northern landscape for hunting, relaxation, and artistic inspiration left its traces as buildings that were to promote pleasure, something that for long periods had been the right of the royal family and nobility and later also of the better bourgeoisie. Summer houses were palaces, manors, and large villas that served as refuges from the stifling conditions in the crowded city behind the ramparts. Inspiring northern Zealand developed a tradition of good-quality, beautiful summer houses, often designed by the period's best architects. Painters and poets, especially in the Romantic Age in around 1800, did their part to make a place for northern Zealand in the national consciousness as the ideal of harmony between nature and culture.

This provides some of the explanation of why so many old buildings north of Copenhagen have been chosen for this guide. But the tradition of good building in this region continued even after the city ramparts were penetrated and more democratic building began. Or to put it in a different way: the more or less well-to-do Copenhagen builders at the end of the 19th century and in the 20th also preferred to settle in the lovely landscape to the north, and they frequently employed the day's best architects. Right up to the very present, the attractions and traditions of the north – which began as one of nature's whims in the ice age – have had a decisive influence on Copenhagen's building and urban planning.

The areas west and south of Copenhagen, put to more practical use, also developed their architecture throughout the centuries, but they managed without help from famous architects. Dragør in Amager (J 136) is an example of an unplanned town that developed in its own way in the course of the 18th century into a homogeneous unit which, after today's norms, is very good architecture. In the west and south, deliberately planned architecture left decisive marks during this century's explosive urban development. This growth especially took the form of completely new conurbations, such as the towns on Køge Bay, Albertslund, and Høje Taastrup, and major traffic facilities like Kastrup Airport.

Good architecture

The concept "good architecture" is an indefinable one that can thus comprise both anonymous buildings in a community and major projects designed by an architect who expresses both himself and a large, international clientele. This is a large field that is not fully elucidated in this guide because it covers a decidedly urban area in which deliberately planned architecture has dominated.

The choice of subjects for this guide was made spontaneously by a group of experts who then made adjustments to their selection after thorough discussions. The subjects can consequently be viewed as reflecting what a contemporary Danish group of experts considers to be good, distinctive architecture. The some 300 subjects do not, however, provide a sufficiently good picture of Copenhagen's best architecture. Many were left out after careful consideration because of space limitations. In addition to taking architectural quality into account, the experts also evaluated whether the subjects reflected a characteristic development when they were built with regard to form, technique, or their relationship to history and society. These aspects also expand our concept of what is good architecture, and in this respect Copenhagen and its environs have a wealth of examples. Within this field, architecture moves effortlessly between sublime art and buildings of historical interest. Here Copenhagen does not differ from other major cities. Nonetheless, Copenhagen's architecture – country manors from the 19th century, public housing from the 1920s, and contemporary commercial buildings – has its own special tone that can be distinguished from that of all other cities. The subjects in the guide were chosen in order to bring out this special Copenhagen tone as it is found in houses, parks, and plans, giving as many nuances as possible.

The merchants' harbor

The oldest building in the guide is the House of the Holy Ghost, erected in the latter half of the 15th century as the hospital of a monastery founded in 1296. The building is the oldest in Copenhagen that has been preserved in its entirety, and is consequently the city's oldest piece of architecture. But Copenhagen's history is much longer. There was evidently a trading post near present-day Slotsholm in around 800. The site was mentioned for the first time by Saxo Grammaticus in an account of the year 1026. A number of papal briefs from the end of the 12th century give it the Latin name Hafnia (harbor), corresponding to the oldest Danish name for the place: Hafn. Written sources from the 13th century give the name Køpmannæhafn (merchants' harbor), clearly the source of the city's present name, and showing that it was a trading post. The area around Hafn was owned by the landed gentry in the early Middle Ages. One landowner was the Bishop of Roskilde, Absalon, who was also a great warrior. In 1167, Absalon built a fortress at Hafn,which consequently gained military importance in the period's wars against the Wends. Remains of Absalon's fortress can be found under Christiansborg Palace, and its builder is considered the founder of Copenhagen.

After Absalon's death in 1201, his lands in Køpmannæhafn fell to the bishopric in Roskilde, which retained them for more than 200 years, until the king, Erik of Pomera-

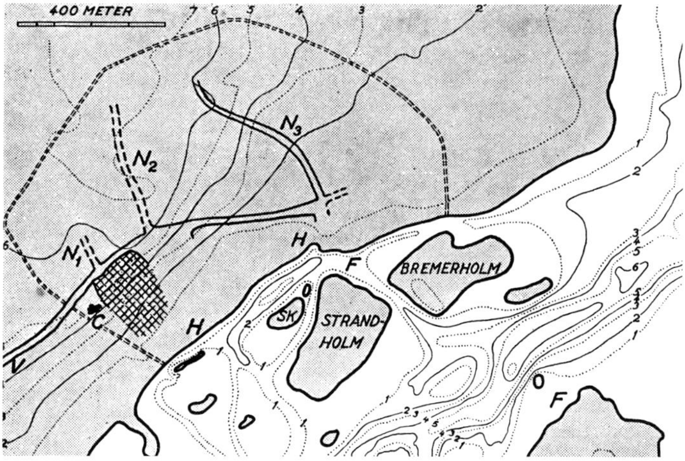

"Hafn" before Absalon

Copenhagen in around 1500

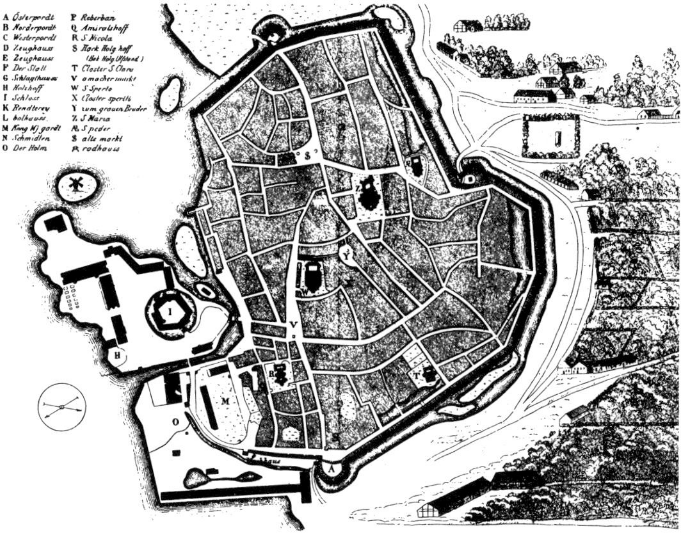

Copenhagen in around 1600

nia, captured the city in a coup in 1417. After the Reformation in the 16th century, when the state confiscated church property and the central administration had grown, the little town on the Sound was officially acclaimed the capital of the Kingdom of Denmark and Norway. At the time, Denmark also covered Scania, Halland, and Blekinge, east of the Sound, so the capital lay in the middle of the kingdom, but was smaller than Malmö, Næstved, Odense, and Viborg. The little capital had two exit roads, one in the southwest, about where present-day Vestergade runs, and another that followed the course of present-day Købmagergade. Staggered at Gammel Torv veje, the two roads met by a ferry and a square, present-day Højbro Plads and Amagertorv. The structure of the city itself at this point has consequently not changed since the Middle Ages. Then, as now, Amagertorv was the city's central market place, a high point on today's elongated market, the Strøget mall. And close by it, a bit west of the square, was the Church of the Holy Ghost, the monastery, and the House of the Holy Ghost, chronologically number one in this guide (F 1). Gothic architecture is represented only by this little hospital building.

Copenhagen's secular Medieval buildings are gone or survive only as ruins. Some are hidden, like the remains of Absalon's fortress under Christiansborg, where they are nonetheless accessible. Others can be seen above ground, such as the ruins of Jarmer's Tower on Jarmers Plads, named after the Wend chieftain Jaromar, who took part in one of the many conflicts between the bishopric in Roskilde and the king in the 13th century. The tower was was built in the 16th century, part of the city's Medieval fortifications, but in the 17th century it was covered by Christian IV's Western Ramparts. As a whole, fortifications were decisive for the formation of old Copenhagen, and especially during Christian IV's reign (1588-1648), the town was given a framework that still plays a role for its form and life. The largest single monument in the fortifications was the Citadel (F 11), which still gives a vivid impression of the ramparts' size and forms, but the Christianshavn Ramparts (I 15) also convey this carefully conceived past glory. The fortifications around the inner city and Christianshavn were built in several stages over the ensuing centuries, and when Copenhagen's days as a fortified city ended in 1856, this magnificent architectural work reflected the art of war and urban ideals of the Renaissance and the Baroque.

The great builders

Christian IV was in all ways a Renaissance prince. As a builder (and perhaps an architect) he created some of Copenhagen's largest and most valuable buildings, making Dutch Renaissance a characteristic style for the city. It can be seen in such buildings as Rosenborg Palace (F 3) and the Bourse (F 4), and the style of royal edifices was copied in town houses, as shown by the house on Amagertorv (F 6). The town houses on Strandgade (F 7) from the same period are more anonymous, although they also had decorations in the style of the day. Together with the buildings in Magstræde (F 13), the basic features of these buildings give us a picture of 17th-century Copenhagen. Christian IV was also an innovator when it came to ordinary housing. He made a decisive break with the familiar urban and housing patterns with the erection of Nyboder (F 9), intended to house the navy's permanent staff: ordinary people. For more than 350 years, the buildings have been a clear and strong source of inspiration for numerous Danish housing complexes. The Renaissance king made his most decisive mark, however, on urban planning. Copenhagen was expanded enormously under Christian IV with New Copenhagen, between Rosenborg Palace and the Citadel, and with the planning of the Christianshavn quarter, which was founded as an independent seaport in 1618 and was incorporated into Copenhagen in 1674. The plan for Christianshavn was drawn up by the Dutch fortifications engineer Johan Semp, who employed the theories of the Italian ideal cities. At the beginning of the 17th century, Christian IV had a naval

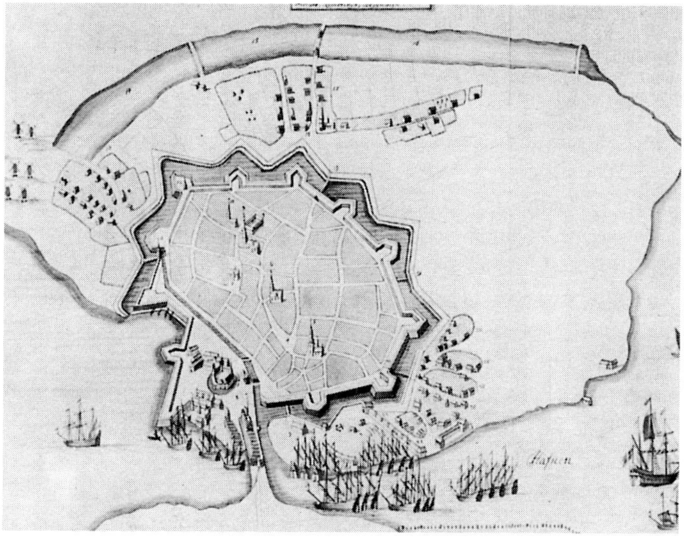

Copenhagen in Christian IV's time

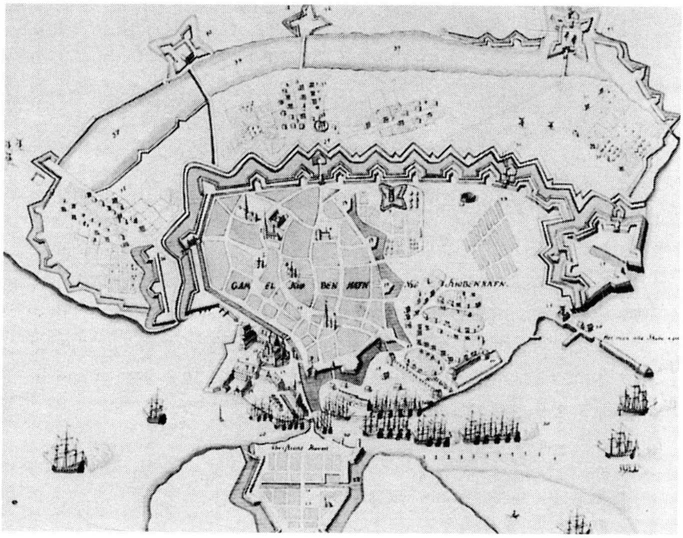

Copenhagen in 1654, after the death of Christian IV

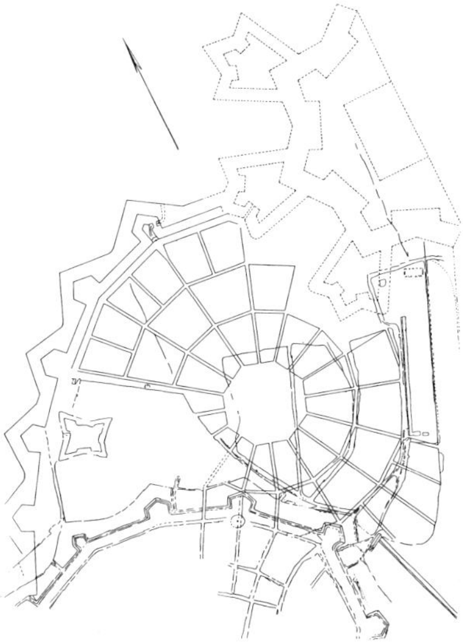

The octagonal plan

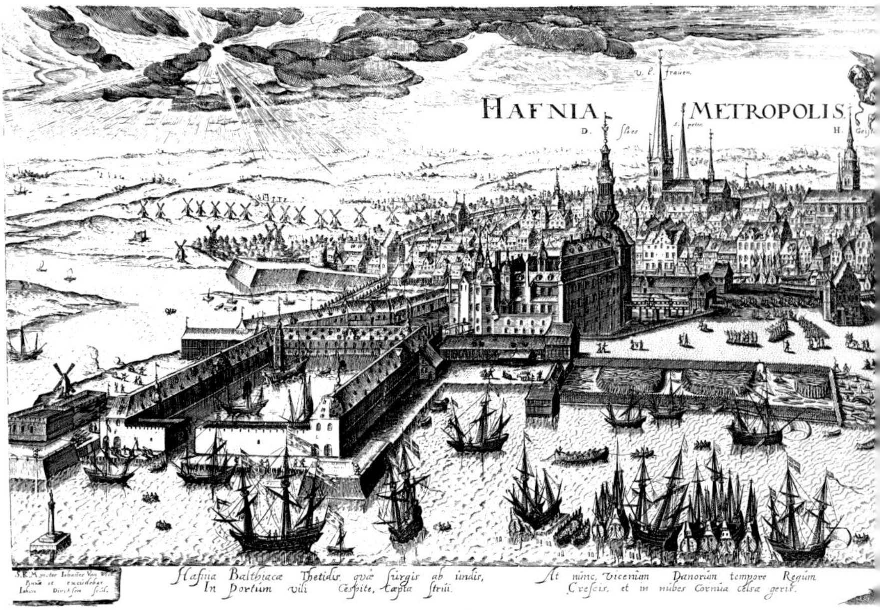

harbor built on a site occupied today by the Royal Library's garden. Built around the harbor were the Provision Yard and the Armory, and the entire complex made up what was called the marine arsenal.

At the end of the 17th century, the expanded city was fortified against the outside world with sturdy architectural symbols of church and state. The Church of Our Savior (F 17) was built in Christianshavn, Charlottenborg Palace (F 16) was the first major building on the newly designed Kongens Nytorv square (F 2), and the enormous ramparts of the Citadel were raised outside New Copenhagen. The Kingdom of Denmark and Norway had been harshly amputated when peace was concluded in 1658 and Scania, Halland, and Blekinge had to be ceded to the Swedes. Suddenly, the Danish capital was the kingdom's border town in the east, and the Citadel provided the necessary defense on that flank. The Reformed Church (F 18) was also built at this time and bears witness to a degree of religious tolerance in 17th-century Copenhagen. The opera house in Fredericiagade (F 20) gives us a glimpse of Copenhagen as a cultural city at the beginning of the 18th century, and the Red Mansion on Slotsholmen (F 21) from the same period was an administration building for the increasingly organized state, which since 1660 had been personified in the absolute monarch. One such monarch, Frederik IV, built a summer house on high Valby Hill west of the city in 1700. Over the decades, the house grew and was transformed into the stately Frederiksberg Palace (H 19), surrounded by romantic, popular Frederiksberg Gardens.

Fires and urban construction

Everything that urban planning, architecture, and the initiative of ordinary people had painstakingly built up could be destroyed in a few hours. This happened in Copenhagen's great conflagrations, the first of which broke out in 1728. The fire had plenty to feed on in the city's old half-timber houses. This provided a lesson for the future, and building was regulated to better resist fires. When the "conflagration houses" were built after 1728, Copenhagen changed its appearance, from half-timbered facades to at

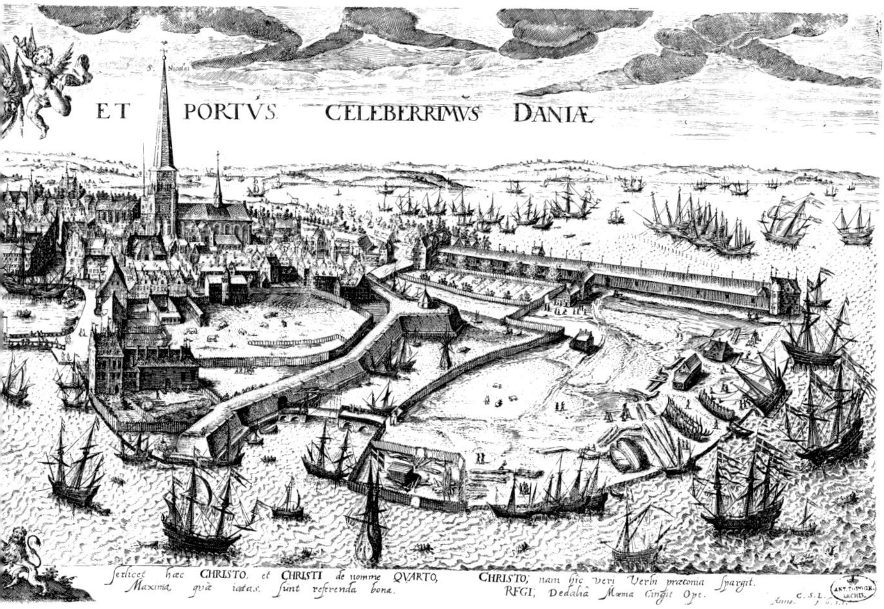

Prospect of Copenhagen in 1611, after Johan van Wick

Reesen's plan from 1611

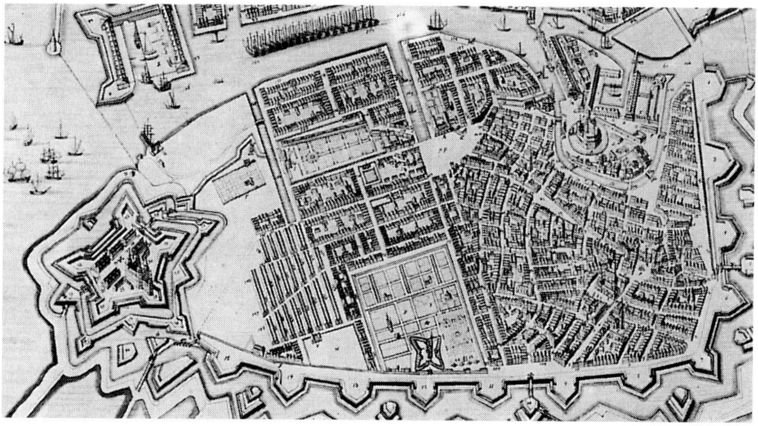

least street facades of plastered brick. A well-preserved example of these houses is a row of tall, narrow buildings with gable attics on Gråbrødre Torv (F 22). At the same time as the city was being rebuilt after the fire, the king and state made their mark with impressive architectural works. The first Christiansborg (F 25) was a Baroque palace, as large and magnificent as anything elsewhere in Europe, but it only stood for some 50 years before it was also consumed by fire. Christian VI's Christiansborg had hardly been finished before his successor, Frederik V, began to lay out an entirely new quarter, Frederiksstaden, in 1749. It was to be the city of the nobility and merchants, and both the urban plan and the buildings were the greatest achievement of Nikolai

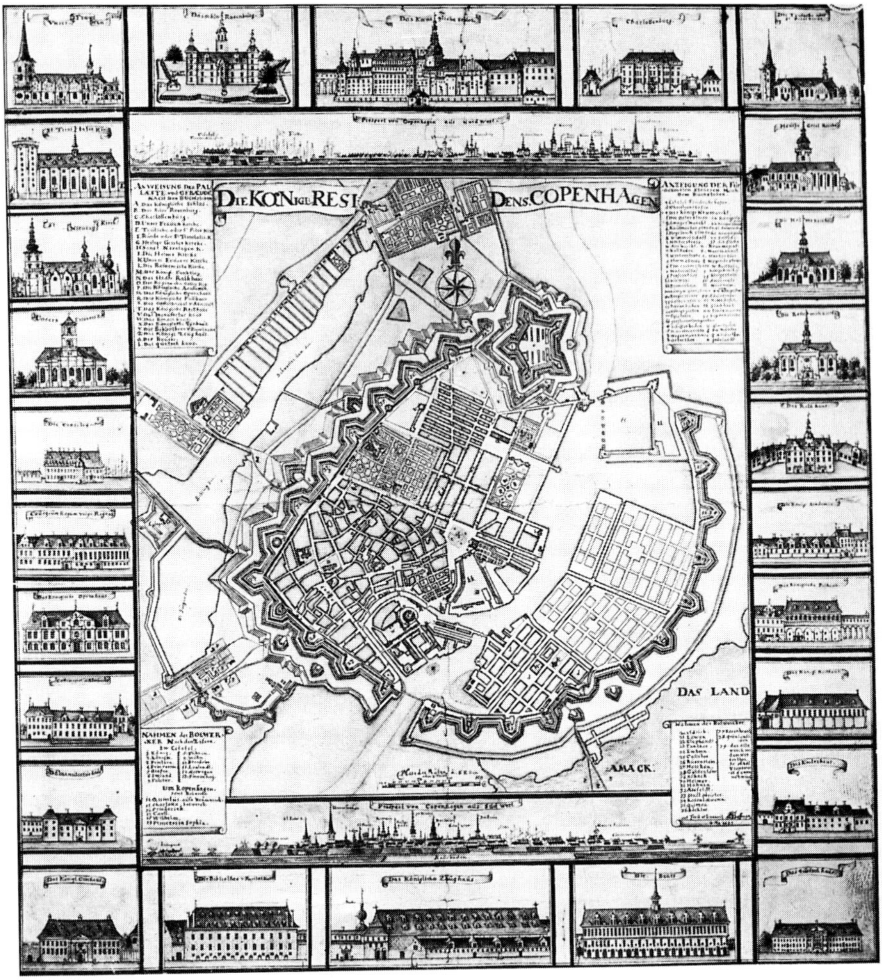

An ideal plan, 1687

The bombardment of Copenhagen on July 26, 1700, seen from the sea

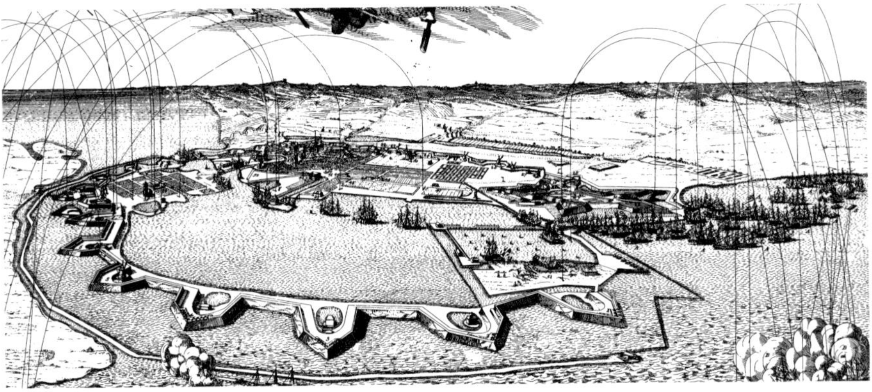

Eigtved, the architect who, with his elegant Rococo buildings, more than anyone else struck the lovely tone that is so distinctive of Copenhagen. It culminated in the palaces around Amalienborg square (F 32), but can also be found in Eigtved's other buildings in Frederiksstaden, for example a building in Amaliegade (F 36) and Frederik's Hospital (F 33).

At around the middle of the 18th century, Copenhagen's harbor also underwent major expansions. This was the time when great fortunes were made in overseas trade, especially with the East. On the Christianshavn side, Nikolai Eigtved left yet another elegant trace, even though it was just a warehouse (F 27), and on the five islands east of the entrance to the harbor, large, well-built houses were erected for the navy (F 29). The dynamics of the city could not be contained within the ramparts. It spread to large manors in the extensive wooded areas and hunting grounds in the north. The royal family sought unspoiled nature and isolation in the Hermitage (J 26), and the aristocracy followed the same pattern, although on a smaller scale, with manors such as Frederiksdal (J 30) and Schæffergården (J 31). The concept "maison de plaisir" was introduced and set the standard for numerous buildings to come.

Map showing the fires in the center of Copenhagen
A. 1728
B: 1795
C: 1807

Below: The Copenhagen fire of 1795

A Classical opening

What is now the Royal Danish Academy of Fine Arts was founded at Charlottenborg Palace in 1754, with Nikolai Eigtved as its first director. He died shortly afterward and was replaced by Nicolas-Henri Jardin, who was brought in for the job direct from France. In this way, Denmark made contact with the newest architectural current abroad, Classicism, without the usual delay. Jardin's influence was spread through a fairly small number of buildings, such as Bernstorff Palace (J 40), the Sølvgade barracks (F 43), and further work on the domed church in Frederiksstaden (F 82) that had been begun by Eigtved but neither architect proved able to complete. It actually was not finished until the end of the 19th century at the initiative of the magnate C.F. Tietgen, with Ferdinand Meldahl as the architect, and by then Classicism had gone out of fashion. Jardin's work at the Royal Danish Academy of Fine Arts was important for

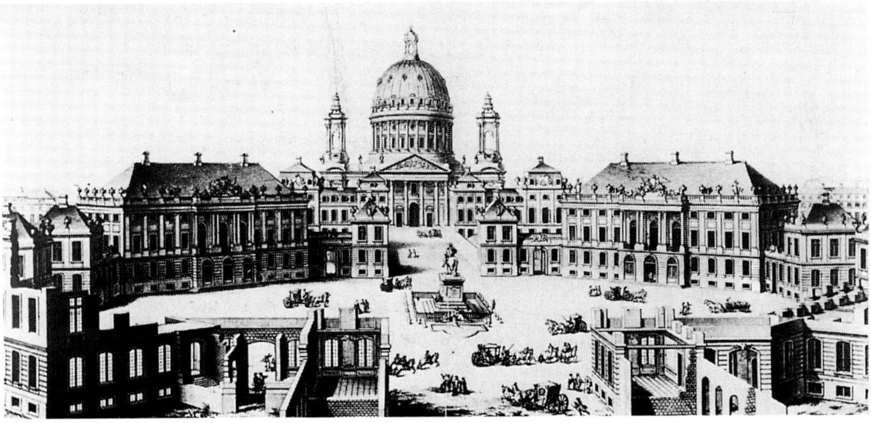

Amalienborg. Prospect

spreading Classicism's new message. Of his pupils, C. F. Harsdorff is the one who stands out as its great exponent. He was also a teacher at the academy, but the building that he erected adjacent to Charlottenborg (F 45), in particular, served as a model for ordinary builders and their clients. It laid the basis for the many town houses with a Classicist look that give a crisp, refined resonance to the city's distinctive architectural tone.

Two major conflagrations changed the city at the end of the 18th century. The magnificent Baroque Christiansborg Palace was consumed by a fire in 1794 that left only the buildings around the riding grounds standing, and in 1795, the entire city, from Holmens Church to the Western Ramparts, was gutted by a fire. Both conflagrations opened up the way for a new orientation in architecture in the direction of Classicism, which provided guidelines for much of the ordinary construction on the site of the fires. For public and monumental building, the mantle had been assumed by one of Harsdorff's pupils, C.F. Hansen. His Classicism was much more striking and theatrical than the style championed by his teacher, which might be why C.F. Hansen is viewed today as the Classicist par excellence. Another explanation for C.F. Hansen's standing is his great productivity. Besides major projects in Copenhagen, he also designed numerous buildings as provincial master builder in Holstein, in addition to building churches elsewhere in Denmark. The Napoleonic Wars were a time of unrest, and in Denmark they culminated with the bombardment of Copenhagen by the English in 1807. As a result, Denmark went bankrupt in 1813, and the union with Norway was dissolved shortly thereafter.

This was not a good climate for large-scale construction. C.F. Hansen's major work was in fact done on a tight budget and often on the ruins of older buildings whose blackened walls had to be reused: the Classicist Christiansborg Palace, which burned down in 1884, had itself been built on the ruins of the Baroque palace; the Church of Our Lady (F 56) was built on the site of several earlier churches; and the city hall and courthouse on Nytorv square were erected where the city's old town hall had been destroyed in the fire of 1795. C.F. Hansen's buildings created the image of monumental Copenhagen, and his Roman-inspired Classicism gave Denmark a place in international architecture for the first time. He also lived to a very ripe old age, so to younger generations of architects it probably came as a relief when the long Hansen era came to an end with his death in 1845.

Great freedom

Radical changes took place in Denmark in general and Copenhagen in particular in the mid-19th century. The city had reached a dangerous state of insufferable overbuilding and stinking filthiness. But things were also happening. The first steam locomotive traveled between Copenhagen and Roskilde in 1847. The absolute monarchy was abolished in 1848, and democracy, ensured by the new constitution, was adopted in 1849. The demarcation terrain outside Copenhagen's ramparts was opened up for construction in 1852. Five thousand inhabitants of Copenhagen died of cholera in the summer of 1853. Copenhagen's status as a fortified city was abolished in 1856. An ordinary citizen of Copenhagen in those days could certainly be overwhelmed by all of these events. Architecture also made a number of turnabouts after the long period with stringent Classicism. The teacher-pupil relationship still carried weight, but the jumps were larger between one generation and the next. M. G. Bindesbøll was at the academy while C.F. Hansen was a professor and director, but the Classicism of the Thorvaldsen Museum (F 62), Bindesbøll's first independent building, was entirely different from Hansen's. It was colorful and sensual, and took an unfettered approach to the Classical

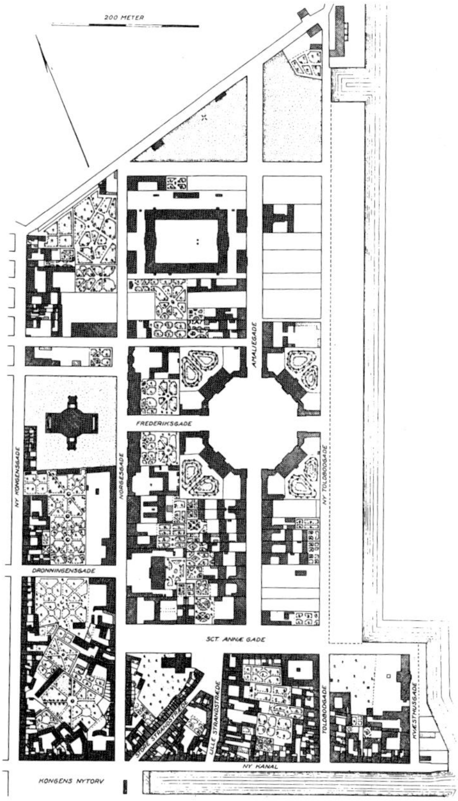

Frederiksstaden

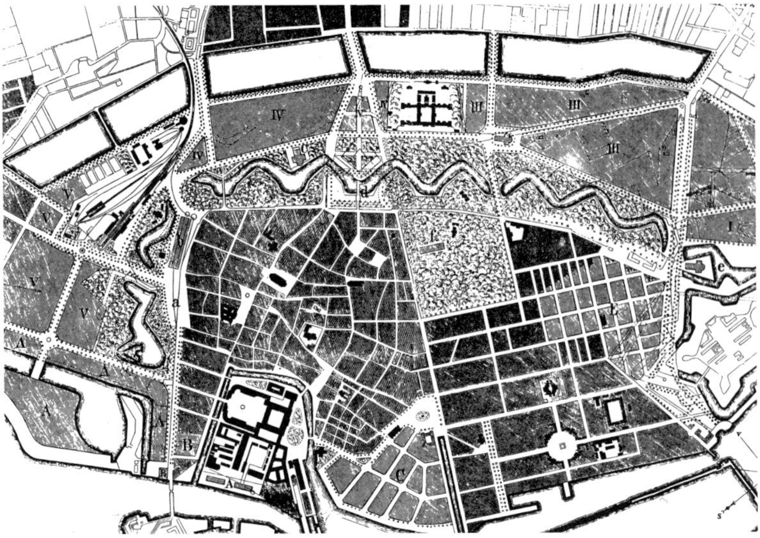

Ferdinand Meldahl's plan from 1866

past. Bindesbøll was as a whole an original architect. When the Danish Medical Association wanted to build housing outside the city for the survivors of the cholera epidemic, Bindesbøll was asked to draw up the plans. He did in the course of a few weeks, and nonetheless created a scheme that has inspired housing ever since. The Medical Association's housing scheme (C 64), known as Brumleby, on Øster Fælled commons has withstood political forces and many other kinds for nearly 150 years; its latest restoration is to be completed in 1996.

As early as 1843, nine years before the ramparts were demolished, the Tivoli Gardens (F 61) were laid out in the military zone, but this popular recreational area was

Peder Madsens Gang

unable to absorb all the press from the crowded city. Liberation from the close confines that had surrounded Copenhagen for centuries was followed by a liberation in architecture. The University Library (F 66), built between 1857 and 1861, was the start of Historicism, which made free use of models from the history of architecture in order to create the right atmosphere for a building's location and function. Liberalism swept the country in both architecture and politics. The liberal attitude to architecture's basic rules might break out in theatrical stagings, which were found especially toward the end of the century, for example in Søtorvet (E 75), but the period also created solid, stringent works such as the Municipal Hospital (F 67), which was built between 1859 and 1863, designed by Christian Hansen, an expert in Antiquity. A brewery-owner by the name of J.C. Jacobsen liberated himself in 1846 from centuries of beer-brewing traditions in the city and moved his brewery all the way to Valby, which had clean water, among other things. The result was the Carlsberg Breweries (H 63), a pioneering enterprise in the new age of industrialism whose buildings include a great deal of fine architecture. This general liberation was also expressed as individualism in the housing of ordinary citizens. The country's first villa quarters were laid out in the 1850s in Frederiksberg on Gammel Kongevej and in Østerbro in the Rosenvænget quarter. Villas in general have not, however, been included in this guide.

The price of freedom

A distinctive feature of this period of liberation, however, was that the increasing volume of building was divided into two types. One type of building came about in the usual way. It consisted (and consists) of a process in which a client needed a building for a specific purpose, and hired an architect to design a project and oversee the work of building. The other kind of building, which predominated, came about in a new way. Anyone at all who had the money and imagination bought a piece of the large area outside the city that had now been liberated from military restrictions and could be

Rosenvænget, Copenhagen. From Illustreret Tidende, 1863

settled largely without civil restrictions as well. The price of land increased with unprecedented speed so everything had to be done quickly. Mr. Anyone-at-All had his building knocked together as quickly and cheaply as possible. The building was supposed first and foremost to earn money. Of course it did contain a few housing units, but this was of secondary importance since there was such a great demand for housing that renting them out was not a problem. This is how most of Copenhagen's quarters just outside the ramparts were built in the latter half of the 19th century. Speculation in land and housing had become a common phenomenon that legislation was only able to stop slowly, in keeping with changes in the political climate. By our standards, building techniques were not bad in those days since they were based on a long tradition, but the housing density was unbearable. For good reason, this guide gives no examples of the period's slum housing, but sober, high-quality buildings were also built outside the ramparts at the time. One example is the rather anonymous building on Gasværksvej (E 287), which is now part of the major urban-renewal project in Vesterbro.

The beginnings of political change could be seen as early as 1865, when the Workers' Housing Society was founded on November 20th at a meeting of workers at the Burmeister & Wain shipyard, where two physicians, F.F. Ulrik and Emil Hornemann,

Slum housing in Bremerholm

lectured on working-class housing conditions. The physicians urged the participants to take their housing situation in their own hands by founding a building and savings society. They openly acknowledged that the motive for their suggestion was a desire to maintain the prevailing social order. A worker who owned his own home would be less revolutionary, they believed, and perhaps they were right. The society quickly got under way and as early as 1866, the topping off ceremonies were held for the first 10 houses, built on Sverigesgade in Amager, followed by a high degree of building activity far into the present century. One of the Society's largest projects was the "Potato Rows" (F 77), whose 480 houses reflect the clients' middle-class ambitions and desire to own their own homes. The physicians were right in this respect. There was nothing revolutionary in this housing area except for the original constellation of clients, which was an honest countermove against the wild speculation in the areas just outside the ramparts.

The view from a hilltop

While activity in Nørrebro and Vesterbro was most hectic, a few oases were kept open, for example around the former military ramparts. Large parks such as Østre Anlæg (F 72), the Botanical Gardens (F 73), and Ørsted Park (E 75) date from this period. Defense was still a hot political issue at the end of the 19th century, but now it was a question of fortifications farther outside the city. The Western Ramparts ran from Utterslev Mose to Avedøre and today form a unique, continuous recreational area. The same period witnessed the construction of major cultural institutions such as the Royal Theater (F 74), the Royal Museum of Fine Arts (F 83), the Marble Church (F 82), and the Ny Carlsberg Glyptotek (F 84), which also marked the end of Historicist architecture. While the century came to a close, architects were beginning to tire of using international models from the past. Instead they became aware of their Danish and Scandinavian heritage. A portent of new times came as early as 1886 with the Abel Cathrine Foundation (H 80), but National Romanticism, as the trend was later called, reached a culmination in Copenhagen City Hall (F 85), completed in 1905, with which the architect Martin Nyrop created a monument to democracy, a union of art and popular culture that was rich in images. The turn of the century was like a hilltop from which it was possible to see in many directions. And this is what art did, and architecture with it, by making use of the many new potentials. The painter-architect J.F. Willumsen struck a festive note with the Free Exhibition Building (F 91). The Art Nouveau movement of the south was tempting and inspired Anton Rosen's many buildings in Denmark and Copenhagen in particular, for example the exuberant Palace Hotel (F 102) and the advanced hotel and commercial building in Vesterbro (E 96). Ulrik Plesner's housing complex, Åhusene (E 89) and ved Danas Plads (E 97), were lush and liberated adaptations of both Danish and English building. New technology was reflected tentatively in e.g. the Østre Elektricitetsværk electric power plant (F 93), while the Main Railway Station (E 95) was still a sign that national and popular elements provided an anchorage. The Free Port was laid out in the 1890s with the use of the newest technology in building and construction, for example using reinforced concrete as the material for Warehouse 1 (F 86).

Ny Carlsberg Glyptotek, 1892-1894

The beginning of the 20th century was both promising and threatening. In around 1900, a number of surrounding municipalities were incorporated into Copenhagen Municipality, which tripled in size as a result. This was intended to ease the pressure from the enormous population increase that Copenhagen had been plagued by for some decades, and still suffered under, but it also required planning. An international urban-planning competition was consequently announced in 1908 for the newly acquired areas. It was won by Carl Strintz, the city surveyor from Bonn, whose proposal was a mixture of German Romanticism with winding roads and English ideas about

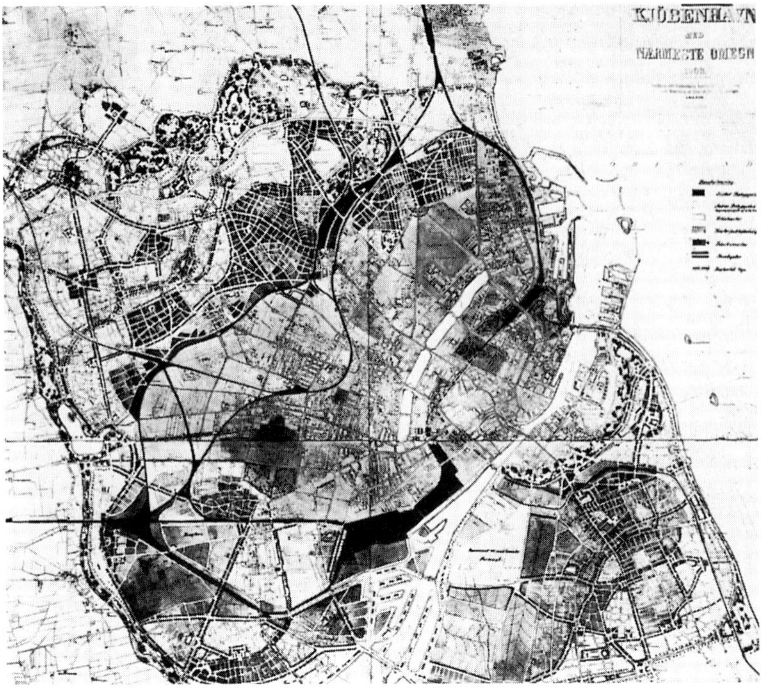

Carl Strintz's plan from 1908

garden cities. The proposal did not leave many tangible traces, but the idea of planning on a large scale, urban planning, had been introduced in Copenhagen. The housing shortage and feverish, uncontrolled housing construction were among the threats. In 1907, after hectic building for five years, there were 10,000 empty apartments. At the same time, many poor families lived in housing with more than four people per room. Tension in housing construction had become too great, and the bottom fell out of the housing market. Banks and contractors went bankrupt, and building stopped completely, resulting in both an increased housing shortage and unemployment in the ensuing years.

Maturing in difficult times

This crisis was the introduction to fruitful developments in Danish housing construction. The working and middle classes began to play a role as builders because they organized themselves, and their building fell into two categories from the very start: the garden house and the urban apartment. A strong source of inspiration came from England with the garden city movement founded by the urban planning theoretician Ebenezer Howard. His writings, such as Garden Cities of Tomorrow from 1898, were a reaction against industrialism's slum cities in England, which were far more overwhelming than Copenhagen's. Germany contributed the idea of housing societies, which had built working-class housing in major industrial towns. A common feature of the two movements was that land and housing were to be common property, more or less following the practice of the cooperative societies that had shown their viability in Denmark for half a century. The year 1912 was a turning point. The two movements each founded a society that was to influence developments far into the future. F.C. Boldsen, a lawyer from Randers who was an enthusiastic adherent of Howard's garden cities, took the initiative to found the Danish Garden House Society. The society's board members were the architects Martin Nyrop, Anton Rosen, and Egil Fischer, the art historian Vilhelm Lorentzen, and the labor unionist Jens Christian Jensen, who was chairman of the house carpenters, a profession that had an unemployment rate of 75% at the time. And this was also one of the motives for founding the Workers' Housing Society, at the initiative of Jens Christian Jensen – in close cooperation with the cooperative movement in Copenhagen.

Both societies quickly turned their ideas into buildings. The Grøndalsvænge quarter in Nørrebro (E 106) was started in 1914 by the Danish Garden House Society, and the Workers' Housing Society inaugurated its first building in 1913, on Nyelandsvej (E 108). The houses on Grøndalsvænge were an exponent of the Bedre Byggeskik (better building practices) movement, which was initiated by the Federation of Danish Architects when they founded their "design aid service" in 1907. For a small fee, the architects offered to supply the country's small-scale builders with designs for their new houses. The goal was to bring a bit of aesthetic order to building in the countryside and suburbs and it was so successful that this help became a popular, aesthetic movement. It aimed at an economic and ecological simplicity based on good Danish crafts traditions and both classical and local ideas of form.

In 1915, the movement organized itself as the Society for Better Building Practices, which continued operations until the end of the 1940s. Its 40 years of work to promote better building left their mark throughout the country as simple, sensible, robust houses that today are still among the most coveted homes. The Workers' Housing Society, later the Workers' Cooperative Housing Society (AAP), was the country's first non-profit housing society. In the course of the century, it proved a decisive factor for housing and urban development throughout the country, with a production of nearly 450,000 units. The building on Nyelandsvej set the standard, with its heavy, red-brick walls and traditional approach, for the many housing blocks in Copenhagen in the ensuring couple of decades. The Copenhagen Public Housing Association (KAB), founded in 1920 at the initiative of F. C. Boldsen, concentrated from the beginning on garden houses and realized its ideas with a radical and innovative approach with such housing developments as Bakkehusene in Bellahøj (E 117) and Studiebyen in Hellerup (B 114). Several of those behind the founding of the Society for Better Building Practices and the two housing societies also took the initiative to found the Danish Urban Planning Laboratory in 1921 as a reaction against the country's provincial towns, which were growing wild. The laboratory is still an important archives and debate forum for Danish urban planning.

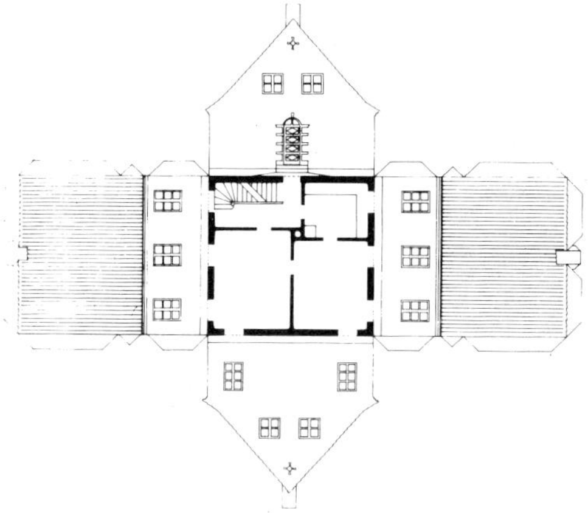

A folding house from the Society for Better Building Practices

Classicism again

Despite the resolute initiatives taken by housing societies, the housing shortage became so severe during the First World War that the authorities had to take an active

role in housing construction for the first time. Copenhagen Municipality built both temporary emergency housing, which in several cases had many fine qualities but has been demolished, and permanent housing, which supplemented the ring of housing blocks around the older quarters. The apartment blocks on Struenseegade (E 112) that were designed by Povl Baumann are a well-formulated prototype of this building and housing form, and Kay Fisker's Hornbækhus (E 116) is a monumental culmination in the development of the large apartment block. The closed city-block form was opened to provide sun and air in Classens Have (F 119) and Solgården (B 124), and as a result paved the way for the demands made of housing that Functionalism later emphasized. Classens Have represented Neo-Classicism. The new interest in things Classical had been awakened in a rather ridiculous way by the "spire affair." The brewery owner Carl Jacobsen (who gave his name to the Carlsberg brewery) offered in 1910 to pay for a new spire for the tower of the Church of Our Lady since he felt that the old one was not impressive enough. The idea sparked off a heated debate among architects, the oldest of whom welcomed the idea while the young ones, lead by Carl Petersen, believed that the spire would compromise C.F. Hansen's Classicist masterpiece. The young architects won the fight. The tower got no spire, but the conflict had created a movement that acknowledged the Classical core in Danish architecture and signalled a renaissance for C.F. Hansen's architecture. Neo-Classicism reached an artistic and theatrical culmination in the Police Headquarters (I 111), completed in 1925. But it was also vociferously criticized by young architects, who with Poul Henningsen in the lead published the satirical, radical periodical Kritisk Revy. This waggish publication gave the first inkling of the century's most important movement in society and culture: Functionalism.

Making things work

Functionalism made its breakthrough in Scandinavian and Danish architecture in the product and housing exhibition arranged in Stockholm in 1930 by what was then called the Swedish Society of Industrial Design. In Copenhagen, the city architect Poul Holsøe was one of the first to respond to the new signals, which were expressed clearly and consistently in the "white meat market," built between 1931 and 1934 (H 133). At the same time, Arne Jacobsen gave his own elegant version of the white style in the Bellavista housing scheme, Bellevue Theater, and Bellevue sea baths (J 134). The consistent, Functionalist housing form, free-standing, parallel blocks, got its first clear exponent in the Blidah Park housing scheme in Hellerup (J 138). In commercial buildings, Nørrebro Station (E 126) and the Vesterport office building (E 134) provide examples of the smooth transition from Neo-Classicism to Functionalism, while Hotel Astoria (E 140)

Carl Petersen and Ivar Bentsen: competition project for an office building on the former railroad yards, 1919

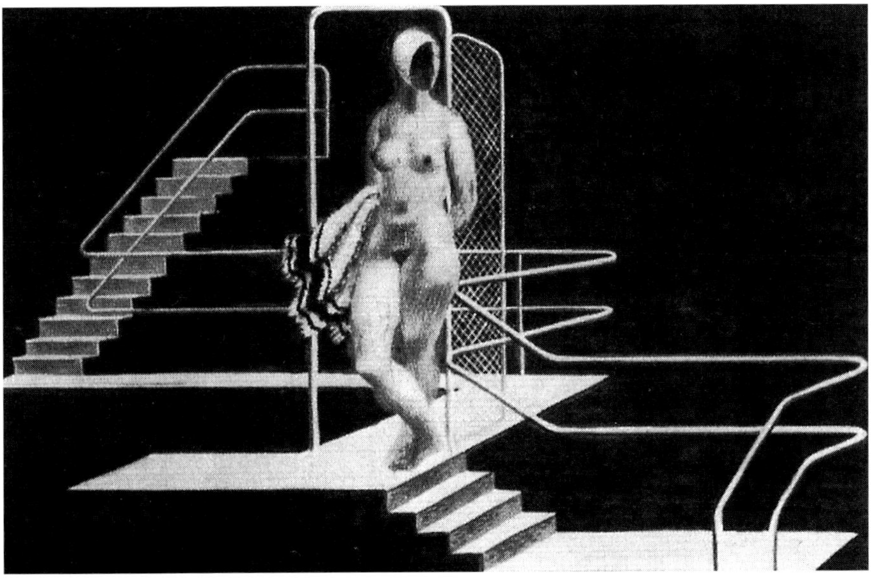

Sikker Hansen and Arne Jacobsen, curtain for the Bellevue Theater, built in 1935-1936

is an expressive and liberated exploitation of the new potentials in form, materials, and structures. The same can be said of the residential building and post office on H.C. Ørstedvej from 1939 and the School on the Sound (I 150), which further broke with box-shaped Functionalism. Functionalism's major achievement in housing construction was the balcony, which was used for a completely new facade type in Ryparken (B 131) and Storgården (B 139), where the repetition of the many little "armchair balconies" makes an overwhelming effect. The balcony was also a leading motive in the powerful Vestersøhus, designed by Kay Fisker and C.F. Møller in 1939 (E 144), but here it was restrained by an architecture that simultaneously reflected an awareness of tradition and was an expression of powerful, personal form. The two architects had experimented back in 1929 with the new idiom in an advanced residential building on Vodroffsvej (E 125) and had together with their colleague Poul Stegmann been responsible for building Århus University since the early thirties. These buildings were exponents of what was later called "the functional tradition," a pragmatic line in Danish architecture that can be traced all the way back to M.G. Bindesbøll and still exerts a tangible influence. In Denmark, Functionalism was given its most striking and personal form of expression in the completely new and important commissions for the state, with Vilhelm Lauritzen as the architect. The Radio Building (E 151) and Kastrup Airport (H 157) were radiantly clear, sensitive solutions to problems that had no traditional answers, and both are key works in the architecture of the time and the entire century.

The city of Copenhagen was given a comprehensive and largely continuous system of parks. Important parts of it run along the municipal border, from Lake Emdrup in the north, through Utterslev Mose (A 148), parts of the Western Ramparts (A 81), then south through Krogebjergparken, Damhusengen, and Damhussøen (D 149), then further through Vigerslevparken (G 122) to Valbyparken (H 147) at Kalvebod Strand.

War and common sense

The Second World War and the occupation of Denmark put an end to the experiments of the thirties in art, culture, and society. Architecture in the forties was largely subdued and centered on the functional tradition as a matter of national principle. The Atelier Houses (B 164) from 1943 were a poetic expression of both a Spartan time and cultivated restraint. In the almost contemporary Bispeparken housing scheme (B 161), Functionalism's achievements were combined with the functional tradition to form a pattern that was to dominate public housing construction for a couple of decades to come. Søllerød Town Hall (J 163), which was inaugurated in 1942, had been designed by Arne Jacobsen and Flemming Lassen in 1939 and served as a clearly conceived type model for Functionalism's Danish town halls. During the war, Copenhagen undertook the period's largest urban-renewal project in the deteriorating quarter around Borgergade and Adelgade. New buildings took the place of old. Dronningegården (F 165), which was begun in 1943, has a composite look of monumentality from the past and the complex situation of the day, but its architectural qualities are also linked with the functional tradition.

Far into the post-war period, housing construction was characterized by the simple common sense of the functional tradition. Collaboration between public housing societies and architects in this period yielded fruitful results that have never been surpassed since. Søndergårdsparken (J 168) from around 1950 clearly follows traditional demands for form and material and was also an example of the desire of the Danish Public Housing Association (DAB) to experiment with low-rise house forms and new housing types. The association's Bredalsparken (J 172) was built at the same time, a very large park scheme with a well-conceived relationship between the complex's staggered blocks and the spaces between them. The population of Denmark, and especially of Copenhagen, grew unprecedentedly in the post-war period. Drastic measures had to be taken to avoid a housing shortage and to ensure the rising housing standard that all expected as the economy began to prosper. The methods were planning and industrialization. In 1947, the regional planning office, under the leadership of the architect Peter Bredsdorff, set forth a plan for the Copenhagen region. It showed residential areas placed along five "fingers" that stretched out from the central city, and was quickly known as the "finger plan." As a simple symbol of a plan based on existing developments, the sketch also took on an important professional and political significance in the years to come.

The idea of establishing a wooded area around Copenhagen to create some of the qualities found in northern Zealand, natural or man-made, had been conceived in the twenties. The "green report" of 1936 on a system of recreational areas for the residents of the capital sought to extend Copenhagen's system of parks with connected systems of paths, excursion roads, and green areas in greater Copenhagen. In legislating the preservation of large agricultural tracts, it was recommended that continuous systems of nature reserves be established and that state forests be planted in unwooded areas. In 1967, Parliament and the municipalities involved revived these plans, which now cover some 1,500 hectares of forests and grazing lands.

Planning manifested itself on the state level with the founding of the Ministry of Housing and Building and the State Building Research Institute in 1947. Now the state

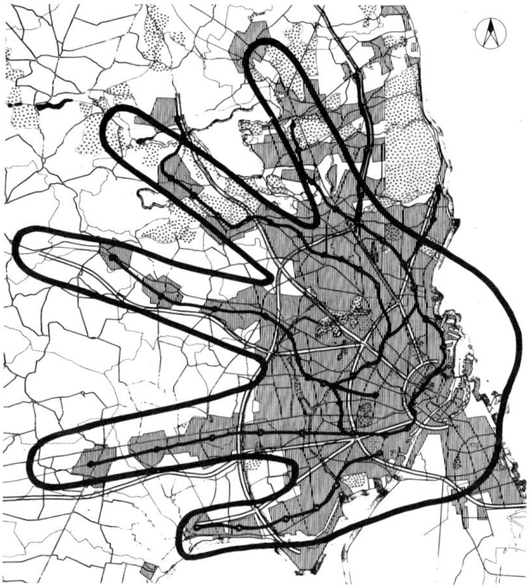

The "finger plan", 1947

wanted to take an active part in the building and housing market, and state subsidies were provided so that more industrialized processes could be used in housing construction. One of the first projects of this kind was high-rise housing in Bellahøj (B 180), an experiment with both new building techniques and the form itself, since buildings of this height were completely new in Denmark. The Modernist urban architecture that had been outlined by the Swiss architect Le Corbusier was consequently introduced in Denmark, but it was given an even more radical expression in the Milestedet housing scheme in Brøndby (G 188), built between 1953 and 1958. Some architects felt that rationalization in the high-rises had been carried too far at the expense of housing quality and ordinary human considerations. This attitude was supported by sociological studies, but industrialization in housing construction continued.

Loners and masterpieces

Modernist architecture was often given a mechanical and unarticulated expression in industrialized housing construction. Arne Jacobsen, in contrast, was able right to his death in 1971 to bring the Modernist idiom to a point of personal perfection and simplification that made his buildings internationally renowned. This is true of such projects as the office building for Jespersen & Søn (E 186) and Rødovre Town Hall (D 189), both from 1955; SAS Royal Hotel (E 200) from 1960; and Danmarks Nationalbank (F 215) from 1971. Individually refined yet type-like, these projects are among the culminations in architecture this century. Another great architect in the post-war period was Kay

Fisker, who carried on his unerring version of the functional tradition in such projects as the Voldparken housing development (A 171) and Voldparken School (A 174), both from the fifties. Jørn Utzon won international renown in 1957 with his winning project for the Sydney Opera House, but in the years just before, he had created the atrium house schemes in Elsinore and Fredensborg, providing a model for housing construction a couple of years later, though they are outside the scope of this guide. Jørn Utzon has built very little in Denmark, but his organically stringent architecture is represented here by Bagsværd Church (J 228), from 1976, and the Paustian House (C 260), from 1987. Seven Houses on Piniehøj in Rungsted (J 204) exhibit consistent, simplified architecture inspired by American work from the time and traditional Japanese architecture. Their architects, Jørgen Bo and Wilhelm Wohlert, had worked a few years before with the same motives in the Louisiana Museum of Modern Art in Humlebæk, a complex that has won international fame.

Debate and reaction

Utzon's atrium houses were one of the sources of inspiration for the extensive, low-rise housing suburb Albertslund Syd (J 205), which was built between 1963 and 1968 as an initial experiment with industrialized dense/low-rise housing. During this same period, the monumentally high housing development Høje Gladsaxe (A 214) was built as the heretofore most radical example of rational high-rise housing. The two projects sparked off a heated debate about low- versus high-rise housing, but time has shown that low-rise is preferable. The building industry, which was geared to large-scale production, did, however, leave one last monument: the Brøndby Strand housing development (J 218), which was completed in 1973, when the Danish housing industry boom

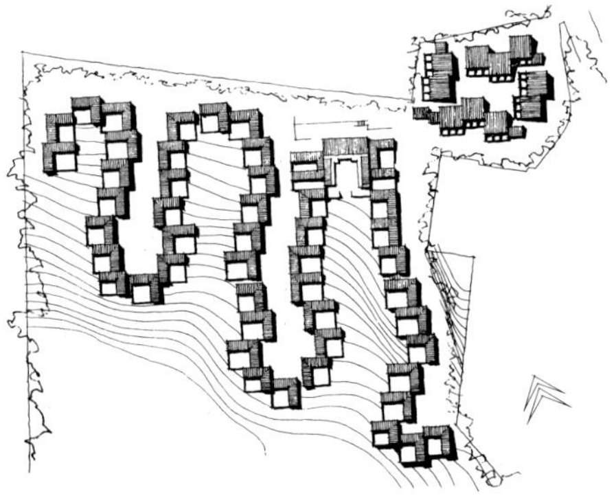

Jørn Utzon's atrium houses in Fredensborg, built in 1962-63

culminated with an annual production of 50,000 units. The reaction to large-scale industrialized building was inspired by the state itself. The State Building Research Institute announced a competition in 1971 for dense/low-rise housing. It was won by Tegnestuen Vandkunsten's radical proposal that called for resident democracy and provided intrepid, informal solutions to everything from the problems of national planning to the furnishing of individual rooms. The proposal was carried out on a modest scale in the Tinggården development in Herfølge (outside the scope of this guide), which with its relaxed, visually rich architecture nonetheless had a major influence on the housing construction of the period. The rebellious atmosphere of the time also manifested itself in the founding of the "free city" of Christiania in Christianshavn in 1971.

Fællestegnestuen stood behind two important experiments in combining a garden house with an urban apartment. Farum Midtpunkt (J 219), from 1974, is a compact structure of parallel terrace houses, while Solbjerg Have (D 236) in Frederiksberg, from

1980, is a block that combines high, terse street facades with fragmented terraced facades on the courtyard. Both developments were unique, with distinctive qualities that did not serve as models for others. Following the State Building Research Institute's competition, dense/low-rise housing gradually dominated. Galgebakken (J 225) in Albertslund Nord, from 1974, experimented with types of housing and "neighborhoods,"

The beginnings of Christiania in 1971

and a couple of years later, the neighboring housing development, Hyldespjældet (J 226), demonstrated how a Casbah-like entity could be built up from concrete elements. The client for both developments was Vridsløselille Cooperative Housing Society, which also built Gadekæret (J 231) in Ishøj in 1979, using concrete elements for a scene modeled on old Danish villages. Dense/low-rise building reached an architectural culmination in Tegnestuen Vandkunsten's Fuglsang Park (J 242) housing development in Farum, from 1983, with housing placed adjoining A5 Tegnestuen's congenial Stenvad School, forming a uniform entity. Similar originality and lushness can be found in Vandkunsten's almost contemporary double development in Værløse, Hesselbo and Nørgårds Plantage (J 242).

Public monuments

While housing construction came to grips with large-scale production and rationalization, the public sector made its mark with monumental projects. In the same period, until the mid-seventies, Copenhagen County Hospital in Herlev (J 209) and Copenhagen Municipal Hospital in Hvidovre (G 212) were built according to two diametrically opposed principles. The former, 120 m tall, is a magnificent sculpture in the Copenhagen skyline, while the latter is a low, sprawling complex with a structural, Modernist idiom. The Technical University of Denmark in Lyngby (J 199) was built over a period of several years before 1974 and is the model of the day's ideals of rationality and structural organization. The Panum Institute in Nørrebro (E 230) is an expression of similar ideas, but in a highly concentrated form and a Brutalist idiom.

The guide gives four examples of the period's new churches. Three are by Johan Otto von Spreckelsen, who won the competition for the new arch in Paris in 1983. Like this major international creation, Sankt Nikolaj Church in Hvidovre (J 201), Vangede

Church (J 227), and Stavnsholt Church in Farum (J 240) were built over squares and cubes. These churches demonstrate the architect's intense work with the relationship of geometry, form, and light. A completely different approach to church construction is taken by Inger and Johannes Exner in their Church of the Resurrection in Albertslund (J 243), from 1984; its forms, light, and material create rooms that are saturated with atmosphere and mysticism.

In order to direct a major part of the urban growth in the capital towards the south, Parliament adopted a law in 1961 on planning the Køge Bay area. The expansion of this strip city is unique because of its extent and the recreational values that have been added to the area through planning. It has gained an architectural attraction in Køge Bay Coastal Park with a Museum of Modern Art (J 295), to be inaugurated in 1996.

Arken – The Museum of Modern Art, Køge Bay

Old virtues

In the mid-eighties, there was a new interest in high-rise housing, and once again, the state helped provide inspiration. The Ministry of Housing and Building's competition in 1983 for industrialized apartment houses was won by Arkitektgruppen i Aarhus. The Engen housing development in Rødovre (D 264) is one of several projects that were carried out according to the winning project's building system. At the same time, pension funds proved a new kind of client for housing construction. Without the constraints that limited imagination in public housing, they made use of a more ambitious architecture that often followed the day's demand for formalism and a smart lifestyle. The Dalgas Have housing development (E 265) and Copenhagen Business School (E 251) in Frederiksberg at the end of the eighties are an entire urban quarter in this spirit, designed by Henning Larsens Tegnestue. The school was moreover inspired by the office's internationally famous project, the Ministry of Foreign Affairs in Riyadh, Saudi Arabia.

Less formal, but with an appeal to the period's terse lifestyle, is Tegnestuen Vandkunsten's elegant and poetic Dianas Have in Hørsholm (J 279), from 1992. The formalistic architecture nonetheless was given its most radical and comprehensive expression in the new town of Høje Taastrup (J 257), built after a winning proposal from Jacob Blegvads Tegnestue in a competition from 1978. The town is the clearest example of Neo-Rationalism in Denmark, and the arches over its railway station (J 258) have made Høje Taastrup "the city of arches."

Regeneration and the future

Throughout the entire latter half of this century, urban renewal has been a challenge in Copenhagen, as it has been in other cities. As noted earlier, the beginning was made in the district around Borgergade and Adelgade during the Second World War. Urban renewal around Bremerholm (F 216) in the late sixties was drastic, but left both distinctive new buildings and the old city block described. The design of Pistolstæde (F 221) in 1971 reflected an interest in preserving old buildings for their picturesque value alone, and Sofiegården in Christianshavn (I 220), from the same period, was a talented proposal for fitting in new buildings with old surroundings. These approaches were not taken in the late seventies when the slums of Nørrebro in the "black rectangle" (E 234) were to be tackled. Urban renewal on this scale proved explosive, as demonstrated by confrontations between Nørrebro's inhabitants and the authorities in 1980. The new buildings in Nørrebro furthermore failed to convince posterity of the necessity and justness of this kind of urban renewal. When the blocks on Rigensgade (F 233) and on Gammelholm (F 254) were renovated in the early eighties, a more sensitive approach was taken, and some of this work was actual restoration. In instances where smaller-scale renovation and pure infill were concerned, contemporary architecture was better able to come into its own. And it did so distinctively in Tegnestuen Vandkunsten's Garvergården in Østerbro (C 263) and "the blue corner" in Christianshavn (I 268), both from 1991. It is difficult to find a balance in infill between artistic and urban elements, but Henning Larsen's stringent, poetic BT-huset (F 284), from 1994, keeps it in exemplary fashion.

Renewal of the existing city will undoubtedly account for more than new construction in the foreseeable future, although Copenhagen's role as the "cultural capital of Europe" in 1996 resulted in a few major projects, such as the extensions to the Royal Library and the Royal Museum of Fine Arts, which will not be completed until 1997.

The Royal Library, extension 1995

Urban renewal and/or expansion have been discussed in conjunction with the new urban quarter planned for Vestamager, Ørestaden. When it comes to urban renewal, the debate still centers on preservation versus new construction, for example in the country's largest urban-renewal project so far, which is now in progress in Vesterbro and will continue into next century. The renovation of one of Vesterbro's solid, old buildings (H 280) shows that the architecture of past and present and ecological technology can form a synthesis that bodes well for the future. It is a matter of preserving that distinctive Copenhagen tone.

Olaf Lind, December 1995

O3
20
E47
E55
16
2
21
211
81
208
MØRKHØJ
HUSUM
LEV
HF. MOSEHØJ
HILLERØDMOTORVEJEN
MOTORRINGVEJEN
SAXE MØLLEVEJ
MØRKHØJ BYGADE
GYPEN
KAGSÅVEJ
PRÆSTEBRO
TRANSFORMERVEJ
DYNAMOVEJ
TURBINEVEJ
GENERATORVEJ
OKTOBERVEJ
JULIVEJ
AUGUSTVEJ
SEPTEMBERVEJ
MAJ ALLÉ
JUNI ALLÉ
APRILVEJ
DEBELVEJ
ILBJERG ALLÉ
RYBJERG ALLÉ
BREUMVEJ
NISSUMVEJ
EJSINGVEJ
OTTINGVEJ
KREJBJERGVEJ
ÅSTEDVEJ
TORUMVEJ
STAVNSBJERG ALLÉ
ONSBJERG ALLÉ
LILLEGÅRDS ALLÉ
JEBJERG ALLÉ
ROSLEV ALLÉ
DURUP ALLÉ
PILE KROGEN
PILEGÅRDSVEJ
KILDEAGER
NOVEMBERVEJ
MULDAGER
KAGS LØKKE
KAGSBRO
HUMLEBJERG
HAMPELAND
ABILDHØJ
Lundevang Skole
TV-Byen
Mørkhøj Kirke
MØRKHØJVEJ
MØRKHØJ PARKALLÉ
Mørkhøj Skole
Blaagaard Statsseminarium
Nørre Gymnasium
Plejecentret Bystævneparken
BYSTÆVNET
VOLDPARKEN
HF. ROSEN VANG
HF. BIRKE VANG
ÆRTEBJERGVEJ
HØRTOFTEV
BOTOFTEV
TOFTAGERVEJ
GÅRD TOFTE VEJ
TOFTEN
HUSTOFTEVEJ
STOREGÅRDSVEJ
EL.st
FREDERIKSSUNDSVEJ
HUSUM TORV
ÅGERUPVEJ
JYDERUPVEJ
MARBJERGVEJ
GERLEVVEJ
GLUMSØVEJ
EDERLANDSVEJ
HAVMANDSVEJ
EMTEDALEN
KLINTEKONGE VEJ
TUKSHØJEN
HAVFRUEVEJ
Korskirken
SVANEREDEN
PILEBRO
KLOKKEDYBET
RYTMEVEJ
SONATEVEJ
MENUETVEJ
AFLØJEN
VOLDFLØJEN
BÅNFLØJEN
Kloakpumpest
VIEMOSEPARKEN
SEHOLMENE
KAGSMOSE
BOSERUPVEJ
HERSLEV VEJ
KORNERUPVEJ
KATTINGVEJ
BOGENÆSVEJ
KLOSTER MARKSVEJ
BJERGMARKSVEJ
KONGEMARKSVEJ
TRAPPEHØJEN
Husum St.
ISLEVHUSVEJ
VINDINGEVEJ
MINDSTRUPVEJ
SVOGERSLEVVEJ
STENLØSEVEJ
STENMAGLEVEJ
TUNET
TERSLØSEVEJ
Korsager Skole
GISLINGEVEJ
BJERGSTEDVEJ
GADSTRUPVEJ
GREVINGEVEJ
GYRSTINGEVEJ
KORSAGER ALLÉ
HUSUM VÆNGE
SMØRUMVEJ
TÅSTRUPVEJ
LUNDEVEJ
Husum Kirke
BRUNEVANG
ISLEVHOLM
DYBEKÆR
KAGSVANG
VIRDINGEVEJ
BYPORTEN
DYSSEVÆNGET
VÆNGELEDDET
VESTER
KANSAGER
ØSTERLÅGEN
BAKKEKAMMEN
BROVÆNGET
MØLLEBAKKEN
AVENDINGEN
LØKKEN
SKRÅNINGEN
KILDELØBET
ISLEVBROVEJ
ISLELUND
VED VANDLØBET
VED TOLDGRAVEN
TORBISTVEJ
Vandværk
KROGEBJERGPARKEN
SLOTSHERRENS HAVE
STENLILLEVEJ
MERLØSEVEJ
Husum Skole
KYRINGEVEJ
TJÆREBYVEJ
HUSUMPARKEN
NORDRUPVEJ
Børneinst.
SNERTINGEVEJ
VEKSØVEJ
SKENSVEDVEJ

GLADSAXE
STADION
GLADSAXEVEJ
HØJE GLADSAXE
GLADSAXE
214
A
RUNDGÅRDEN
GUSTAV WIEDS VEJ
MARIENBORG ALLÉ
WERGELANDS ALLÉ
Marielyst Skole
HØJE GLADSAXE TORV
Søborg Gymnasium
Haralds kirken
Høje Gladsaxe Skole
Bagsværd Sogialpæd Sem
SKOLESVINGET
DALEN
DALTOFTEVEJ
NORDTOFTEVEJ
HOLMEVEJ
MARS ALLÉ
URANIENBORG ALLÉ
VENUSVEJ
BAKKEDRAGET
HØJMARKSVEJ
GRØNNE MOSEN
HØJVANGEN
HØJTOFTEVEJ
GRØNNEMOSE ALLÉ
MAGLE TORV
Søborgmagle Kirke
TVÆR
SYD
LANGE
MARKSVEJ
TOFTEVEJ
MOSESKRÆNTEN
KÆLKEBAKKEN
HELLESKRÆNTEN
TOPPEN
HØJE GLADSAXE VEJ
HILLERØDMOTORVEJEN
TINGBJERG ÅS
VESTGAVL
SOLGAVL
FUGLEGAVL
TRAPPEGAVL
STENGAVL
VINGEGAVL
GAVLHUSVEJ
VIRKE
FELTET
GRO
STEDET
STRÆDE
ARKADERNE
HÆKKEVOLD
SKOLESIDEN
TÅRNHUSSTRÆDE
BYGÅRD
TERRASSERNE
Tingbjerg Hallen
Tingbjerg Skole
HELLE
BORG
Tingbjerg Kollegiet
RUTEN
VED BYGÅRDEN
1
HARESKOVVEJ
148
UTTERSLEV MOSE
16
MOSESVINGET
STIEN
ANDE
STORKEBAKKEN
NEBBEGÅRDSBAKKEN
MOSEBAKKEN
SKOLEVANGEN
STUBBEVANGEN
Voldparkens Skole
174
ÅKANDEVEJ
F. ENGHAVEGÅRD
HF. BELLEVUE
HF. TREKANTEN
HUSUM IDRÆTS PARK
Husumvold Kirke
GADELANDET
PILESVINGET
RUGVEJ
GÅSEURTVEJ
KIRKEMOSE
HF. BRØNSHØJHOLM
DALVANGEN
MELLEMVANGEN
BYTINGET
BYVANGEN
HØJLANDSVANGEN
ASTERSVEJ
GRABYNKE
KLINTEVEJ
LØVETANDSVEJ
IRISVEJ
HIRSEVEJ
KABBELEJEVEJ
PRÆSTEGÅRDS ALLÉ
HVEDEVEJ
HAVREVEJ
BRØNSHØJ KIRKEVEJ
VIKKE VANGEN
EGE VANGEN
TJØRNE VANGEN
PILE VANGEN
ELLE VANGEN
BAUNEVANGEN
KIRKETOFTEN
BRØNSHØJ KIRKEGÅRD
Brønshøj Kirke
BRØNSHØJHOLMS ALLÉ
RISVANGEN
ENIGHEDS ALLÉ
211
BRØNSHØJ PARKEN
Bellahøj Kirke
Bellahøj Skole
SVENSKE LEJREN
SOLKROGEN
SONNERUPVEJ
SOLSIKKEVEJ
Skt. Antoni Kirke
Plejehjem
VEKSØVEJ
HERFØLGEVEJ
PRÆSTE KÆRVEJ
HOLCKS PLADS
FREDERIKSSUNDSVEJ
HVALSØVEJ
TØLLØSEVEJ
KNABSTRUPVEJ
HAVDRUPVEJ
STAVNSTRUPVEJ
NORD
FELDVEJ
ELMELUNDEVEJ
RYTTER
SKOLEHØJ
BRØNSHØJ TORV
BRØNSHØJ
Brønshøj gl. Skole
HAGESTEDVEJ
FJENNESLEVVEJ
LISELUNDVEJ
IDRÆTS ANLÆG
BRØNSHØJGÅRDVEJ
LEJREVEJ
ASTRUPVEJ
KRABBESHOLMVEJ
TUXENSVEJ
HABETS ALLÉ
ARNESVEJ
DEGNEMOSE ALLÉ
ROSTGAARDSVEJ
SKOVVEJ
STRUPVEJ
BROKSØVEJ
VALLØVEJ
SVEND GØNGES VEJ
SPARTA
HØJSTRUPVEJ

A81 **Vestvolden with Kagmosen * and Brøndbyskov**

1888-92, ca. 1970

Client: The provisional government

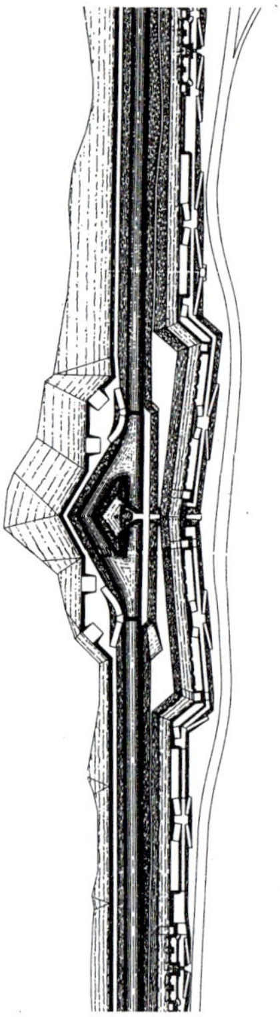

Double traverse

The Vestvold ramparts or the West Enceinte, was built as part of Copenhagen's fortifications toward the countryside. It runs over 15 kilometers from Utterslev Mose heath in the north to Køge Bugt bay in the south. Together with the coastal defenses and the northern forts, the complex was one of the strongest city defence systems of the time. The ramparts are up to 100 meters wide. On the inner edge there was a railway line, this was followed by Voldgaden road flanked by trees from where ramps and steps led up to the different embankment terraces. On the other side of the moat, the glacis rise up to the covered way and a slightly sloped ravelin planted with thornbushes and brambles. Along the embankment, there are 15 canon emplacements on traverses staggered at intervals of 600 meters so they could be fired along the ramparts without hitting each other.

In 1920, Vestvolden was retired as a military complex, and has gradually become a recreational area, near Husum in the 1930's and in other places during the 1970's. The complex was declared a national landmark in 1994. Adjacent to Vestvolden are a number of other significant recreational areas. Kagmosen marsh has ca. 40 acres, half of which is water and marshes. It was regulated in 1939-41 and is now a bird sanctuary and lay-by for migrating birds.

The 175 acre Brøndbyskov forest was planted on an open field in the sparsely wooded area in 1953-54 by Brøndbyerne Municipality according to an arrangement with Copenhagen Municipality. Today the area is predominantly a beech forest.

Utterslev Mose and Brønshøj Kirkemose **A148**

1937-43

Client: Copenhagen Municipality
Landscape architect: Jacob Bergmann, Copenhagen Municipal Park Department

There are only a few areas in the greater Copenhagen area that can be predetermined as parks or green areas for natural reasons as they are difficult to build on due to their ground water characteristics. Some examples of these are the lakes in Copenhagen, Emdrup Lake, Grøndals Park, Krogebjerg Park, Damhusengen Park and Damhus Lake, Vigerslev Park and Utterslev Mose marsh and Brønshøj Kirkemose marsh.

Utterslev Mose marsh has 500 acres of which about half is under water. It is Copenhagen's largest park and runs from Bispebjerg Park Allé in the east to Vestvolden toward west. It is a significant link in the chain of park areas that ring Copenhagen. It was established as part of a job creation program from 1937-43. While the area was controlled by the Copenhagen Water Works it was used to recover water by ground pumps in the marshes. It is a very scenic area with an extensive net of paths. The landscaping was done with respect for the area's natural flora and consists of groups of hawthorn, willows, etc. In other areas, the cutting of trees, and reeds for roofing has created magnificent vistas across the meadows and water areas. Bird life has been protected by digging canals to create inaccessible islands. Utterslev Mose, with its wealth of birds and fish offers excellent opportunities for nature studies. Its athletic fields, playgrounds and skating rinks provide many sites for sports and recreation.

Bibliography: Havekunst 1940, 122

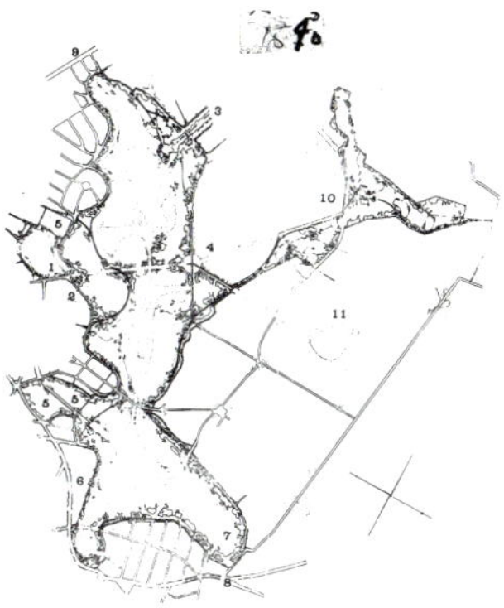

1:80.000

A171

The Voldparken housing scheme

Kobbelvænget, Arildsgård, Voldparken, Husum
1949-51

Client: The Workers' Cooperative Housing Association (AAB)
Architect: Kay Fisker
Landscape architect: C.Th. Sørensen

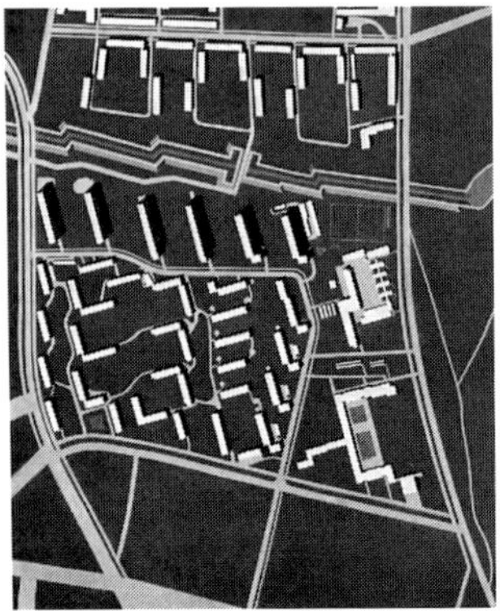

This scheme with its 1400 units was one of the largest post-war projects and the last to be built by traditional building methods, in the spirit of the functional tradition. Kay Fisker's buildings for AAB are at the eastern end of the scheme, which as a whole was planned by municipal architect F.C. Lund, Edvard Heiberg, Karl Larsen, and V.S. Jørgensen. The broad roof eaves and the recessed balconies are simple effects employed with a great mastery so that the buildings are distinctive in their placement and relationship to the terrain. The varying heights of the blocks can be easily read in the strong, horizontal shadows on the facades. The yellow brickwork and the fiber cement panels used as roofing and on the balcony railings give the scheme a light and unifying expression. As a whole, these features make Fisker's buildings the most homogeneous of the entire scheme. The proximity to Vestvolden and Utterslev Mose and the careful design of the spaces between the buildings evokes an almost parklike character. Of the many common facilities, Kay Fisker also designed the Voldparken School. (A 174)

Voldparken School

Åkandevej 31, Husum
1951-57

Client: Copenhagen Municipality
Architect: Kay Fisker
Landscape architect: C.Th. Sørensen

The design of the school started in 1944, and construction work took place in two stages, which were completed in 1951 and 1957. The classrooms are grouped in one- and three-story buildings, which together with buildings with large common rooms, surround the schoolyard. It is not an original type. Its qualities can be found in the powerful architectural expression, a masterly interplay of distinct brick volumes and large roof surfaces. The materials are identical with those used in Kay Fisker's neighboring Voldparken housing scheme: yellow brick facades and pale grey corrugated fiber cement roofing. It is an ideal background for the buildings' precise and distinctive play of light and shade and forms a fine contrast to the surrounding park areas.
Bibliography: Tobias Faber a.o: Architect Kay Fisker. 1995

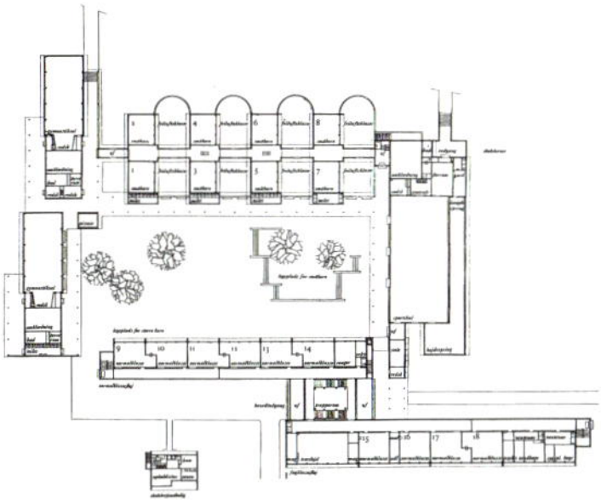

1:3000

A175

The Tingbjerg housing scheme

Ruten et al. Husum
1950-71

Client: Copenhagen Public Housing Association (KAB) and the Social Housing Association (FSB)
Architect: Steen Eiler Rasmussen
Landscape architect: C.Th. Sørensen

With its 3000 units, the scheme has the size of a small town. The original idea was that Tingbjerg should be an independent town unit, which beside offering a variety of housing types, should also include businesses, shops and institutions. The scheme is formed after the classic town ideals with streets and squares, though augmented with a high-rise building. The business intentions never materialized, and the urban character is somewhat diluted by the openness of the plan and the lack of urban functions. Tingbjerg is an example of an idealistic housing and city planning project, with a somewhat dry, academical character, however the housing units have many qualities in terms of human scale and the well designed details such as the French windows with sliding shutters.

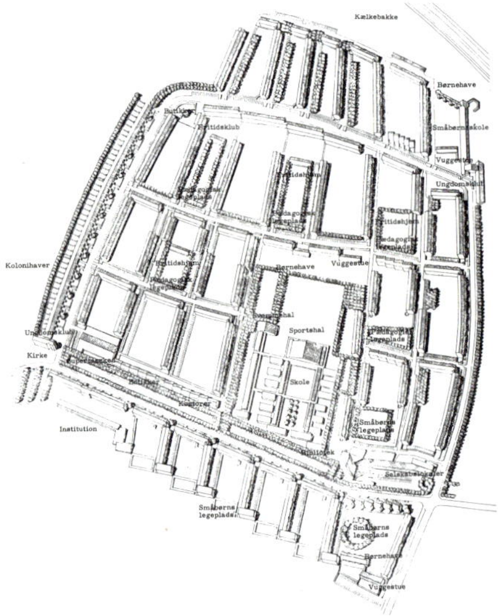

Blaagaard Teachers' College

Mørkhøj Parkallé, Søborg
1962-66

Client: Blaagaard Seminarium, Gladsaxe Municipality
Architect: Jørgen Bo, Karen and Ebbe Clemmensen
Landscape architect: J. Palle Schmidt

Together with the Enghavegård School, the teachers' college constitutes a building complex used daily by ca. 2000 people from 6-70 years old. Due to its size, the scheme has a town-like character. The plan has a flexible structure that complies with the landscape and its use, and alterations and additions occur regularly. The school and the college are connected by a "bridge building" that houses common functions. From the center of the area, where the assembly hall is, the sports halls protrude toward east and the teachers' college toward south. The freestanding building toward west houses facilities for art subjects. The different elements in the complex are placed at different heights according to the terrain grade. This gives an interior character of a hilly urban landscape with an outer organic rhythm.
Bibliography: Arkitektur DK 1969, 54

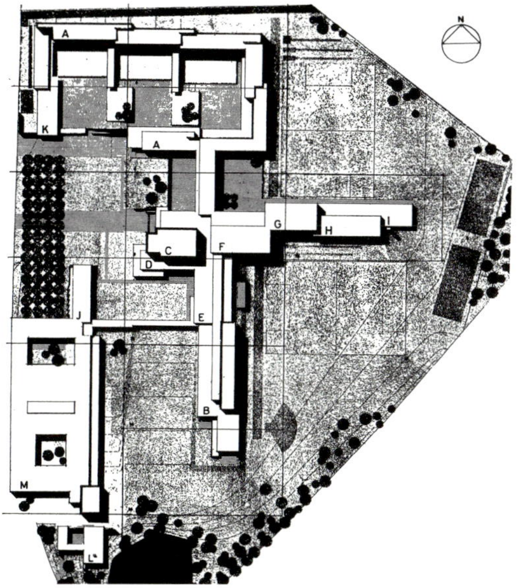

1:5000

A214

The Høje Gladsaxe housing scheme

Høje Gladsaxe on Gladsaxevej, Gladsaxe
1963-68

Before renovation

Client: Five public housing associations, administrator: Arbejderbo
Architect: Hoff & Windinge, Juul Møller & Agertoft and Alex Poulsen. A5 Tegnestuen (renovation)
Landscape architect: Sven Hansen, Morten Klint and Andreas Bruun

The scenic quality of the site near the Utterslev Mose moor was a decisive consideration in the choice of the building form, which was based on architect Vilhelm Lauritzen's master plan from 1943. By concentrating the 2000 apartments in five large high-rise blocks, flanked by a number of lower blocks, the landscape toward south was freed for recreational use. The building system was part of the so-called Ballerup Plan, and the industrialized building process employed at Høje Gladsaxe was the fastest and most advanced at that time. There are 1435 units in the high-rise buildings and 486 in the low blocks, with relatively deep apartments in both building types. In every way, the scheme marked the culmination of modernism's ideals, both regarding the landscape treatment, architecture, technical standards and the character of the living facilities. Its coherent, radical form aroused a debate in contrast with the low-rise new town in Albertslund, built during the same period (J 205). An extensive renovation in 1991-93 included closing off the open balconies with glass, which has greatly affected the architectural expression.
Bibliography: Arkitektur DK 1969, 24

After renovation

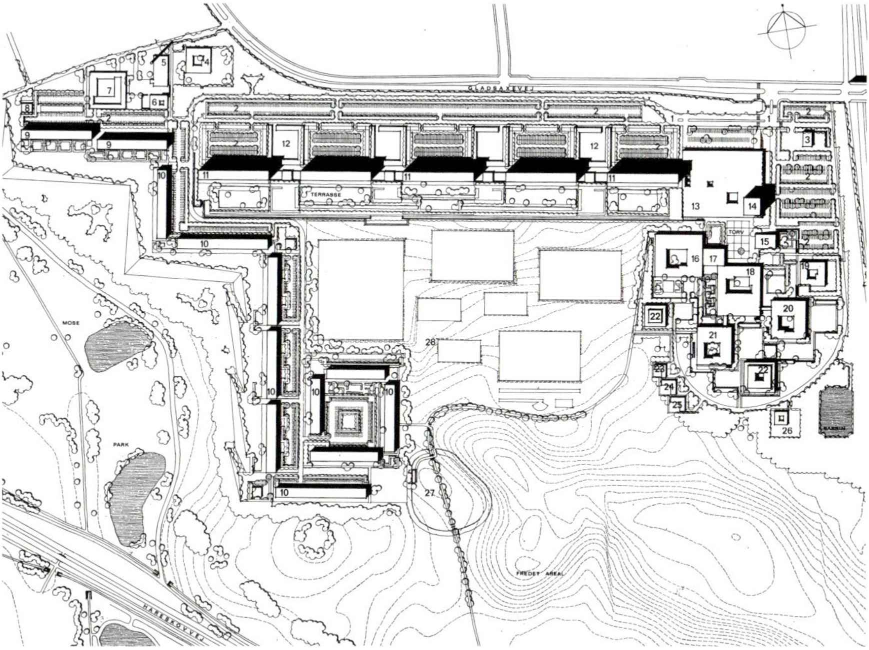

1:10.000

SØBORG
WERGELANDS ALLÉ
RUNEBERGS ALLÉ
SELMA LAGERLØFS ALLÉ
MAGLEGÅRDS ALLÉ
NIELS BOHRS ALLÉ
SØBORGHUS ALLÉ
SØBORG HOVEDGADE
DALSTRØGET
MUNKEGÅRDSVEJ
RØNTOFTEVEJ
ALMINDINGEN
HULKÆRVEJ
THULEVEJ
Dyssegård St.
DYSSEGÅRDSVEJ
MUNKELY
MINDEVEJ
PLANTEVEJ
VANGEDEVEJ
KNUD RASMUSSENS VEJ
SØNDERDALEN
GRØN TOFTEN
ESKEAGER
LANGAGEN
VESTER DALEN
SØNDER GÅRDSVEJ
SØNDERENGEN
SLETTEVEJ
BUEN
KANAL
177
DYSSEGÅRDSPARKEN
ELLEMOSEVEJ
THOR LANGES ALLÉ
GLADSAXEVEJ
STJERNEBORG ALLÉ
LAUGGÅRDS VÆNGE
Vandværk
BÆKKEBO
VED RENDEN
VENUSVEJ
ENGKROGEN
MOSEVEJ
SØBORGHUS PARK
RØDKLØVERVEJ
KIÆRS ALLÉ
LAUGGÅRDS ALLÉ
MAGLE DALEN
KIRSTENS ALLÉ
MAGLESTIEN
MAGLE KROGEN
DUNHAMMERVEJ
ENGBLOMMEVEJ
HVIDKLØVERVEJ
TREKLØVERVEJ
GULKLØVERVEJ
STENKLØVERVEJ
IDRÆTSANLÆG
FIRKLØVERVEJ
MOSEKROGEN
MOSEPARKEN
MOSESKELLET
DALMOSEVEJ
FREDERIKSBORGVEJ
NØKKEROSEVEJ
Emdrup skole
Emdrup gård
C. J. FRANDSENS VEJ
EMDRUPGÅRDSVEJ
EMDRUP ENGVEJ
EMDRUP MOSEVEJ
EMDRUP KÆRVEJ
LAVTOFTEVEJ
HAVEVEJ
HØJMOSEVEJ
EMDRUPVEJ
EMDRUP
MAGLE TORV
GRØNNEMOSE ALLÉ
Torgmagle Kirke
164
RØRMOSEVEJ
GULDSTJERNEVEJ
PRAGTSTJERNEVEJ
FLADSTJERNEVEJ
SKOVSTJERNEVEJ
BØLLEGÅRD ALLÉ
KANTORPARKEN
Håndværker kollegiet
MAGLEGÅRDS ALLÉ
MOSEVANGEN
BISMOSEVEJ
ENGBLOMMEVEJ
VED VIGEN
Emdrup Kirke
BLÅMUNKEVEJ
RINVEJ
ROSMA
BISPEBJERG PARKALLÉ
UTTERSLEV MOSE
TONEMESTERVEJ
HENRIKSVEJ
JEPPES ALLÉ
OLDFUXVEJ
PERNILLEVEJ
MAGDELONEVEJ
ORGELBYGGERVEJ
RÅDVADSVEJ
FILOSOF VÆNGET
VILHELM BIRKEDALS VEJ
BISPEBJERGVEJ
115
Grundtvigskirken
MOSESVINGET
SVANESTIEN
BISPEBJERG TORV
PÅ BJERGET
JENSEN KLINTS PLADS
BJERG VÆNGET
Ø2
FOLEVADSVEJ
ØREVADS VEJ
Bispebjerg Krematorium
C. J. BRANDTS VEJ
PETER NORDAHLS VEJ
RØNNINGS VEJ
TAGENSVEJ
BERGS VEJ
JACOB LIND
LÆRKEBAKKEN
MAGESTIEN
ENGSVINGET
STØVNÆS ALLÉ
BISPEBJERG KIRKEGÅRD
BISPEPARKEN
CHARLOTTE MUNCKS VEJ
UTTERSLEV
HORSEBAKKEN
161
HYRDEVANGEN
RAVNEHOLMSVEJ
RÅDVADSVEJ
HYRDELEDET
VÆBNERVEJ
TÅRNBLÆSERVEJ
GRANLIEN
HJORTHOLMS ALLÉ
SKOLEHOLDERVEJ
GRAVERVÆNGET
KLOKKERHØJEN
MØLLERLOODEN
POSTHOLDERVEJ
FUGLEFÆNGERVEJ
Ungdomsskolen i Utterslev
PRÆSTELÆNGEN
DEGNESTAVNEN
RINGERTOFTEN
142
Bispebjerg Sk
BOMSLUTTERVEJ
MAGISTERVEJ
HOVMESTERVEJ
UTTERSLEV TORV
HF
UTTERSLEVDAL
RENTE
MESTERVEJ
DORTHEAVEJ
TOFTEN
BIRKEDOMMERVEJ
TOMSGÅRDSVEJ
Børneinst.
SKOVLØBERVEJ
TINGSKRIVERVEJ
LANDFOGEDVEJ
RIDEFOGEDVEJ
TOLDSKRIVERVEJ
146
Grundtvigs skolen
TRYKKERVEJ
FRIMESTERVEJ
SLOTSFR
Efterslægtselskabets Gymnasium
Utterslev Kirke
NORD STIEN
RYTTERBAKKEN
SVENDELODDEN
MESTERSTIEN
SMEDETOFTEN
Stadsgartn.
BIRKEDOMMERVEJ
HARESKOVVEJ
UTTERSLEVVEJ
UTTERSLEV GÅRD
SØKKELUNDSVEJ
DORTHEAVEJ
Km. pl.
Plejehjemmet Dorotheagården
STIKKERVEJ
PERLE
Tagensbo Kirke
LANDSDOMMERVEJ
OLDERMANDSVEJ
GEMMET
MØNTMESTERVEJ
PARK STYKKET
TVÆRVANGEN
HYRDEVANGEN
RENTEMESTERVEJ
PETER IPSENS ALLÉ
BISPEVEJ
VAGTMESTERVEJ
TØJMESTERVEJ
SPORMAGERVEJ
SADELMAGERVEJ
BUNTMAGERVEJ
TØNDEBINDERVEJ
STENHUGGERVEJ
TEGLBRÆNDERVEJ
BISIDDERVEJ
FREDERIKSSUNDSVEJ
Brandst.
HULGÅRDS PLADS
KEDELSMEDEVEJ
PROVSTEVEJ
THORAVEJ
FREDERIKSBORGVEJ
SKAFFERVEJ
BYGMESTERVEJ
RENTEMESTERVEJ
Bellahøj Bad og Hal
BORUPS ALLÉ
THEKLAVEJ
LILLE THEKLAVEJ
HOUMANNS ALLÉ
GLASVEJ
Bellahøj Kirke
VED BELLAHØJ
180
Frederikssundsvejens Skole
UGLEVEJ
STÆREVEJ
SNEPPEVEJ
BROFOGEDVEJ
BLYTÆKKERVEJ
REBSLAGERVEJ
Bellahøj Skole
16
ØRNEVEJ
Busanlæg
FREDERIKSSUNDSVEJ
PLUMSVEJ
DREJERVEJ
Tekn. Skole
179
Kapernaums Kirke
BELLAHØJ
STÆREVEJ
RØRSANGERVEJ
MÅGEVEJ
MUSVÅGEVEJ
MATTERGALEVEJ
ALEXANDERVEJ

B
HANS JENSENS VEJ
C. V. E. KNUTHS VEJ
HELLERUP KIRKEGÅRD
Skt. Therese Kirke
Rygård Skole
Rygårds-centret
Hellerup St.
GENTOFTE
IDRÆTS ANLÆG
LYNGBYVEJ
NIELS ANDERSENS VEJ
BERNSTORFFSVEJ
TUBORGVEJ
Skt. Lukas Stiftelsen
STUDIEBYEN
RYVANGEN
SØHOLM PARK
EMDRUP SØ
EMDRUP SØPARK
EMDRUPVEJ
RYPARKEN
Ryparkens Hallen
VOGNMANDS MARKEN
Svanemøllens Kaserne
IDRÆTSANLÆG
EMDRUP VÆNGE
Lundehus Kirke
Emdrup Bad
Emdrup Søgård
LERSØ PARKALLÉ
Lundehusskolen
HF. VENNERS LYST
HF. FREM TIDEN
KOLONIHAVEPARK
HF. ØBRO
HF. BLOMSTEN
HF. ALDERSRO
Kommunens Gartneri
Busanlæg
Meteorologisk Institut
Ryparken St.
KILDEVÆLDS PARKEN
Kildevælds Kirke
HF. 4. MAJ
1921
Stadsing. Dir.
SANKT KJELDS PLADS
JAGTVEJ
FÆLLED
ØSTER ALLÉ
UNIVERSITETSPARKEN
Zoologisk Museum
Datalogisk
Aug. Krogh Inst.
50
114
104
124
131
176
178
217

B50

Søholm *

Søholm Park 1, Hellerup
1806-09

Client: Merchant Joseph Nathan David
Architect: Christian Frederik Hansen

The drawings for Søholm are generally attributed to C.F. Hansen, while his young project architect, Peder Malling, who thirty years later was responsible for Copenhagen University's main building on Frue Plads, is believed to have supervised the project. At that time, the building consisted only of the five-bay main building. The wings were added in 1858, and later there were major alterations to the roof and interior. In 1982, the building was taken over by the Architects Pension Fund, which carried out an extensive restoration to return the house to its original condition with the addition of several contemporary, exclusive details. This restoration was supervised by Preben Hansen's Tegnestue under the leadership of David Bretton-Meyer.
Bibliography: A.L. Thygesen and H. Lund: C.F. Hansen. 1995. Arkitektur DK 1985, 140

Bispebjerg Hospital

Bispebjerg Bakke 25-31, Bispebjerg
1908-13

Client: Copenhagen Municipality
Architect: Martin Nyrop
Landscape architect: Edvard Glæsel

The hospital complex is formally organized along a central axis, stepping down a southeast oriented slope. The main entrance in the administration portal is monumental and gives the institutional character inherent in the main disposition. The patient buildings, with the large windows, are freestanding, although the four buildings at the base of the complex are connected in pairs, by covered passageways, with the surgery buildings. Despite its symmetry, the spacious scheme has an almost rural atmosphere, and was Denmark's first pavilion hospital. The proportions of the buildings and the picturesque details in the brickwork and half-timber contribute to the friendly, humane environment, which is enhanced by the gardens.

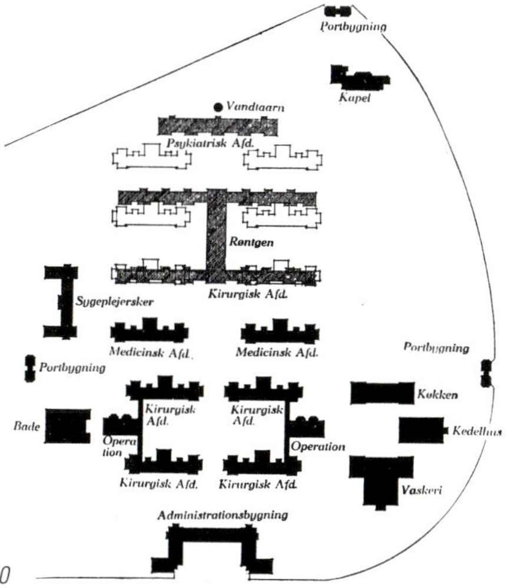

1:10.000

B104

Fælledparken *

Østerbro
1906-14

Client: Copenhagen Municipality
Landscape architect: Edvard Glæsel, Copenhagen Municipal Park Department

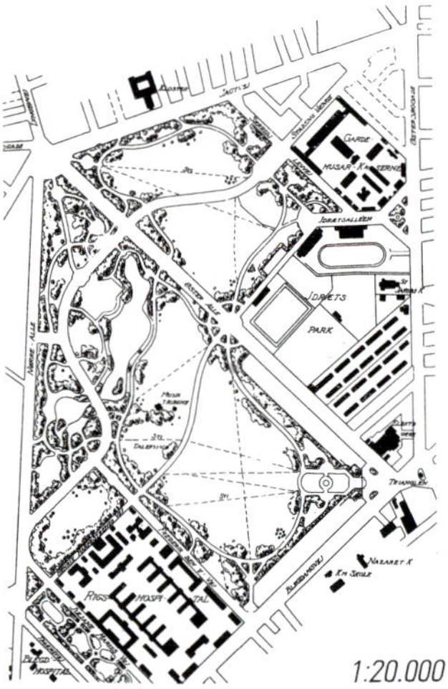

Fælledparken was established at the beginning of the century and represented a new concept in park design compared to earlier parks, in that it was planned from a utilitarian point of view with large open lawns for ball games, meetings, public festivals and concerts. Originally there were eight playgrounds, some with wading pools and sand areas. The park lies in an area formerly used as a military exercise area up until the turn of the century. Based on a 1906 competition won by O.K. Nobel and Svend Koch, landscape architect Edvard Glæsel and the municipal engineer designed a project in which the large lawn areas were edged by powerful groups of trees, usually beeches, along the adjacent roads. During the sixties, an open air swimming pool and a wading pool were established on the opposite side of the winding Borgmester Jensens Allé, and during the 1980's a large skate board and roller skating area was established.

Sømarksvej ved Rygårds Allé 76, Hellerup
1920-24

Client: Copenhagen Public Housing Association (KAB)
Architect: Edvard Thomsen, Anton Rosen, Ivar Bentsen, Thorkild Henningsen, Kay Fisker
Landscape architect: G.N. Brandt

KAB was especially interested in low-rise housing during the first years after its founding in 1920, and the association wanted to experiment with architecture and building methods. From the very beginning, it worked with the leading architects of the time. This entire program was manifested in Studiebyen, which KAB hoped would be "an encyclopedia of low-rise housing". Under the leadership of KAB's own architect, Peter Nielsen, over a score of architects worked on the design of the 104 houses, including Edvard Thomsen, Anton Rosen, Ivar Bentsen, Thorkild Henningsen, Kay Fisker, and G.N. Brandt, who was the municipal gardener in Gentofte and was responsible for the garden plans. Both individual houses, double houses and row houses were represented, and experiments were made with new materials and structural designs – with dispensations from the building codes – in order to find the most practical and inexpensive solutions. In an attempt to harmonize the aesthetics of the scheme, each architect, when possible, designed two houses opposite each other.

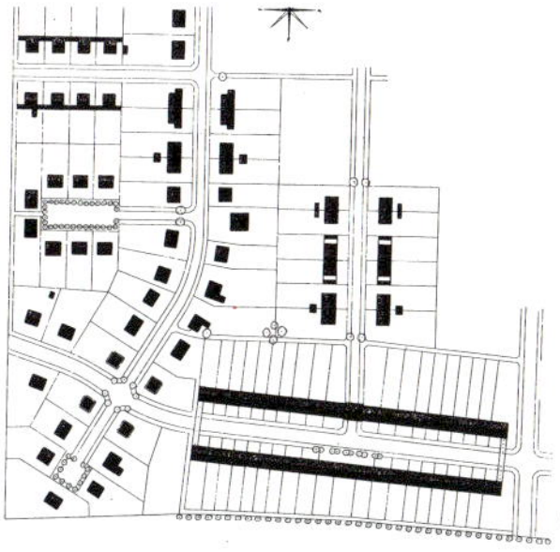

1:8.000

The gate building facing Rygårds Allé suggests an attempt to emphasize the quarter's special identity

B115

Grundtvigs Church

På Bjerget, Bispebjerg
1921-40

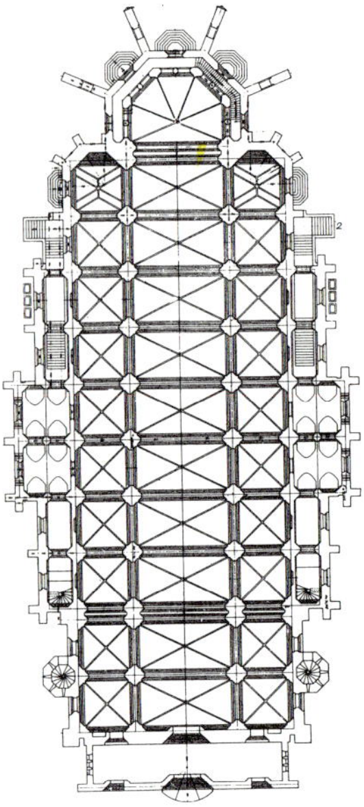

1:1000

Client: The State, Copenhagen Municipality and a private committee.
Architect: Peder Vilhelm Jensen-Klint

The poet priest, N.F.S. Grundtvig's (1783-1872) influence on the Danish intellectual life was and is monumental. The monumentality of the church built with a massive joint effort to honor him, is thus appropriate, especially because the expression is subtle and mild. This is evident in the tower facade with the Danish village church metaphor and the cathedral size organ facades, in the three-aisled church space by the ethereal light effects, and in general in the homogeneity and simplicity provided by the yellow brick, the church's sole building material and decorative element. The Gothic suggestions yield to the architect's very personal design. He described the building as an oversized village church. After P.V. Jensen-Klint's death in 1930, the supervision of the church building was completed by his son, Kaare Klint. The buildings surrounding the church, På Bjerget 1-36, were built in 1924-36 from drawings by these two architects. The low, uniform buildings emphasize the greatness of the church and form a harmonious town and park space around it. The site planning of the church and its surrounding buildings on Bispebjerg was done by architects Charles I. Schou and Georg Gøssel.

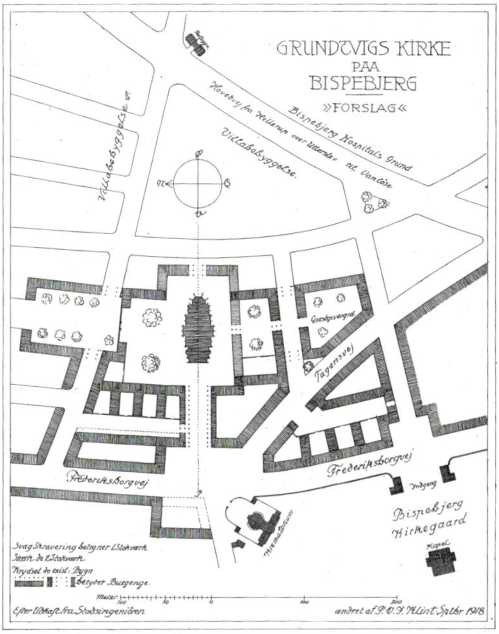

GRUNDTVIGS KIRKE
PAA
BISPEBJERG
»FORSLAG«
Bispebjerg Hospitals Grund
Hovedvej fra Hellerup over Utterslev til Vanløse
Villabebyggelse.
Villabebyggelse
Gjæstgivergrd.
Tagensvej
Frederiksborgvej
Frederiksborgvej
Indgang
Bispebjerg
Kirkegaard
Krematorium
Kapel
Svag Skravering betegner 1. Stokværk
Stærk do 2. Stokværk
Krydsel do exist: Bygn
betyder Buegange.
Meter 100 50 0 100 200
Efter Udkast fra Stadsingeniøren
ændret af P. V. J. Klint Sptbr 1918

1:8000

B124

The Solgården housing block

The block formed by Vejrøgade, Skt. Kjeldsgade,
Ourøgade, and Langøgade, Østerbro
1929

Client: Copenhagen Public Housing Association (KAB)
Architect: Henning Hansen
Landscape architect: C.Th Sørensen

When completed, the 186 unit housing block had many new features. The opening of the block's corner towards south-west was a step towards the breaking up of the large city block. The solar orientation of the living rooms, and the placement of the main entrance in the rear courtyard were also new features, which Henning Hansen had previously experimented with at his housing project from 1921 at Vilh. Thomsens Allé 4-40. The single stairway system found in some areas of Solgården, was also uncommon at that time, as were the small rooms for children in some of the apartments. The south and west facades are pulled back from the street line to allow the sun into the ground floor apartments where there are brick walls to screen the small gardens. The symmetrically organized facades and end walls have a neo-classicistic character, but the different innovative features seem to be a harbinger of functionalism.

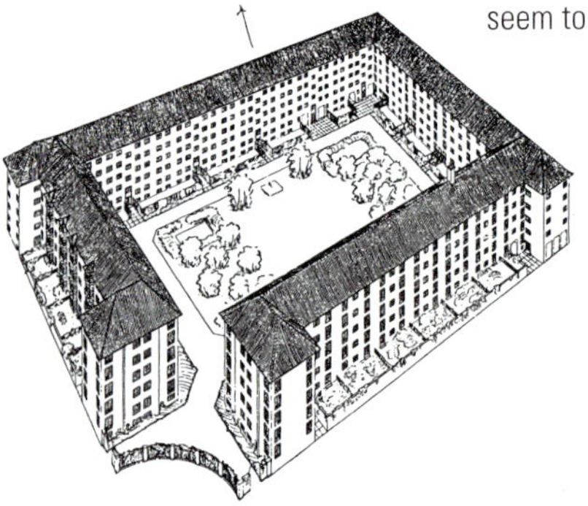

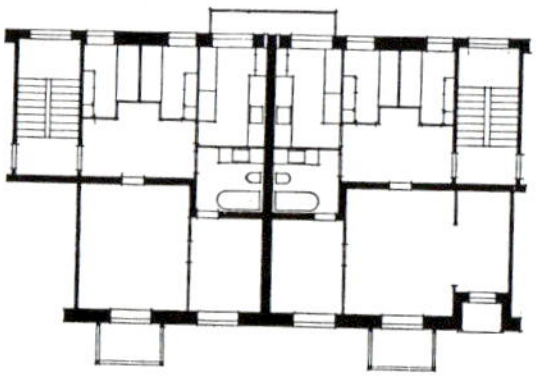

Ryparken housing scheme

Ryparken, Hellerup
1931

Client: A consortium led by attorney Rasmus Nielsen (later the Society for Social Housing, FSB)
Architect: Povl Baumann, Edvard Heiberg, Karl Larsen and Frederik Wagner
Landscape architect: C.Th. Sørensen

Functionalism's new public health requirements for housing were first clearly evident in Ryparken's subdued blocks, which were organized in relation to the sun. The scheme was a radical break with previous housing ideals. The sun worshipper's attribute, the balcony, was employed here for the first time in such a uniform and consistent fashion that it became the scheme's primary motif. The space between the buildings was thoughtfully landscaped with playgrounds and other elements so that these facilities are a fine supplement to the formal site plan and the monotonous buildings. A recent renovation with new plastic windows and alterations of the balconies has destroyed much of the scheme's original character.
Bibliography: H.E. Langkilde: Povl Baumann. 1991, 157

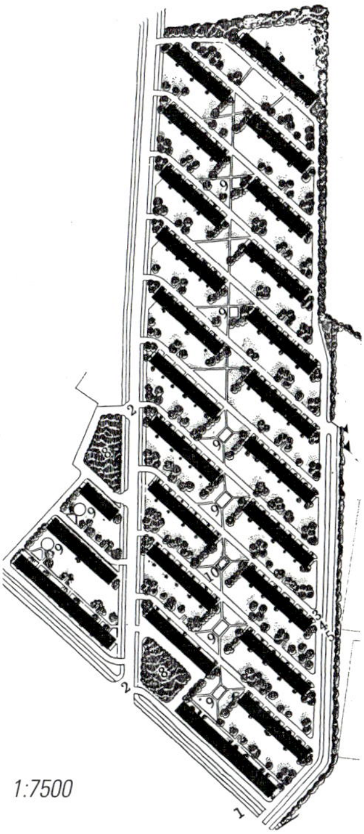

1:7500

The open areas around the buildings were landscaped as open lawns with groups of different kinds of willow trees, and as a new feature for the time, large screened playgrounds with sandboxes and wading pools. Near Lyngbyvej road there is an unusual gathering place consisting of a graveled area with parasol-trimmed hawthorns.

B142 **The Storgården housing project**

Tomsgårdsvej 70-110, Bispebjerg
1935

Client: The Society for Social Housing, FSB
Architect: Povl Baumann & Knud Hansen
Landscape architect: C.Th. Sørensen

The most prominent elements on Storgården's 280 meters of facade are the balconies, which with their formally organized, uniform repetition evoke a new kind of monumentality. The balconies are modest in size, but carefully designed and positioned. The long, straight building has a modest yet refined flare at the end wall towards north, which emphasizes the firm architectural bearing. The 210, small, two-room apartments, have an extra room: the balcony, which provides extra space and light. On the garden facade, the balconies' form, as an enlarged lounge chair hung lengthwise on the facade, evokes the feeling of a private space. The balconies facing Tomsgårdsvej were removed in connection with a renovation, but the building is still an impressive monument to the small, functionalistic high-rise apartment. The project's recreational area, shared with Bispebjerg School, is more varied than the spaces surrounding the traditional functionalistic housing block, and the landscaping offers a fine contrast to the monumental apartment block.
Bibliography: H.E. Langkilde: Povl Baumann. 1991, 162

1:5000

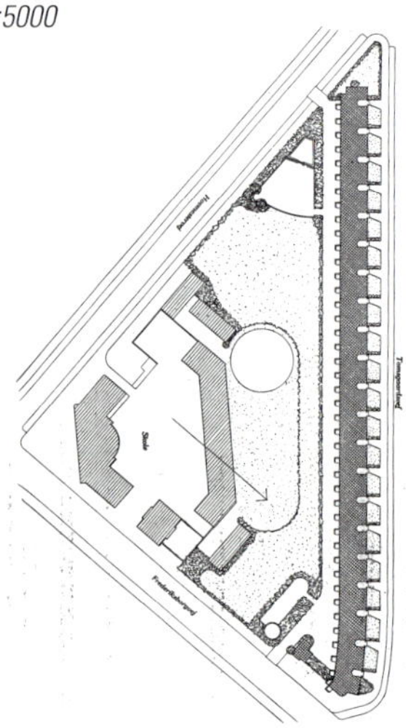

Grundtvigs School **B146**

Magistervej 4, Nørrebro
1937-38

Client: Copenhagen Municipality
Architect: Municipal architect Poul Holsøe and F.C. Lund

The scheme has a symmetrical organization with the classrooms in a south oriented three-story wing. The special-subject rooms form the two sides of the central main hall, which has large windows toward north and south.
The plan displays a traditional, formal attitude, while the cubistic building forms with their flat roofs and modernistic materials and colors lean toward the liberal school architecture of the 1940's. The pompous ceremonial character of the main hall is emphasized by the axial view towards north through the park wedge in the Bispebjerg housing area to Grundtvigs Church.

B161

The Bispeparken housing scheme

Between Frederiksborgvej, Tagensvej and Tuborgvej, Bispebjerg
1940-42

Client: The Society for Social Housing, FSB
Architect: Kooperative Arkitekter, Ivar Bentsen, Kaare Klint, Valdemar Jørgensen, Knud Thorball, Magnus Stephensen, Harald Petersen, Frederik Wagner, Knud Hansen and Vagn Kaastrup.
Landscape architect: C.Th. Sørensen

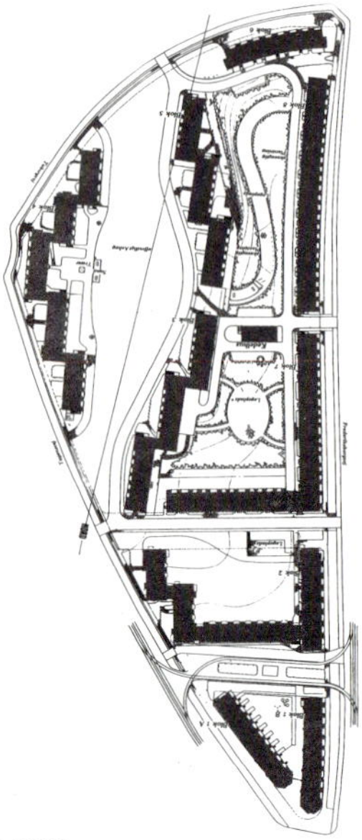

1:6000

On Grundtvig Church's visual axis there is a large, open green bordered by different types of hawthorns. Within the housing area there are still several fine groves of birch trees, but most of the open areas today are occupied by parking, sheds, Laundromats and a day-care center. These buildings are of red brick in a quality far inferior to the precision of the housing blocks.

Public housing increased in scope at the end of the 1930's and with the rent support law in 1938, which was primarily aimed at large families, it received a decisive take-off towards its great future development. Bispeparken was a manifestation of the cooperative spirit, both in the design of the large garden housing scheme with the many small apartments, the client constellation, and the collaboration between several architects. The site plan was done by Ivar Bentsen and Kooperative Arkitekter, while the design of the individual blocks also involved Kaare Klint, Valdemar Jørgensen, Knud Thorball, Magnus Stephensen, Harald Petersen, Frederik Wagner, Knud Hansen and Vagn Kaastrup. The unconstrained site plan had a traditional touch in its symmetrical organization toward southeast and in the axial effect toward Grundtvigs Church, but the staggered blocks gave a new and varied depiction of the urban home. The balcony/bay motif was popular and was given a variety of forms by the different architects. The small apartments with a children's room was now a regular feature.

The Atelierhus housing scheme *

Grønnemose Allé 21-49, Emdrup
1943

Client: The Society for Social Housing, FSB
Architect: Viggo Møller-Jensen
Landscape architect: C.Th. Sørensen

The war and the tenants' modest financial resources were the reasons that this housing scheme had to be austere. The three groups of staggered row houses were built for young artists and were originally heated by tiled stoves, and the electrical installations were exposed, while the simple materials like the mortar brushed brickwork, corrugated asbestos cement roofing and tarred woodwork were combined in such a sober and sensitive way, that the architecture still expressed quality. The scheme also represented an innovation in row house design as the shift between the living quarters, studios and outbuildings gave a richly varied interplay of sheltered outdoor spaces around the units. The site by Utterslev Mose marsh and the common parklike area around the pond contributed to the exceptionally pleasant housing environment. Architecturally, the Atelierhusene represent an extension of the functional tradition, and the scheme has been the paradigm for a number of housing schemes that followed, even though its purpose and design were aimed at a special group of tenants.

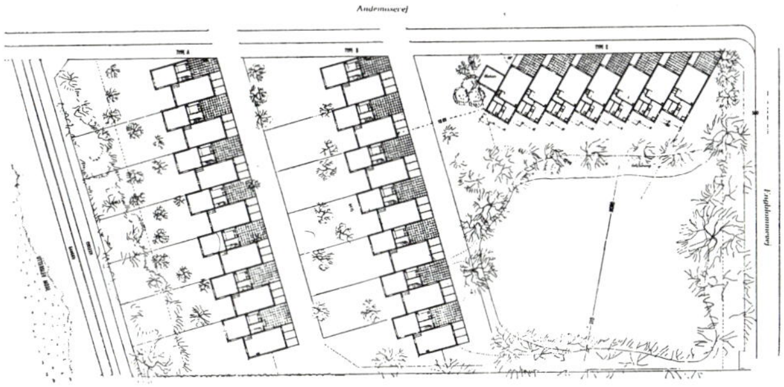

1:2000

B176 **Lersø Parkallé and Bispebjerg Parkallé**

1930-47

Client: Copenhagen Municipality
Landscape architect: V. Fabricius Hansen, Jacob Bergmann, Copenhagen Municipality's Park Department

Lersø Parkallé and Bispebjerg Parkallé form a green link between Fælled Park and Utterslev Mose. Lersø Park Allé's character of a road in a wild, scenic space is unusual and impressive. The lawns on both sides, with parallel paths for pedestrians and bicycles, vary in width from 10 to 100 meters and are landscaped with spread groups of large ash and bird cherry trees as well as broad clusters of hawthorn. Running crosswise along Strødamvej road, with its pollarded willows, lies a belt of ca. 400 tract gardens. They were established in 1946-47 and have connecting paths to Lersø Park Allé and Lersø Park.

Dyssegårds Park * B177

Ved Renden, Gentofte
1949-50

Client: Gentofte Municipality
Landscape architect: Aksel Andersen

The small, functional and unpretentious local park is situated in a low-lying area adjacent to the Dutch-like Gentofte Rende channel with rows of chestnut trees toward west. To the east it is bordered by a row of large weeping willows. Broad hedges of cherry plum, bird cherry, oak and hornbeam create spaces for three, grass, playing fields. Toward north there is a small pine woods that also has a playground. The edge facing the villa quarter has a beautiful, almost circular stone wall.
Bibliography: Arkitektur DK 1990, 180

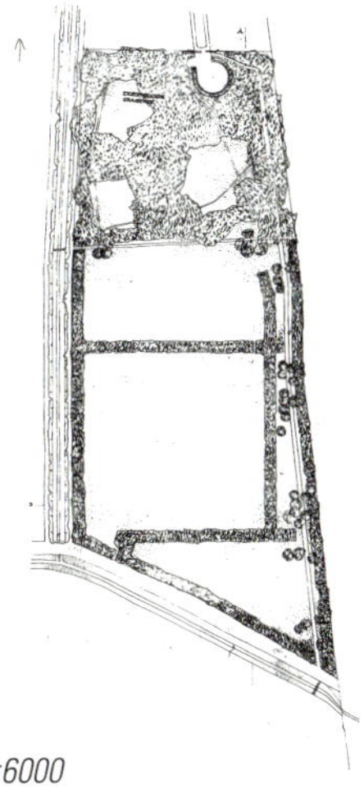

1:6000

B178

Mindelund memorial park

1946-1950
Tuborgvej 35, Hellerup

Client: The national government and the Church Ministry
Architect: Kaj Gottlob
Landscape architect: Aksel Andersen

During World War II, the German occupational forces used a corner of the military training area at Ryvangen to execute members of the Danish resistance. After the war, the Mindelund memorial park was established here in an existing wooded thicket. The execution site in the south corner is now marked by three wooden posts and a memorial plaque with a verse by the poet priest Kaj Munk. The central space is square in form and bordered on three sides by a stone wall with bushes and trees. On the fourth side there is a memorial hall. From the entrance to the north, one is led from the low-lying Tuborgvej road through a ten meter high portal up to the park. The entrance portal is built together with a covered pergola and the low memorial hall to the east. The memorial hall has a wall with memorial plaques for 151 resistance folk killed in action, with unknown burial places. The portal effect at the entrance continues through the long access path, and between the path and the wall there is a long narrow space with trimmed beeches. On the other side of the path, the memorial park is divided in three areas. In a clearing in the forest there is a burial area for 31 resistance members whose bodies were returned to Denmark after the war. In the forest, which unfortunately suffers from the Dutch elm disease, there are a number of burial plots in an irregular staggered circular pattern. On a large lawn with scattered hawthorn trees lies the central, rectangular burial area with a stone marker raised two steps above grade. A wide border of yews forms a background for precise rows of heather covered, identical burial plots and memorial plaques for 196 resistance members that were executed by the Germans. The monument, "The mother with the dead son" by sculptor Axel Poulsen is centrally placed behind the memorial plaques.
Bibliography: Arkitektur DK 1990, 190, Havekunst 1949, 44

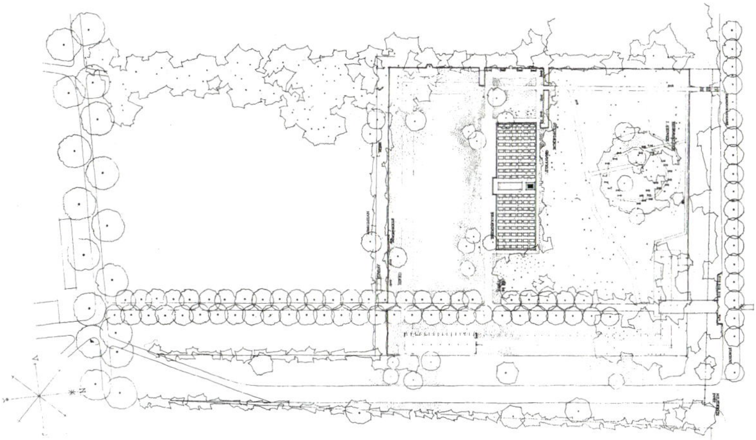

1:5000

B179

Bellahøj open air theater

Bellahøj, Brønshøj
1950

Client: Copenhagen Municipality
Landscape architect: C.Th. Sørensen

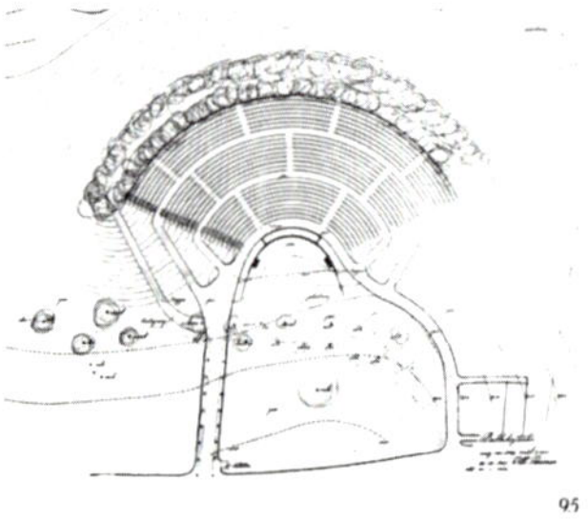

An open air theater was built on an east facing slope near Bellahøj with room for over 2000 spectators. The theater is built into an artificial curved hill consisting of surplus earth from the nearby housing project. The main access path is an old, trimmed linden tree alley that ends at the large theater bowl. From the alley there are three stairways that each lead to a separate seating area.
The 3:1 grade of the slopes results in seat risers that are 40 cm. high and 120 cm. wide seat treads, which offers a comfortable width. Two measured rows of linden trees mark the upper edge of the theater.
The Bellahøj theater bowl has a 120 degree circle sector, while some of Sørensen's other open air theaters have other shapes depending on the local conditions, such as at the Frilandsmuseet open air museum, at Roskilde Folkepark and Boeslunde near Slagelse.
Bibliography: Steen Høyer and Sven-Ingvar Andersson: C.Th. Sørensen – en havekunstner. 1993

The Bellahøjhusene housing scheme — B180

Ved Bellahøj, Brønshøj
1951-56

Client: Four public housing associations
Architect: Svenn Eske Kristensen, Edvard Heiberg, Karl Larsen, Ole Buhl and Harald Petersen, Dan Fink, A/S Dominias arkitektafdeling and Stadsarkitektens Direktorat
Landscape architect: C.Th. Sørensen

Denmark's first real high-rise scheme was fostered by the winning proposal in a 1944 competition for the planning of the Bellahøj area. The winners, Tage Nielsen and Mogens Irming introduced le Corbusier's vision of skyscraper cities with wonderful views over an open, surrounding landscape. However here, the space between the buildings was carefully planned and landscaped as auxiliary spaces to the park surrounding the Bellahøj estate. The high-rise blocks were an experiment, as were the new building methods, such as the slip-form cast concrete. The so-called tower blocks lie in pairs, staggered around an elevator and stairwell with a glass facade. The scheme has 1300, predominantly small apartments with common facilities such as a restaurant and shop. The buildings vary slightly as the northern area was designed by S.Eske Kristensen, Edvard Heiberg, Karl Larsen, Ole Buhl and Harald Petersen. The southern area was designed by Dan Fink, A/S Dominia's architect department and the Municipal Architects office.

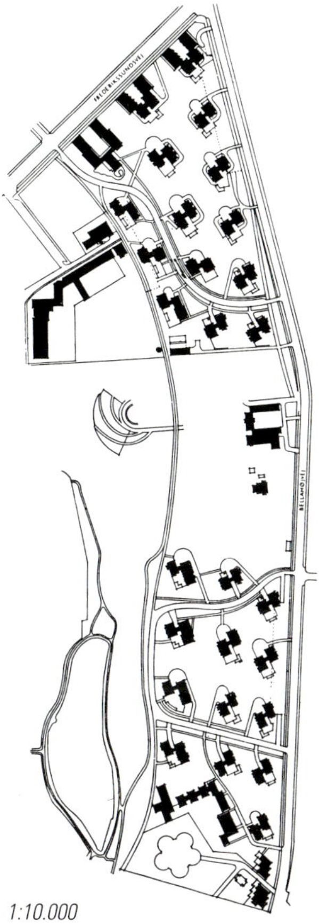

1:10.000

The green areas surrounding the Bellahøj housing scheme were also designed by C.Th. Sørensen. The tower blocks lie on a raised site in a park-like area with spread groups of ash trees.

B217

Lyngbyvej road

From Hans Knudsens Plads to Vangede
1965-74

Client: The Danish government, department of highways
Landscape architect: Edith and Ole Nørgård

Lyngbyvej is an old king's road, which has had the same route since the 1760's. In the 1960's, due to traffic intensity, plans were made to widen the road to a six-lane highway with two-lane, one-way local access roads on both sides as well as the necessary cross bridges and tunnels.
From Hans Knudsens Plaza to Vangede the road is rhythmically divided in a series of clearly separate sceneries. Along the sunken stretches, which were necessary to separate crossing traffic, there are up to seven meter high sheet pilings, from which creepers and wisteria hang like large green curtains.
The placing of trees emphasizes the road's rhythmic division. In the densely built areas, where the road is sunken, there are trees planted along the upper edge of the retaining walls with a precise and uniform size. Originally they were primarily elm with willows by Gentofte lake. Where the road runs on grade, the landscaping is scattered in groups, often of light locust trees. This is also true of the side areas along the exits to Bernstorffvej road and at Vangede. The small plots that remained after expropriations all are uniformly landscaped.
The highway fixtures such as crash barriers, railings, lighting, etc. all have the same form language and a limited use of materials and colors, so that they appear as part of a whole.
Bibliography: Havekunst 1968, 87

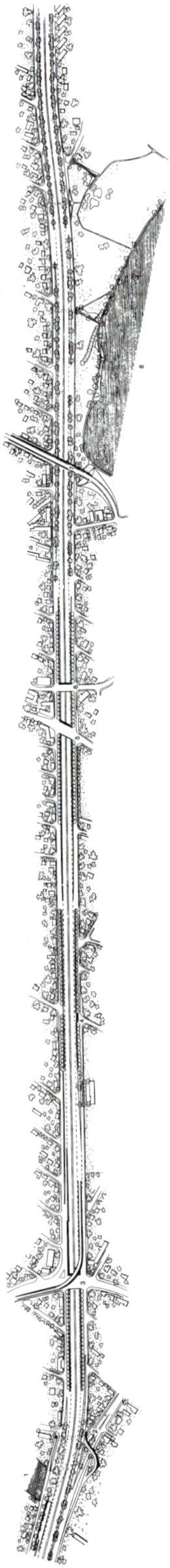

1:20.000

152
105
Hellerup Lystbådehavn
HELLERUPVEJ
STRANDPARKSVEJ
Bernadotte skolen
Gl. Hellerup Gym
SANKT PEDERS VEJ
STRANDVEJEN
FREDERIKKEVEJ
MARIEVEJ
HELLERUP
CALLISENSVEJ
CAROLINEVEJ
NORDKROG
EHLERSVEJ
TUBORGLINIEN
Kl.pumpest.
Gasværket
Nokken
292
HANS BEKKEVOLDS ALLÉ
TUBORG BOULEVARD
TUBORGVEJ
O2
Eksperimentarium
TUBORG HAVN
TUBORG HAVNEVEJ
NORGESMINDEVEJ
Plejehjemmet Norges Minde
Tuborgs bryggerier
STRANDAGERVEJ
GAMMEL VARTOV VEJ
EVANSTONEVEJ
SVANEMØLLEBUGTEN
ROSBÆKSVEJ
Kbh.s Børnehavesem.
VED ELTHAM
SCHERFIGSVEJ
Kirke
ENG SKIFTEVEJ
STRANDØRE
Skt. Joseph Søstrene
KILDE
VÆNGET
O2
RYVANGS ALLÉ
VANGEHUSVEJ
SOLVÆNGET
SØLUNDSVEJ
ØSTERLED
STRANDPROMENADEN
Svanemøllens Kaserne
SVANEVÆNGET
SVANEMØLLE HAVNEN
BELLMANNSGADE
EDVARD GRIEGS GADE
Svanemøllen St.
Kl.pumpest
SVANEMØLLEHAVEN
STRANDVÆNGET
87
KILDEVÆLDSGADE
Svanemølle hallen
Øresundshospitalet
Svanemølle værket
LAUTRUPSKAJ
260
KALKBRÆNDERILØBSKAJ
SUNDKROGSGADE
CONTAINERVEJ
STUBBELØBGADE
LANDSKRONAGADE
CARL NIELSENS ALLÉ
LAUTRUPSGADE
KALK BRÆNDERI HAVNEN
NYGÅRDSVEJ
Strandvejs skolen
78
Østre Gasværk
KALKBRÆNDERIHAVNSGADE
SIONSGADE
HJORTØGADE
ORIENT PLADS
TÅSINGEGADE
263
NYBORGGADE
STRANDBOULEVARDEN
POUL HENINGSENS PLADS
JAGTVEJ
ØSTERBROGADE
VORDINGBORGGADE
Davids kirke
KOLDINGGADE
ÅRHUSGADE
ØSTBANEGADE
ÅLBORGGADE
ØSTERFÆLLED TORV
NORDBAS
VIBORGGADE
PARKEN
GUNNAR NU HANSENS PLADS
Færdsels lege plads
Idrætshuset
Svømmehal
IDRÆTSANLÆG
Nordhavn St.
UNICEF PLADS
248
ØSTERBRO
GAMMEL KALKBRÆNDERI VEJ
NORDRE FRIHAVNSGADE
MARMORVEJ
MELLEM BASSINET
Det sociale Højskole
Fibiger Instituttet
PARKEN
64
Brumleby
ØSTER ALLÉ
Ingrid Jespersens Gym

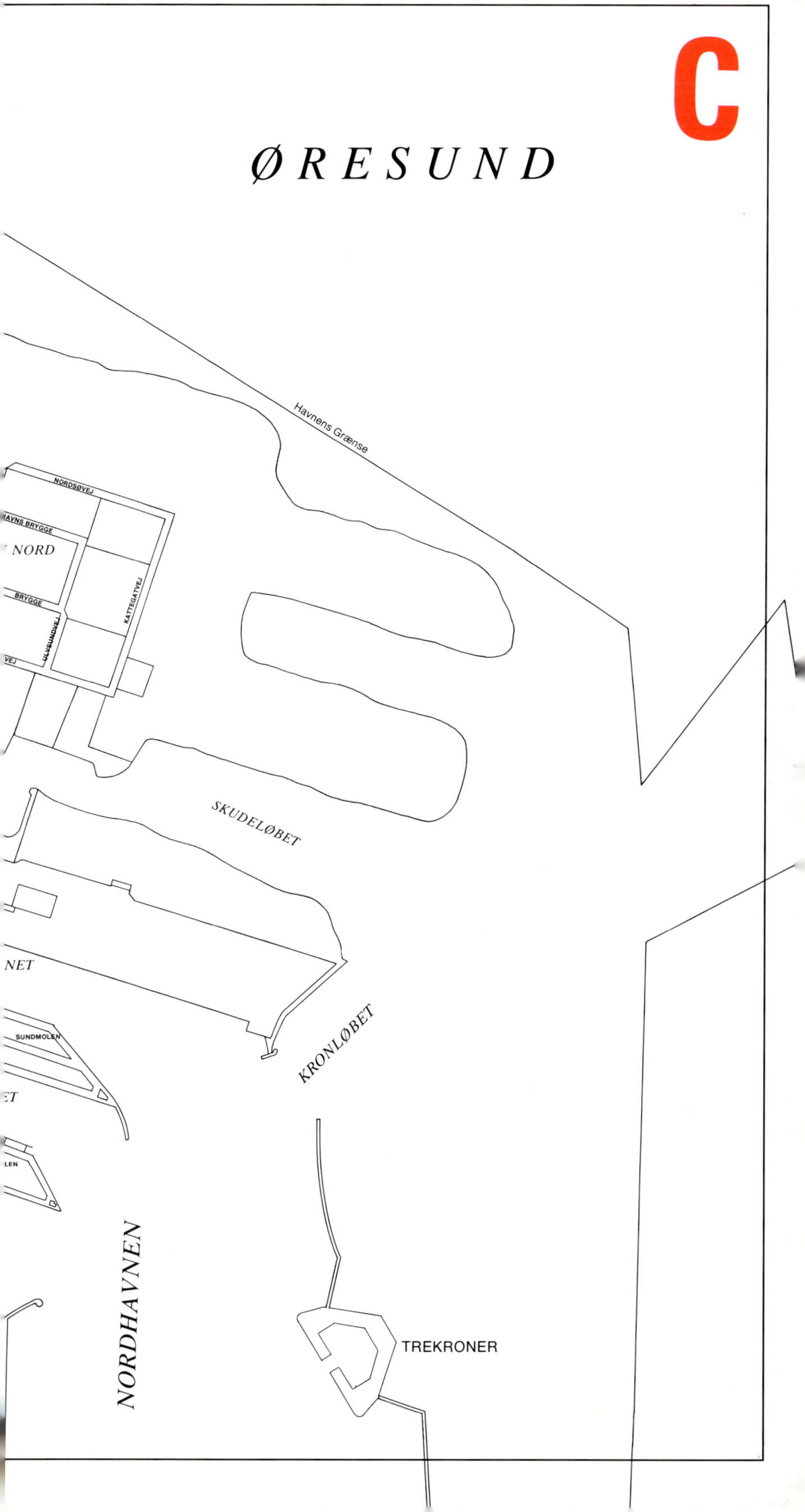
C
ØRESUND
Havnens Grænse
NORDSØVEJ
KATTEGATVEJ
ULVSUNDVEJ
NORD
SKUDELØBET
SUNDMOLEN
KRONLØBET
TREKRONER
NORDHAVNEN

C64

Brumleby (The Medical Association housing scheme)*

Brumleby No. 312-481, Østerbro
1853-72

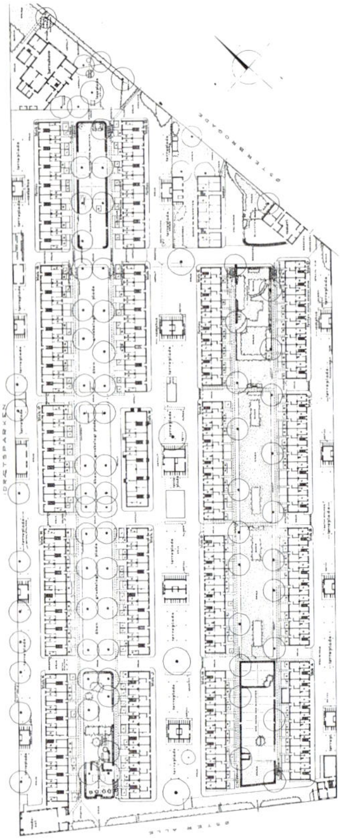

1:3000

Client: The association for the building of healthy and inexpensive housing for the needy classes (The Medical Association)
Architect: Michael Gottlieb Bindesbøll and Vilhelm Klein

In the summer of 1853, Copenhagen was ravaged by a severe cholera epidemic during which ca. 5,000 people died within a few months. As a result of this catastrophe, doctor Emil Hornemann led the initiative to build a new housing area outside the city embankments on the Øster Fælled plane. The project was financed by contributions, and architect M.G. Bindesbøll produced the drawings in a few short weeks so that construction was started already at the end of 1853. During the four years that followed, 240 units were built. A continuation in 1866-72, designed by architect Vilhelm Klein brought the total number of units up to 550. A new feature in the scheme was a series of common facilities including a kindergarten, bathhouse and meeting hall, as well as Copenhagen's first cooperative store. From the beginning, the Medical Association housing was considered a landmark in the area of social-philanthropic housing, both at home and abroad. Since than the scheme has inspired a number of housing projects. After many years of discussion, the scheme was declared an historic building site in 1959. This resulted in a major renovation project started in 1990 and due for completion in 1996. This work is being done by the Copenhagen Urban Renewal Company and led by Dominia. Royal Building Inspector Gehrdt Bornebusch is the architect with Lone van Deurs as the landscape architect.
Bibliography: E. Hansen and M. Philer: Lægeforeningens Boliger på Østerbro. 1971

Østre Gasværk, Gasholder building * C78

Nyborggade 17, Østerbro
1881-83

Client: Copenhagen Municipality
Architect: Martin Nyrop

The cylindrical, domed building originally housed a telescoped gasholder of the type that is usually exposed. With an outer diameter of 47 meters, it is one of Denmark's largest domed buildings. The dome, which is crowned by a lantern, has a slender steel construction, which when built, was considered an engineering marvel. The elaborate brick cylinder, with its round windows in round arched openings appears somber and heavy like a mausoleum. The historical orchestration of utilitarian buildings was typical of the period, but this early work by the architect also has an elementary expressive power in the interplay between the main form and the ornamentation. Since 1979 it has been used as a theater.
Bibliography: Jørgen Sestoft: En bygning på Østre Gasværk. 1985

Building association housing, Kildevældsgade C87

Kildevældsgade et al, Østerbro
1892-1903

Client: The Workers' Building Association
Architect: Frederik Bøttger

With this scheme of 393 houses, architect Bøttger could celebrate his 1000th house designed for the Workers' Building Association. His interest for architectural style was clearly expressed in the thoroughly decorated facades. The arrangement of the scheme around streets and small squares created a fine composition of urban spaces, quite different from the Building Association's standard street buildings. The units here are also larger than normal. As a whole, the architecture clearly expresses the middle class ambitions that were a major incentive for the Workers' Building Association.

C105

Hellerup Strand Park

Onsgårdsvej, Strandparksvej, Hellerup
1912-18

Client: Gentofte Municipality
Architect: Edvard Thomsen
Landscape architect: G.N. Brandt, E. Erstad-Jørgensen, Gentofte Municipal Park Department

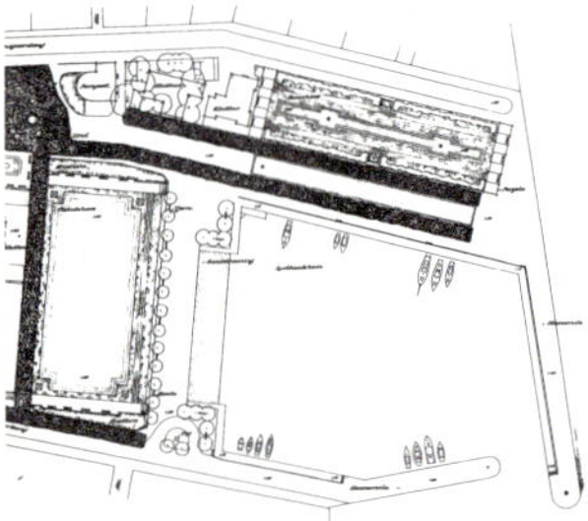

1.5000

Hellerup Strand Park is a modest 5 acres, but is still one of Copenhagen's finest parks. It lies between high-rise housing and a villa quarter, and has direct access to a yachting harbor established in 1910.

The neoclassicistic plan is based on a free composition of rectangles, each with its own function and formed by space-defining hedges and trees. The harbor is flanked by two flower gardens, with perennials and roses, that run out to the beach area.

The perennial garden was established in 1921 by G.N. Brandt and E. Erstad-Jørgensen. It has a slightly recessed lawn bordered by perennial beds with trellis gazebos in each of the four corners. A trimmed linden arcade separates the garden from the tennis courts behind.

The simple, compact rose garden was designed by G.N. Brandt and architect Edvard Thomsen in 1918. In the center there is a lawn with sandstone vases. Along the sides there are beds of roses terminated with rose covered pergolas.

Bibliography: Arkitektur DK 1990, 42, Havekunst 1962, 34

Unipac **C248**

Unicef Plads, Frihavnen
1983

Client: Foreign Ministry, department A
Architect: Tegnestuen Vandkunsten
Landscape architect: Tegnestuen Vandkunsten

Unipac is a subdivision of Unicef, UN's children's foundation, which offers aid during wars and catastrophes around the world. The building houses a distribution center for the supplies to be shipped abroad. An existing warehouse is used for storage. A production building was added with workshops and secondary rooms as well as an administration wing. In between the latter functions is a 120 meter long "street", which gives access to the various departments. Along the street, adjacent to the offices, a raised area serves as an informal "sidewalk" and gathering area. In keeping with the straightforward lay-out, the architecture is cheerful and unpretentious, and composed of simple, inexpensive materials – a democratic framework for one of the traditionally hierarchic UN organizations.
Bibliography: Arkitektur DK 1985, 224 and 1994, 198

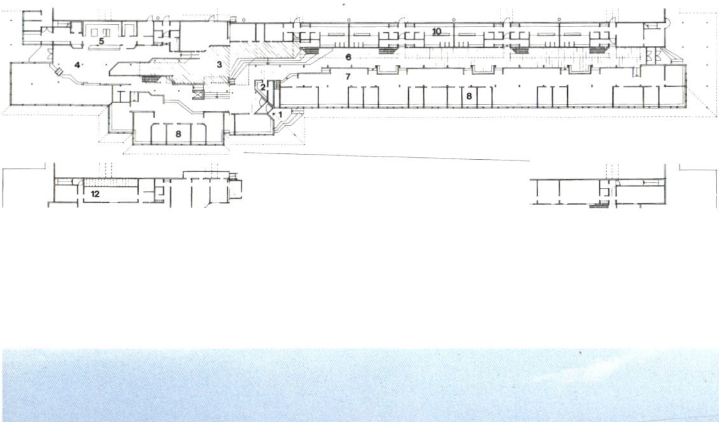

1:1500

C260

Paustians Hus

Kalkbrænderiløbskaj 2, Østerbro
1986-87

Client: Paustian A/S
Architect: Utzon Associates
Landscape architect: Utzon Associates

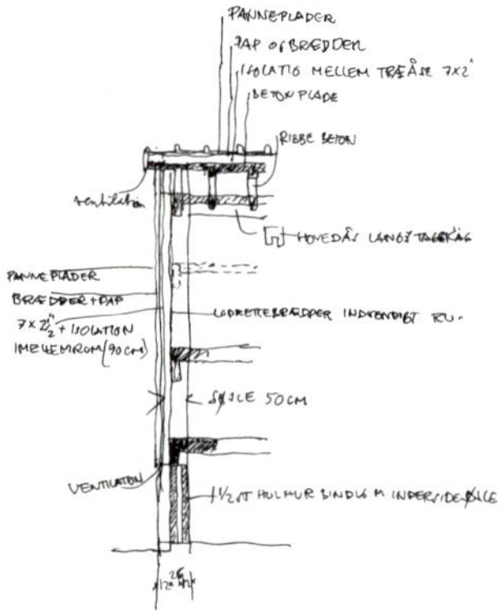

A forest of columns, is the initial impression given by this building, in which furniture is exhibited and sold. The columns have different heights according to the slightly sloped saddle roof, which they support together with several decks of varying size. In the center of the building, there is an open space rising to the roof. This is surrounded by other areas on various levels and with different ceiling heights. The general impression is one of a bright pattern of varied spaces that, as intended, give spatial associations with the Danish beech forest. The structure forms a robust and pleasant framework for the functions it encloses. Toward the harbor waters, the forest of columns implies the soulful interplay between building and nature, one that is characteristic for Jørn Utzon's great works.
Bibliography: Arkitektur DK 1989, 353

The Garvergården housing scheme **C263**

Masnedøgade, Tåsingegade, Østerbro

1988

Client: Pension Funds' Joint Administration (PFA-Pension)
Architect: Tegnestuen Vandkunsten
Landscape architect: Tegnestuen Vandkunsten

The area of urban renewal grew in importance during the 1980's and proposals ranged from careful adjustment to radical innovation. Garvergården is a clear example of the latter mixed with an understanding of the history of the place and a good portion of humor. The building scheme is partly based on a converted shoe factory from the 1870's. The factory's shed roof section is recreated in the facade siding facing Masnedøgade street. The corner between this and Tåsingegade street is marked by artfully exaggerated pathos, the northeastern corner is similarly emphasized by a six-story, oblique building. Along Tåsingegade street the building edges back and forms a small crooked urban square. The scheme's relation to the surroundings is quite informal and the 71 units are clearly oriented inwards to the courtyard, which with its landscaping, stairs and niches forms an urban garden. Despite the visual challenge, Garvergården displays a straightforward intention for integration with the surrounding neighborhood as is evident in the way that pedestrians are invited to pass through the courtyard.

Bibliography: Arkitektur DK 1994, 224

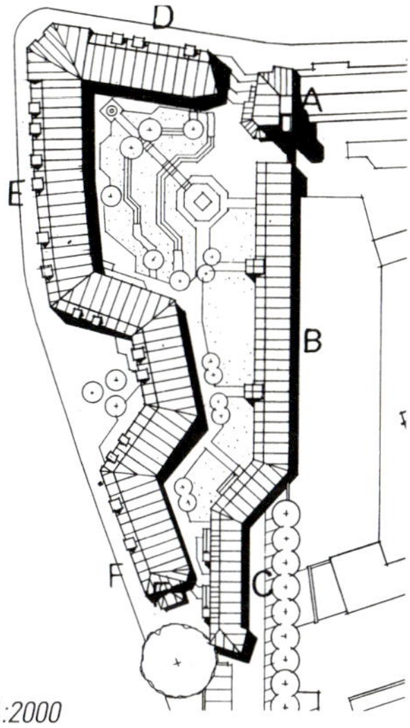

1:2000

C292

Tuborg Nord housing and commercial buildings

Strandvejen 66, Hellerup
1994-96

Client: Interessentskabet Tuborg
Architect: Henning Larsens Tegnestue
Landscape architect: Stig L. Andersson

The scheme consists of three simple geometric building forms: a straight wing, a square building block and a truncated cone. On the ground floor, the forms are tied together by a foyer, which gives access to a supermarket in the building block's roofed atrium, to the offices on the lower two floors and to the apartments on the top floors of the wing and the block. On the ground floors facing Strandvejen road, there are shops and a cafe with the spectacular room in the cone. This space is 15 meters high. Along the wall there is a stairway and a freestanding elevator that give access to a rooftop restaurant, where a panorama room offers a 360-degree view. The precise form of the cone, with its shiny metal siding, offers a distinctive bearing point in Strandvejen's multifarious architecture.

1:2000

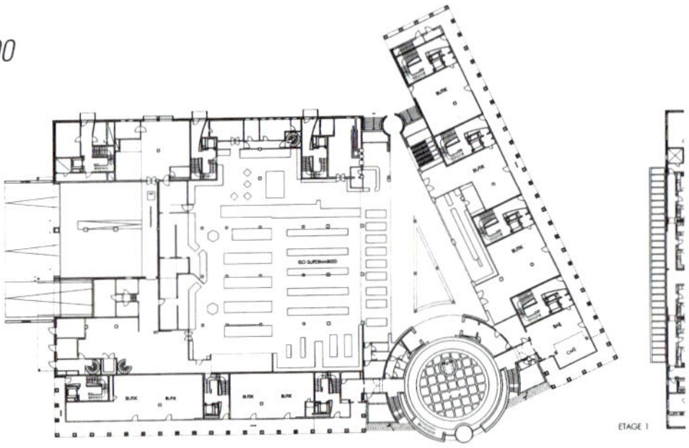

HUSUMPARKEN
Børneinst.
NORDRUPVEJ
VEKSØVEJ
KROGEBJERGPARKEN
KILDELØBET
Vandværk
SLOTSHERRENS HAVE
AVEDØNINGEN
DYSSEVÆNGET
SPANGEN
PILELY
ÅDIGET
TÅRNVEJ
VED VANDLØBET
VED VOLDGRAVEN
TORBISTVEJ
SNERTINGEVEJ
VALLEKILDEVEJ
BOESLUNDEVEJ
SMØRUMVEJ
SOLRØDVEJ
SLOTSHERRENSVEJ
SLOTSHERRENS ENG
LILLE VANG
BJERNEDEVEJ
DALBYVEJ
FAKSINGEVEJ
KONGSTEDVEJ
ÅRSLEVVEJ
Broparken
Plejehjem
Skøjtehal
SLOTSHERRENS VÆNGE
LISEBERGVEJ
RØDOVRE STADION
Islev St.
TYBJERGVEJ
KÆRBYVEJ
HORSEVÆNGET
ELSTEDVEJ
NORDBYVEJ
RINDBYVEJ
SØNDERVIGVEJ
KNUDSBØLVEJ
BROBØLVEJ
OKSBØLVEJ
BRABRANDVEJ
Rødovre Sportshal
KROGEBJERG
KROGEBJERGPARKEN
HARBOØREVEJ
FUGLAGERVEJ
BORGVEJ
LERCHEN
EGEMARKSVEJ
ROSHAGEVEJ
BILLESBORGVEJ
NØRAGER PLADS
NØRAGER
ØRHAGEVEJ
RAUNSTRUPVEJ
181
FORTVEJ
STOVBYVEJ
NØRUPVEJ
VEDERSØVEJ
Tinderhøj Skole
JUELSMINDEVEJ
ELSTEDVEJ
SANDHØJEN
BIRKHOLMVEJ
GJORSLEVVEJ
HJORTDALSVEJ
FLINTERUPVEJ
VANDVÆRKSVEJ
Vandværk
SVANKÆRVEJ
ERIKS
HØJRISVEJ
RØDOVREVEJ
ENGBOVEJ
HORSHØJVEJ
VESTERVIGVEJ
THORSMINDEVEJ
VANGSÅVEJ
SØNDERVIGVEJ
SEL SØ VEJ
TYBJERGVEJ
SNYDEBRO
JYLLINGEVEJ
TUDS
NØRREGÅRDSVEJ
ENGDIGET
264
KÆRVEJ
KROGEBJERG
TIPS
AGER VEJ
TOFTEVEJ
LYNGVIGVEJ
AGGERVEJ
LYNGHOLMVEJ
RØN ALLÉ
BJERGVEJ
SCHWEIZERDALSTIEN
SIMMEL
Grøndalslund Kirke
SCHWEIZERDALSPARKEN
ENGDIGET
FERRINGVEJ
TYBO
BUL
SCHWEIZERDALSVEJ
RØDOVRE
KARLSKÆR
KÆRDALS
VOLDUMVEJ
DAMHUSENGEN
VANLØSE
VANLØSE BY
GRØNLUNDS ALLÉ
ALLÉ
ALLÉ
TOFTØJEVEJ
Damsøgård Plejehjem
TÆBYVEJ
TÆBYVEJ
HANSTHOLM
RÅDHUSSTIEN
249
EGEGÅRDSSTIEN
RØDOVRE
NÆSBYVEJ
BYSTRÆDET
SYV STENSVEJ
DILVEJ
EGEGÅRDSVEJ
BRØNDUMVEJ
HJERTINGVEJ
STA
VEJLBYVEJ
TYBORØN ALLÉ
LUCERNESTIEN
Politi
Kulturhus
266
GUNNEKÆR
Rødovre Skole
Rødovre Gård
KIRKESVINGET
HYLTEBJERG
RISAGERVEJ
TÅRNVEJ
Dommerkontor
Rådhus
182
190
189
Bibl.
VED RÅDHUSET
BIRKMOSEVEJ
ØVREVEJ
RØDOVREVEJ
Rødovre Kirke
KIRKESTINGET
Eng Skrænten Plejehjem
DOKTOR HAVEN
BIRKAGERVEJ
RØDOVRE PARKVEJ
ELVER
GÅRDSVEJ
SORTEBRO
149
Rødovre Centrum
PRÆSTEBAKKEN
ANNEXGÅRDSVEJ
SKANDERUPVEJ
BRANDHOLMS ALLÉ
MINERVA VEJ
AMORINVEJ
HØJNÆSVEJ
AXEL
CHRISTIANS
PIL
DAMSVEJ
AURORAVEJ
Vandtårn
HIMMELKOL
HØJ
DAL
SYLVESTER VEJ
Brandholmskolen
Valhøj Skole
RØNNE HOLMS VEJ
DIANAVEJ
DAMHU
Børneinst.
LUNAVEJ
RØDAGER ALLÉ
RØDAGER ALLÉ
STELLAVEJ
VALHØJ
HENRIK DAVLINGS ALLÉ
SØTORPVEJ
JUNOVEJ
RISUMS ALLÉ
TÅRNVEJ
VEDELVEJ
ANNEXGÅRDSVEJ
AURORAVEJ
ENGGÅRDSVEJ
VERONIKAVEJ
VALHØJS ALLÉ
VALHØJS ALLÉ
CHRISTIANSDAL
HØJNÆSVEJ
RØDOVREVEJ
DIANAVEJ
Børneinst.
BRANDHOLMS
AXELHØJ
KEMPS
GREDSTENSVEJ

D
VANLØSE
IDRÆTS ANLÆG
BRØNSHØJGÅRDVEJ
BRØNSHØJVEJ
FJENNESLEVVEJ
LEJREVEJ
HØJSTRUPVEJ
TRYGGEVÆLDEVEJ
BÆKKESKOVVEJ
LYSTRUPVEJ
BROKSØVEJ
VALLØVEJ
SPANAGERVEJ
SONNERUP VEJ
GAUNØVEJ
GAVNØVEJ
HVALSØVEJ
EDELSMINDEVEJ
LILLIENDALSVEJ
TÅRNHOLMSVEJ
LINDHOLMSVEJ
HAVDRUPVEJ
ÅSTRUPVEJ
JÆGERSPRISVEJ
MULLERUP VEJ
BORREBYVEJ
BASNÆSVEJ
BELDRINGEVEJ
ENGELHOLM
THURE
Vand tårn
SVEND GÖNGES VEJ
TUXENSVEJ
KARLSTADS ALLE
ARNESVEJ
DEGNEMOSE ALLE
DEGNEMOSEN
ROSTGAARDSVEJ
HABETS ALLE
Vandrehjem
Højdereservoir
HERBERGVEJEN
RINGHOLM
TORPSTIEN
NÆSBYHOLMVEJ
FELDTVEJ
GÅRDVEJ
SANDBY
TORBEN
AGGERSVOLDVEJ
ANNEBERGVEJ
FUGLSANG ALLÉ
El. St.
BRØNSHØJVEJ
HEGNSHUSENE
BELLAHØJVEJ
PRIMULAVEJ
GODTHÅBSVEJ
Frederikshøj
Rødkilde Skole
Bellahøj Skole
BELLAHØJVEJ
HOLSTEINBORGVEJ
VANLØSEHØJ
Kirkebjerg Skole
SKJULHØJ ALLÉ
SLOTSHERRENSVEJ
SVENSTRUPVEJ
RISBYHOLMVEJ
BÆKKESKOVVEJ
BORREBYVEJ
DØNNERUPVEJ
SALTØVEJ
KIRKEBJERG ALLE
FLORAS ALLÉ
TRYGGEVÆLDEVEJ
HØJSTRUPVEJ
HAVDRUPVEJ
EGELYKKEVEJ
MARKSKELLET
Advents kirken
SALLINGVEJ
DYBENDALSVEJ
TULIPANVEJ
LIMFJORDSVEJ
THYVEJ
ABAKKEVEJ
ÅDALSVEJ
RANDBØLVEJ
SKIBELUNDVEJ
KNIVHOLTVEJ
SPØTTRUPVEJ
BELLISVEJ
LUPINVEJ
GYVELVEJ
MIMOSAVEJ
SYRENVEJ
REBILDVEJ
VANLØSE ALLÉ
SKALBAKKEN
JYLLINGEVEJ
HØG
HOLTVEJ
CLAUSHOLMVEJ
BANGSBOVEJ
BANGSBO PLADS
KATRINEDALSVEJ
Katrinedals Skole
Van løse Kirke
STOVRINGVEJ
KATHOLM
RYGHOLM
BRATSKOVVEJ
JERNBANE ALLÉ
TIRSBÆKVEJ
KALØ
BØRGLUMVEJ
DRONNING LUNDVEJ
TUSTRUPVEJ
KATRINEDALS VEJ
ESKÆRVEJ
KILHOLMVEJ
BANGSBOVEJ
ABAKKEVEJ
ÅLØKKEVEJ
DYBENDALSVEJ
GRØNDALS PARKVEJ
HERLUFSHOLMVEJ
VANLØSE ALLÉ
APOLLOVEJ
JUPITERVEJ
O2
Km. Pl.
ÅLEKISTEVEJ
VERAS ALLÉ
Vanløse St.
KLINGSEYVEJ
GRØNNEHØJ
HOLMESTIEN
RUNDHOLMEN
LØVHOLMEN
INDERTOFTEN
JYDEHOLMEN
LINDEHØJEN
GRØN VANGEN
GRØNDALS
GRØNBAKKEN
RINGPARKEN
C. F. RICHS VEJ
BERNHARD
BANGS ALLÉ
LAURITZ SØRENSENS VEJ
Hyltebjerghallen
Hyltebjerg Skole
Hyltebjerg Kirke
BOGHOLDER ALLÉ
BOBAKKEN
BYHØJEN
TORNESTYKKET
FLAKHOLMEN
KASTANIE ALLÉ
HANE
HYLTEBJERG ALLÉ
BRED
LINDE ALLÉ
NEDERTOFTEN
KÆRHOLMEN
RYDSLETTEN
STILLEDAL
GENNEMLØBET
ARNESTEDET
HAVE
KROGEN
VED GRÆNSEN
BUEN
FINSENSVEJ
LORENZENS VEJ
Gasforsyningsanl.
EINER-JENSENS VÆNGE
FLINTHOLM ALLÉ
236
Plejehjem
SOLBJERG HAVE
El. st.
128
GRØNDALSPARKEN
GRØNDALSPARKVEJ
PETER GRAUS VEJ
Falkonergårdens Gymn.
CHRISTIAN PAULSENS VEJ
FREDERIKSBERG IDRÆTSPARK
Damsøbadet
Sønderjylland skolen
Frederiksberg Kommunes Gartneri
SØNDERJYLLANDS ALLÉ
HENNING MATZENS VEJ
REGENBURGSVEJ
A. D. JØRGENSENS VEJ
MØRK HANSENS VEJ
JUNGGREENSVEJ
GUSTAV JOHANNSENS VEJ
C. N. PETERSENS VEJ
N. JESPERSENS VEJ
PHILIP SCHOUS VEJ
JULIUS VALENTINERS VEJ
H. SCHNEEKLOTHS VEJ
Lindevang Skole
P. G. RAMMS ALLÉ
EWALDSENSVEJ
EMIL SLOMANNS VEJ
Flintholm Kirke
Peter Bangsvej St.
Lindevang Kirke
HATTENSENS ALLÉ
LAURIDS BINGS ALLÉ
CARL PLOUGS VEJ
DALGAS BOULEVARD
HVIDTJØRNEVEJ
DYSSEAGER
ÅBJERGVEJ
LANGKÆRVEJ
VINKELAGER
BUSKAGER
DAMSTIEN
DAMHUSDÆMNINGEN
ÅLEKISTEVEJ
HF. ZENIA
HF. LINDEVANG
HF. GRÆNSEN
PETER BANGS VEJ
O. V. KJETTINGES ALLÉ
BENDZVEJ
Børneinst.
Skt. Marie K
J. C. SCHIØDTES VEJ
K. B. Hallen
Tennishal
Frederiksberg hallen
JENS JESSENS VEJ
MARIELYSTVEJ
JOHAN OTTOSENS V
GOLDSCHMIDTSVEJ
HOFFMEYERSVEJ
GLAHNS ALLÉ
FREDERIKSBERG KOMM.
BORGMESTER GODSKESENS PLADS
JOAKIM LARSENS VEJ
GENERAL BAHNSONS VEJ
Plejehjem
Johannes skolen
Søndermarks Skolen
ALSTRUPVEJ
SÆBYHOLMSVEJ
SÆBYHOLM VEJ
ALHOLMVEJ
PETER BANGS VEJ
LANGVADDAM
SAXHØJVEJ
KJERSTRUPVEJ
ULRIKSDALVEJ
RÅDMAND STEINS ALLÉ
CAMILLA NIELSENS VEJ
ROSKILDEVEJ
156

D128

Grøndals Park

Grøndalsparkvej, Vanløse
1930-39

Client: Copenhagen Municipality
Landscape architect: Valdemar Fabricius Hansen, Copenhagen Municipal Park Department

The Vanløse area contains several parks and park belts located on low-lying sites that are thus not well suited for buildings. This is true of Grøndals Park, a small strip that winds its way for three kilometers between railway tracks and roads from Damhussø lake toward northwest to Grøndalsvænge Haveby. The school and tract gardens on Grøndalsvænge Allé are connected to the park and were originally established as a functional attraction together with the lawns and shrubbery. The park is primarily for strolling with many seating areas and small playgrounds. With its simple pattern of lawns it is especially noteworthy for its unusual lushness with dense groups of varied plants: hawthorn clusters, pine groves, yews and several freestanding willows.

Damhuseng, Damhussø * and Krogebjerg Park D149

Rødovre, Frederiksberg
1939-45

Client: Copenhagen Municipality
Landscape architect: Jacob Bergmann, Copenhagen Municipal Park Department

Krogebjerg Park, Damhuseng field and Damhussø lake form a major park in the outer park system, which primarily runs along the municipal border from Emdrupsø lake in the north, through Utterslev Mose, parts of Vestvolden and southward through Krogebjerg Park, Damhuseng and Damhussø, and from there on through Vigerslev Park to Valby Park at Kalvebod Strand. Damhuseng and Damhussø were established as job creation programs when the areas were acquired from Copenhagen's Water Works. Emphasis was placed on preserving and maintaining the beauty of the existing landscape as well as employing indigenous bushes and trees. In addition a network of walks and bicycle paths was established. From Vestvold, Krogebjerg Park forms a narrow, sometimes hilly park belt with large groups of birch and pines, ash and willows that form a beautiful background. The original waterlogged area has been drained so that it can be used for playing fields.
Damhussø lake's large 100 acre water surface forms a distinctive break in the urban context. The lake was created by damming Harrestrup Å stream during the seventeenth century.
Bibliography: Havekunst 1940, 134

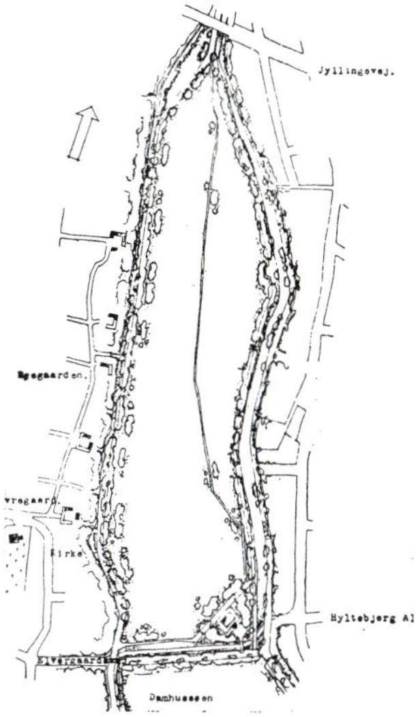

1:20.000

D181

The Islevvænge housing scheme

Fortvej 50-90, Tårnvej 409-525, Knudsbølvej 17-101, Rødovre
1951

Client: The Danish Public Housing Association (DAB)
Architect: Arne Jacobsen
Landscape architect: J. Palle Schmidt

The short dead-end streets and the staggering of the buildings closely tie the low blocks to the gentle hilly site. The form idiom employed with these nearly 200 buildings is concise and cubistic, and the distinctive tall chimneys make the scheme appear especially low. There are two building types, with different roof forms and brick colors. The austere expression was influenced by the especially meager conditions existing after World War I, but there is also a similarity to a project designed by Arne Jacobsen as early as 1928. Islevvænge is thus an adaptation of early functionalism, but it is also a product of his unfailing infallible design. Later renovations have resulted in unfortunate changes in roofing materials on some of the buildings.
Bibliography: Arkitekten U 1954, 374 and Arkitekten 1967, 389

The housing units each have a small garden, from which narrow paths run out to the long common green - as at Søndergårdspark. Toward west the green is terminated by the old Vestvold embankments.

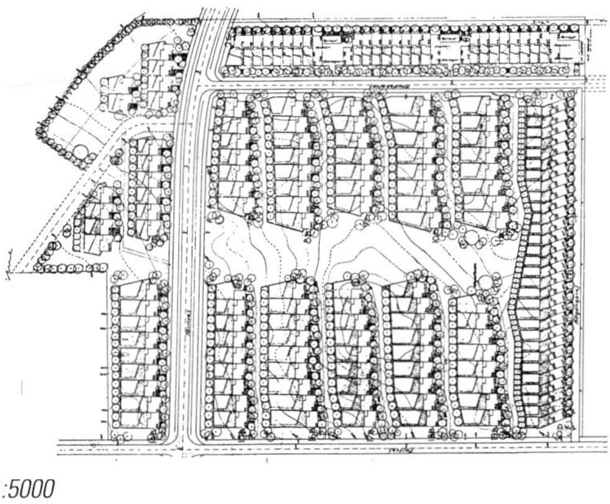

1:5000

The Carlsro housing project

D182

Tårnvej 205, Borgmester Gustav Jensens Vej, Rødovre
1951-53

Client: The Danish Public Housing Association (DAB)
Architect: P.E. Hoff & B. Windinge, Juul Møller & Agertoft, A. Poulsen
Landscape architect: Aksel Andersen, J. Palle Schmidt

The cooperative ideals were tried on a grand scale with this project that consists of 900 units made up of 600 small row houses and a 200 meter long six-story block with shops and common facilities on the ground floor. The radical concept can be attributed to DAB's director, Erling Knudsen, who defended large-scale housing projects from the viewpoint of housing and social policies. Carlsro was thus an omen of the even larger projects that followed. The contrast between the large block and the many small row houses is dramatic, and as an architectural and social experiment, Carlsro fostered many professional debates in the years following its completion. The cooperative facilities are no longer as large as originally planned.

1:10.000

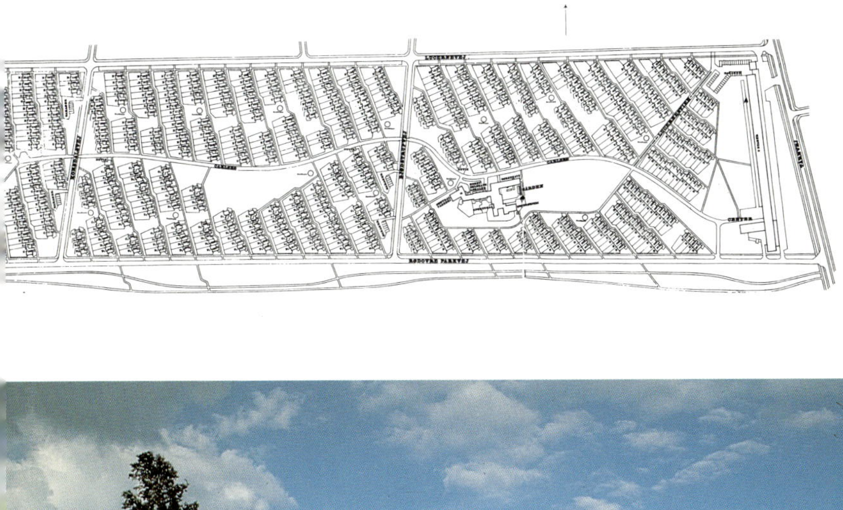

D189

Rødovre town hall *

Rødovre Parkvej 150, Rødovre
1954-56

Client: Rødovre Municipality
Architect: Arne Jacobsen
Landscape architect: Arne Jacobsen

An office building and a town council hall are the two basic elements in this scheme. The motif is similar to that at the Søllerød town hall (J 163). The office building is similar in type to A.Jespersen & Søns' headquarters (E 186) with a structure consisting of double rows of columns and cantilevered beams that bear the steel and glass curtain wall facade. The end walls are closed and sided with stone. The town council hall is based on the same principle with two closed end walls and two glass facades, but the system is turned so that the buildings are perpendicular to each other and are connected by a glass corridor. The refined play of extremely simple effects is obvious when moving around the buildings, and it is evident at the main entrance, which is marked by a simple canopy, in the foyer with a light, open, suspended stairway, and in the town council hall's sober and precise interior. The town hall lacks the traditional monumentality but it has a discreet dignity that makes it an architectural monument.

Bibliography: Arkitekten M 1956, 153

1:1000

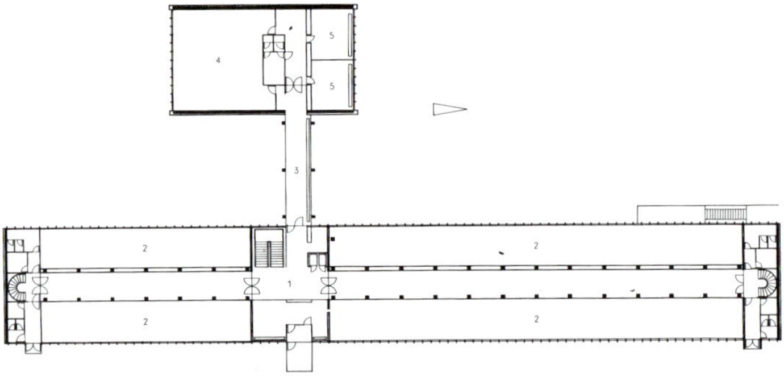

Rødovre main library D190

Rødovre Parkvej 140, Rødovre
1969

Client: Rødovre Municipality
Architect: Arne Jacobsen

The two Arne Jacobsen buildings that lie opposite each other on the town hall square in Rødovre, the town hall from 1955 and the main library, are architectural contrasts. The town hall is light and transparent while the library is heavy and closed – a contrast that appears more architecturally than functionally motivated in the case of the library. The black marble facades surround the low rooms like an uninterrupted cloister wall, with daylight access from the roof and courtyards. Only the roof lantern over the main hall breaks with the extremely low heights of the facades and rooms. The library was one of the architect's last works. The aesthetic simplicity that controls the building was a natural extension of his personal form.
Bibliography: Arkitektur DK 1970, 138

1:1200

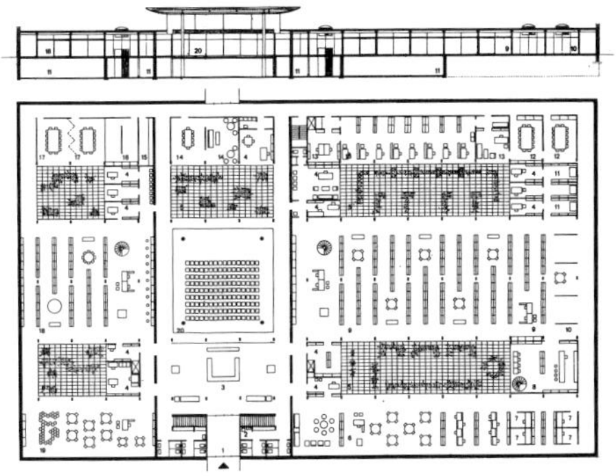

D236

Solbjerg Have

Lauritz Sørensens Vej, Solbjerg Have, Frederiksberg
1977-80

Client: Frederiksberg United Housing Associations
Architect: Fællestegnestuen
Landscape architect: Ginman, Harboe and Borup

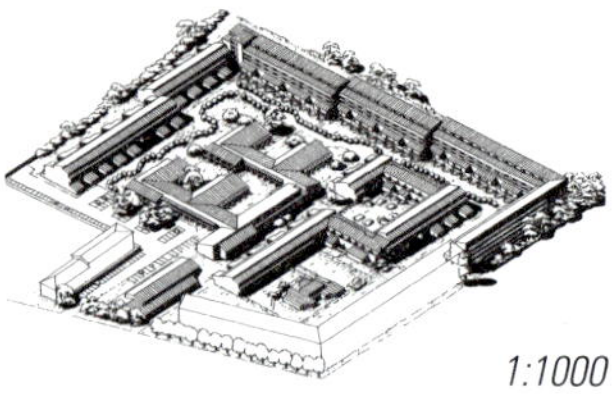

1:1000

From time to time efforts have been made to combine the urban housing type with the garden house. This was the basic idea behind the first functionalistic housing blocks and the postwar park housing schemes. It was also the concept employed at Farum Midtpunkt, which the architects designed a few years earlier. At Solbjerg Have, they created a successful union of the urban housing's dense and intense atmosphere, and the more informal, nature oriented home. This union occurs in the six-story perimeter blocks where the ordinary family units are located. Toward the streets, the perimeter buildings appear as city blocks with a scale and mass similar to the neighboring buildings. Toward the inner courtyard, the facades are broken down by a varying terrace formation facing the low buildings in the center that house a nursing home, day-care centers and sheltered units for the elderly. Each of the 480 units has access to a small garden, though the smallest units only have balconies. The richly varied facades reflect a similar complexity in the 300 units in the perimeter blocks, of which there are 48 types ranging from one to six rooms, on one or two levels. The choice of facade materials is equally varied, but the simplicity, texture and natural colors on the surfaces help to maintain a total impression of homogeneity. The large existing trees presented a fine basis for the landscaping of the courtyards and path network, which produce the air of a lush urban park.
Bibliography: Arkitektur DK 1980, 261

1:1000

Solbjerg Have's court facade

The Sibeliuspark housing scheme **D249**

Tæbyvej, Egegårdsvej, Rødovre
1984-86

Client: Rødovre Public Housing Association and Building Company in association with DAB
Architect: Fællestegnestuen A/S
Landscape architect: John Alpass Aps

The Egegårds quarter is an industry zone in which Silbeliuspark was placed as part of a housing and work place integration experiment. The scheme consists of row houses and multistory units, with 169 units of varying sizes in addition to 36 supplementary rooms and 22 youth units. The living units are primarily oriented inwards with separate outdoor recreational and play areas as well as path networks. There is a richly varied urban atmosphere with a well-designed juxtaposition of different materials, forms and colors. Contact with the surrounding neighborhood is by way of portals that contribute to the dense urban atmosphere. Toward south, the scheme's main thoroughfare opens to the surrounding industrial area.
Bibliography: Arkitektur DK 1987, 271

D264

The Engen housing project

Rødovrevej 226, Rødovre
1988-89

Client: Rødovre Public Housing Association, Admin.: DAB
Architect: Arkitektgruppen i Aarhus
Landscape architect: Arkitektgruppen i Aarhus

In 1983, the Ministry of Housing arranged a competition for "future multistory housing". During the 1980's, the winning proposal resulted in five building projects including "Sø-fronten" on Vodroffsvej road. The project proposed a column/deck construction with mechanical equipment cores. At the Engen scheme, the facade freedom inherent in the system was used to adapt the building to the sloping site. This gives the building a light and airy character. Access to the units is from the south side by way of steel and glass stair towers, which stand like sculptures in front of the facade. In this way, as a new feature, the balconies become part of the access area. For the sake of the experiment, the 51 units are all very different with diagonally placed mechanical equipment cores as a common feature.
Bibliography: Arkitektur DK 1992, 30

1:1250

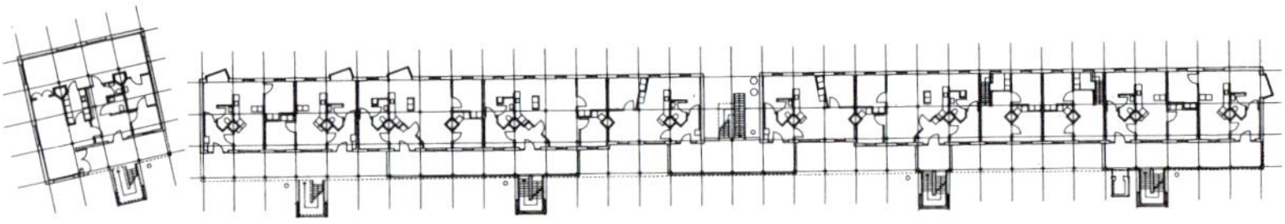

Viften cultural center **D266**

Rødovre Parkvej, Rødovre
1989

Client: Rødovre municipality
Architect: Dissing + Weitling a/s

This building represents the final stage in Rødovre's municipal building trilogy that started with Arne Jacobsen's town hall in 1955 and continued with his library in 1969. The culture center, as the town hall and library, is an isolated building without a strong urban character. On the other hand it clearly signals its function. The theater is a closed block, discretely broken by the bulge of the stage. Opposite this, the fan-shaped, zinc covered side building, with the foyer and cafe, opens naturally to the plaza, and the round stair tower stands functionalistically and expressively as the scheme's main pivot point. In a subdued fashion, the culture center terminates the collection of modernistic architecture at this site.
Bibliography: Arkitektur DK 1991, 146

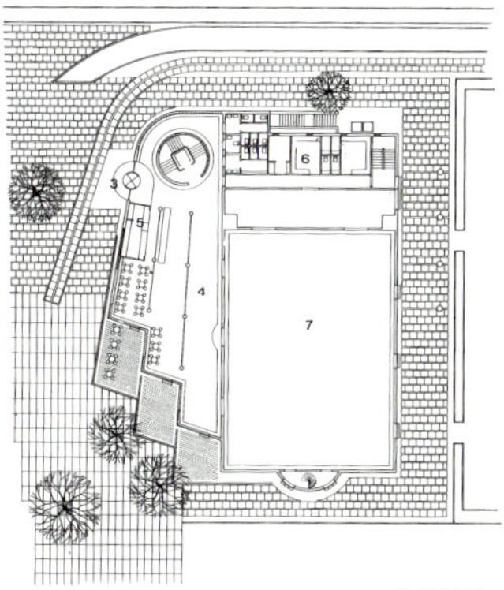

1:1000

16
Busanlæg
BELLAHØJ
Ø2
CAMPINGPLADS
Grøndal Centret
GEN FORENINGS PLADSEN
RØDKILDE PARK
110
121
117
118
106
143
108
265
251
58
HVIDKILDEVEJ
HULGÅRDSVEJ
HILLERØDGADE
BORUPS ALLÉ
BISPEENGBUEN
Fuglebakken St.
Vandværk
Grøndals Kirke
Grøndalsvængets Skole
Kapernaums Kirke
Tekn. Skole
Advent Kirke
NORDRE FASANVEJ
MARIENDALSVEJ
KRISTIAN ZAHRTMANNS PLADS
Skolen på Duevej
Godthåbsvej St.
GODTHÅBSVEJ
GRØNDALSVEJ
FEMTE JUNI PLADS
C. F. RICHS VEJ
Frederiksberg Hospital
Skolen på la Cours Vej
Frederiksberg Varmeværk
Handelshøjskolen
Lindevang St.
Solbjerg St.
Frederiksberg St.
FINSENSVEJ
Forvaltnings højskole
Lindevangskolen
Godthåbs Kirken
Frederiksberg Seminarium
Skolen på Nyelandsvej
Tekn. Skole
IDRÆTS ANLÆG
Pædagogisk Center
FREDERIKSBERG SVØMMEHAL
HF. KILEN
Handelshøjskolen
Domhus
Bibl.
Politist.
SMALLEGADE
FALKONER ALLÉ
Rådhus
4. Maj Koll
PETER BANGS VEJ
Emmaus Kirke
Diakonisse Stiftelsen
DRONNINGENSVEJ
KRONPRINSENSVEJ
SØNDRE FASANVEJ
FREDERIKSBERG
FREDERIKSBERG HAVE
FREDERIKSBERG RUNDDEL
Storm P. Museet
Frederiksberg Kirke
Haveselskabets Have
SOLBJERG KIRKEGÅRD
ZOOLOGISK HAVE
Idrætsanlæg
Frederiksberg Slot
ROSKILDEVEJ
PILE ALLÉ
ALLÉGADE
JACOBYS ALLÉ

E
UNIVERSITETSPARKEN
FÆLLED
Zoologisk Museum
Datalogisk
Aug. Krogh Inst.
H. C. Ørsted Institut
IDRÆTSANLÆG
NØRRE ALLÉ
Otto Mønsted Hallen
Rigsarkivet
Danm. Højsk. f. Legemsøvelser
Biol. Inst.
Universitets bibl.
Studentergård
Rigshospitalet
JULIANE MARIES VEJ
TAGENSVEJ
FREDERIK V's VEJ
FREDRIK BAJERS PLADS
Tandlægehøjskolen
Panum Instituttet
230
BLEGDAMSVEJ
FREDENSGADE
De Gamles By
Fosdagården
Kollegiegården
Rådmandsgade
RÅDMANDSGADE
MIMERSGADE
Samuels K.
Skole
Kingos Kirke
Nørrebro Hallen
BALDERSGADE
HEIMDALSGADE
HAMLETSGADE
BALDERS PLADS
NANNASGADE
VULKANGADE
YDUNSGADE
FREJASGADE
THORSGADE
ODINSGADE
P. D. LØVS ALLÉ
GULDBERGSGADE
GULDBERGS PLADS
ARRESØGADE
NØDDEBOGADE
FENSMARKGADE
SJÆLLANDSGADE
JAGTVEJ
NØRREBROGADE
NØRREBROS RUNDDEL
Stevnsgades Skole
STEVNSGADE
Stefans Kirke
NØRREBRO PARKEN
Havremarkens Skole
JULIUS BLOMS GADE
HUSUMGADE
Anna Kirken
KRONBORGGADE
HEINESGADE
FYENSGADE
PRINSESSE CHARLOTTES GADE
Sions Kirke
Sjællandsgades Skole
FREDERIK VII's GADE
MEINUNGSGADE
NØRREBRO
ASSISTENS KIRKEGÅRD
42
Jagtvejens Skole
Metropolitanskolen
Blågårdsskolen
Hellig Kors Kirke
Hellig Kors Skole
Brorsons Kirke
211
112
129
Døves Kirke
ÅBOULEVARD
Den kgl. Vetr.- og Landbohøjskole
Statens Veterinære Serumlab.
Statens Husdyrbrugsforsøg
Skolen på Inge mannsv.
Skt. Thomas Kirke
ROLIGHEDSVEJ
Hermes hallen
H. C. ØRSTEDS VEJ
Skt. Josephs Plejehj.
Skole
MOSAISK KIRKEGÅRD
Bethania Kirken
273
272
SANKT HANS TORV
Skt. Johannes Kirke
Bernh. Inst.
Plejecentret Sølund
Københavns Amts Sygehus
Brandst.
FÆLLEDVEJ
NØRREBROGADE
Sakraments Kirke
Blågårds Kirke
Kristuskirken
239
107
260
41
75
SØTORVET
DRONNING LOUISES BRO
SORTEDAMS SØ
PEBLINGE SØ
ØSTER SØGADE
NØRRE SØGADE
89
141
88
Bethle.
Kristi K.
Teknisk Skole
Radio
151
ROSENØRNS ALLÉ
HERMAN TRIERS PLADS
156
Forum
JULIUS THOMSENS PLADS
Handelshøjskolen Københavns skolen
GYLDENLØVESGADE
Katolsk Apostolisk Kirke
Gevinde Danner Huset
65
Den kgl. Vetr.- og Landbohøjskole
Skolen ved Bülowsvej
Vajsenhuset
El. St.
Medborgerhus
ØRSTEDS-PARKEN
76
155
NØRRE FARIMAGSGADE
144
186
Hans Nansens Gård
Skt. Markus K.
Martins Kirke
Ebenezer Kirke
Apostolsk Kirke
Skt. Jørgens Gymnasium
97
Frederiksberg Gymn.
SØ
SØGADE
KAMPMANNSGADE
SKT. JØRGENS
VESTER
Ole Rømers Hus
Kommune Information
Vesterport St.
H. C. ANDERSENS BOULEVARD
274
200
130
VESTERBROGADE
El. St.
Immanuels Kirke
Kapt. Jonsen Sk.
90
125
Tycho Brahe Planetarium
267
GAMMEL KONGEVEJ
International Schools
Skt. Hjerte Kirke
140
95
Københavns Hovedbanegård
Det Ny Teater
98
Vesterbro Studenterkursus
162
Skole
FREDERIKSBERG ALLÉ
VESTERBROGADE
Elias Kirke
Maria Kirke
REVENTLOWSGADE
BERNSTORFFSGADE
ALHAMBRAVEJ
H. C. ØRSTEDS VEJ

E41

The Lakes *

1720's. 1928

Client: Copenhagen Municipality
Architect: Poul Holsøe
Landscape architect: Valdemar Fabricius Hansen, Copenhagen Municipal Park Department

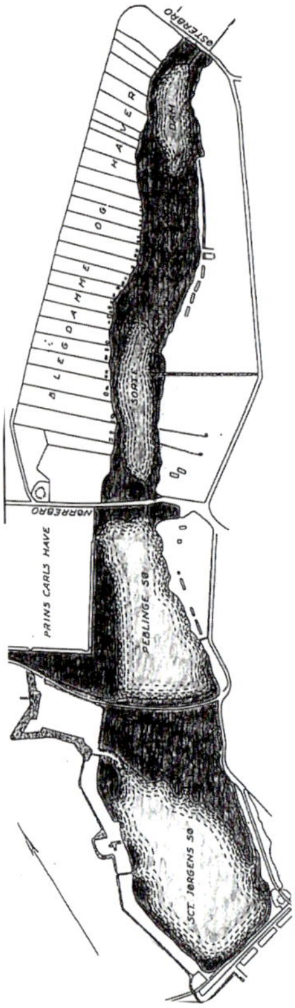

1:30.000

The Copenhagen lakes, Sortedams Sø, Peblinge Sø and Sankt Jørgens Sø run from north to south in an almost three kilometer long curve. As a reservoir for the city water works until the 1960's, and as a protective element, the lakes have been important to the city, especially due to the peaceful beauty the large water surfaces provide.

After an extensive renovation and cleaning in the 1720's, the lakes were given a regular shape and surrounded by rows of trees along precisely formed embankments. In keeping with a 1928 proposal by municipal architect Poul Holsøe and municipal gardener Valdemar Fabricius Hansen, stone walls and promenades were established along Peblinge and Sortedams Sø, with wide terraces at Østerbrogade street and an embankment at Gyldenløvsgade street. Stone walls were built below the banks and rows, and horse chestnut trees were planted along Østerbrogade and Nørre Søgade.

Through the years, the lakes have been used for bathing, ice skating and sailing. In the 1990's, the promenades and banks were renovated and a number of recessed seating areas were established along Sankt Jørgens Sø, with a different relationship to the water surface than at the other lakes. At the Søpavillion building, new fountain gardens with stairs leading to the water were established, and Sankt Jørgens Sø is now terminated by a new terrace complex in front of the Planetarium.

Assistens Cemetery

Kapelvej, Nørrebro
1760, 1806, 1828, 1853, 1861

Client: Copenhagen Municipality
Landscape architect: Copenhagen Municipal Park Department

In 1760, the first part of the cemetery was established as an auxiliary cemetery for the churches within the city gates. In 1806, in accordance with a plan by city surveyor Rawert, the cemetery was enlarged toward north along Nørrebrogade street up to Jagtvej. Later expansions occurred in 1828, 1853, and in 1861 when a special area for Catholic and Russian orthodox burials was established. The cemetery is surrounded on almost all sides by a wall, and several of the interior areas are also marked by brick walls. As early as 1879 it was decided that the cemetery was to be discontinued in 1980, a date that has now been extended to 2020. It was also agreed that the area should be converted to a park. The cemetery has a romantic expression with large, rare trees and is divided up by a through-going avenue of Lombardy poplars. There are many fine monuments and gravestones, of which almost 1800 are considered worthy of preservation. A number of them were done by sculptors like Wiedewelt, Abildgaard, Weidenhaupt and Dajon. The cemetery has a great cultural historical significance, therefore plans have been made to divide it into four areas. The oldest area will become a museum area where the historical cemetery environment will be preserved and recreated. Most of the 1806 expansion will be converted to a memorial park. The central area will continue as a cemetery, and the edge toward Jagtvej and Hans Tavsens Park to the south will become a park with lawns and groups of trees around the remaining grave monuments such as H.C. Andersen's burial site.
Bibliography: Landskab 1988, 130

1:12.000

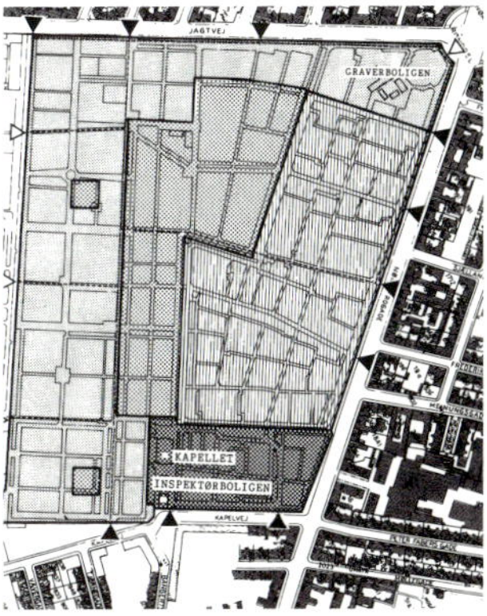

E58 **The Royal Danish Horticultural Society's Garden**

Pile Allé 4, Frederiksberg
1884, ca. 1906, 1955

Client: The Royal Danish Horticultural Society
Landscape architect: August Flindt, E. Erstad-Jørgensen, I.P. Andersen, Eywin Langkilde, and others.

The Horticultural Society was founded in 1830 to promote horticulture and landscape gardening. Flindt produced the first plan in 1884 with winding paths. In the beginning of this century, E. Erstad-Jørgensen incorporated several areas that are still evocative, such as the rose garden, the area around the hill and the lake. For many years the Copenhagen gentry found inspiration for their villa gardens here. In 1955 an exhibition was arranged where the landscape architects of the time each designed a garden with a special theme: the grey-blue and the evergreen garden, the children's garden etc.
Bibliography: Havekunst 1955, 47

E65 **The Royal Veterinary and Agricultural University ***

The Royal Veterinary and Agricultural University * **E65**

Bülowsvej 13, Frederiksberg
1856-58

Client: The Royal Veterinary and Agricultural University
Architect: Michael Gottlieb Bindesbøll
Landscape architect: J.S. Benzien and others

The Royal Veterinary and Agricultural college was founded in 1856 the same year that M.G. Bindesbøll died. However the original main building was built according to his drawings. It is governed by a symmetrical axis marked by the projecting frontespiece and the characteristic, heavy corner pilasters. The facades are yellow Flensborg brick and the roofing is black glazed tile. Although the building has traces of both classicism and historicism, one also senses Bindesbøll's will to create a simple and functional architectural expression. In 1959-60 a major addition was carried out by Architects Steen Eiler Rasmussen and Mogens Koch (Thorvaldsensvej 40) and from 1995 new buildings were designed by architects Erik Møller & Jens Fredslund as well as Dissing + Weitling. The scenic garden surrounding Bindesbøll's buildings was established in the 1850's by head gardener J.A. Benzien. It includes a large study collection of plants. The professors at the university have left their mark on the garden as can be seen by professor Georg Georgsen's neoclassicistic areas from the 1930's: the hedge garden on Rolighedsvej road, and a prim, recently renovated rose garden. In the 1960's, professor Georg Boye established the court gardens by the large high-rise building. In 1994, Andreas Bruun created a new arrival plaza in front of the main building.

E75

Søtorv *

Søtorvet, Ny København
1873-76

Client: The Copenhagen Building Society
Architect: Vilhelm Valdemar Petersen and Ferdinand Meldahl

During the 1870's, Copenhagen's cultural life and politics were oriented toward Europe. In terms of architecture, F. Meldahl was especially interested in the international style, with the reconditioned Paris as his ideal. Meldahl is presumed to have been responsible for the plans for Søtorv square. With its axis running down Frederiksborggade street and the later Dronning Louise's bridge, it should serve as a new and metropolitan gateway to Copenhagen. The buildings along the square are formed as mansions in a French inspired renaissance style with towers and spires on the accentuated corners. There is a theatrical, evocative orchestration in complete compliance with the Meldahlian attitude. As opposed to other buildings of the time, the courtyards in the Søtorv blocks are planned with consideration for light and fresh air. Some of the facades facing the square have been disfigured by bombastic facade signs.

Ørsteds Park * E76
1876-79

Client: Copenhagen Municipality
Landscape architect: Henry August Flindt

1:5.000

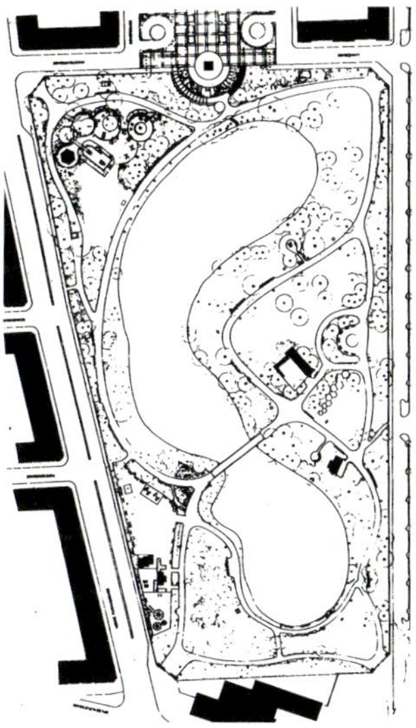

Ørsteds Park, just as Tivoli, the Botanical Gardens and Østre Anlæg was established on the remains of Copenhagen's old ramparts. Inspired by Adolphe Alphand's parks in Paris, landscape architect Henry August Flindt designed the park, which is surrounded by a cast iron fence with distinctive entrances designed by architect J.D. Herholdt. The dismantled defence complex is still reflected in the plan. The embankments and the moat have been partially preserved, but the steep slopes have been given a softer form, and the straight edges of the moat have been curved to form a long pond, the surface of which is the park's unifying spatial element. A network of winding paths runs through the park, and a single bridge crosses the pond, Fredrik VII's iron bridge, which previously crossed the moat at Nørrebro passagen. The existing trees were incorporated in Flindt's park complex and the new landscaping included exotic trees, bushes and groups of flowers to enhance special vistas and planted areas. Along the west side of the park there is a playground, and to the northwest: a cafe. There are also a number of monuments: J.A. Jerichau's bronze statue of statesman Anders Sandø Ørsted from 1902, Einar Utzon-Frank's statue of Thorvaldsen from 1930, as well as several casts of well known classical statues such as "the Wrestlers" and "the Grinder". The park is a lovely example of the nineteenth century scenic park ideals.
Bibliography: Arkitektur DK 1990, 161

E88

Søpavillonen *

Gyldenløvesgade 24, Indre By
1893-94

Client: Copenhagen's Skating Club
Architect: Vilhelm Dahlerup

The intense urban development at the end of the nineteenth century in the "bridge quarters" north and west of the lakes necessitated the building of bridges across the lakes. V. Dahlerup participated in this work and was responsible for the design of Dronning Louise's Bridge between Frederiksborggade street and Nørrebrogade street in 1885, and Fredens Bridge between Sølvgade and Fredensgade streets in 1904. At the same time, the bridge at Gyldenløvsgade was refined by the addition of a festive pavilion on Peblingsø lake, which was built as a restaurant for the active ice skating life of the time. The building is completely of wood and has two towers reminiscent of Turkish minarets.

The Åhusene housing scheme * E89

Åboulevarden 12-18, Indre By
1895-98

Client: Private consortium
Architect: Ulrik Plesner

The housing scheme represented a breakthrough for Plesner, who designed the facade for No. 12-14 and the plans for No. 16-18. The plans and facades are composed as an architectural whole in which the street facade has a picturesque symmetry and a strong relief. Part of the facade is pulled back from the street line to create small garden areas. Plesner had a very personal and frank way of cultivating textural effects in the red Danish brick, but there are also inherent English features in the sandstone sided bays. In addition, the facades are beautifully modeled and the building's mass and the sweeping mansard roof and pediments have Baroque roots.

1:1250

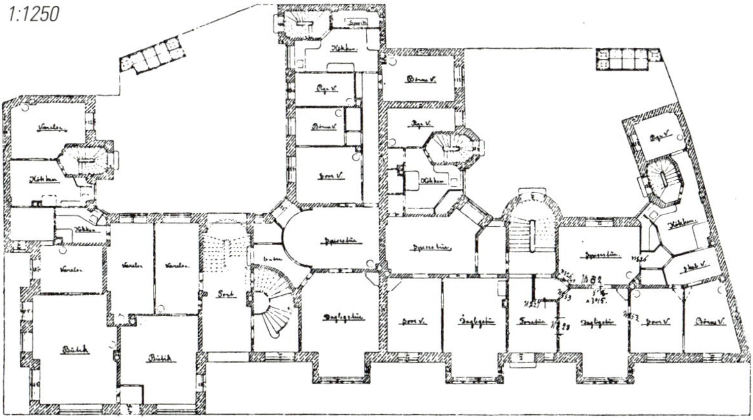

E90 The Institute of Physical Training *

Vodroffsvej 49-51, Indre By
1897-98

Client: Physical training teacher N.H. Rasmussen
Architect: Peder Vilhelm Jensen-Klint

The baroque manor house facade, the heavy rounded windows and the bold red brick facades place the building in a national romantic context. The facade details and the interior are well-designed and expressive. The details have an art nouveau character, a favorite style for many years in the Danish folk high school movement, which both the client and architect subscribed to. The movement's special blend of physical and spiritual schooling can be read in the inscription over the main entrance "Stand straight and speak the truth". The building still serves its original purpose.

E95 Copenhagen's main railway station *

Copenhagen's main railway station * **E95**

Banegårdspladsen 5-7, Indre By
1904-11

Client: The Danish State Railways (DSB)
Architect: Heinrich Wenck

Copenhagen's first railway station was built in 1847 in connection with the first railway line, which ran from Copenhagen to Roskilde. Wenck's building replaced J.D. Herholdt's main station from 1864 and like the town hall built just before, it was an indication of Copenhagen's enormous growth at the end of the nineteenth century. There is also an architectural relationship between the two buildings, which both are rich with imagery and possess a national form idiom with many fine stone and brickwork details. The formal functional requirements for the station had a great influence, and the impressive timber structure in the main hall and platform halls is well-integrated in the national romantic architecture. Originally there was a clear separation of arrival and departure traffic in the main hall. The large "service island" in the center, which provided the separation, was removed in connection with an extensive renovation by architects Dissing + Weitling A/S started in 1978. Smaller service islands now lie along the central axes. The new furnishings have a formal and smooth expression, which in general, forms a fine contrast to the old, pleasant details. The furnishings were designed by PLH architects in collaboration with DSB's building department.
Bibliography: Arkitektur DK 1980, 72 and 1986, 126

1:2000

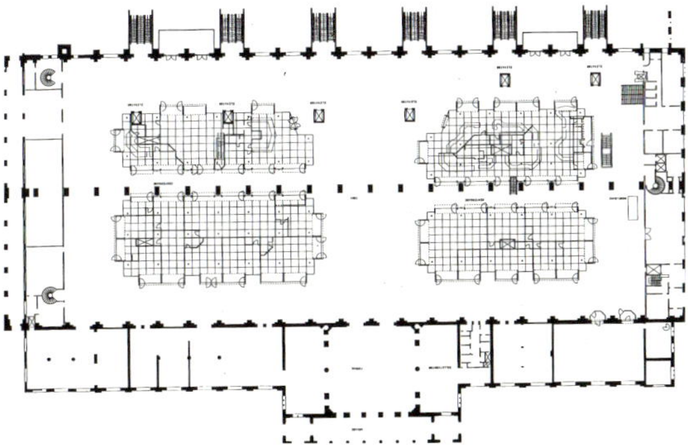

E97

Housing

Danas Plads 10-20, 11-13, 22-24, and 19-23, Frederiksberg
1906-09

Client: Master builder J.P. Wissing
Architect: Ulrik Plesner and Aage Langeland-Mathiesen

For his time, Plesner's architecture offered an outspoken and very personal contribution to the national romantic style, which was often attributed to his Jutland heritage. Plesner, who was also inspired by English architecture, gave the buildings on Dana Plads a neobaroque character with exuberant forms in robust red brick. The result was a homogeneous quarter in this urban area, and consisted of the two corner buildings on Vodroffsvej street as a distinctive and symbolic entrance. As opposed to Langeland-Mathiesen, Plesner did not cultivate the Jugend style, but some of his buildings were decorated by jugend artist Thorvald Bindesbøll.

Hotel and office building * E98

Vesterbrogade 34, Vesterbro
1906

Client: Master carpenter Kaas-Rasmussen
Architect: Anton Sofus Rosen

Originality, experiments and a receptiveness for international trends were some of Anton Rosen's characteristics. His office was a youthful inspiration for many architects who became the avant-garde of the architecture that followed. The building on Vesterbrogade street is an early attempt with a non-bearing facade, a curtain wall, in the American tradition. With its simple grid and the large, very fragmented glass areas, the facade has a modernistic attitude with the many ornaments that are subordinate to the clear primary structure. As infill housing, it is a textbook example of the fine balance between new and old.

E106

The Grøndalsvænge housing quarter

Quarter between Hulgårdsvej, Hvidkildevej,
Grøndalsvænge Allé and Godthåbsvej, Brønshøj
1914-20

Client: The Garden Housing Association Grøndalsvænge
Architect: Poul Holsøe and Jesper Tvede

The first years of the public housing movement saw two different directions: urban housing and garden housing. Grøndalsvænge is the first example of garden housing. The Danish Garden Housing Association collaborated in the building of Grøndalsvænge. The association's director, F.C. Boldsen was inspired by the English theorist Ebenezer Howard, whose ideas about garden cities had a decisive influence on city planning in the United States and Europe. During 1914-1920, P. Holsøe and J. Tvede were responsible for the site plan and design of the buildings. All of the 339 units were built during the period up until 1928. The winding roads in the quarter were influenced by older, romantic urban ideals put forward by the Austrian city plan theorist Camillo Sitte, and the buildings' "Better Building methods" style resulted in an almost rural atmosphere. "The National Association for the Advancement of Better Building Methods in Rural Areas" was founded in 1915 as a reaction to the increasingly uncontrolled building activity in many of Denmark's new provincial towns. The varied housing types at Grøndalsvænge make up a homogeneous whole with Better Building Methods' unobtrusive mixture of high quality craftsmanship traditions and the neoclassicism that thrived at that time.

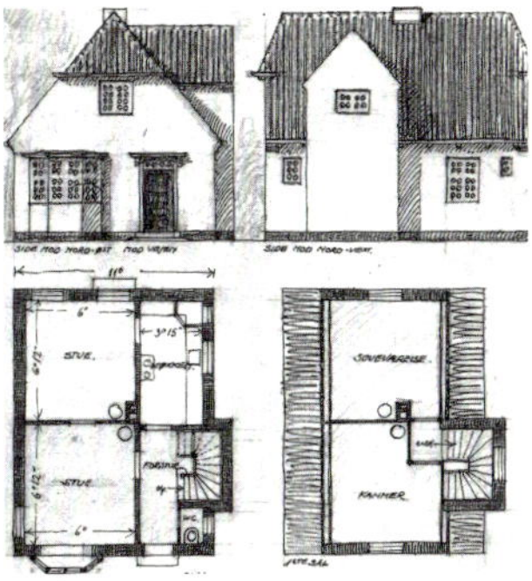

GRØNDALSVÆNGE
Nº 8B & 8A
HUSLEJE 34 Kr. 75 Øre
OM MAANEDEN m.
KÆLDER UNDER
DET GRØNNE.

1:400

LYNGBYGADES FORLÆNGELSE.
GODTHAABSVEJ
1ste SEKTION.
2den SEKTION.
3die, 4de SEKTION.

Haveboligforeningen
Grøndalsvænge

E107

Blågårds Plads
Nørrebro
1912-1916

Client: Copenhagen Municipality
Architect: Ivar Bentsen

This square takes up an entire city block that was formerly commercial space. It consists of a paved, recessed 30 x 50 meter area. A low granite wall separates the area from the street and sidewalks. The wall contains 22 sculptures that depict the life of the working class. The individual sculptures were done by Kai Nielsen in collaboration with architect Ivar Bentsen. The square is surrounded by a wide graveled area with two rows of large park lindens, which were planted already in 1900. This urban space has suffered from the local urban renewal efforts and has thus lost much of its original magic.

E108

Housing block
Nyelandsvej 57-63, Frederiksberg
1913

Client: The workers' Housing Association (later AAB)
Architect: Viggo Alexander Thalbitzer

The architect was also the originator of the idea with this building that contained the first public housing in Denmark. It came about as a collaboration between the Cooperative societies, and this new housing movement was considered a parallel to the cooperative movement. The architecture has certain national romantic characteristics, but there are also new details such as the corner windows and balconies. This building type: the large red brick city block, later took on certain neoclassicistic elements and was characteristic for many of the urban housing projects built up until the middle of the 1920's by the Workers' Housing Association (from 1917, the Workers' Cooperative Housing Association – AAB).

Housing E110

Vestergårdsvej (opposite Genforenings Plads), Brønshøj
1917

Client: The Workers' Building Association of 1865, now KSB
Architect: Povl Baumann and Ivar Bentsen. Kooperativ Byggeindustri (KBI), (renovation)

The grand housing scheme on Genforenings Plads was built during and after World War I. A part of this project, which was characteristic of the period, was the U-shaped building on Vestergårdsvej. It heralded a new form of large-scale building with smaller apartments. The main form of the scheme was a forerunner to the larger city block, which was typical of the new building projects during the following twenty years. The upper floor was added to the original project for economical reasons, and gave the neoclassicistic facades a mild and plain tone. In his book about Povl Baumann, H.E. Langkilde calls the scheme "a folksy breakthrough in urban housing". The building was renovated in 1994 in collaboration with the Copenhagen Urban Renewal Company.
Bibliography: H.E. Langkilde: Povl Baumann. 1991,107

E112 **Housing Block**

Between Struenseegade and Hans Tavsensgade, Nørrebro

Client: Copenhagen Municipality
Architect: Povl Baumann

The housing shortage, which worsened during World War I, culminated in 1918 and the municipality had to step in as builder for a number of major housing projects. The housing scheme along Struenseegade reflected the city's tense housing situation, the tight economy and neoclassicism's firm grip and unusually clarified form in the large projects. The regular, rectangular city block was developed here as a prototype for a number of building schemes that followed and came to dominate Copenhagen's northern suburbs. The street facades are imposing yet simple with a precise numerical proportioning, and with ornamentation confined to the area around the entrance doors. The apartment plans are tightly organized with consideration for daylighting and furnishing, and do not pretend to be more than they are. The smooth, pale rear facades cannot relieve the effect of the somewhat narrow courtyard, but attempts were made to create a common area. The small urban apartment had now become a serious architectural project.
Bibliography: H.E. Langkilde: Povl Baumann. 1991, 115

E116 **The Hornbækhus housing block ***

The courtyard at Hornbækhus is unusually large. The spaciousness is maintained as the center area is a large lawn, and the playground, clothes yard, etc. are placed on the long side and screened by shrubbery. At both of the entrances at the ends, there are small squares marked by trees and paved with the same beautiful granite sett pavers used on the paths along the buildings.

The Hornbækhus housing block * **E116**

The city block made up of Ågade, Skotterupgade,
Borups Allé and Hornbækgade, Nørrebro
1922-23

Client: The Hornbækhus Cooperative Housing Association
Architect: Kay Fisker
Landscape architect: G.N. Brandt

The housing scheme represents the peak of the large housing block epoch both in its enormous size and in its stringent architecture. The 290 apartments have living rooms facing the street, and kitchens and bedrooms toward the courtyard regardless of solar orientation, and thus the project was a continuation of traditional urban housing. On the other hand, the continuous and landscaped courtyard was a new feature. The almost 200 meter long facades were a culmination of the so-called kilometer style, and the uniform rhythm of windows had a monumental effect. The neoclassicistic order was achieved by pilasters in the corners, although their symmetry can hardly be recognized in the long facades, and the window rhythm continued past the stair landings. Consistency, precise proportioning and careful detailing are the special characteristics and qualities of this building. The kilometer style offered certain financial advantages, which were important during the housing shortage, but the many repetitions in plan and facade dictated by the style soon became a constriction, and from the middle of the 1920's, new directions were sought in both architecture and urban planning.

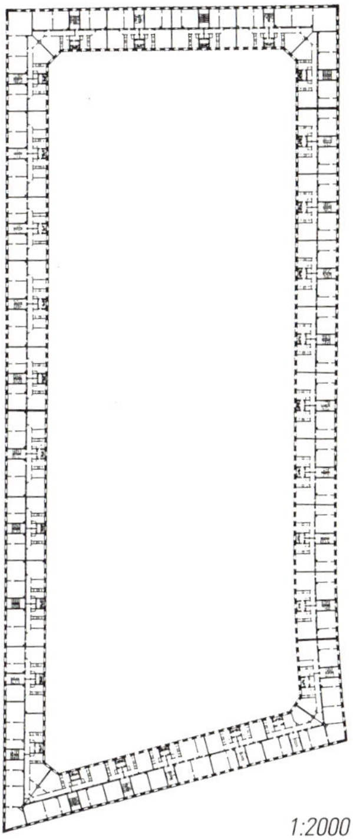

1:2000

E117

The Bakkehusene housing scheme *

Hulgårdsvej, Markvej, Bakkevej and Rødkildevej, Brønshøj
1921-23

Client: Copenhagen's Public Housing Association (KAB)
Architect: Ivar Bentsen and Thorkild Henningsen

KAB was founded in 1920 on the initiative of attorney F.C. Boldsen, who served as director from 1920-45. One of the association's main purposes was to further the building of low-rise worker housing. Bakkehusene's 171 row house units were KAB's first housing project. The ideological basis originated with F.C. Boldsen who was interested in the English garden city movement, and the architects who returned to the Danish building tradition. The row house was a familiar street house in the old rural towns, and the simple, subdued architecture that without any special style provides a framework for the basic functions was known from some of M.G. Bindesbøll's works such as the Medical Association housing (F 9). The architects continued this line in Danish architecture, which later became known as the functional tradition. However Bakkehusene is also characterized by the traditional craftsmanship cultivated in the "Better Building Methods" movement. In addition to the sensible plan solutions, the gardens represented the major innovation in these working class housing units, and still represent one of the great qualities. At first, many felt that the buildings were too austere and thus ugly. The first tenants were not workers but artists and middle class. Today the Bakkehusene scheme is considered one of Copenhagen's most desirable housing areas and represents a monument in public housing history.

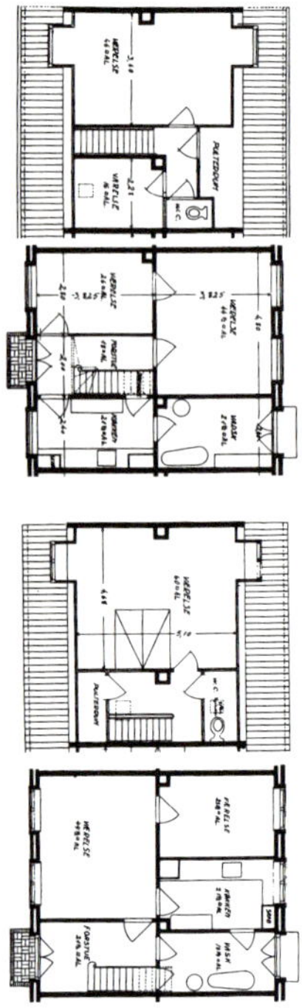

1:400

The Bakkehusene scheme is divided in two by Rødkilde Plads, which is a unique and distinctive park space. A large, sloping and almost square plane is flanked by full-crowned linden trees

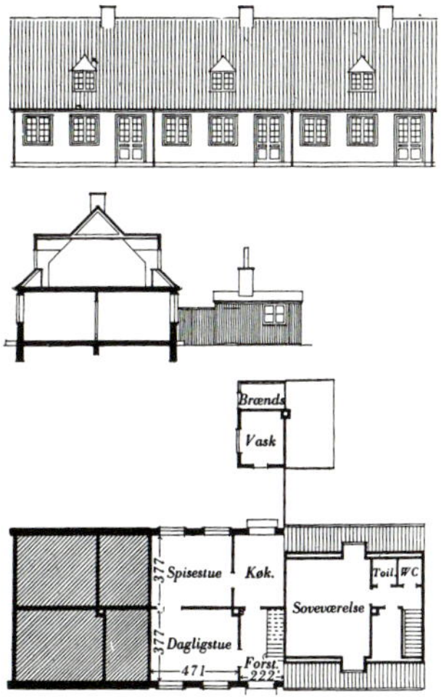

Brænds
Vask
Spisestue
Køk.
Toil.
WC
Soveværelse
Dagligstue
Forst.
377
377
471
222

1:500

1:5000

E118 **Row houses ***

Hulgårdsvej 54-70, Brønshøj
1924

Client: Private consortium
Architect: Thorkild Henningsen

When the Bakkehusene (E 117) proved to be unattractive as worker housing, Thorkild Henningsen developed a more exclusive form of row housing. Here the home as a private area was emphasized as opposed to Bakkehusene's common facilities. The row houses on Hulgårdsvej road reflect this development in the small shifts between the street facades, in the alternating red and reddish-yellow brickwork, and in the stairways that are alternately parallel and perpendicular to the facades. In addition, screened verandas were built toward the gardens. Just like the Bakkehusene, these row houses were influenced by the proportioning and detailing of the "Better Building Methods" movement.

E121 **The Vibevænget housing scheme**

Side streets to Nattergalevej, Brønshøj
1927

Client: Copenhagen Public Housing Association KAB
Architect: Povl Baumann
Landscape architect: C.Th. Sørensen

Traditionally the living room faces the street and the secondary spaces face the paths and gardens, but the freestanding apartment block was an innovation, and the Vibevænget housing scheme is considered the first detached block housing in Denmark. This signaled a radical break with the traditional urban street building and the large blocks of the period. The detached block later became a standard housing type in the functionalistic period. As in many of his other schemes, Povl Baumann fostered a new architectural concept that brought new qualities to the small apartment unit.

Housing * **E125**

Vodroffsvej 2A and 2B, Frederiksberg
1929

Client: A/S Vodroffsborg
Architect: Kay Fisker and C.F. Møller

This building represented a radical break with the past. With its cubistic forms and continuous bands of windows it was clearly inspired by the Bauhaus tradition, however the yellow and red brick surfaces made it a Danish version of international functionalism. It was criticized for being an "unreasonable brick building with a reinforced concrete idiom", but it was also an undaunted signal of new times. The staggering of the six stories facing the lake and the five toward the street was elegantly conveyed in the end wall toward south, where the lake side's red spandrels are woven together with the yellow ones on the street side. As a whole, the building has a sculptural effect that lives up to its fashionable location on the lakes.

Nørrebro Station * **E126**

Lundtoftegade 147, Nørrebro
1930

Client: DSB
Architect: DSB's chief architect, Knud Tanggaard Seest

This station was built especially for passenger traffic in connection with the establishment of the elevated railway tracks through the Nørrebro quarter. It is symmetrically placed in relation to the tracks, which gives a certain air of neoclassicism, but the form idiom is functionalistic with a fine sculptural accent in the clarified building masses. The barrel vault roof is an interesting feature with its decorative, diagonal timber cross framing. On the other side of Nørrebrogade, on Lyngsies Plads, lies a station for the Slangerup line built in 1906 and designed by DSB's chief architect Heinrich Wenck. The building is somewhat similar to Østerport Station (F 234), which was also designed by Wenck and built in 1897. Both stations were recently renovated.

E129

Housing

Part of the block, Ågade, Hans Egedes Gade, Brorson's Church, Henrik Rungs Gade, Nørrebro
1930

Client: Copenhagen Municipality
Architect: Povl Baumann

Baumann designed about 2/3 of the buildings on this site, which is a narrow irregular property. The perfectionism that radiates from these buildings with the finely rounded brickwork at the site's sharp and blunt corners. Baumann's deep interest for brickwork aesthetics is evident in the elaborate bond in red and yellow brick, which gave the building the nickname "the linoleum building", and was inspired by the opera house on Fredericiagade street (Østre Landsret, F 20). The facade pattern harmonizes perfectly with the rhythm of the windows. The building primarily contains apartments of 100-170 sqm, which according to the standards of the time were well-equipped and had bathrooms.
Bibliography: H.E. Langkilde: Povl Baumann. 1991, 179

1:1200

Vesterport office building

Vesterbrogade 8, Indre By
1930-32

Client: The Old Railway Property Company
Architect: Povl Baumann and Ole Falkentorp

In many aspects, this large building complex was an innovation, and rental space for several different firms was a new feature. The supporting structure of rolled steel sections was similar to the American skyscraper principle. The new, light facade construction was emphasized as the primary architectural motif, and this was also an innovation compared to the heavy brick buildings of the time. Vesterport is functionalistic in its concept, but there are classical motifs in the symmetrical treatment toward Vesterbrogade street, and the fine, patinated copper facade siding provides a textural treatment that is atypical of functionalism.

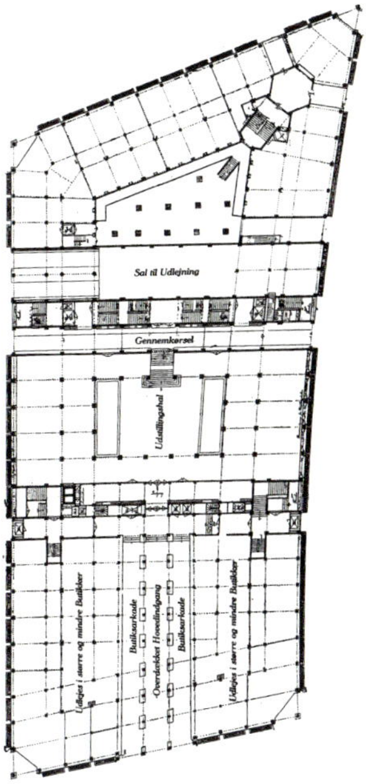

1:1500

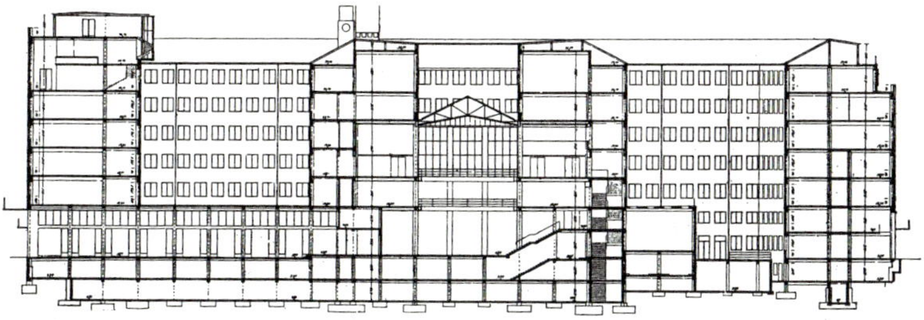

E140

Hotel Astoria

Banegårdspladsen 2-4, Indre By
1934-35

Client: The Danish National Railways, DSB
Architect: Ole Falkentorp

The extremely narrow site was a decisive factor in the form of this building and its protruding facades. Yet the form also implies an expressiveness, a symbol of speed and comfort corresponding to the notion of a modern railway hotel. The building's horizontal force is emphasized by the elegant stair tower at the southern end and by DSB's winged wheel symbol that crowns the north end of the building. The hotel rooms and corridors have an air of an exclusive sleeping car interior, and the building contains many other refined details resulting from the scarcity of space. The unusual building form required a structure of reinforced concrete.

E141

Bethlehem Church

Åboulevard 8, Indre By
1936-38

Client: The Copenhagen Church Building Fund
Architect: Kaare Klint

The kinship between this church and Grundtvig's Church is obvious. Part of this influence lies in the early sketches by the architect's father, Grundtvig's Church architect, P.V. Jensen-Klint. The site is narrow and thus the short, three-aisled church appears forced up to a cathedral-like height. The walls, columns and vaults are of exposed yellow brick, giving the space the characteristic Klintish homogeneity together with the cabinetmaker's attention to details. The street facade, which is flush with, and built together with the neighboring buildings, discreetly marks the church in the street scene. The towering Gothic character of the facade does not really come into its own in this constricted urban situation.

Novo Nordisk factory E143

Nordre Fasanvej 215, Frederiksberg
1935/1969

Client: Novo Industri
Architect: Arne Jacobsen

The factory was originally located in a number of existing old buildings on the site. As an addition to these, Arne Jacobsen designed the new three-story building built in 1934-35, facing Nordre Fasanvej road. The white facade, the rounded corners and the dark granite stuccoed spandrels are a fine example of Jacobsen's personal and always well-designed version of functionalism. The light fire stair located in a glass shaft is a refined detail. Jacobsen also designed the large complex for enzyme production located behind the old building and along Hillerødgade road. It represents a stringent and modernistically simplified architecture in which certain functional elements are emphasized as part of the sculptural composition.
Bibliography: Arkitektur DK 1969, 85

E144

The Vestersøhus housing scheme *

Vester Søgade 44-78, Gyldenløvesgade 21-23, Indre By
1935-39

Client: Contractors A. Nielsen, C. Nielsen and director P. Christiansen
Architect: Kay Fisker & C.F. Møller

The balcony was the thirties' great contribution to housing, and it was further refined at the Vestersøhus scheme. In earlier housing with smaller apartments, the balcony was hung on the facade. Here it was both built-in and built-out. This produced a screened corner recessed from the facade line, the living room next to the balcony thus had a corner window, and the protruding railings with rounded corners provided a rhythmic facade motif. The standard balcony is spacious, but those on the upper floors stretch over two bays as a terrace. The long railings here give the facade rhythm a certain tension. The railings' thin, flat steel sections are a further refinement of the monumental and sculptural facade facing Vester Søgade. On the corner of Gyldenløvesgade street, the transition between the two buildings is elegantly resolved by a staggering of the brickwork and windows. The building's grandiose expression is in keeping with the large, well-appointed apartments, which were equipped with refuse chutes and in some cases separate baths and toilets. In 1994-95, the windows were replaced with respect for the original sill and frame dimensions.

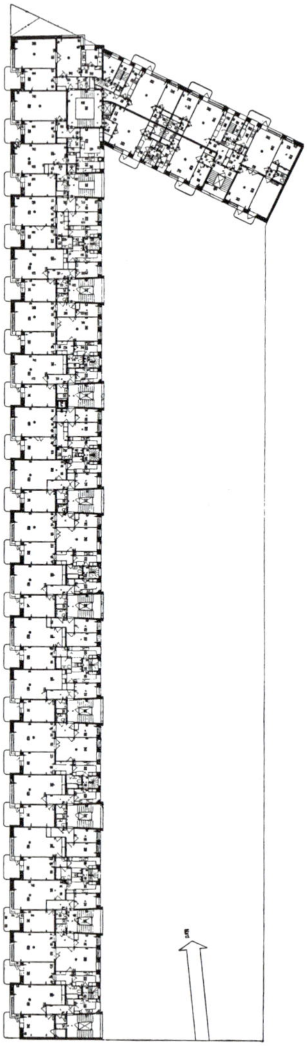

1:1000

1:600

E151

Radiohuset *

Rosenørns Allé 22, Frederiksberg
1936-42 (opened 1945), 1956

Client: The national government
Architect: Vilhelm Lauritzen
Landscape architect: G.N. Brandt
Engineer: Chr. Nøkkentved and Ludvig Birch (Birch & Krogboe)

Since its completion, the building has been the headquarters for Denmark's Radio broadcasting. The main entrance faces Rosenørns Allé street. There are two administrative wings and a building with 12 sound studios of varying size. From Julius Thomsensgade street there is access to "Studio 1", a concert hall that seats 1200. Above the studio building there is a roof terrace with access from the canteen. It was designed by G.N. Brandt, but no longer has its original form. This building was the first of its kind in Denmark as was an example of the special Nordic transition between functionalism and modernism. The architect's design and delicate choice of materials give the well-disposed building a poetic grace. The maple paneling in the concert hall was originally pale but now has a refined reddish patina. Before its completion, the scheme received massive public criticism for its lack of monumentality. Though on its opening in 1945, the press was unanimous in its praise. Today the Radiohus is not only considered a pioneer work in this type of building but also one of this century's important architectural works.
Bibliography: L. Balslev Jørgensen, J. Sestoft, M. Lund: Vilhelm Lauritzen. 1994, Havekunst 1941, 73-80 and 1958, 84

1:1400

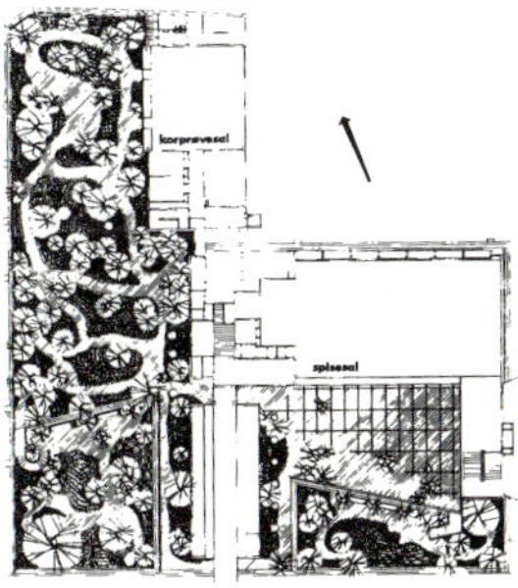

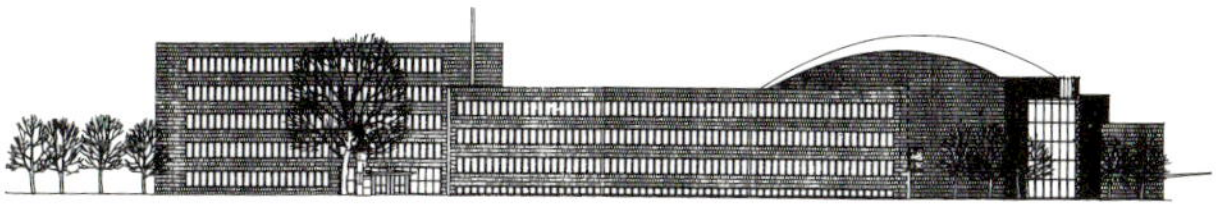

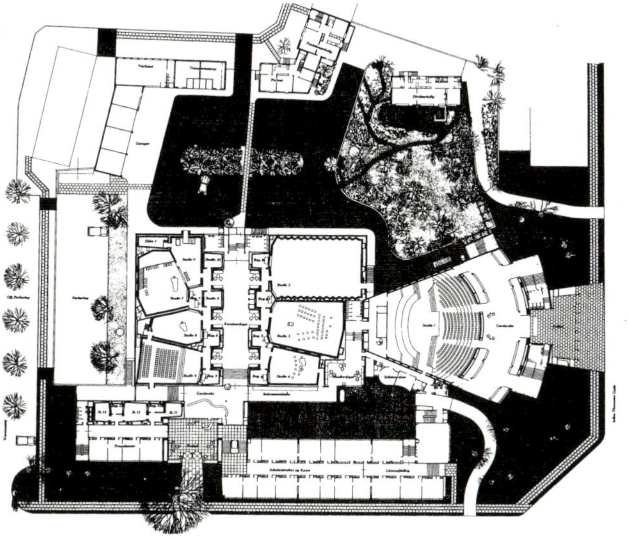

G.N. Brandt and Aksel Andersen designed two unique and lush gardens on the Radiohus roof on the second and third floors. The scheme consists of a pergola covered terrace outside the canteen with a richly varied landscaping. Long, grey concrete pavers were laid, with broad joints, as winding paths between the plants. In a continuous green carpet of ivy, barrenwort and saxifrage were flowering bushes, fruit trees and laciniated trees. Recently the gardens have been altered due to a roof renovation. Despite the protected status of the garden, the alterations lack a sense of the qualities inherent in the existing paving patterns and landscaping.

E155

Industriens Hus

Corner of Nørre Voldgade and Larslejstræde, Indre By
1939

1:1000

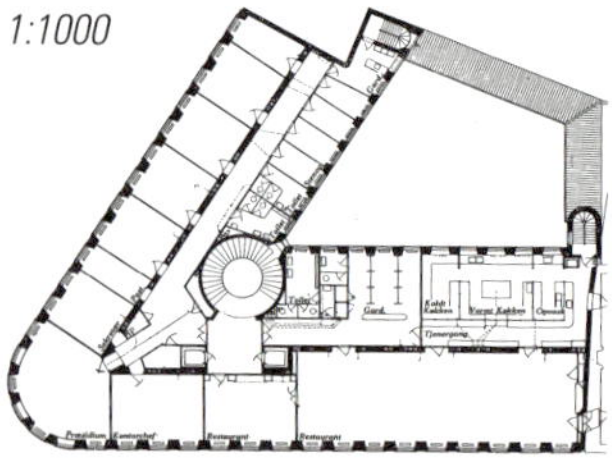

Client: The Industrial Branches and the Steel Industry's Amalgamation
Architect: Povl Baumann

Baumann's project for this office building was chosen from a closed competition in 1938 that reflected the contemporary discord between neoclassicism and functionalism. With total regard for this either-or debate, Baumann chose an architecture that respected the existing neighboring buildings but with his own interpretation. Each floor has a special window type with diminishing heights upwards, and the format and division are English inspired as are the stuccoed, white painted window recesses on the ground floor. This building is one of many examples of the exceptional perfectionism that is characteristic of Baumann's work. Here, it is evident in the street facade brickwork, with the strong protruding joints, which are still intact. The angle-shaped building has a central corridor with offices toward the street and secondary spaces facing the small five-sided courtyard. At the junction of the two corridors there is a delicately detailed circular stairway that runs up to a roof lantern.
Bibliography: H.E. Langkilde: Povl Baumann. 1991, 184

Housing and post office **E156**

H.C. Ørsteds Vej 54, Frederiksberg
1939

Client: Painting contractor Johan Thomsen
Architect: Edvard Thomsen

New materials and new structural ideas were extensively tested in this building with its bearing cross walls, cantilevered balconies of reinforced concrete, and facade areas of glass block. It has a complex functionalistic expression that reveals both the architect's joy of exploring new ideas and his personal form attitudes. The street facade with the angled, protruding balconies that follow a precise facade grid is both complex and sculptural – a form idiom inspired by the Bauhaus school. Spatial economy was also one of functionalism's characteristics. The units have access from balcony corridors on the courtyard facade, and the placement of the stairs outside the building gives room for as many of the 50 sqm apartments as possible. The apartment plans are also economical in their disposition with American style Murphy beds. The recessed upper floor is the result of building code that set a maximum cornice height, and the irregular form of the site can be read in the building's shifting facade.

Havemann's department store **E162**

Vesterbrogade 76-78, Vesterbro
1939

Client: Havemanns Magasin
Architect: H. Ortmann and V. Berner Nielsen

Although the building's name has been changed to Føtex, its function remains the same. The elegant functionalistic facades fit effortlessly into the gaudy Vesterbrogade townscape. The asymmetrical placement of the glass bay and the tower accent the main entrance, and the smooth tiled facades provide a simple, effective expression in keeping with the building's function and location. This expression is further underscored by the small clusters of florescent lights on the facades, which in a simple manner and in keeping with the form idiom, mark the building in the flickering night scene.
Bibliography: Arkitekten M 1943, 13

E186

A. Jespersen & Søn office building

Nyropsgade 18, Indre By
1955

Client: A. Jespersen & Søn
Architect: Arne Jacobsen

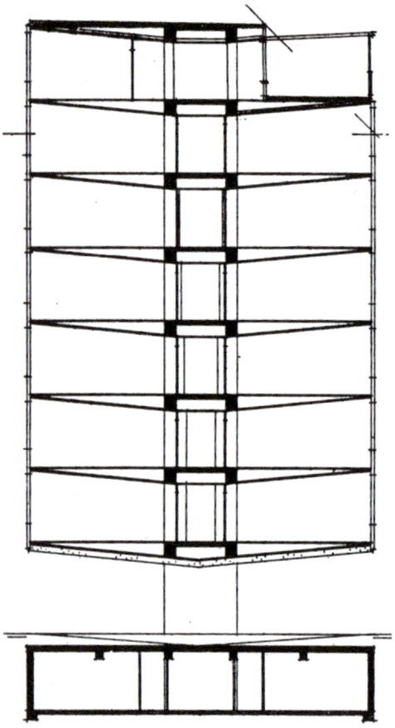

1:400

The arrival of new business structures during the 1950's led to an increasing need for administration facilities and with that, office buildings. The building on Nyropsgade street, with its extreme simplification is an architectural and structural prototype of the modern office building of the time. The facade facing Nyropsgade finds its strength through its disciplined proportions and discreet choice of materials and color. The glass in the nonoperable windows and the grey-green glass spandrels have the same reflective features and give the facade a weight and intangibility that is secured by the elegant grid of mullions and the dark, closed towerlike slab at the end. The consistency of this curtain wall is in keeping with the consistency of the supporting structure, where two columns alone bear the building. Under this floating mass there is vehicle access to the courtyard and parking area. Higher up in the building, the columns split into pairs, straddling the corridor, while the rest of the floor area is free of structural members. The subdivision of offices is thus achieved with light, glass walls and cabinets. On the upper floor there is a canteen with a terrace facing the courtyard. The building is one of Arne Jacobsen's most important works and represents the American inspired modernism that he advocated so much.
Bibliography: Arkitektur DK 1958, 109

SAS Royal Hotel

Vesterbrogade and Hammerichsgade, Indre By
1956-61

Client: Scandinavian Airlines System, SAS
Architect: Arne Jacobsen

This 18-story skyscraper, resting on a low two-story block in the middle of the city, was Copenhagen's first taste of modern metropolitan architecture with an obvious reference to Skidmore, Owings & Merrill's Lever House in New York City. The building was, and still is, a striking feature of Copenhagen's skyline. It stands out due to its size, but also because of the eminent and precise proportioning of the high and the low blocks, and the tower block's delicately divided reflective surface that deliberately blends with the clouds and sky. As with some of Arne Jacobsen's large buildings, the structure is subordinate to the precise exterior form described by the curtain walls. The low flat block contains the foyer, restaurant and hotel administration, and originally an SAS booking terminal. The tower block contains the hotel rooms, and a restaurant and observation area on the top floor. The SAS Hotel was the most striking example of Arne Jacobsen's total design, in that he also designed all the furnishings, fixtures and even the dinnerware. In recent years the interiors have been redone with a total disrespect for the unique coherence in Arne Jacobsen's work.
Bibliography: Arkitektur DK 1960, 209

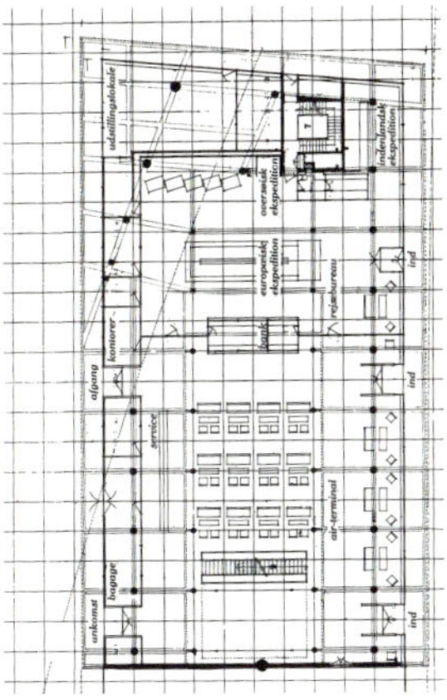

1:1000

E211

The Zealand regional archives, annex

Jagtvej 10, Nørrebro
1963-66

Client: Ministry of Culture
Architect: Eva and Nils Koppel
Landscape architect: Edith and Ole Nørgård

The first regional archives building was built in 1891-92 with Martin Nyrop as architect. It is a functional, disciplined building with less ornamentation and ebullience than Nyrop's other buildings. The annex respects the older building but has a will of its own in the urban context. The one-story connecting building contains offices, canteen, exhibition and meeting rooms gathered around an atrium garden. The new archives building has six low stories, of which two are below grade. The slightly sloped, closed facades are sided with rough hewn black slate. The building is a somber monolith, and in itself a clarified solution to the problem but also reflects the lack of sense for the situation so typical of the 1960's.
Bibliography: Arkitektur DK 1967, 265

E230

Panum Institute

Blegdamsvej 3, Nørrebro
1971-90

Client: Ministry of Education, department of buildings
Architect: KKET, Eva and Nils Koppel, Gert Edstrand, Poul Erik Thyrring
Landscape architect: Edith and Ole Nørgård

As part of Copenhagen University, this institute (named after doctor P.L. Panum, 1820-85) houses the health and medical institutes, the faculty of science offices, and the dental college. This broad range of activities is the reason for the extensive size of the scheme. It is divided in three parts with the class rooms in a low building toward west, the laboratories in five traverse wings in the center and the service rooms in the tall, long building along Tagensvej road. The partially closed facade toward Tagensvej serves as a traffic noise screen, and the distinctive, diagonally cut brick facade follows the path of the fire stairs. The enormous building masses behind the brutalistic exterior are clearly structured for their function and location.
Bibliography: Arkitektur DK 1976, 223

Blågården E239

Blågårds Plads, Nørrebro
1979-81

Client: The Association for Social Housing, FSB
Architect: Kooperativ Byggeindustri A/S
Landscape architect: Bruun, Samuelsen & Ulfstedt and Lone van Deurs

Prior to renewal activities in the 1980's, the inner Nørrebro quarter was an extremely dense and dilapidated area. The comprehensive urban renewal plans were approved in 1979 and implied a reduction in density of 50%. The building project that followed met violent protests from the tenants. In "the Black Quadrangle", the area around Blågårds Plads, almost all of the existing buildings were torn down, and the new building project totally changed the street structure. The Blågården project is characteristic of the standardized housing, which in a variety of types, now fills the neighborhood. Large building depths, prefabricated brick facade elements and standard details are the basic elements in an architecture strongly criticized for its lack of expressiveness. With its ultra-rational building process and architecture, Nørrebro's renewal was a turning point after which urban renewal now implicates the tenants to a greater degree and places more weight on the preservation of important features and details in the old city quarters and their buildings.
Bibliography: M. Kjeldsen: Industrialized Housing in Denmark. 1988

Courtyard in the Dossering block E260

Baggesensgade, Wesselsgade, Korsgade, Peblinge Dossering, Nørrebro
1988

Client: Copenhagen Urban Renewal Association
Landscape architect: Lone van Deurs

The long, narrow block contains a series of courtyards connected with small passages. Each space has its own character, but the mutual use of used, smoothly worn granite cobblestones, the detailing of the blue-painted fence and trellises as well as the distinctive, familiar plants along the new stuccoed facades create a context in the modest and pleasant everyday complex.
Bibliography: Landskab 1993, 16

1:2000

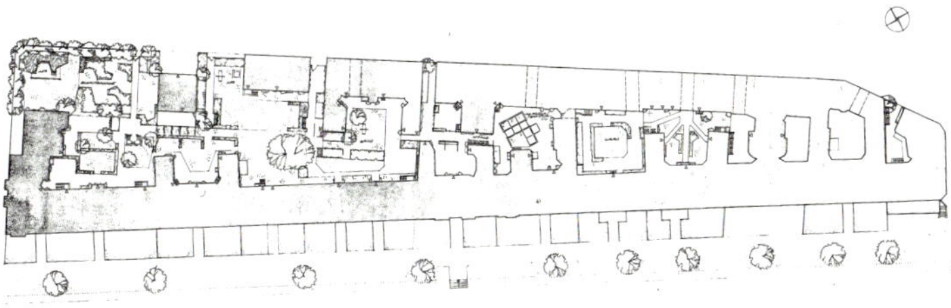

E251

Copenhagen Business College

Dalgas Have 15, Frederiksberg
1985-89

Client: The Danish Society of Engineers' Pension Fund
Architect: Henning Larsens Tegnestue
Landscape architect: Ginman, Harboe and Borup

Despite its great size, the school is part of a larger whole that also includes the Dalgas Have housing scheme (E 265). The whole is an urban quarter with the school as the large monumental front. The building's symmetrical main form with the semicircular center part and its blinding whiteness are typical classicistic motifs – most known from the building where the color and form have made it a symbol, "The White House" in Washington D.C. from the 1790's, designed by James Hoban and Thomas Jefferson. In a more recent sense, the building is inspired by the Italian-German neorationalism. The exterior is dominated by an absolute classical formality, which is broken on the interior by surprising effects. The ca. 150 meter long, 3-story center "street" runs through the length of the building and has a slight bend in the center – a modern break with the classical perspective. In addition, this common space has a certain Islamic touch in its details, a fountain and reflecting pool at the bend of the road, the pastel colored towers at either end and low-hanging mosquelike lighting fixtures, all inspired by the architect's previous project for the Foreign Ministry in Riyad. The building is a refined play with ethnic and universal effects and with classicism as a solid background.
Bibliography: Arkitektur DK 1989, 62

The Dalgas Have housing scheme

Dalgas Have, Frederiksberg
1989-91

Client: The Danish Society of Engineers' Pension Fund, PKA
Architect: Henning Larsens Tegnestue
Landscape architect: Ginman, Harboe and Borup

Special tax laws made it attractive during this period for the so-called institutional building clients to invest in large housing schemes, which until then had been primarily public housing. One of these large private projects was Dalgas Have, the most obvious example of the turn taken by architecture and housing needs in a formal direction. The white buildings illustrate the renewed interest in the classical form ideals inspired by Italian neorationalism and traditional English classicism. The enormous scope of the building scheme justified the basic concept that dealt with both urban structure and architecture. Apart from the disciplined complex with axes and symmetry, Dalgas Have has 16 tower blocks that form a fluid and less formal boundary to the surroundings. The building form has a clear reference to the old villas in the nearby Frederiksberg quarter. The design of the ca. 500 units respects the formal fundamental principle without any particular innovative housing features, however there are many common facilities.
The Business College is part of Dalgas Have's architectural whole, which further underscores the scheme's formality.
Bibliography: Arkitektur DK 1992, 10

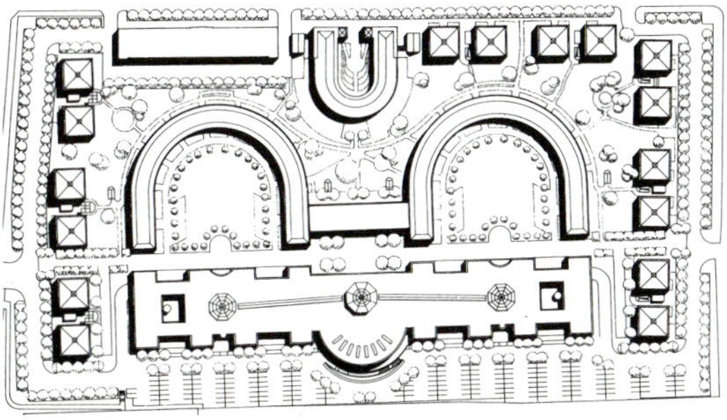

1:5000

E267

Tycho Brahe Planetarium

Gl. Kongevej 10, Indre By
1988-89

Client: Urania Foundation
Architect: Knud Munk

The site on the edge of Sankt Jørgens lake makes the planetarium one of Copenhagen's most conspicuous buildings. The architecture is strong and with a distinctive character that lives up to its function and demanding role. Toward the city, the geometrically precise cylinder is surrounded by lower buildings with irregular forms. Toward the lake, the entire clear form of the cylinder is reflected in the water. It is the simple and dramatic contrasts that securely tie the building to the site. The architectural effectivity is followed up by the super graphics on the cylinder's two facades: the horizontal curved with the brickwork stair pattern, and the sloping roof with the herringbone pattern. There is also a drama about the interior. The exhibition area under the planetarium hall is dimly lit to aid spectators in adjusting their eyes to the darkness of the planetarium. As opposed to the refined exterior, the interior detailing is rough, like the steel stairway that climbs around the cylinder. The building's main hall is also dramatic with the steeply stepped seating under the large domed screen where the stellar drama unfolds. Regardless of its function the building is an architectural monument.
Bibliography: Arkitektur DK 1991, 172

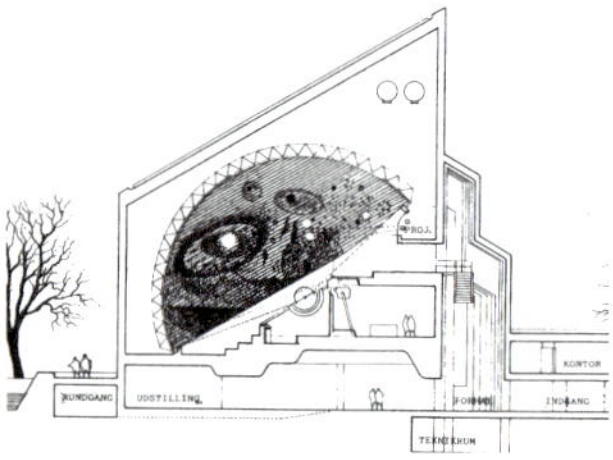

1:1250

Senior housing E271

Mariendalsvej 14-18, Frederiksberg
1992

Client: The lawyers and Economists' Pension Fund
Architect: Box 25 Arkitekter
Landscape architect: Peter Holst

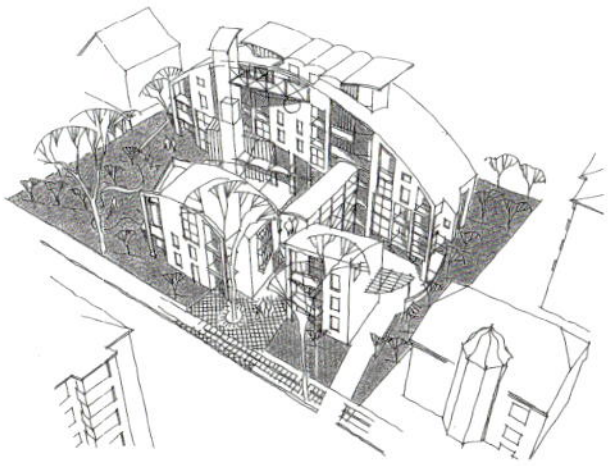

As an alternative to the standard, subsidized housing for the elderly, this scheme was designed with emphasis on both individual needs and communal spirit. In addition, there were a number of ecological and urban architectural efforts, which formed the basis for the public subsidies. The character of the site determined the division of the scheme into a large building facing the heavily trafficked Ågade street, and the two tower blocks on Mariendalsvej road that refer to the many large villas in the neighborhood. The expressive and delicate architecture offers many visual sensations, which reflect the architectural goals. The well-equipped common facilities, such as the exercise room and rooftop swimming pool, illustrate a level of quality far above standard. The 22 different units are somewhat small due to the large common facilities, but all have solar oriented balconies. The curved roof surface toward south has solar collectors, ventilation exhaust heat is retrieved and rainwater is collected for use in toilets, etc.

Bibliography: Arkitektur DK 1993, 354

E272 **Sankt Hans Torv**
1993

Client: Copenhagen Municipality
Landscape architect: Sven-Ingvar Andersson
Sculptor: Jørgen Haugen Sørensen

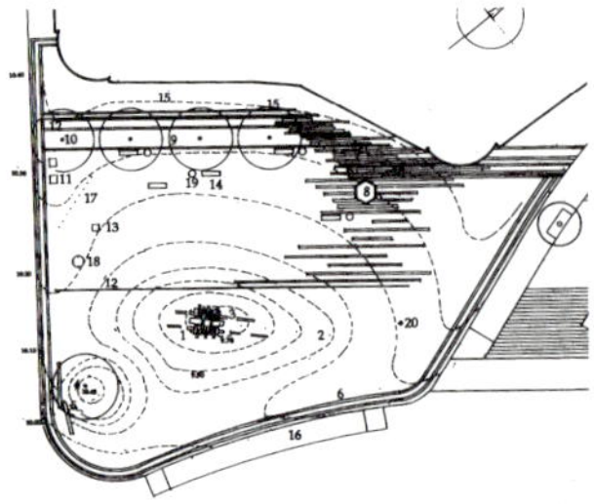

The square is formed by the space where six streets run together. The terrain slopes gradually downwards toward the granite sculpture "The house that rains" where it forms a hollow. It then rises upwards toward a small knoll with a linden tree, a counterpoint to the hollow. The sculpture is a card house of Portuguese granite, with rough hewn stone beams wedged together. The sculpture's main axis is twisted slightly in relation to the directional pattern of the granite sett paving and border slabs. A single jet of water rises from the paving and is regulated by the air temperature.
Bibliography: Landskab 1994, 110

E273 **Infill housing**
Egegade 20, Nørrebro
1993

Client: The Trade Union Housing Association
Architect: Tegnestuen Møllen

This infill housing building respects the neighboring building with its curved facade and cornice height, but is also contemporary both in terms of architecture and building methods. The asymmetrical street facade is subdued with modernistic features, but there is also a discreet ornamentation with the small railings by the windows. The structure is primarily steel, sided with fiber cement, plasterboard and lightweight concrete – a building method that facilitated building work on the narrow site. There are five, one-story, two-room units and two, two-story, three-room units. In addition there is also a common room in the high basement. Access to the units is by way of a portal.

Axeltorv **E274**

1990-91

Client: Scala I/S
Architect: Mogens Breyen

Axeltorv square in front of the Scala shopping mall is an example of an urban space, where art and architecture have been integrated. Parallel with a row of linden trees running the length of the square, sculptor Mogens Møller placed a row of nine bronze vases, with figures representing the nine planets of the solar system. These amphoras stand on a small strip of red granite, unequally spaced, to correspond proportionally with the distance between the planets. The different figures spray water mist, while a circular pool with gilded decorations has a smooth reflecting surface that marks the center of Axeltorv square.
Bibliography: Arkitektur DK 1991, 263

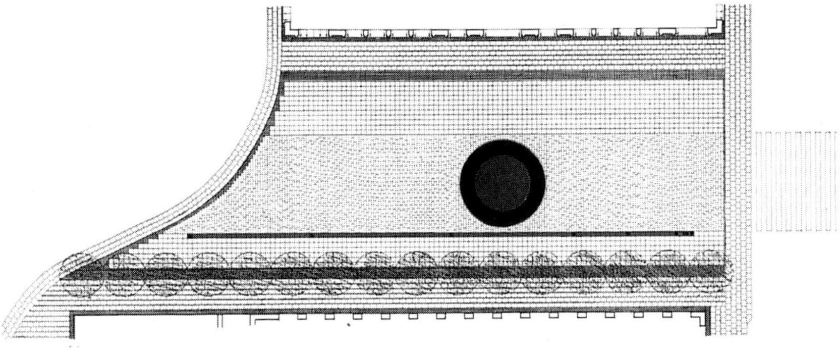

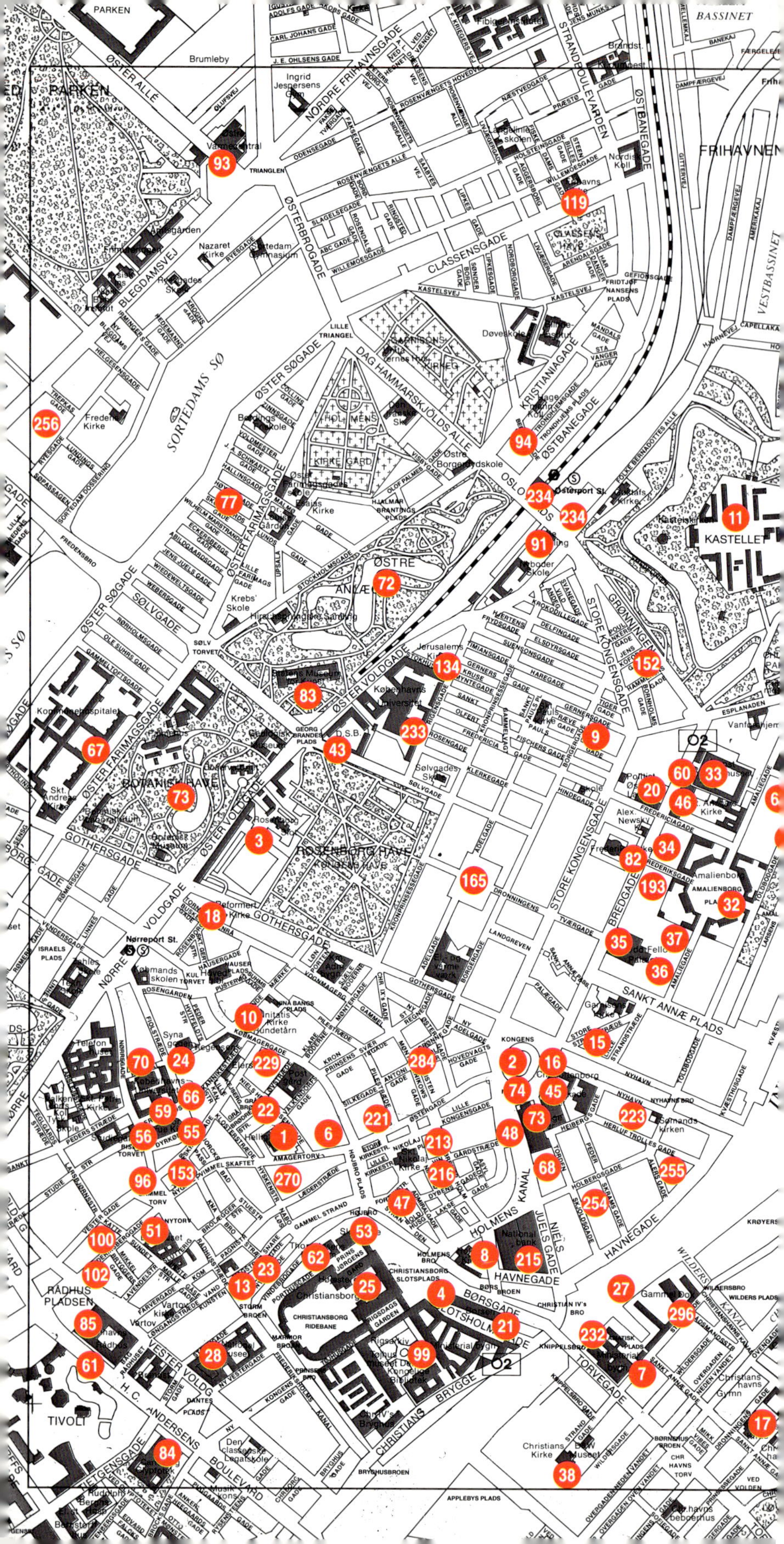
PARKEN
BASSINET
ØSTER ALLÉ
Brumleby
CARL JOHANS GADE
J. E. OHLSENS GADE
Ingrid Jespersens Gym.
NORDRE FRIHAVNSGADE
STRANDBOULEVARDEN
ØSTBANEGADE
FRIHAVNEN
Østre Varmecentral
TRIANGLEN
ODENSEGADE
ROSENVÆNGETS ALLÉ
HOLSTEINSGADE
WILLEMOESGADE
CLASSENSGADE
ØSTERBROGADE
SLAGELSEGADE
ABC GADE
KASTELSVEJ
FRIDTJOF NANSENS PLADS
VESTBASSINET
CAPELLAKAJ
BLEGDAMSVEJ
Nazaret Kirke
RYESGADE
LILLE TRIANGEL
DAG HAMMARSKJÖLDS ALLÉ
GARNISONS KIRKEGÅRD
Døveskole
KRISTIANIAGADE
SORTEDAMS SØ
ØSTER SØGADE
Frederiks Kirke
HOLMENS KIRKEGÅRD
Østre Borgerdydskole
OSLO PLADS
Østerport St.
KASTELLET
ØSTBANEGADE
FOLKE BERNADOTTES ALLÉ
ØSTER FARIMAGSGADE
ØSTRE ANLÆG
STOCKHOLMSGADE
STORE KONGENSGADE
GRØNNINGEN
ESPLANADEN
SØLVGADE
SØLV TORVET
Statens Museum for Kunst
Jerusalems Kirke
Københavns Universitet
ØSTER VOLDGADE
GEORG BRANDES PLADS
Kommunehospitalet
BOTANISK HAVE
Geologisk Museum
ROSENBORG HAVE
Sølvgades Skole
Alex. Newsky Kirke
FREDERICIAGADE
AMALIENBORG
GOTHERSGADE
KRONPRINSESSEGADE
DRONNINGENS TVÆRGADE
LANDGREVEN
BREDGADE
AMALIEGADE
Reformert Kirke
Nørreport St.
NØRRE VOLDGADE
SANKT ANNÆ PLADS
KØBMAGERGADE
Trinitatis Kirke Rundetårn
KONGENS NYTORV
NYHAVN
Telefon
Københavns Universitet
Frue Kirke
AMAGERTORV
Sankt Nikolaj Kirke
HOLMENS KANAL
National bank
HAVNEGADE
NIELS JUELS GADE
Holmens Kirke
Christiansborg
BØRSGADE
SLOTSHOLMSGADE
CHRISTIANSBORG SLOTSPLADS
CHRISTIANSBORG RIDEBANE
Rigsarkiv
Tøjhus Museet
Det Kongelige Bibliotek
Ministerial bygn.
CHRISTIANS BRYGGE
TORVEGADE
Christianshavns Gymn.
RÅDHUSPLADSEN
VESTER VOLDGADE
Rådhus
TIVOLI
H. C. ANDERSENS BOULEVARD
Glyptotek
Christians Kirke
BRYGHUSBROEN
APPLEBYS PLADS
VED VOLDEN
93 119 256 94 234 234 11 77 91 72 152 134 83 9 67 233 43 60 33 20 46 73 3 34 82 165 193 32 18 35 37 36 10 15 229 284 2 16 70 24 66 74 45 223 59 22 221 73 55 56 1 6 213 48 153 270 216 68 255 96 47 254 51 53 100 8 215 102 62 23 13 25 4 27 296 85 21 232 28 99 61 7 17 84 38

F
LYNETTELØBET
LYNETTEN
LYNETTE HAVNEN
Renseanlæg Lynetten
PRANKAJ
PLADSKAJ
REFSHALEVEJ
NORDRE REFSHALE BASSIN
224
REFSHALEØEN
SØNDRE REFSHALE BASSIN
REFSHALEVEJ
LYSTBÅDEHAVN
29
SIXTUS
29
QVINTUS
QVINTI LYNETTE
REFSHALEVEJ
MARGRETHE HOLM
Amagerværket
FLÅDENS LEJE
NYHOLM
CHAR LOTTE AMALIES BASTION
Kl.pumpest.
KRAFTVÆRKSVEJ
Amagerforbrænding
1. REDAN
DOKØEN
29
HOLMEN
FREDERIKSHOLM
FREDERIKS BASTION
29
29
2. REDAN
FORLANDET
KRAFTVÆRKSVEJ
29
STADSGRAVEN
HF. STRANDLYST
Københavns Go-kartbane
CARL BASTION
REFSHALEVEJ
Kl.anl.
ARSENALØEN
3. REDAN
HF. STRANDHØJ
H. F. PRØVESTENEN
VILHELMS BASTION
HF. ROSEN
HF. KLØVERMARKEN
KLØVERMARKSVEJ
REFSHALEVEJ
SOFIE HEDEVIGS BASTION
HF. KLØVERBLOMSTEN
4. REDAN
CHRISTIANIA
HF. SOMMERLY
Kl.pumpest.
Kl.pumpest.
ULRIKS BASTION
STADS GRAVEN
RAFFINADERIVEJ
5. REDAN
KLØVERMARKEN
Lille Havfrue
LANGELINIEKAJ

F1

Helligåndshuset and church

Niels Hemmingsensgade 5, Indre By
13th Century, 1732

Client: Originally a Catholic convent
Architect (restoration): Herman Baagø Storck
Landscape architect: Edith Nørgård

The various buildings in the church complex contain the remains of a convent, founded in 1296. The late Gothic "Helligåndshus" is from the second half of the 15th century. It was originally a hospital and is now the only wholly preserved medieval building in Copenhagen. Today it is used for exhibitions etc. The church was built in the middle of the 15th century and was destroyed by the Copenhagen fire of 1728. Parts of the medieval outer walls still remain. A restoration in 1878-80 involved the rebuilding of the tower from 1594, but also destroyed much of the complex's historical authenticity. Griffenfeld's Chapel was built in 1673 and restored in 1956 by the Royal Housing Inspector, Thomas Havning.

Kongens Nytorv F2

Indre By
1600's, 1800's, 1900's

Client: Copenhagen Municipality
Landscape architect: E. Erstad-Jørgensen, Copenhagen Municipal Park Department

Kongens Nytorv square is surrounded by buildings on all five sides. It was paved with cobblestones in 1670 and the "l'Amoureux" equestrian statue of Christian V was raised in 1688. The statue was surrounded by a large ring of trees, which were removed in the middle of the 1800's when the innermost trees were planted: a dozen freestanding elm trees. In 1908, Erstad-Jørgensen planted a parterre with ornamental boxwoods. Eight years later the ring was again established with elm trees, which today are square-trimmed annually. During the 1990's the square was renovated. New cobblestone paving was laid, the parterre was replanted and the trees suffering from the Dutch elm disease were replaced.
Bibliography: Landskab 1992, 74

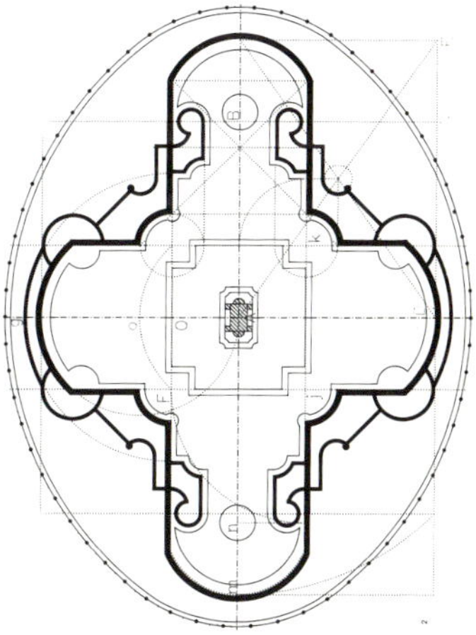

F3

Rosenborg Castle *
Øster Voldgade 4 A, Ny København
1606-34

Client: The national government
Architect: Christian IV

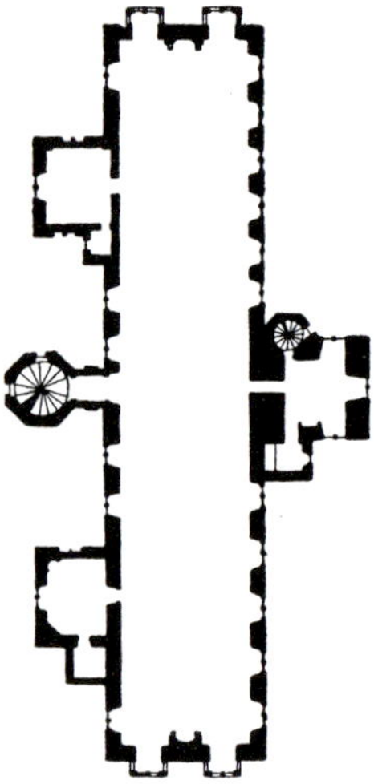

1:750

The castle was originally a two-story "summer house", built in 1606-07 as a sanctuary in relation to the old Copenhagen Castle. In 1613-17, the castle was lengthened, an extra story was added as well as a 50-meter high tower on the west side. The stair tower on the east is from 1633-34. The king is said to have had a decisive influence on the design of the tower, perhaps aided by architects Hans van Steenwinkel the younger and Willum Cornelisz. Despite the long period of realization, the castle as a whole, is a fine example of Dutch renaissance. The ground floor interior, with private quarters for the king and queen, is basically unaltered, the middle floor was partially changed during the reign of Frederik IV, and the great hall on the upper floor still bears witness to the castle's original splendor. In the early 18th century, the outer walls were painted grey in the style of the time, and in the early 19th century, to restore the original appearance, it was painted brick red with black joints. In 1866, architect Ferdinand Meldahl started an extensive restoration that included the removal of the paint and the replacement of large areas of sandstone. The roofing was originally slate, but was replaced in 1712 and later with copper. The castle has never served as the official residence for the royal family, but has housed many official ceremonies and events.

Kongens Have * F3

Indre By
1600's, 1721-49, 1963

Client: Christian IV
Landscape architect: Johan Cornelius Krieger, The Royal Castles and Gardens

Christian IV began work on the Kongens Have garden in 1606. The first known survey from 1649 shows a division of the flat areas in uniform squares, a chessboard pattern that still has traces in the path system. Around 1700, linden alleys were planted along the main paths. The two trimmed alleys, Damegangen, and nearest the castle, Kavallergangen, are from that period. The Swan fountain in the ring of old linden trees lies where the original plan showed a junction of the diagonal paths. Until 1783, the military exercise area south of the castle was part of the garden, with a fancy parterre designed by Krieger, who also built the orangery along Vestervoldgade street. At the end of the 1700's, the garden was opened to the public, and a wrought iron fence, with small pavilions designed by architect Peter Meyn, was built about 1800. The alleys were pruned around 1950 and since the 60's the garden has been renovated according to a design by The Royal Castles and Gardens with architects Knud Preisler and Ingwer Ingwersen. This includes the characteristic row of trimmed chestnut trees along Gothersgade, the unique crocus carpet axis between the castle and Kronprinsessegade street, and a fine, renaissance inspired rose garden between the moat and Husalléen.

Bibliography: Havekunst 1964, 141, Landskab 1993, 114

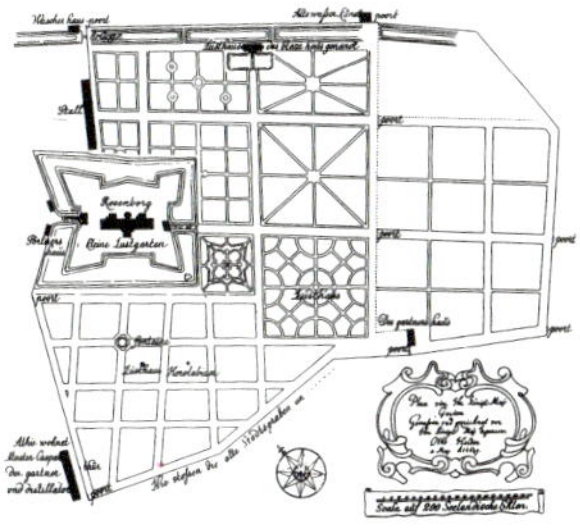

Heider's plan, 1649

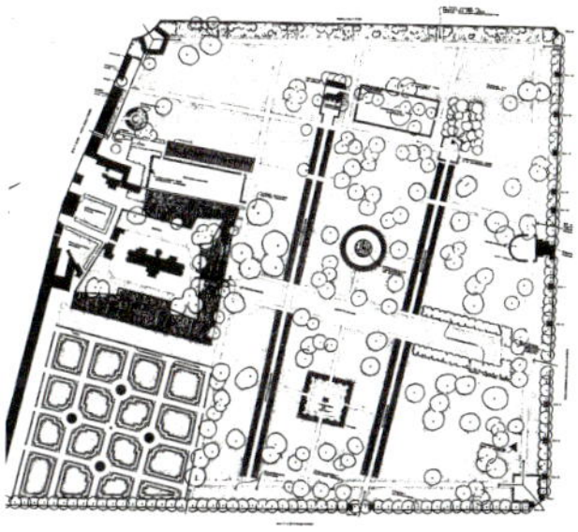

F4

Børsen, the stock exchange *
Slotsholmsgade og Børsgade, Indre By
1619-25

Client: The national government
Architect: Lorenz and Hans van Steenwinkel et al

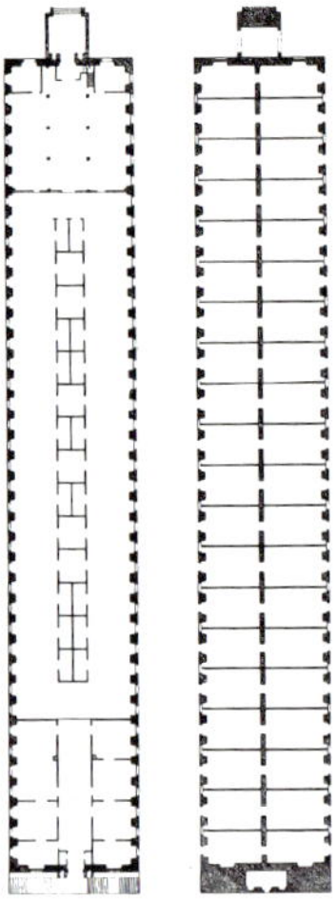

The building was built on an embankment between Slotsholmen and the first Knippelsbro bridge, which was built at the same time. At first it served as a simple trading hall with a packing room in the basement and shops and offices on the upper floor. But King Christian IV wanted a more magnificent building and in 1624-25 the "Dragon spire" was added by Ludvig Heidtrider, who was actually a fireworks designer. The dormers facing the canal were added then, and later came the richly ornamented gables. In 1772-77 the dragon spire was restored. In 1857, the building was converted to a stock exchange with a large trading hall, in connection with a large rebuilding project by architect H.C. Stilling. In 1880-83, the original red-flamed yellow brick was covered with the thin red brick tiles, which exist today, and a dormer was added on the Slotsholmsgade facade. In 1902-06, the sandstone figures were renewed. The building was again restored in the 1920's and 1950's. Thus there is not much of King Christian IV's original building remaining, but it is one of the most popular buildings credited to this great building enthusiast. It no longer serves as a stock exchange, but as office space for trade organizations in the Merchants' Guild.

City mansion * F6
Amagertorv 6, Indre By
1616

Client: Mayor Matthias Hansen
Architect: Unknown

The early seventeenth century was a vigorous period for architecture as can be seen by the many large building projects initiated by King Christian IV. During this time several mansions were built in the Dutch renaissance style, brought here by the Dutch master builders, but only a few of these remain. This house is a handsome example with the typical twin-dormers and many festive details, which form a fine interplay with the new paving on the square. The facade facing the square is intact although with some restored or replaced, sandstone ornaments. The interior of the former merchant's house is totally altered and the building serves today as a shop for the Royal Copenhagen Porcelain factory.

Gentry housing * F7
Strandgade 30-32, Christianshavn
1624-36

Client: Mayor Mikkel Vibe
Architect: Unknown

The original dormers and ornamentation, typical of the time, have completely disappeared, despite being spared during the Copenhagen fires. Several rebuilding projects took place in the early 1800's when No. 32 had an extra story added. Despite this, there are typical renaissance features. No. 30 has limestone fascia boards and window arches. On the end wall of No. 32, facing Sct Annægade there are traces of the original brick patterns. In 1943-45, No. 30 was restored by architect Harald Hauberg, and is still one of the city's most well preserved gentry residences from the renaissance.

F8

Holmens Church

Holmens Kanal, Indre By
1619

Client: The national government
Architect: Peter de Duncker et al

In 1619, Christian IV built a church for the royal navy in an old anchor smithy built by Frederik II in 1562. The smithy buildings and the elaborate renaissance gables, which still face the canal, were designed by Peter de Duncker. In 1641-43, the church was converted to a cruciform church, and the new gables were built similarly to the old one. This project was designed by Leonhard Blasius. The long chapel along the canal was built in 1708 from drawings by J.C. Ernst. The sacristy was built in connection with an extensive rebuilding project in 1872 supervised by Ludvig Fenger. At the same time, the Kongeport portal was moved here from Roskilde Cathedral. Holmens church has avoided damage by wars and fires and thus much still remains – especially the interior – as it was in the middle of the seventeenth century.

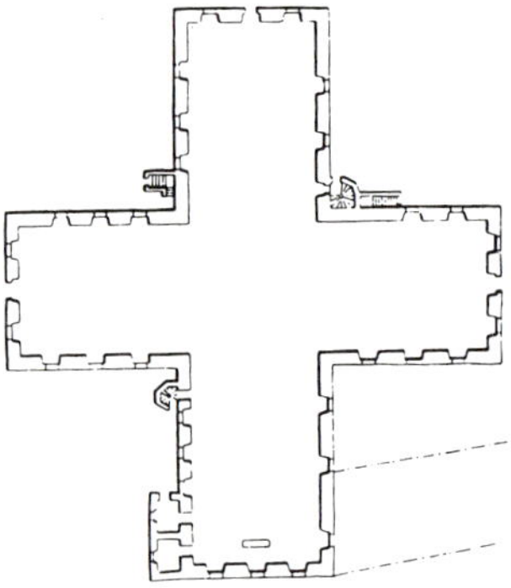

1:1100

Nyboder housing scheme * **F9**

Quarter between Store Kongensgade and Øster Voldgade, Ny København
1631-1758

Client: The national government
Architect: Hans van Steenwinkel the younger, Leonhard Blasius, Philip de Lange

The construction of this large scheme was started in 1631 and at Christian IV's death in 1648 it consisted of about 600 housing units, which were reserved for navy personnel. The housing scheme was later enlarged and altered, but the original one-story building types can still be seen on Sct. Poulsgade 20 where the "Nyboders Mindestuer" are located. The two-story building type that now dominates the quarter, was added in 1758 and designed by Philip de Lange. Nyboder was a radical departure from the seventeenth century housing culture in the crowded, twisted city within the ramparts. The scheme's formal, military arrangement with long, narrow blocks along straight streets was not without quality both in terms of housing and aesthetic value. This could be found in the simple, functional details, the good proportions and color. The arrangement of the housing blocks, with small "cabbage gardens" between the house rows, offered a necessary supplement to the daily housekeeping. It was also a sound principle for the distribution of light, air and traffic and has served as a model for many housing schemes since. Nyboder's fundamental character is so lasting, that the quarter is still one of the city's most desirable living areas. Around 1900, there were plans to demolish the entire quarter to build new private housing, but fortunately these were dropped for economical reasons.

Bibliography: Jørn Ørum-Nielsen: Længeboligen. 1988, 82

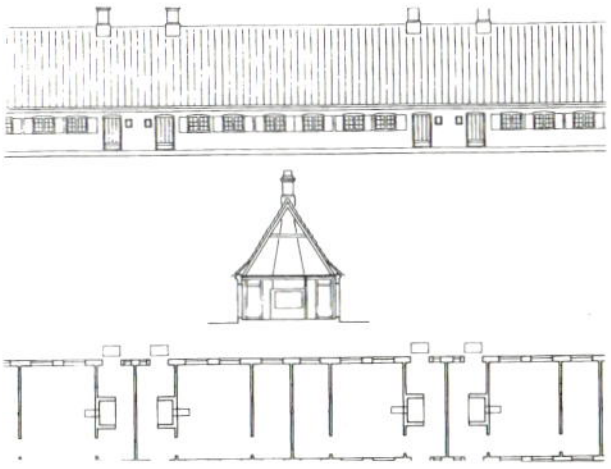

Oldest row

F10

Trinitatis Church, Round Tower *, parish hall, and rectory, Trinitatis Church square

Købmagergade, Indre By
1637-56

Client: The national government
Architect: Jørgen Scheffel, Hans van Steenwinkel the younger, I. & J. Exner
Landscape architect: Sven-Ingvar Andersson

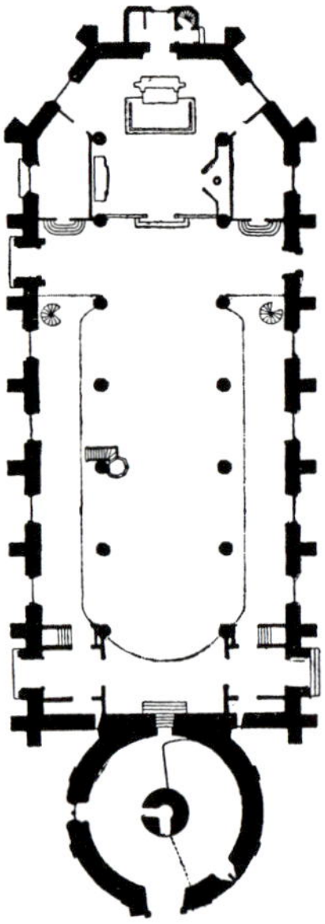

1:1000

The church and the Round Tower (which has no sacral function) served the university and the sciences. The church was a parish church for students. The church attic housed the university library and royal collection of antiquities. On the roof of the Round Tower, there was an observatory. As with other Christian IV's building works, he had a great influence on the design of the Round Tower. It was completed in 1642 and is characterized by its alternating red and yellow brickwork, which was covered with stucco from 1870 to 1952. The spiral ramp leading 210 meters to the top of the tower can be negotiated by horseback and coach, which was perhaps used to transport the sensitive and heavy astronomical instruments. The gothic influenced church was completed in 1656. Possibly the architects were Jørgen Scheffel, Hans van Steenwinkel and Leonhard Blasius. The 1728 Copenhagen fire destroyed the roof and the library as well as the church's furnishings. The baroque interior, which was built after the fire, still gives the church its characteristic style despite several restorations. The most recent was completed in 1985 by architects Inger and Johannes Exner, who also designed the parish house and rectory in 1982. In collaboration with landscape architect Sven-Ingvar Andersson, the Exners' designed the poetic Trinitatis Church square, where the old corbel stones from the Round Tower balustrade lie as animal-like sculptures.
Bibliography: Arkitektur DK 1985, 98

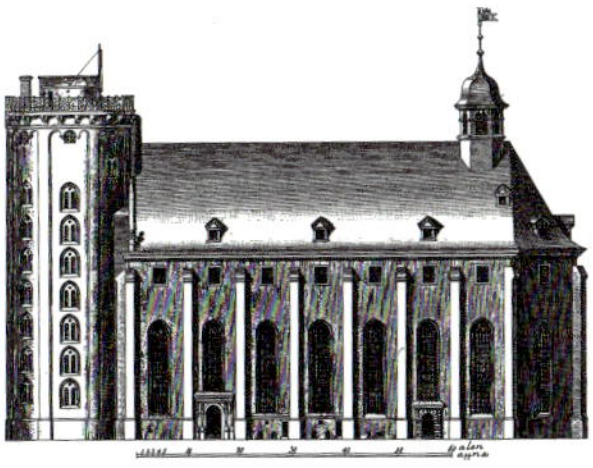

Between the neighboring building and the parish hall there is access to the square from Pilestræde street up a sculptural stairway centered on a series of ramps. The change in grade is about one meter and the stairs also resolve the difference in paving pattern orientation between the church square and the alley. When the Round Tower was restored, the old sandstone corbels from the platform were laid out on the church square's granite paving and down along the ramp.

1:1000

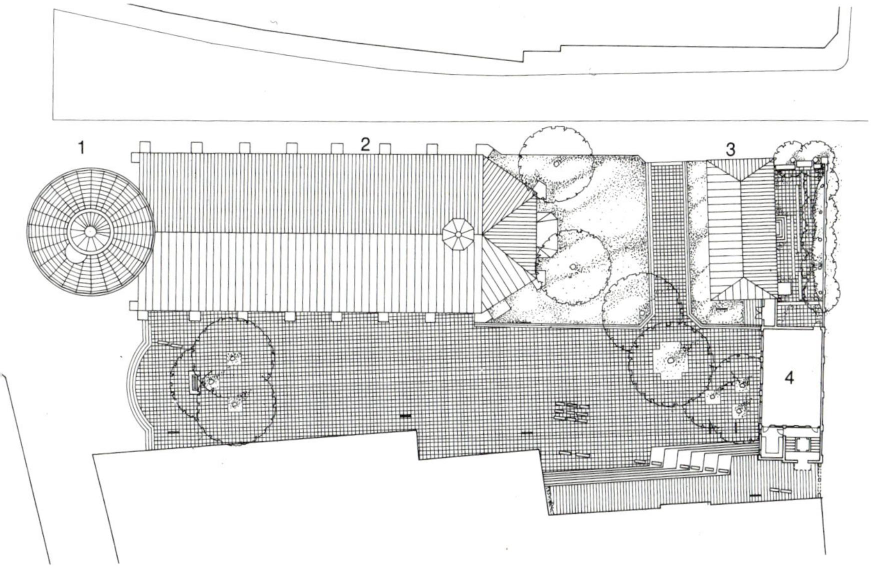

F11

Kastellet (the Citadel) and Kastel park *

Main entrance Esplanaden, Ny København
1662-64, ca. 1900, 1989

Client: Frederik III
Architect: Henrich Rüse et al
Landscape architect: Edvard Glæsel, H.A. Flindt, Copenhagen Municipal Park Department

The Kastellet complex was the result of Copenhagen's expansion under Christian IV, and the conclusion of peace with Sweden in 1658, in which all Danish possessions east of the Øresund strait had to be surrendered. Christian IV's son, Frederik III summoned the Dutch engineer Henrich Rüse to design this enormous defense complex, which was formed according to the most advanced warfare strategies of the time. The outer form is a five-pointed star, while the buildings within the fortification are controlled by two perpendicular axes oriented toward the points of the compass. The east/west axis is defined by the headquarters building built in 1725 and the Kastel Church built in 1704. The north/-south axis is marked by the "Norway gate" and the "Zealand gate". Some of the Kastellet's other buildings, such as the housing blocks for the troops, are very distinctive. As the Kastellet gradually lost its military significance, many changes were made in the buildings and the embankments. The church was restored in 1985-87 by the Defence Construction Service. There are still some military functions within the Kastellet complex. The fortification originally consisted of five bastions and a moat, which was a twin moat facing land. Toward the strait, there were two low outer embankments, along the present Langelinie. The five pointed star consists of 20 meter high embankments.
The area surrounding the fortifications has been gradually converted to a continuous promenade from Grønningen out to the Langelinie complex, designed by H.A. Flindt and architect Vilhelm Dahlerup. The Esplanaden area was created at the end of the 1780's as a pedestrian park with alleys. About the turn of the century, Edvard Glæsel designed Kastel Park, now known as Churchill Park. The impressive Gefion fountain by sculptor Anders Bundgaard marks the entrance to the promenade.
During the 1990's, the embankments were renovated by PLH Arkitekter in collaboration with the Defence Construction Service, so that the complex, with the geometrically precise earth forms, is sharply defined. Much of the nineteenth century shrouding growth has been cleared and the railway tracks passing through the area have been removed. A new bridge from the Zealand Ravelin to the King's Gate replaced the embankment from the foregoing century.
Bibliography: Arkitektur DK 1990, 332

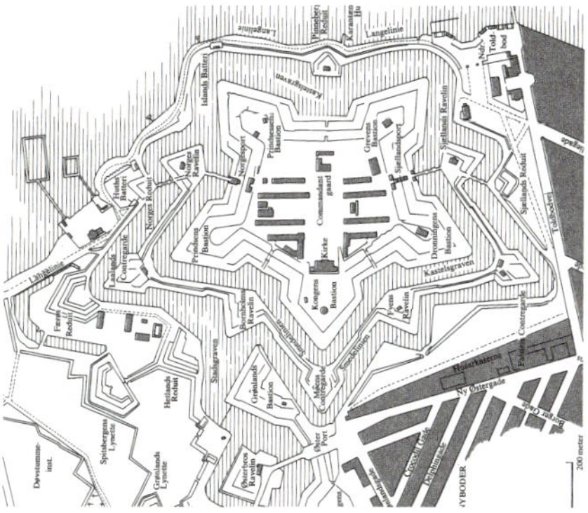

Langelinie
Pinneberg Reduit
Langelinie
Kastelsgraven
Islands Batteri
Prindsessens Bastion
Grevens Bastion
Norgesport
Sjællandsport
Sjællands Ravelin
Norges Ravelin
Norges Reduit
Commandant gaard
Kirke
Prindsens Bastion
Dronningens Bastion
Kastelsgraven
Sjællands Reduit
Toldbodvej
Langelinie
Laalands Contregarde
Kongens Bastion
Bornholms Ravelin
Fyens Ravelin
Færø Reduit
Fyens Contregarde
Stadsgraven
Hetlands Reduit
Grønlands Bastion
Møens Contregarde
Ny Østergade
Øster Port
Spitsbergens Lynette
Døvstumme-inst.
Grønlands Lynette
Østerbros Ravelin
NYBODER
200 meter

F13

Gentry housing *
Magstræde 17-19, Indre By
ca. 1640

Client: Unknown
Architect: Unknown

The regular gable house with one gable facing the street was characteristic for the housing built by Copenhagen's gentry during the last half of the 1600's and well into the 1700's. These houses, which escaped the city fires of 1728 and 1795, are good examples of this house type. They have renaissance features but without the heavy ornamentation typical of the Dutch renaissance used on the King's buildings and the larger city mansions. The two houses, with their common stairway, have facades of large, coarse medieval brick and are natural elements in Magstræde street's homogeneous street scene.

F15

Gentry housing *
Nyhavn 9, Indre By
1681

Client: Unknown
Architect: Unknown

The building is Nyhavn's oldest and is of the so-called "conflagration house" type, which were established according to standards laid down after the city fire in 1728, but were characteristic of the gentry housing already at the end of the 1600's. A very pristine group of these houses can be found on the south side of Gråbrødretorv square, built in the 1730's (F 22). Apart from the windows on the ground floor, the small, skewed gable building in Nyhavn is almost intact in its original form. The date 1681 is formed by the iron ties on the street facade.

Charlottenborg palace * **F16**

Kongens Nytorv 1, Indre By
1672-83

Client: Ulrik Frederik Gyldenløve
Architect: Evert Janssen

The client for the palace was Frederik III's son and governor of Norway. As the largest palace on the new Kongens Nytorv square, it was a significant manifestation of the absolute monarchy. In connection with the center wing with the cupola room, Lambert van Haven is the only architect known to have been involved with the building. There are certain Dutch features in the dark red brick, Dutch clinker, and sandstone ornaments. Some building materials came from Kalø castle in Jutland. Charlottenborg is the oldest major monument for Danish baroque architecture, and the formal axial symmetry is evident in the main plan, which originally included a magnificent garden running the length of Nyhavn canal. The great hall, facing Kongens Nytorv square was rebuilt by architect C.F. Hansen in 1827-28, while the baroque splendor is still evident in the tripartite arcade in the low, middle wing and its lavish cupola room above. Since 1753 Charlottenborg has been the home of the Royal Danish Academy of Fine Arts. In 1996, the architecture school moved to the Holmen area.

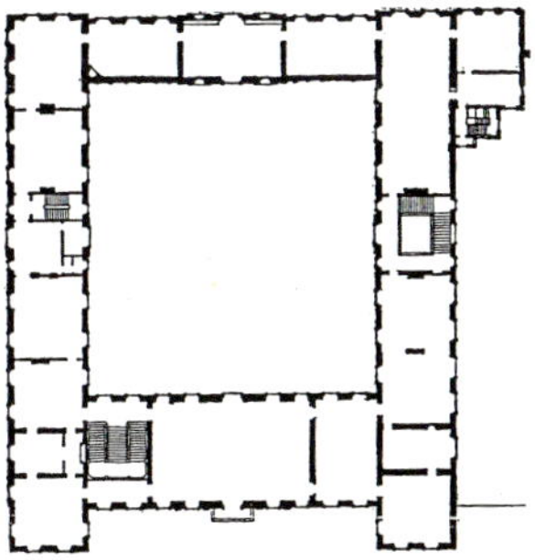

1:1500

F17

Vor Frelsers Church

Sankt Annæ Gade 29, Christianshavn
1682-96

Client: The Zealand diocese and the Crown (Frederik V)
Architect: Lambert van Haven and Lauritz de Thurah

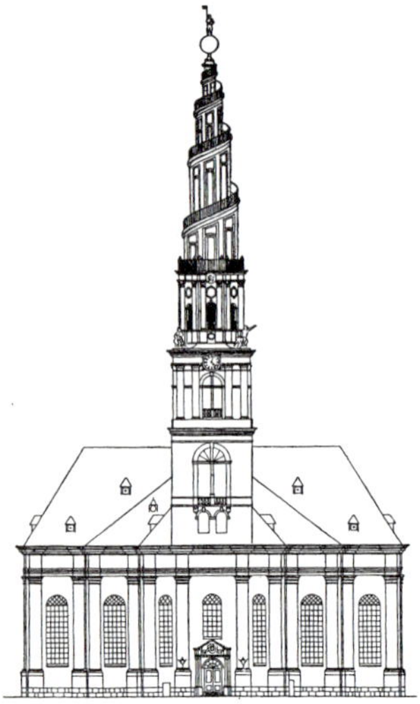

1:1200

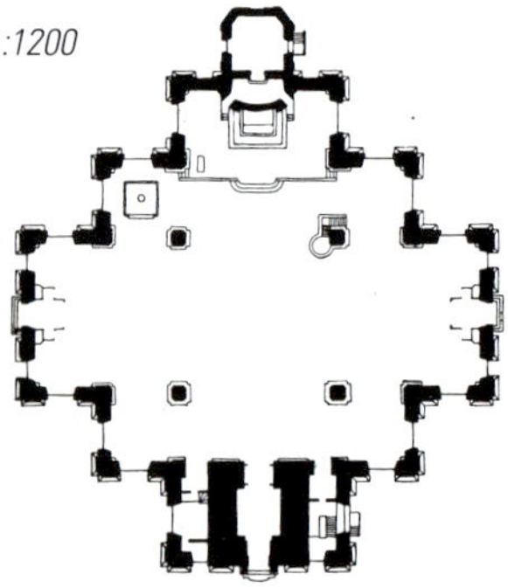

Construction of the church took place over many years and with great difficulties. The marshy site required major landfill work and the financing of the building had to done through contributions from the country's other churches. The church's architect, Lambert van Haven died in 1695 and at the consecration in 1696, much of the furnishings were unfinished. The spiral spire, which is now one of Copenhagen's most distinctive, was first finished in 1752. It was designed by Lauritz de Thurah, who mentions the Roman church, San Ivo della Sapienza, as his source of inspiration. Vor Frelsers Church is Denmark's first baroque church, and there are traces of Dutch influence on the exterior, with the tall windows, dark red brick, and the heavy sandstone cornices. The cruciform church space is voluminous and bright, and contains many exciting furnishings, such as the monumental organ from 1698 designed by sculptor Christian Nerger, who also did the two elephants that appear to support the organ. The altar is from 1725 and was designed by Nicodemus Tessin, and the pulpit is from 1773 by C.F. Harsdorff.

The Reformed Church * F18

Gothersgade 111, Indre By
1688-89

Client: The German-French Reformed Community in Copenhagen.
Architect: Henrik Brockman

During the last half of the 1600's, Copenhagen housed a large community of Dutch, German and French Calvinists. Queen Charlotte Amalie, who came from Germany, was a member of this religious community and offered both financial and moral aid, so they could build their own church across from the Rosenborg palace. The church was built according to drawings by the Dutch master builder, Henrik Brockam, who was also a member of the community. The building is Dutch baroque as is the Vor Frelsers Church built at the same time. However, the white church interior, with its flat ceiling and daylighting from all four directions, is marked by the formality of its confessional function. The pale wooden furnishings were added after 1728 when the church was damaged by the great Copenhagen fire. A distinctive feature here is the placement of the pulpit just above the altar, and the Queen's box opposite the altar and pulpit.

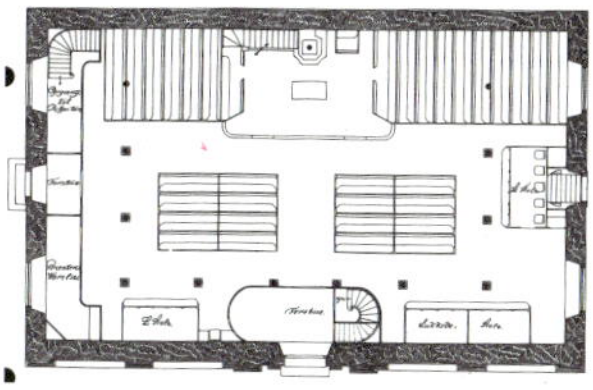

1:1200

F20

Østre Landsret high court (former opera house) *

Fredericiagade 24, Frederiksstaden
1701-03

Client: The national government
Architect: V.F. von Platen et al

At the request of Frederik IV, an opera house was built on this site, presumably with V.F. Platen as architect. However, as early as 1718-21, it was converted to a naval college after drawings by J.C. Ernst. From 1861, the building served as barracks until the parliament moved in after the Christiansborg fire in 1884. Following the change of the Danish political system in 1901, the building lying parallel with Bredgade street was built after a design of Martin Borch. Ever since the Parliament moved back to the new Christiansborg in 1918, the building has housed the Østre Landsret high court. The oldest building in the complex, with its large pilasters, has a Dutch baroque character, while the diagonal brick pattern is an Italian inspiration, similar to the building from 1901.

The Red Palace *

Slotsholmsgade 4, Indre By
1715-20

Client: The national government
Architect: Johan Conrad Ernst

The palace, which is also called the chancellery building or the department building, was originally, and still is, the home of Denmark's central administration. The plan is an irregular, three-winged complex designed by the executive master builder, J.C. Ernst in an Italian Baroque style. The facade toward Slotsholmgade street is stately and formal and is dominated by a colossal, semicircular pediment decorated with a sandstone relief with a bust of Frederik IV surrounded by a grand panoply or fan of banners and weapons. The interior is well preserved and has many of the original stucco ceilings, painted ceilings, wallpaper and tapestries.

F22

Gentry housing *

Gråbrødretorv 1-9, Indre By
1729-32

Client: Several including fishbleeder Hans Lau (No. 1)
Architect: J.C. Krieger

This row of houses is one of the few examples of attached "conflagration houses", the standard house type prescribed after the Copenhagen fire in 1728, according to a prototype by the chief national building master J.C. Krieger. The street facade had to be brick, while the rear facades and side buildings could be half-timber. These requirements were later eased as few could afford to follow them. However, Krieger's prototype had an effect on the new gentry housing built after the fire, in that it gave a somewhat homogeneous character to the city, with uniform street facades, without relief, but often with strongly characterized gables. In 1904, painter Jens Møller-Jensen took the initiative to have the facades painted in the original, bright colors, a practice that has been respected since.

City mansion * F23

Nybrogade 12, Indre By
1732

Client: Court confectioner J.H. Ziegler
Architect: Philip de Lange

The building shares an entrance portal with the neighboring building built in 1748 for merchant Frantz Rausch. As opposed to the "conflagration houses" that had smooth, brick facades instead of the traditional half-timbered, the frontispiece here has heavy sandstone ornaments that continue up to the gable. The sweeping forms are also repeated in the wrought iron railing in front of the windows on the piano nobile and the top floor. The style is inspired by south German baroque, and some of the facade details can be seen on other buildings by Philip de Lange, such as the post office on Købmagergade 33. The merchant, Frederic de Coninck owned the building from 1770-83 and the poet priest N.F.S. Grundtvig lived here in 1852.

Gentry house * F24

Fiolstræde 18, Indre By
1734

Client: Unknown
Architect: Unknown

The building's half-timbered construction did not fulfill the requirements placed on ordinary buildings after the city fire of 1728. However, these requirements were eased for a brief period, and this building survived both the great fire of 1795 and the English bombardment in 1807, which otherwise destroyed much of Fiolstræde street.
The half-timber facades and gable toward both Fiolstræde and Krystalgade streets reveal how much of Copenhagen looked before the 1728 fire. A similar example of half-timbered buildings from that period can be seen at Gammel Mønt 41. Fiolstræde 18 was restored in 1990-91.

Christiansborg Palace, The equestrian grounds and Marmorbro bridge *

Frederiksholms Kanal, Indre By
1733-45, 1918

Client: The national government
Architect: Elias David Hausser, Nicolai Eigtved and Thorvald Jørgensen

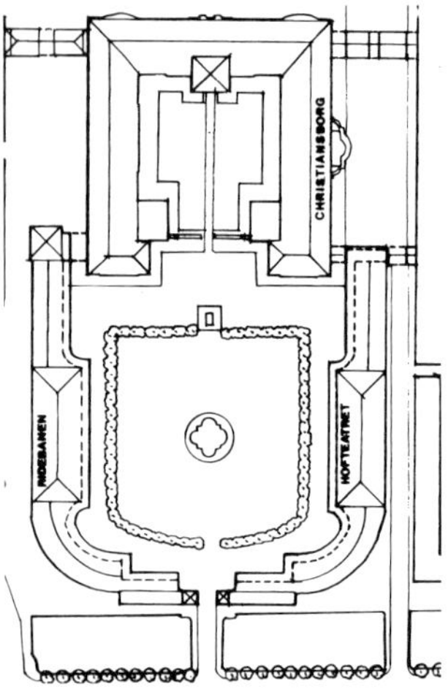

The equestrian ground buildings and the Marmorbro bridge are the only remains of the original Christiansborg Palace built by Christian VI in 1733-45 with E.D. Hausser as architect. This magnificent building, which burned down in 1794, was meant to manifest the absolute monarchy and with its more than 300 nobly equipped rooms, it was an unusually expensive accomplishment for the time. The German master builder Hausser was the chief supervisor and gave the building a Viennese baroque look. Nicolai Eigtved, who was a champion of the French rococo, designed the statuesque Marmorbro bridge and the two pavilions at its end. He was also responsible for the manège hall, while the Court Theater opposite designed by Nicolas-Henri Jardin. The second Christiansborg was designed by C.F. Hansen and built in 1803-28. This large classicistic monument burned down in 1884 with only the partly damaged palace church remaining. In 1905 an architect competition was arranged for the design of the third Christiansborg. The winning proposal was by Thorvald Jørgensen in a heavy, neobaroque style, which only in a few of its decorations reflected the change of political system that had occurred a few years earlier. When the palace was completed in 1918, its architectural expression seemed antiquated compared to the contemporary trends.
Bibliography: Christiansborg Slot 2. ed. K. Hvidt, S. Ellehøj and O. Norn.1975

F27

The Foreign Ministry and Eigtved's warehouse (Asiatisk Kompagni's office building and warehouse) *

Strandgade 25, Christianshavn
1738 and 1781, 1748-50, 1976-82

Client: Asiatisk Kompagni
Architect: Philip de Lange, Nicolai Eigtved, Erik Møllers Tegnestue

The westernmost of the almost identical palacelike buildings was built in 1738 as an office building for the Asiatisk Kompagni during the grand days of the company's overseas trade. The late baroque street facade is heavy and dignified with its red brick, strong pilasters, protruding pediment and mansard roof. The building to the east was built 43 years later, and has an identical street facade to its western twin. However its function was that of a warehouse and thus the interior was quite different, which can be seen by the gable hoist on the rear facade. The buildings were renovated and rebuilt in 1982 by Erik Møller's Tegnestue A/S, and are now used as offices for the Foreign Ministry.
When the warehouse was built, King Frederik V lived at Christiansborg from where he could see the building, therefore the facade facing Christiansborg was carefully designed. With this facade as well as the roof, Eigtved gave the prosaic warehouse some of the distinguished character and quality found in his light and elegant rococo palaces. In 1916, two bays with a hoist gable were torn down at the end of the building facing the harbor thus destroying the symmetrical division of bays. In 1976-82 architects Erik Møller's Tegnestue A/S converted the warehouses to office space and reception rooms for the Foreign Ministry.
Bibliography: Arkitektur DK 1983, 30

Gammel Dok warehouse, Architecture and Building Export Center and The National Workshops **F27**

Strandgade 27, Christianshavn
1882 and 1984-86

Client: De forenede Oplagspladser og Værfter i Kjøbenhavn
Architect: H.C. Scharling and Erik Møllers Tegnestue

The original warehouse was a two-story building with a slate roof. A rebuilding project in 1920 added another floor and the enormous tile roof, which includes three attic levels. It is a utilitarian building with no special architectural style, but has a structure and materials characteristic of the quality warehouses of the time. In 1984-86, the building was converted to "The Gammel Dok Architecture and Building Export Center" and to "The national workshops for the visual arts" with Erik Møller's Tegnestue A/S as architects.
Bibliography: Arkitektur DK 1986, 150

F28

Prinsens Palæ – The Danish National Museum *

1742-45, 1991

Client: The national government
Architect: Nicolai Eigtved, Bornebusch Tegnestue

The palace was built as a residence for the crown prince who ascended the throne as Fredrik V in 1746. After that, the palace was the home of a number of noble families and Court officials. The Academy of Sciences and Letters was also located here, and from 1849, the collections were gathered that later became the National Museum. The palace plan is a three-winged complex with the middle wing elegantly pulled back from the canal street, and the low, portal wing facing the street conceals a cour d'honneur courtyard. Behind the palace there was a garden that ran out to Vester Voldgade street. Eigtved thus created Denmark's first French rococo palace. Several of the original rooms in the main wing are preserved and are now part of the National Museum. In 1938, architect Mogens Clemmensen completed a conversion of the entire city block to a museum, and the palace was given a pastichelike addition toward Stormgade. A new organization of the collections, and an extensive rebuilding project was completed in 1991 with Bornebusch Tegnestue A/S as architects. The Løvegård atrium was given a glass roof creating a bright and exciting lobby from which one can gather information about the museum's extensive collections.

Bibliography: Arkitektur DK 1982, 182 and 1992, 389

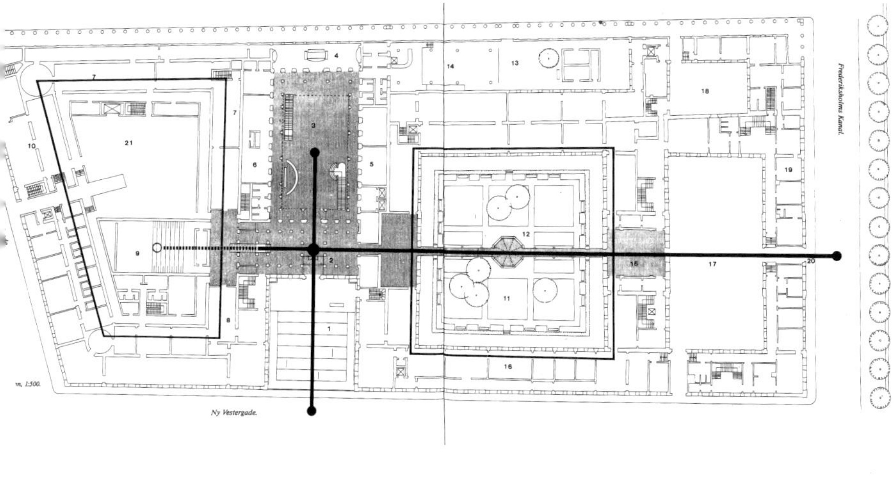
Frederiksholms Kanal.
Ny Vestergade.
m, 1:500.
1
2
3
4
5
6
7
8
9
10
11
12
13
14
15
16
17
18
19
20
21

F29

Buildings at Holmen (the Royal Dockyards) *

Prinsessegade, Christianshavn
1742-72

Client: The national government
Architect: Philip de Lange et al

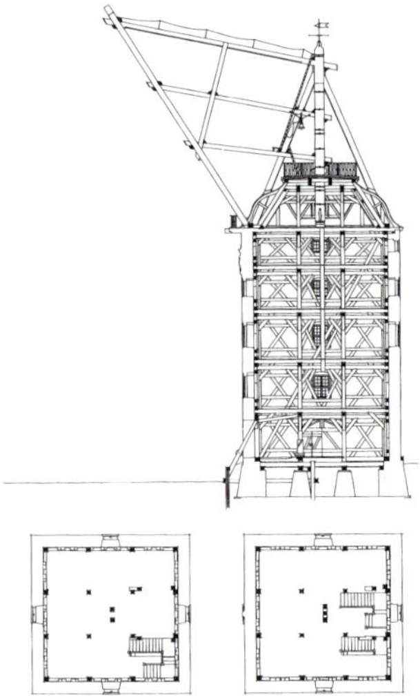

The area east of the entrance to Copenhagen harbor has been part of the city's coast defenses since 1680, when the fleet moved from the city harbor. The five islets that make up Holmen: Nyholm, Frederiksholm, Arsenaløen, Christiansholm and Dokøen, were all created by landfill. Nyholm's Main Guard is a fine little baroque building with a protruding frontispiece with a loggia for the guards, and a hefty spire topped by an enormous crown. The building was designed by Philip de Lange and built in 1744. Directly south is the Rigging Crane, also by Philip de Lange. It was built in 1746 as a brick-faced timber structure, and its characteristic silhouette is a symbol for the Holmen. Philip de Lange also designed the Arsenalgård on Arsenaløen, and the Main Storehouse and the Rigging Loft on Frederiksholm, of which the latter two were given an extra story in 1860. The Arsenalgård has a gaily decorated Kongeport, which connects the scheme's two wings. In 1995, most of the naval activities were moved from the Holmen, and the area is being converted to a Center for Artistic Studies, thus opening the entire area to the public.
Bibliography: Miljøministeriet: Bygninger og anlæg i Københavns Havn. 1988

F32

Amalienborg Palace *

Amalienborg Slotsplads, Frederiksstaden
1750-60

Client: The noble families Moltke, Løvenskjold, Levetzau and Brockdorff
Architect: Nicolai Eigtved

The four palaces and the palace square are the stately center of Frederiksstaden, a new city quarter founded in 1749 on the initiative of Frederik V. The plan lies at the junction of Frederiksgade and Amaliegade streets and forms an octagonal square at the center. From here there is an axial effect along Frederiksgade with the Marmor Church as a magnificent climax. Joint standards for the buildings determined a common height for windows and cornices, and Eigtved's fast grip on the street buildings is evident in Amaliegade 17 (F 36). The church was not built according to Eigtved's drawings, but the four palaces and the palace square were his major work. As the most significant work in Danish rococo architecture it can be compared to the best in Europe. The four identical palaces radiate a natural elegance and reserved stateliness, and together define the palace square as a precise, spacious and exclusive urban space with Saly's masterly equestrian statue of Frederik V from 1768 in the center. Some of Eigtved's magnificent interiors have been preserved, as have fine examples of interiors from other periods.
The colonnade crossing Amaliegade was built in 1794 according to drawings by C.F. Harsdorff. At that time, the Crown had taken over three of the palaces, and since then one of the Amalienborg palaces has served as the royal residence with the palace square as a national assembly place.

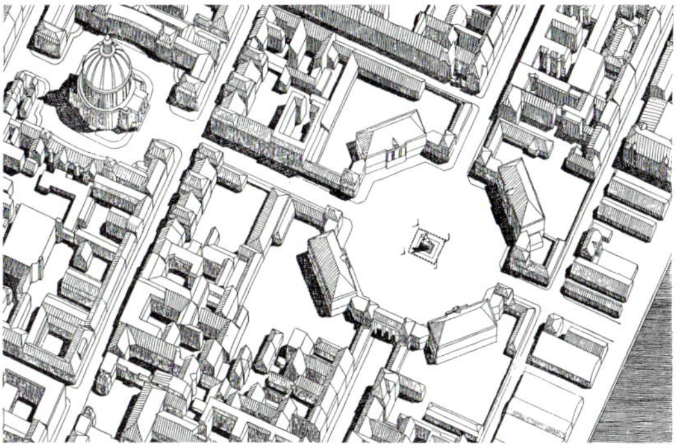

F33

Kunstindustri Museum (Frederik's Hospital) *

Bredgade 66-72, Frederiksstaden
1752-54

Client: The national government
Architect: Nicolai Eigtved and Lauritz de Thurah

The Royal Frederik's Hospital was the first treatment hospital in Denmark. It was built during the last years of architect Nicolai Eigtved's life. After his death, Lauritz de Thurah took over and built four pavilions, two facing Bredgade street and two at the opposite end toward Amaliegade. The hospital's design was unparalleled at the time. The rooms had large windows facing the garden courtyard with grass and trees, and the pavilions housed a pharmacy, bath and maternity hospital. Eigtved's scheme is a collection of elegant buildings with cocked eaves and a hipped roof on the main buildings. It was a major work in both Copenhagen rococo and in his own production. Thurah's pavilions have a heavier, baroque character as can be seen by the mansard roofs. In 1910, the hospital was moved to the present State University Hospital and the buildings were purchased by bank director Emil Glückstadt, who donated them to the Kunstindustri Museum of applied arts in 1919. In 1921-26, the building complex was renovated and converted to a museum by architects Ivar Bentsen and Kaare Klint. Hanne Kjærholm's Tegnestue was responsible for a redesign of the entrance and public facilities in 1995. The old pharmacy furnishings can be seen at the Medical History Museum at Bredgade 62.
Bibliography: Havekunst 1931, 37

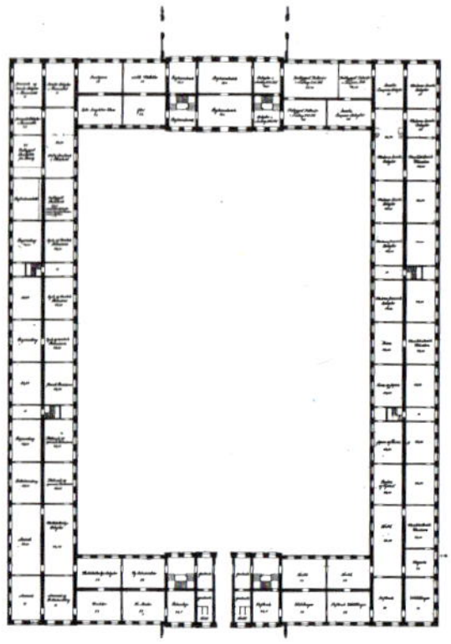

1:2500

The courtyard was renovated by G.N. Brandt in 1923-24 so that it consists only of a lawn with cobblestone paths between two alleys of linden trees. Niels Skovgaard's spring, "the Sea Horse", lies in the shadow of the trees. The benches and the rest of the sculpture are located along the tree rows to simplify the general impression.

Bernstorffs and Dehn's mansions * F34

Bredgade 42 and 54, Frederiksstaden
1752-56

Client: Foreign Ministry, Count J.H.E. Bernstorff and Privy Councillor, Baron F.L. Dehn
Architect: J.G. Rosenberg

Like a portal on the Frederiksgade axis between Amalienborg Palace Square and the Marmor Church, this duet of identical buildings plays an important role in the architectural pattern of Frederiksstaden. N. Eigtved was most likely the architect behind the scheme, which was detailed by J.G. Rosenberg. The five-bay facade division used in Eigtved's other mansions in Frederiksstaden is also evident here but in a more voluminous version. All the buildings have mansard roofs, and the facades are richly decorated at the eaves and over the windows. Originally, the mansions were splendidly furnished and the stairways have been preserved as exceptional examples of Danish rococo interiors. Bernstorff's mansion has seen many uses, it was divided in separate apartments, it was owned by the Crown and it was used by the High Court. In 1921 it was purchased by the Baltic insurance company. Dehn's mansion was originally owned by the nobility, it has also been divided in apartments, and for over a century, has housed the piano manufacturers, Hornung & Møller. In 1984-86 it was renovated by the Pharmacists Society with V. Wohlert as architect.

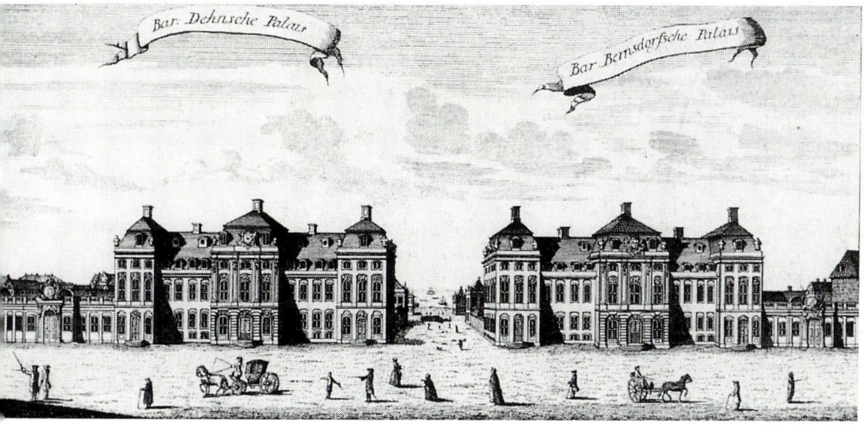

F35

Odd Fellows Palace *

Bredgade 28, Frederiksstaden
1755

Client: Count C.A. von Berckentin
Architect: Nicolai Eigtved

The palace was built the year after Eigtved's death according to his drawings and under the supervision of J.G. Rosenberg. It has the same size and facade pattern as the Amalienborg palaces, but its Frontispiece is sharper and more pompous. Its location as a point de vue for Dronningens Tværgade street, the pulled back position on the site, and the two gate pavilions contribute to the monumental impression. However, the pavilions, which were built in 1885 have an adapted rococo style. During this building period, an excellent, 1500 seat concert hall was added. The architect for these additions was Johan Schrøder. Since 1900, the buildings have been owned by the Odd Fellows order. The complex was restored after an extensive fire in 1992, but the concert hall no longer exists.

City Mansion * F36

Amaliegade 15-17, Frederiksstaden
1754-56

Client: G.W. Bæsecke and J.P. Pfeiffer
Architect: Nicolai Eigtved

The mansion was built after Eigtved's death in 1754 on the basis of his standard drawings for the Frederiksstad plan. The two clients were both master stone masons, and the two buildings were originally mirror images of each other, both inside and out. Since then, the top floor of No. 15 was heightened in 1892. The street facade on No. 17 illustrates Eigtved's unerring and elegant design with its finely coordinated ornamentation. Here one can sense the rococo cultivation of the building structure as a basis for ornamentation, as opposed to the baroque, where the building's mass is emphasized.

City mansion * F37

Amaliegade 25, Frederiksstaden
1755-57

Client: Lauritz de Thurah
Architect: Lauritz de Thurah

The mansion's facade follows the guidelines laid down by Eigtved for the buildings in Frederiksstad, but there is still a great difference between Thurah's design and Eigtved's at Amaliegade 17.
On Thurah's facade, the center part is emphasized and there are arches over the three windows on the piano nobile. With Eigtved's mansion, the side parts are emphasized and the windows are round-headed. The results can be seen as the difference between the baroque and rococo expression. In 1787, the building was converted to the Royal Maternity Hospital by Queen Mother Juliane Marie and now serves as an office building.

F38

Christians Church *

Strandgade 2, Christianshavn
1755-59

Client: The German Community on Christianshavn
Architect: Nicolai Eigtved

The large German Community on Christianshavn took the initiative to build a church in the 1740's. The property was donated by Fredrik V, and funds were raised through collections and lotteries. The church's first official name was the German Frederik's Church. Its present name, Christian's Church, was adopted in 1901 when it became a Danish parish church. In 1832-39, N.F.S. Grundtvig held services there for his free congregation. The church was built according to drawings by Nicolai Eigtved, who died the year before work was started. Therefore it was supervised by his son-in-law, G.D. Anthon, who also designed the spire, built in 1769. The exterior of the church is characterized by rococo's lightness with the yellow Flensborg brickwork and typical Eigtved details such as the structuring of the facade with simple pilaster capitals and the large hipped and cocked tile, church roof. The main church space has a flat plaster ceiling and a theaterlike interior with screened boxes along the short walls and the characteristic grouping of the altar, pulpit and organ opposite the Royal box on the long wall. The interior furnishings could have been inspired by Eigtved's work with the first Royal Theater, built in 1748.

The Danish State Railway Company (DSB) headquarters (Sølvgades barracks) * — **F43**

Georg Brandes Plads 2 (Sølvgade 40), Ny København
1765-71

Client: The national government
Architect: Nicolas Henri Jardin

This building complex was one of Denmark's first large barracks and symbolized the end of private billeting, which was very unpopular both with the soldiers and citizens. The plan was based on Frederik V's face-to-face monogram, and the large, oblique courtyards have a fine spatial tension due to the diagonal axis of symmetry. The facades are almost free of ornament, but the large mansard roof has a certain baroque heaviness. On the other hand, the portal has classicistic features with a relief by sculptor J.F.J. Saly, who as director for the Royal Academy of Fine Arts brought classicism to Denmark. The complex functioned as barracks until 1926. Since then it has been the domicile for DSB.

F44

The blue and the yellow warehouses * , renovation

Toldbodgade 36 and 38, Frederiksstaden
1978-80, 1978-79

Client: Det Blå Pakhus k/s, Cooperative building association Gule Pakhus
Architect: Flemming Hertz and Ole Ramsgaard Thomsen, Hans Munk Hansen
Landscape architect: Hertz & Thomsen, H.M. Hansen

The two warehouses, together with the other preserved warehouses, bear witness to the golden days of Danish overseas trade and the influence on Copenhagen harbor at the end of the 1700's. The blue warehouse was built in 1781-83 with C.F. Harsdorff as architect, and the yellow warehouse in 1777-78 with G.E. Rosenberg as architect. In recent decades the inner harbor and thus the warehouses have lost their original function. Therefore, it was necessary to find a new use for these protected buildings. Housing was a natural solution especially due to the superb location. Despite the large building depth, the architects succeeded in creating some excellent apartment plans. In the "blue" warehouse, which is now red (the reason for this name is unknown), the problem was more difficult due to the extremely large building depth, whereas the dimensions and proportions in the yellow warehouse are similar to an older Copenhagen house. The warehouses are colorful and still meaningful buildings due to their site on the waterfront, where the newer buildings and park complexes are less convincing.
Bibliography: Arkitektur DK 1983, 209 and 215

Harsdorff's mansion * **F45**

Kongens Nytorv 3-5, Indre By
1779-80

Client: Caspar Frederik Harsdorff
Architect: Caspar Frederik Harsdorff

Harsdorff was a professor at the Royal Academy from 1766, and lacked examples of classicistic architecture to show his students. Following a trip to Italy, he decided to castigate the "pernicious taste" that he felt ravaged Copenhagen. Therefore the king, Christian VII bestowed the property next to Charlottenborg on him, and Harsdorff built the mansion as a textbook example for architect students and the city's master builders and clients. As such, the building has many features and details that could be used as patterns for both plans and facades, and Harsdorff's example had a great influence on the design of classicistic Copenhagen. The mansion, which consists of two properties, has three examples of facades, interwoven with the frontispiece. The roof is an ideal example of how to join two roof surfaces on a corner building. The dining room plan, which resolves the corner with a rounded wall, is a feature that still exists in many older apartment buildings in Copenhagen.

Bibliography: H.E. Langkilde: Mellem Byen og Bremerholm. 1984, 90

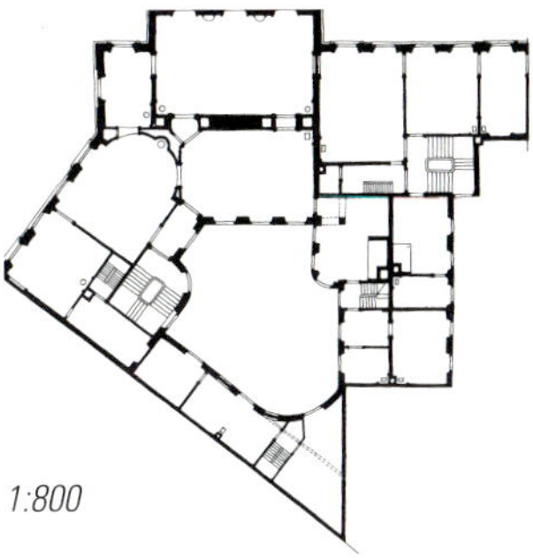

1:800

F46

The Medical History Museum (Academy of Surgeons) *

Bredgade 62, Frederiksstaden
1785-87

Client: The Academy of Surgeons
Architect: Peter Meyn

During the 1700's, the education of surgeons was independent of the university, and this situation was affirmed when the Academy of Surgeons built their own building on a site close to Frederik's Hospital, built 30 years earlier. Peter Meyn, Court master builder, and a student of C.F. Harsdorff, designed the street facade in a heavy classicistic style with a strong quoins and an entrance pediment supported by ionic columns. The auditorium is a well-designed, functional amphitheater space with coffered dome ceiling. The building now houses the Medical History museum, and the auditorium is often used for doctoral dissertations.

F47

Gustmeyer's mansion *

Ved Stranden 14, Indre By
1796

Client: Consul Fr. Ludolf Gustmeyer
Architect: Johan Martin Qvist

J.M. Qvist was a respected mason and master builder who had studied at the Royal Academy under C.F. Harsdorff. His building for Consul Gustmeyer was also influenced by Harsdorff's simple, classicism as can be seen by the location of the oval dining room in the corner between the front and side buildings. The recessed center of the building facade with the ionic columns is also related to the more formal Roman classicism that C.F. Hansen employed during the same period on his buildings in Altona Germany. For many years, the building has been let out for business and housing use. The High Court was located on the piano nobile from 1884-1919, and physicist Niels Bohr was born here in 1885. The entire building was carefully renovated in 1986 by architect David Bretton-Meyer.
Bibliography: H.E. Langkilde: Mellem Byen og Bremerholm. 1984, 117

Erichsen's mansion * F48

Holmens Kanal 2-4, Indre By
1797-99

Client: Shipowner Erich Erichsen
Architect: Caspar Frederik Harsdorff

C.F. Harsdorff died in 1799, while the mansion was under construction, and master builder G. Schaper finished it. The mansion, with its impressive temple facade facing Kongens Nytorv, is the most distinguished example of classicistic housing in Copenhagen. The facade toward Holmens Canal originally had an interplay with the existing Royal Theater designed by Nicolai Eigtved. On the lower floor, there were offices, and the piano nobile's large rooms were exquisitely decorated with paintings and stuccowork by the French architect, J. Ramée. Some of these interior details have been preserved. The building was purchased by the Kjøbenhavns Handelsbank in 1888. It was renovated and the neighboring building was built at Holmens Kanel 4. This work was done by architect F.L. Levy.

F51

City hall, court house and jail *

Nytorv 25, Indre By
1805-15

Client: The municipal authorities and the justice administration of Copenhagen
Architect: Christian Frederik Hansen

The court house's powerful facade facing Nytorv square radiates an august composure and dignity. In a corresponding fashion, the jail facade facing Slutterigade street and the two heavy, ominous bridges crossing Slutterigade have a countenance that could cause many prisoners to repent. C.F. Hansen formed the Roman classicistic building details in an impressive, theatrical orchestration of the complex's solemn and gloomy functions. It was a considerably more impressive classicism than the cool and subdued expression that his teacher, C.F. Harsdorff stood for. The interiors of the city hall and court house were also given a similar, symbolic appearance in the most important rooms, but the effects were primarily achieved with imitated materials due to the modest budget. Along the building's main axis, there is a portico that starts on the exterior with a deep, coffered ceiling and continues inside as a two-story lobby with an enormous ceiling rosette. The axis is terminated by the municipal authority's meeting hall (now the courtroom) with an apselike end wall. The building served as Copenhagen's city hall until 1905, when the new one on City Hall Square was completed. It still serves as a courthouse (Copenhagen City Court), and the jail has been converted to offices. Thus many changes have been made to the interior, but the building's original principal features are intact. The entire scheme was restored in 1991-92 by architects Erik Møller and Jens Fredslund.
Bibliography: A.L. Thygesen and H. Lund: C.F. Hansen. 1995

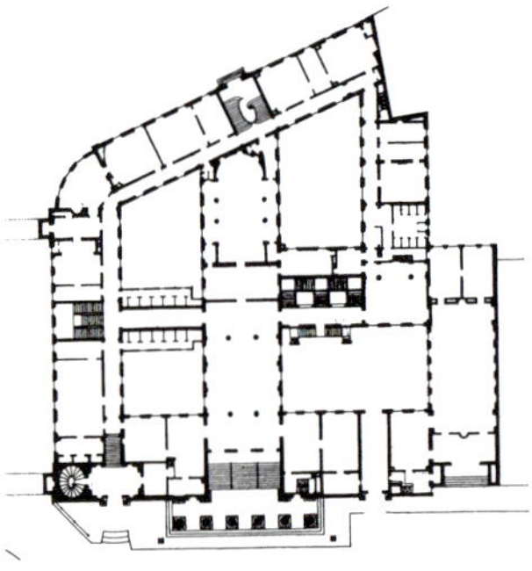

1:2000

F53

Christiansborg Palace Church *

Christiansborg Slotsplads, Indre By
1811-28

Client: The national government
Architect: Christian Frederik Hansen

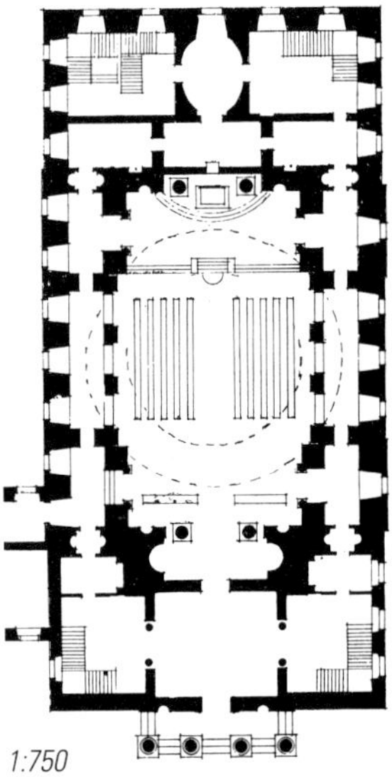

1:750

The first Christiansborg Palace and church burned down in 1794. The palace that was subsequently built after C.F. Hansen's drawings, burned in 1884, but this time the palace church was partially saved. The church was again destroyed by fire in 1992, and the resulting renovation work was not yet finished in 1995. C.F. Hansen's study trip to Italy in the 1780's had a decisive influence on the church. The rectangular form was determined by the church ruins, which Hansen was forced to use. However the squarish, domed space offers a clear indication of his Roman ideals, especially from the Pantheon. The dome is also unusual as from the exterior it appears as a flat sector of a sphere, while on the inside it is a hemisphere. The dome and the simple, formal facade facing the palace square give the building the appearance of a classicistic high place or temple. Europe was at war at that time, and materials for the Palace and church came from many places including Hirschholm Palace in Hørsholm, which was torn down in 1810-12. On the site of the palace, C.F. Hansen designed Hørsholm Church (J 57)

Bibliography: A.L. Thygesen and Hakon Lund: C.F. Hansen. 1995

University Annex (former Metropolitan School) * **F55**

Fiolstræde 4-6, Indre By
1811-15

Client: Copenhagen University and the Church
Architect: Christian Frederik Hansen

As an institution, the school originated in the 1200's. C.F. Hansen's buildings replaced a building destroyed in the 1807 bombardment. Construction work took place at the same time as Vor Frue Church was being built, and there seems to be a deliberate interplay between the school's formal west facade and the church's large round apse. The large interior stairwell takes up the five middle bays, which coincides with the beautifully equipped assembly hall on the top floor. A restoration in 1995 has given the interior a bright and easy atmosphere, and has to a great degree, returned the building to its original appearance. The restoration was supervised by the Royal housing inspector, David Bretton-Meyer.
Bibliography: A.L. Thygesen and H. Lund: C.F. Hansen. 1995

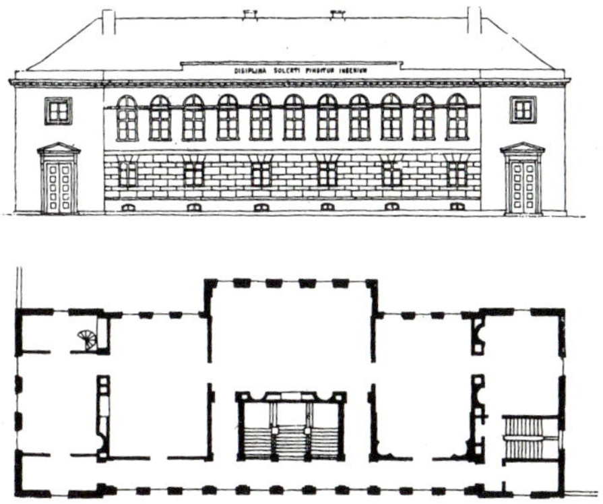

1:750

F56

Vor Frue Church

Nørregade, Frue Plads, Indre By
1811-29

Client: The national government and Copenhagen University
Architect: Christian Frederik Hansen

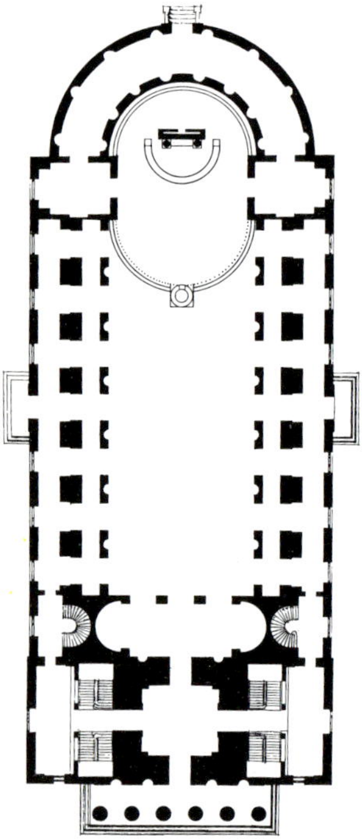

1:1000

The church was built on the ruins of several older churches that were partially destroyed during the bombardment of Copenhagen in 1807. For financial reasons, it was given the same plan outline as the former church, and parts of the outer wall and tower were reused. The facade to Nørregade street has a temple front similar to the Slots Church, but is larger and more ornamented, with six Doric columns as opposed to the four Ionic columns on the Slots Church. The clarified forms have a sensuous geometry in the confused urban space, an effect that is especially strong at the apse. The daylighting in the church room is impressively treated so that the upper part of the space and the curve of the nave have the brightest light, an effect underscored by the grey lower walls and the white upper walls. The light and colors also form a sympathetic background for Bertel Thorvaldsen's sculptures of Christ in the altar niche, and of the apostles along the long walls. In the early 1900's, plans to add a spire to the tower met strong resistance, especially from architects. The spire discussion provoked a renewed interest in C.F. Hansen's architecture and contributed to the neoclassicistic movement around 1920. Architect Vilhelm Wohlert's restoration in 1975-79 returned much of the church's exterior and interior to its original appearance. Since 1924, the church has been Copenhagen's cathedral.
Bibliography: A.L. Thygesen and H. Lund: C.F. Hansen. 1995, Arkitektur DK 1980, 89

F59

Copenhagen University main building *

Frue Plads, Indre By
1831-36

Client: Copenhagen University
Architect: Peder Malling

When founded in 1479, the university was given space at Vor Frue Church school, and has been in this quarter since. The main building's architect, Peder Malling was originally a student and later employed by C.F. Hansen. He was State Master Builder when he did the university building project. His attitudes about the classical ideals were more liberal than his mentor, and the facade facing Frue Plads has features that augur a more imaginative historicism. In the lobby there are frescos by Constantin Hansen with Greek mythological motifs, and the assembly hall is decorated with cultural historical paintings by Vilh. Marstrand and others.

F60

Catholic Church *

Bredgade 64, Frederiksstaden
1841-42

Client: The Roman Catholic church in Denmark
Architect: Gustav Friedrich Hetsch

G.F. Hetsch was C.F. Hansen's son-in-law and also worked for him, but his buildings display a classicism moving toward historicism. The church lies on a narrow site between the Academy of Surgeons and Frederik's Hospital, and only the street facade was designed. The heavy red brick surface is divided in bands by thin courses of yellow brick, and the large cornices and corner towers seem to be inspired by the early Christian churches. The main church room was colorfully decorated by others, after sketches by Hetsch. The tower by the rear facade was built in 1943 from drawings by C.E. Glahn. G.F.Hetsch also designed the Mosaic synagogue on Krystalgade 12, built in 1830-33.

Tivoli F61

Vesterbrogade 3, Indre By
1843

Client: Tivoli
Landscape architect: G.N. Brandt, Aksel Andersen, Georg Boye, Eigil Kjær, Eywin Langkilde, Birgitte Fink

Tivoli was founded in 1843 by festival organizer Georg Carstensen, and with H.C. Stilling as architect. The garden is located on one of Copenhagen's old fortifications. The zigzag pattern of the former embankments is marked by three rows of elm trees, and Tivoli lake is part of the old moat. Tivoli's garden character is preserved and under constant development. An example of this is G.N. Brandt's festive parterre with flowers and fountains from the 1940's, and Eywin Langkilde and Simon Henningsen's illuminated hanging gardens. The children's playground from 1958 was an innovation with play sculptures by Torsten Johansson, Gunnar Westmann and others. The many buildings in the garden, such as the Chinese Tower, The Glass Hall, the concert hall and pantomime theater all have very different architectural styles.
Bibliography: Havekunst 1943, Landskab 1988, 136

KONDITORIET

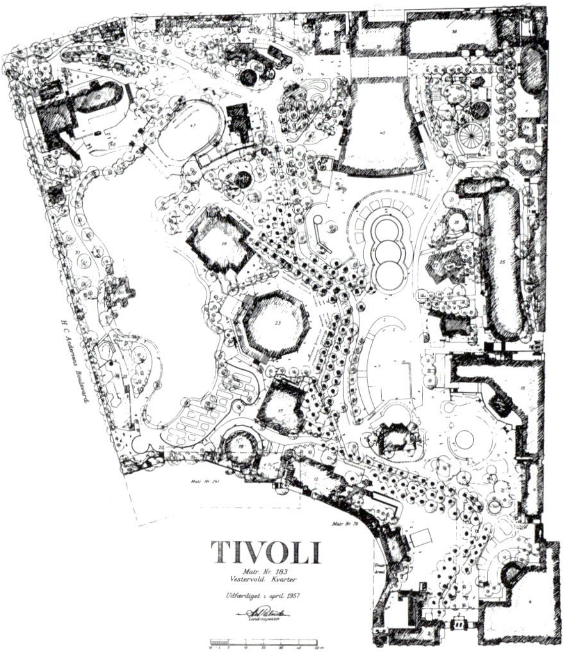
H C Andersens Boulevard
Matr Nr 241
Matr Nr 79
TIVOLI
Matr. Nr. 183
Vestervold Kvarter
Udfærdiget i april 1957
Landinspektør

Pantomime Theater * **F61**

Tivoli, Vesterbrogade 3, Indre By
1874

Client: Tivoli
Architect: Vilhelm Dahlerup

Dahlerup's equilibration with different styles reached its culmination with Tivoli's little outdoor theater, the only place in the world where one can see Harlequin, Colombine and Pierrot of the Commedia dell Arte tradition. Though the architect had never been in China, his exquisite sense for the curious and exotic enabled him to create a magnificent and convincing Chinese pavilion. The curtain has the shape of a peacock tail, which folds together like a fan when the performance begins. The building was restored in 1951 by architect Hans Hansen.

F62 **Thorvaldsen's Museum** *
Porthusgade 2, Indre By
1839-48

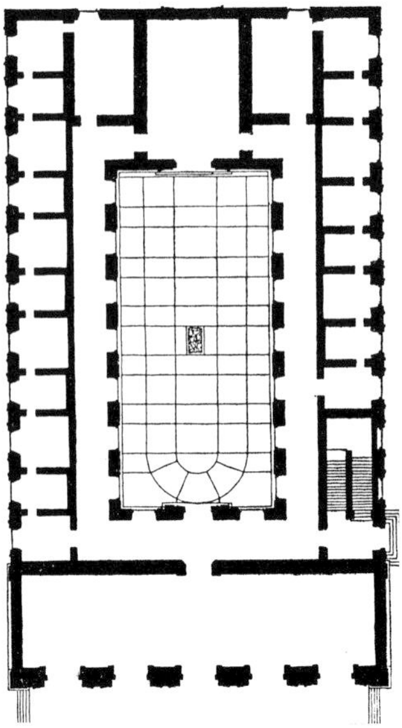

1:1000

Client: The national government and Copenhagen Municipality
Architect: Michael Gottlieb Bindesbøll

On his homecoming to Copenhagen from Rome in 1838, sculptor Bertel Thorvaldsen donated his collections to the city of Copenhagen with the stipulation that a museum be built to house them. The property bestowed by the king was the site of a royal tram depot, and part of this building was included in Bindesbøll's project. The museum's colorful architecture, was inspired by the polychrome Antiquity, and represented a new, more sensual classicism. Bindesbøll also created a subtle interplay with Christiansborg Slots Church, and its copper dome is visible above the museum's entrance facade. The three other facades are decorated with painter Jørgen Sonnes fresco frieze that depicts situations from Thorvaldsen's homecoming. The rooms in the museum were given colors according to the Pompeian tradition with bright colors on the ceilings and walls – an exuberant background for Thorvaldsen's white sculptures. The building was Denmark's first art museum, and is also an expression of the overwhelming personality cult that Thorvaldsen was subjected to. The lower floor was rebuilt during the 1920's by architect Kaare Klint to house Thorvaldsen's collection of studies. In 1968-78 an exhibition of Thorvaldsen's life was arranged by architect Jørgen Bo.
Bibliography: Arkitektur DK 1981, 223 and 1989, 162

F66

University library *

Fiolstræde 1, Indre By
1857-61

Client: Copenhagen University
Architect: Johan Daniel Herholdt

The university library was founded in 1482 and is Denmark's oldest library. From 1657 it was located in the attic of Trinitatis Church, where it was totally destroyed by the city fire in 1728. When the architecture competition for a new library was arranged in 1855, fire safety was emphasized by the use of brick and cast iron columns. There was also a desire that the new building be in harmony with its surroundings. The architecture in Herholdt's winning proposal was entirely new, and represented an exuberant yet disciplined fantasizing with Italian medieval motifs such as San Fermo Church in Verona. At the same time, the building's many fine brick and cast iron details express a strong sense of structural logic and simplicity, as well as the textural effects of the materials. The large library hall is an impressive and portentous space with the atmosphere of a practical work room. And all quite different from the neighboring buildings, especially Vor Frue Church and the Metropolitan School's stuccoed and formal classicism. The library building represented the serious introduction of historicism to Denmark.

1:750

Municipal Hospital *

Øster Farimagsgade 5, Indre By
1859-63

Client: Copenhagen Municipality
Architect: Christian Hansen

The hospital was built as a result of the cholera epidemic in Copenhagen in 1853. Christian Hansen worked for many years in Athens and was well versed in the Greco-Byzantine style, which influenced the hospital's yellow brick facades with red brick bands. The formal symmetry of the plan is based on classic ideals, but is also determined by the function. The common rooms lie along the main axis, and the wings on each side were planned for men and women respectively. There was a hygienic innovation in the large south oriented windows in the patient rooms, and in the service rooms that separated the wards, and as a totally new feature, there was plumbing. In the center building, there is an operating room on the first floor and on the top floor, under the copper covered cupola, there is a chapel decorated with golden ceiling mosaics. The proportions of the building were numerically determined, and the dimensions were so generous that the hospital still can be used today. With its fine brick and interior details, it is one of late classicism's masterpieces, and was a monument to a growing social awareness.

1:4.000

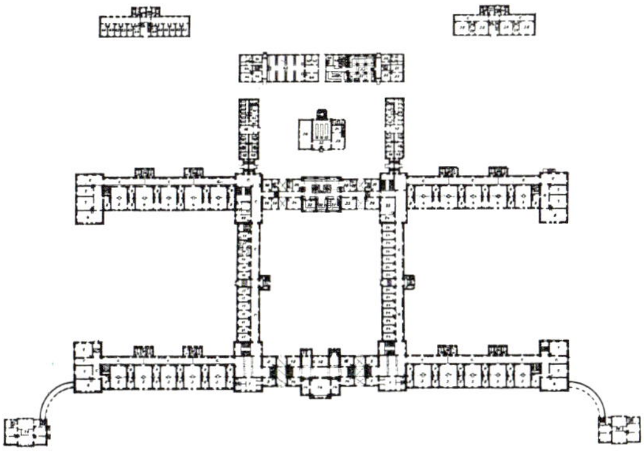

F68

Grøns department store *

Holmens Kanal 7, Indre By
1860-62

Client: Merchant M.E. Grøn
Architect: Johan Daniel Herholdt

The building is one of the first public buildings to be built on Gammelholm after the removal of the naval dockyard. The architecture of the street facade illustrates Herholdt's continued imaginative play with the historical styles, which he started in the University Library. In a functional sense, it represented a new building type, the department store, modelled after the English example with show windows on the ground floor and offices above. It was equipped with many new finesses such as plumbing, gas, central heating, a hydraulic elevator and a kind of intercom, which consisted of talking through the building's hollow cast iron columns. The building was renovated in 1990-91 with Niels Brøns as architect.

F69

The English row houses *

Toldbodgade 71-85, Indre By
1869-73

Client: Det Classenske Fideicommis
Architect: Vilhelm Tvede

In 1866-80, this client/architect team built the now demolished "Classenske Housing" in Frederiksberg, which was an ideal example of how workers' housing should be. The row houses on Toldbodgade street were a similar attempt to create a new ideal for middle class housing according to an English model. The houses lie in opposite pairs as individual buildings, and the main entrance to the high, ground floor is on the courtyard side. The units are all about 400 sqm spread over three floors, and an unusual feature at the time was the bathroom on the bedroom level. The kitchen and servant quarters were in the basement, and as a whole, the buildings illustrated the English housing/social term "upstairs and downstairs". Until 1966, they were rental housing, and now they are much sought-after condominiums.

University administration building (Zoological Museum) * **F70**

Krystalgade 25-27, Indre By
1863-69

Client: Copenhagen University
Architect: Christian Hansen

The building was originally a joint exhibition space for several older zoological collections. Its form is similar to an ordinary city block with a courtyard as a three-story glass-roofed space. A corridor runs around the perimeter of this atrium and gave access to smaller exhibition spaces on each floor. The atrium is profusely decorated with animal motifs etc. The building's architectural style is Italian renaissance. The exhibits had a theatrical atmosphere in keeping with the tradition of the time for zoological museums. The buildings were renovated and rebuilt in 1980-85 by architects Eva & Nils Koppel and Gert Edstrand, and are now used by the university administration
Bibliography: Arkitektur DK 1986, 170

F72

Østre Anlæg *
1873

Client: Copenhagen Municipality
Landscape architect: Ove Høegh Hansen

The park has gradually developed on the old ramparts. Although some of the area was taken over by the Hirschsprungske Collection, and for the new addition to the National Museum of Art, it is still a worthwhile park with popular strolling paths along the lake, beautiful vistas and many recreational possibilities. Denmark's monument in memory of Christian IX and Queen Louise's golden wedding anniversary in 1892 is now placed on the top of Pückler's bastion. A luxuriant rhododendron garden on the edge of the moat was planted in the 1940's, and the rose gardens are a favorite stopping place for the local residents of Østerbro.

F73

Botanical Gardens, greenhouse *
Øster Farimagsgade 2 C
1871-74, 1980-82

Client: Copenhagen University
Architect: Eva and Nils Koppel, Gert Edstrand
Landscape architect: H.A. Flindt

Flindt planned the Botanical Gardens in connection with the other embankment parks. The plan is scenic with trim, curving paths, and the embankments and moat have been extensively remodelled, in some areas to an almost mountainlike height. The garden serves scientific purposes and contains over 20,000 different species of plants, grouped according to botanical systems or geographic principles.

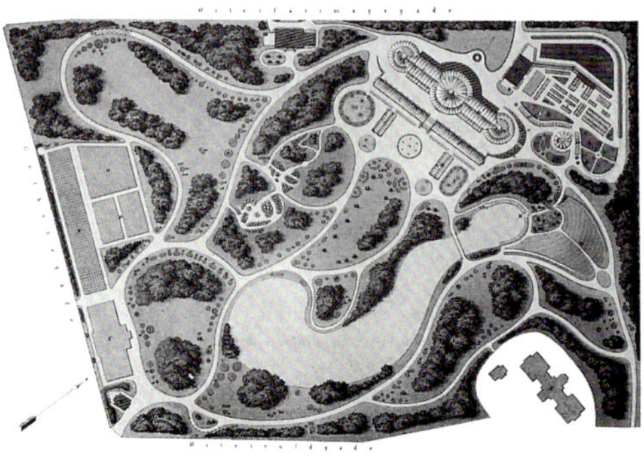

A number of flora groups exist representing the East, the Tropics and southern Europe. The greenhouse lies at an angle, high on the site with a view over the city.
Brewer J.C. Jacobsen donated the greenhouse to Copenhagen University in 1874. It was designed by architect P.C. Bønecke, with the zealous help of J.C. Jacobsen himself, and was inspired by the Crystal Palace in London from 1852. A recent renovation was almost a reconstruction as the building was extremely dilapidated after 100 years of use. A service building on the north side was removed, the wooden window frames were replaced with aluminum, the rusted iron structure was replaced and obvious structural errors were remedied. The alterations respected the original design, such as the preservation of the characteristic cast iron borders on the roofs. The building is a tribute to a period when cast iron and glass produced new architectural expressions.

F74

The Royal Theater * , the old and new stage

Kongens Nytorv 9 and Tordenskjoldsgade 5, Indre By
1872-74, 1929-31, 1983-85

1:2250

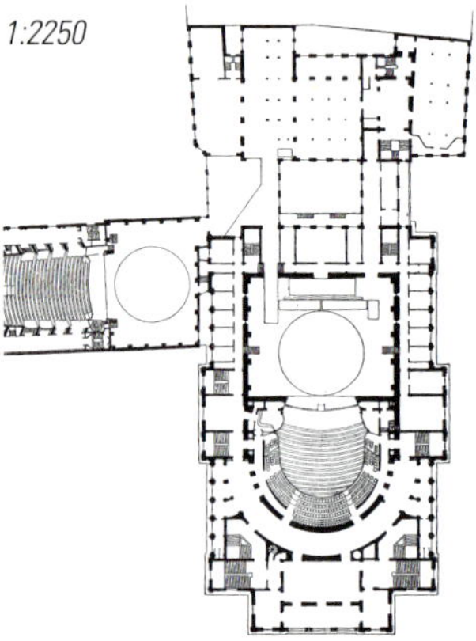

Client: The national government (Ministry of Culture), Ministry of Public Affairs
Architect: Vilhelm Dahlerup & Ove Petersen, Holger Jacobsen

Vilhelm Dahlerup and Ove Petersen's winning proposal for the 1870 theater competition was inspired by the grand metropolitan theater life in Paris and Vienna. Aside from the stage itself, the public areas are also a stage, where one can see and be seen, and it was magnificently decorated with stucco, gold, mirrors and red velvet. The theater hall is a genuine, festive expression of the theater- and cultural style of the time, and the Kongens Nytorv facade marks the theater's monumentality in the Copenhagen townscape. The style is Italian renaissance, which ideally expressed the neo-capitalistic upper class ideals. After the 1978 competition for a new theater, the commission was awarded to Royal Housing Inspector Nils Koppel, and architects Knud Holscher & Svend Axelsson, and carried out in 1983-85. The theater room and the public areas were restored to their original appearance, while the rebuilding work dealt with improving conditions for the actors and technicians. The new facades on Holmens Kanal and Tordenskjoldsgade present the new architecture as a cool and stringent contrast to the old theater.
The "New Stage", also called "Stærekassen", was originally planned for the National Broadcasting Service. The interiors, which already begin in the mosaic decorated portal over Tordenskjoldsgade street, are a unique, bizarre and exuberant fantasy of the art deco style by several artists under the direction of Holger Jacobsen.
Bibliography: Arkitektur DK 1987, 100

The Building Society row houses F77

Side streets to Øster Farimagsgade, Østerbro
1873-89

Client: The Workers' Building Society
Architect: Frederik Christian Bøttger

The 480 row houses are popularly known as the "Potato rows". They were built on the initiative of the workers at Burmeister & Wain's shipyard, who could save money in the building society, and win a house in a lottery. The houses were originally planned with several apartments. An entire house was too expensive for a working class family, and thus many of them rented rooms to others. Despite economical considerations, the street facades of yellow brick with horizontal red bands, have certain late classicistic features. Both in terms of ownership and architecture, the scheme expressed social aspirations. In recent years, most of the houses have been converted to large owner homes, and are among the most desirable in Copenhagen. It was unusual for the architects of the time to become involved with worker housing. On the other hand, Bøttger won several awards in other countries for the 1200 row houses that he designed for the Workers Housing Building Society. This also includes the 400 houses built in 1893-1903 near Kildevældsgade street (C 87)., which are interesting because here he worked with different types of urban spaces other than straight streets.

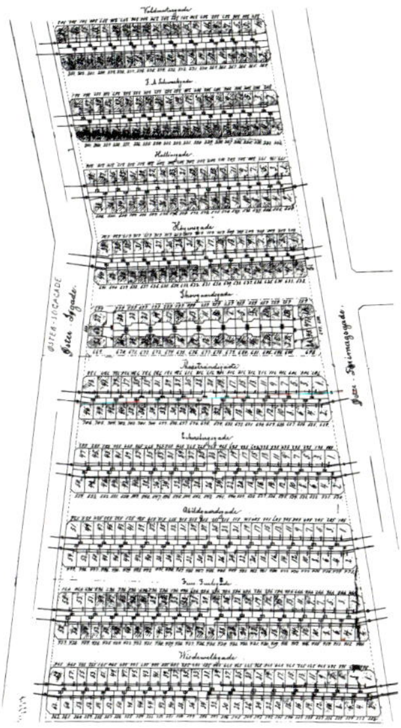

F82

Frederiks Church (Marmor Church)

Bredgade 53, Frederiksstaden
1749-70 og 1875-94

Client: Merchant C.F. Tietgen
Architect: Ferdinand Meldahl

1:1500

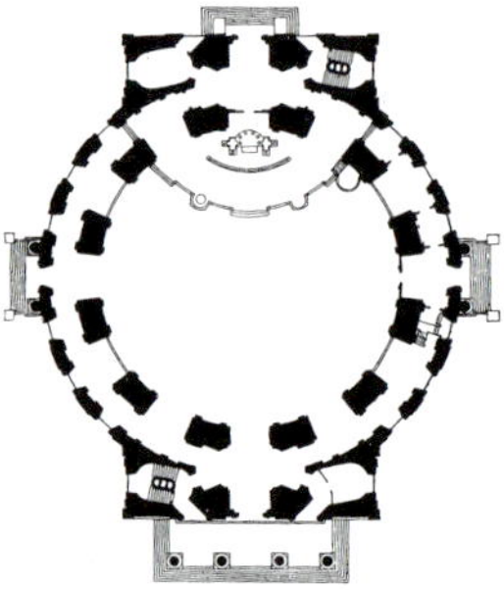

In 1749, the cornerstone was laid for the rococo church, which according to N. Eigtved's drawings was to be the major feature of his plan for Frederiksstaden. After his death in 1754, his colleague Nicolas-Henri Jardin altered the project to a classicistic church in marble, which was so expensive that it was never built. For over 100 years the unfinished building stood as a romantic ruin, until 1874 when C.F. Tietgen purchased both the site and the surrounding properties on the condition that the church be completed. F. Meldahl respected the monumental intentions but gave the church an Italian baroque countenance with Saint Peter's Church in Rome as a model. The copper dome is an imposing element in the Copenhagen skyline, and the buildings around the church, also by Meldahl, form an urban space with a Parisian character. The cylindrical interior is dimly lit from windows in the tambour. The form, color and the symbolic decorations evoke a temple-like atmosphere, unparalleled in Danish church architecture.

The National Museum of Art

Georg Brandes Plads, Ny København
1889-96

Client: The national government
Architect: Vilhelm Dahlerup and Georg E.W. Møller
Landscape architect: (new building) Svend Kierkegaard Aps

The museum design was the result of a competition, and it was built to house the royal art collection after the Christiansborg Palace fire in 1884. A new location was chosen on the old embankments and the building was placed high on the site, which strengthens the effect of its monumental architecture. As a symbol of its function, the entrance facade is decorated with reliefs and statues, and the frontispiece is formed as a powerful, Greco-Roman arch of triumph. The interior was symmetrically arranged around the main room with its magnificent stairway inspired by the ambassador stairway in Versailles. Already at its opening, the museum lacked space, and as part of a rebuilding project in 1966-69, this splendid stairway was removed and the inner courtyard was converted to an exhibition space. In 1993, C.F. Møllers Tegnestue won the competition for an addition to the museum. Their proposal placed the annex along the building's rear facade facing Østre Anlæg park, thus leaving the entrance facade untouched. The park area in front will be altered with a large, curved stairway complex, which will further emphasize the monumental character of the old architecture. The rebuilding project is scheduled for completion in 1997
Bibliography: Arkitekten 1993, 277

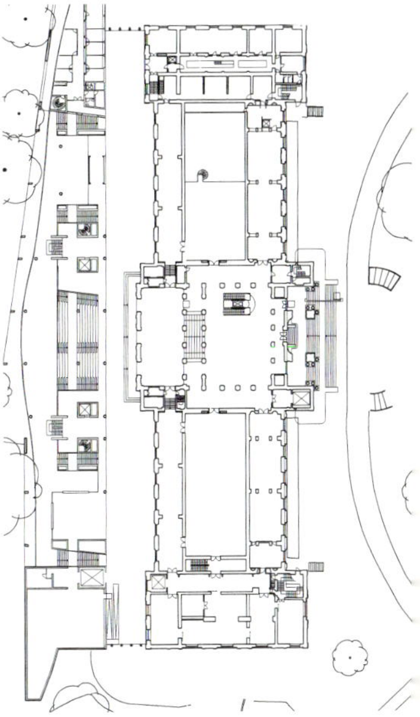

1:2000

F84

Ny Carlsberg Glyptotek *

Dantes Plads 7, Indre By
1892-1906, 1992-96

Client: Brewer Carl Jacobsen, the national government and Copenhagen Municipality
Architect: Vilhelm Dahlerup, Hack Kampmann, Henning Larsens Tegnestue
Landscape architect: Eigil Kiær

The building was created as a framework for Carl Jacobsen's extensive collection of art, which he donated to the state in 1888. The part of the scheme designed by V. Dahlerup faces Dantes Plads and was opened in 1897. Like a magnificent Venetian palace, the entrance facade has an exuberant and polychromatic duality with its patterned red brickwork as a background for the polished granite columns. The richly decorated interior culminates in the winter garden, which is roofed by a large glass dome. In 1901-06, the southwestern part of the museum was built from drawings by Hack Kampmann, whose architecture is more classicistically simplified than Dahlerup's, with the massive garden facade appearing as a fantasia over the mausoleum in Halikarnassos. In 1992, a competition for an addition to the museum was won by Henning Larsen's Tegnestue. His proposal placed the addition as a freestanding building in one of the museum's two interior courtyards. The project is due for completion in 1996.

In 1906, an enormous cast iron and glass dome was built in the central building. A subtropical palm house was established by Eigil Kiær here with such an unusual lushness that even today it is a great attraction.

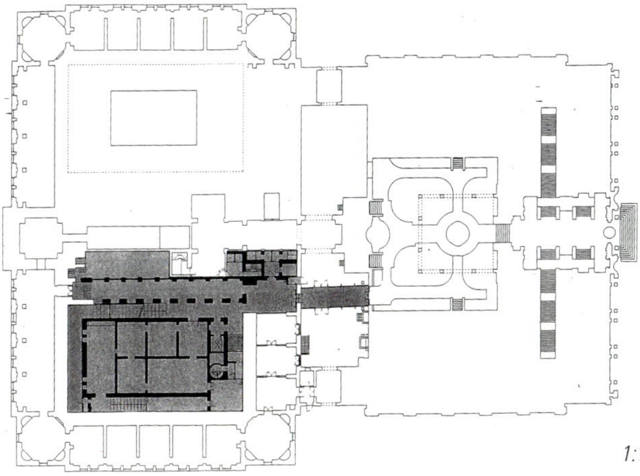

1:1500

F85

Copenhagen City Hall *

Rådhuspladsen, Indre By
1892-1905

Client: Copenhagen Municipality
Architect: Martin Nyrop

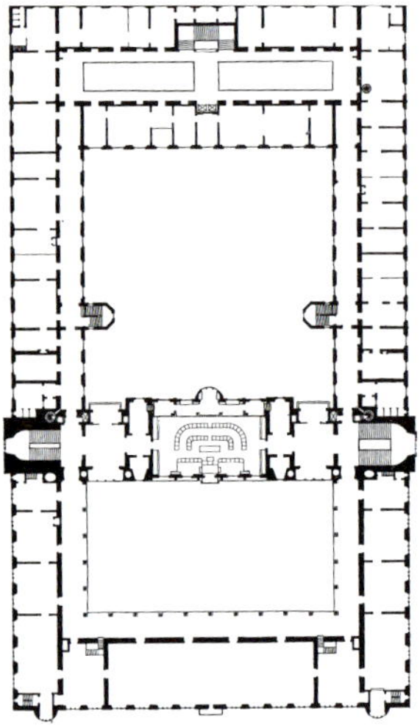

1:2000

At the end of the nineteenth century, Copenhagen's population grew so dramatically, that the city felt this should be expressed by a new city hall. Nyrop's proposal was chosen through a competition, and it marked both a renewal of Danish architecture and a manifestation of his personal design idiom. The city hall came to be a magnificent monument to the national romantic tendencies that broke free from the nineteenth century's foreign inspired architectural styles. Nyrop's version, and this architectural style were enhanced by his pronounced sense of texture, materials and details. The city hall was to be a place for all citizens, and should express the democratic changes in the political system. The huge building complex is symmetrical and only the tower, the city's tallest, breaks this pattern and emphasizes the liberation from historical styles. This asymmetrical placement was inspired by the town hall in Sienna. The building complex is formed as a city block with two courtyards, of which the one nearest the city hall square has a glass roof. Surrounding the spacious city hall main room lie the ceremonial functions such as the assembly hall, the city council meeting hall and the wedding chamber, while the offices lie around the open courtyard and around an imposing, panoptic hall near the rear entrance toward southeast. The city hall square in front of the building was originally formed as a clam shell inspired by the town hall square in Sienna. A similar theme formed the concept for an ongoing renovation by KHR architects due for completion in 1996.

F86

Warehouse 1 *

Østmolen, Frihavnen
1893-94

Client: Private corporation, Frihavnen
Architect: Vilhelm Dahlerup

Copenhagen's Frihavn or free port was established in 1891-93. This marked the first time that reinforced concrete was so extensively used, both in the new dock complex and the buildings. Dahlerup designed the impressive silo warehouse on the Midtermole pier, which burned in 1968. With his design for Warehouse 1, he surrounded an unusually forceful building construction with an exuberantly detailed brickwork. The facades are bearing and the interior structure consists of reinforced concrete decks supported by cast iron columns, encased in concrete. The robust structure and active function are hidden behind a historical, palacelike architecture. Warehouse 1 is now undergoing renovation and will be converted to an office building. The imposing silo warehouse B on the Amerikakaj dock, designed by architect Fredrik Levi in 1903, is also being converted to office space.

F91

Den Frie Udstilling's building *

Oslo Plads, Østerbro
1898

Client: Den frie Udstilling committee
Architect: Jens Ferdinand Willumsen

J.F. Willumsen was part of the group that established the organization "Den frie Udstilling" in 1891 in opposition to the established art world. He worked as a painter, artist-craftsman and architect and always with a radical, expressive idiom that is also evident in the exhibition building. It was originally built at Jarmers Plads at the other end of the city, but was moved to its present site in 1914. It is built entirely of wood. The closed, white-painted facades have simple bright colored decorations. The exhibition spaces have a lightness and a rhythmical progression that make them well suited to their use. The architectural expression is a festive and masterly combination of art nouveau, Asiatic and classical styles and is still a refreshing provocation.

Østre power station F93

Øster Allé 6-16, Østerbro
1900-1902

Client: Copenhagen Municipality
Architect: Municipal architect Ludvig Fenger and Ludvig Clausen

The power station was the city's third central electricity plant and similar to the Gothersgade plant from 1892 and the Vestre works from 1898, Øster power station was given a careful architectural treatment. The project did not economize on materials or details, and the buildings reveal an almost solemn meticulousness in the pioneer work with energy generation. The impeccable brickwork represents a continuation of the historicized Italian inspiration from the 1800's, but it also expresses a certain objectivity in terms of the building's purpose, supplying the new energy form. The objectivity is even clearer in the interior where the visible structure and installations were a sign of the coming functionalism that developed some twenty years later.

Apartment house F94

Østbanegade 11, Østerbro
1903-04

Client: Master painter Chr. Vikke
Architect: Aage Langeland-Mathiesen

This corner building with the huge fronton with arch and fan forms, and the elaborate balcony railings is one of Copenhagen's few examples of the jugend style, the German version of art nouveau. According to one of the architect's employees, the facades were directly inspired by a jugend building in Vienna, where this style was very popular. In the Østerbro quarter, with its large, luxurious buildings, was a building expected to resemble a mansion. This building also has a monumental character, which is reinforced by the rounded jugend forms. The architect worked on several projects with Ulrik Plesner including the large housing complexes on Danas Plads and Islands Brygge.

F96

Apartment house

Gammeltorv 8, Indre By
1905-06

Client: Engineer Hj. Hein
Architect: Ulrik Plesner

This small street building is characteristic due to its symmetry. However, this is broken by the off-center, bay windows and the single balcony on the roof level. These effects were often used by Plesner in his larger schemes, where they contributed to his characteristic exuberance, but here they appear especially strong in their simplicity. The closely spaced window mullions give the building a spirited, impeccable character. The decorations on the gable were by Thorvald Bindesbøll.

F99

The Royal Library Garden

Christians Brygge 8, Indre By
1914

Client: Staten
Architect: Thorvald Jørgensen and Magdahl Nielsen
Landscape architect: I.P. Andersen

Despite the vehement criticism that arose when it was established, this regularly subdivided and richly blooming garden is still very charming. A large square pool in the center is surrounded by trimmed hedges and lawns. A double row of Siberian crab apple trees ends the complex at the Proviantgård. Toward the Rigsarkiv it is terminated by a large bed of perennials.

Office building

Frederiksberggade 16, Indre By
1907

Client: A/S Byggeselskabet Frederiksberggade-Kattesundet
Architect: Anton Sofus Rosen

The jugend style or art nouveau, "the new art" is not especially represented in Denmark, but some of the best examples are by Anton Rosen. The building on Frederiksberggade has a powerful ornamentation, but with its steadfast facade rhythm, it is a well designed street building, which has proven its robustness through changing years in the business world. It still offers a festive, metropolitan deviation in the townscape, and both the windows on the ground floor and the two-story, bay windows above still serve as show windows.

F102

Palace Hotel *

Rådhuspladsen, Indre By
1907-10

Client: Director Anders Jensen
Architect: Anton Sofus Rosen

The hotel complex is a major work in Anton Rosen's production and also in Danish jugend architecture. There is an exclusive cosmopolitan ambience in the massive facade facing the city hall square, and the architect's love of form was given free rein in the sensual entrance and the elegant, slender tower that steals attention from the much higher, neighboring city hall tower. All the hotel's original interiors and furnishings were designed by Anton Rosen, but no longer exist. The building complex runs from the city hall square to Mikkel Bryggersgade street, where the Grand Biograf theater facade has a clear jugend character.

Housing block at Classens Have F119

Classensgade 52-68, Østerbro
1924-25

Client: A subsidiary of Copenhagen's Public Housing Association, KAB
Architect: Carl Petersen, Povl Baumann, Ole Falkentorp and Peter Nielsen
Landscape architect: V. Fabricius Hansen

There were many innovative features in this large block of buildings built on a site formerly owned by the industrial magnate, Frederik Classen in the 1700's. The southern side of the block was held open to the sun, and the apartment living rooms face the courtyard. There is a monumental axial effect running from the portal on Classensgade street to Hardargade street. The neoclassicistic, red brick facades with white window frames have a milder character than in some of the earlier large blocks of buildings, and this effect is strengthened by the romantic gardens. Carl Petersen died before the scheme was completed, but was influential during the project phase.

H.P. Lorentzens Stiftelse F134

Gernersgade 69, Ny København
1933

Client: H.P. Lorentzen's Stiftelse
Architect: Ib Lunding

The street facade is an example of an imaginative and skilful play with functionalism's familiar pattern, such as the round window and asymmetry. The enthusiasm for maritime forms was evident in the small semicircular balconies with ship railings, however the balconies were later removed during a renovation. In the few, but characteristic buildings designed and built by Ib Lunding, there is a cheerful and relaxed approach to functionalism. (see Grønningen 7-9, F152).

F152 **Apartment house**

Grønningen 7-9, Hammerensgade 8, Ny København
1935-36

Client: Daros property company
Architect: Ib Lunding

A completely original building that was unusual for its time and still bears witness to its talented and unconventional architect. The street facades with their heavy red brickwork are boldly penetrated by vertical groups of windows, balconies and bays. The protruding corner windows are especially handsome and bold, and the round, bubbling stair windows have both architectural logic and humor. Among the building's many fine details are the three different entrances, with a variety of round and pointed arched portals and with varied colors of brick. The architecture can be considered functionalistic but with a talent, wit and original interpretation.
Bibliography: Tegl 1994, 13

Stelling building * **F153**

Gammeltorv 6, Indre By
1937-38

Client: Paint merchant firm A. Stelling
Architect: Arne Jacobsen

At the time the building was completed, both its architecture and choice of materials were a startling innovation. The slender reinforced concrete structure is sided with painted steel panels on the two lower floors, while the three upper floors are sided with a continuous surface of glazed tiles. The facades clearly express the building's functional organization with the shop on the ground floor, offices on the upper floors and an apartment on the roof level. The precise proportioning of the facade and the careful detailing make this building an exceptional, refined infill project. Arne Jacobsen was also responsible for the interior design and furnishings in the shop. These elements, which contributed to the building's homogeneity no longer exist.

F165

The Dronningegård housing scheme *

Dronningens Tværgade 23-45, Frederiksstaden
1943-58

Client: Private consortia
Architect: Kay Fisker, C.F. Møller and Sven Eske Kristensen

The comprehensive slum clearance program for the quarter around Adelgade and Borgergade streets in the early 1940's was the largest urban renewal project ever to be undertaken in Copenhagen at that time. The project was the result of a long and complicated planning process with the municipality functioning both as the property seller and planning authority. The scarcities caused by the war were a deciding factor in the choice of materials and building methods. Political policies and the housing shortage led to a very dense housing program with many small apartments. These difficult conditions are reflected in Dronningegård's complex architecture with its mixture of the past and present. The main disposition has a neoclassicistic monumentality, but the division of the eastern and western parts in nine-story, slim buildings with lower intermediate buildings gives the large masses a human scale. This effect is underscored by the gables on the tall buildings, where the high balcony openings also give the scheme an exclusive character. The recessed and protruding balconies on the court facades facing north and south appear as a principal brickwork pattern reinforced by the careful brick detailing throughout the scheme.

Atrium garden on Bredgade F193

Bredgade 40, Frederiksstaden
1958

Client: Baltica insurance company
Architect: Sven Eske Kristensen & Erik Barfoed
Landscape architect: Eywin Langkilde

When the Bernstorffske Mansion was converted to Baltica's headquarters building in 1958, a simple atrium garden was established, where water and grass are part of a refined pattern of cobblestone bands and areas of sett paving. Grey Øland stone was used for the low retaining walls, which protrude into the pools and surround an exquisite mulberry tree. In the smallest pool there is a sculpture "the Sea horse" by Utzon Frank. Large granite blocks are used as stepping stones across the pool and as edging around it.
Bibliography: Arkitektur DK 1990, 184; Havekunst 1958, 70

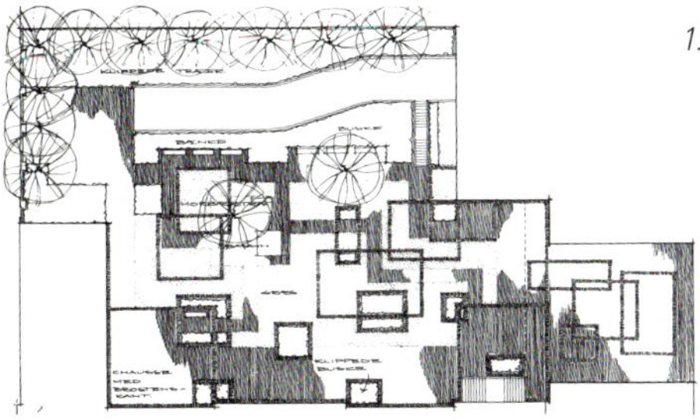

1:1500

Relay station F213

Bremerholm 6, Indre By
1962-63

Client: Copenhagen Power Company
Architect: Hans Chr. Hansen from the municipal architect's department
Landscape architect: Copenhagen Municipal Park Department

Locating a large electrical transformer complex on one of the city's main streets presents a challenge both to the building and the surroundings. No attempts were made with traditional considerations to the neighboring buildings, and the facade toward Bremerholm street is formed as a force field between the low, heavy ground floor and the open ascending upper floor. The field between is a large bronze grate with a discreet grid proportioned in a city building scale. It is a self-aware indication that the building has a special function – which is not outwardly revealed – with a scale, proportions and materials in keeping with a dignified urban building. The station is unmanned, but there is an office on the upper floor.
Bibliography: Arkitektur DK 1972, 161 and 1986, 320

F215

Denmark's National Bank

Havnegade 5, Indre By
1965-71

Client: Denmark's National Bank
Architect: Arne Jacobsen, Dissing + Weitling A/S
Landscape architect: Arne Jacobsen and Eywin Langkilde

A closed competition in 1991 resulted in the choice of Arne Jacobsen's project to replace J.D. Herholdt's bank building from 1870, which was a paraphrase of a Florentine palace. The new building scheme consists of an office building, a mint and a protected courtyard for currency transport. The detailed plan of the scheme is secret. The outward architectural expression corresponds with the safeguarded functions. The similarly subdivided areas of dark tinted glass and the stone sided end walls give the facades a distinguished pomposity, which is in keeping with the building's special status. The main entrance on Havnegade street is extremely discrete, but the space directly inside, the lobby, is one of the few publicly accessible rooms and is an impressive experience. With its cathedral high ceiling, it reaches up through six stories, dimly lit from the side. The only fixed object in the space is a tenuous stairway of glass and steel that disappears up in the darkness of the ceiling. Behind the reserved exterior, there is a theatrical ambience that reaches beyond the historical pathos of Herholdt's palace.
Bibliography: Arkitektur DK 1972, 135, Landskab 1983, 129

The National Bank complex has several courtyards, atriums and roof gardens of varying size. Arne Jacobsen's inspiration for this atrium garden is said to have come from the fallen, overgrown column fragments in the Mediterranean area. White marble gravel forms a floor for the molded, horizontal concrete pipes covered with low creepers.

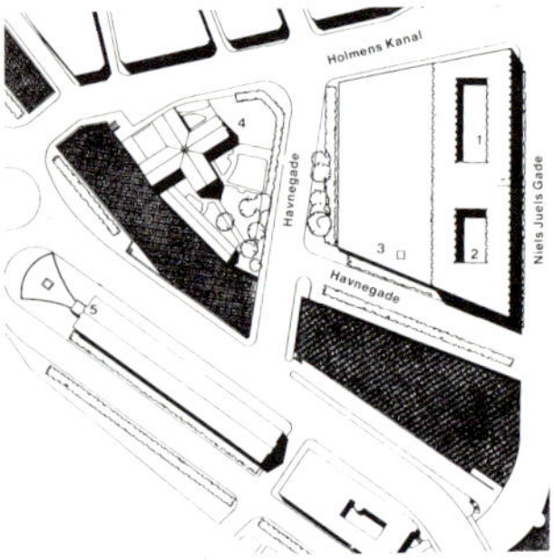

F216

The Bremerholm redevelopment project

Vingårdsstræde, Bremerholm, Dybensgade, Nikolajgade, Indre By
1968-71

Client: Copenhagen Municipality
Architect: Municipal Architect Department – Erik T. Harpøth

This city block was built in 1795-1800, just after the great fire of 1795. The smooth, classicistic facades follow the guidelines for the so-called "conflagration buildings", which are a characteristic feature of central Copenhagen. The restoration took place according to the redevelopment legislation from 1959 that placed requirements on the preservation of buildings of historical or architectural value. At that time, preservation projects of this type were uncommon and thus this was a pilot project. The dense cluster of courtyard buildings was removed and the courts were renovated in collaboration with the tenants. The individual buildings and their details bear witness to a rich and disciplined architectural period in Copenhagen urban housing.
Bibliography: Arkitektur DK 1972, 260

Pistolstræde, renovation and restoration F221

Pistolstræde 4-6, Ny Østergade 11, Grønnegade 18, Indre By
1971

Client: A/S J. Moresco, and F. Birger Christensen
Architect: Erik Møller

The little passageway, Pistolstræde is all that remains of the infamous nineteenth century red-light district, Peder Madsen's Gang. The original buildings along the alley had no special historical or architectural interest. However, after the restoration and rebuilding, the general consensus is that it was a worthwhile endeavor. New public spaces have been created by maintaining some old areas of picturesque quality. This opportunity was a pleasant surprise after many decades of rational, heavy-handed slum clearance. Seen in this light, the Pistolstræde redevelopment project is a pioneering effort for the attitudes that have now won acceptance in the area of urban renewal.
Bibliography: Arkitektur DK 1972, 247

Housing * F223

Nyhavn 18
c. 1770, restored and rebuilt 1972

Client: Denmark's National Bank
Architect: Erik Møller

The original building had three stories, the fourth floor and mansard roof were added in 1846. In 1969, the building was purchased by the National Bank to establish guest apartments for visiting scientists and artists. The renovation included the removal of the attic level and rebuilding the mansard area with a stepped-back glass facade. This level houses a common room for the apartments. In addition to this, the portal was returned to its original form, and an elevator was added in the courtyard. The alterations of the roof have brought the tall building into an improved context with the lower neighboring buildings, and the reddish-yellow facade stucco is a fine contribution to Nyhavn's colorful row of houses.
Bibliography: Arkitektur DK 1972, 243

F224

Lynetten sewage treatment plant

Refshalevej 250, Refshaleøen
1973-80

Client: Copenhagen Municipality
Architect: Martin Andersen, Sv. H. Baggesen and Erik Katborg of the municipal architect's office
Landscape architect: Copenhagen Municipal Park Department

When built, this plant for the treatment of sewage from eight Copenhagen municipalities was one of the largest in the world and the most advanced. The concrete facades are cast in situ. The surface is broken by windows, grates and technical details that strengthen the dynamic, sculptural effect. The varied building sections reflect the functional requirements, as do the colors, which give an almost cheerful character to this secluded urban complex. Blue symbolizes waste water treatment, yellow is for ventilation, red for sludge, etc. The architecture is robust and functional and with its contemporary form idiom it follows Copenhagen's tradition for the careful design of large public facilities.
Bibliography: Arkitektur DK 1981, 166 and 1986, 326

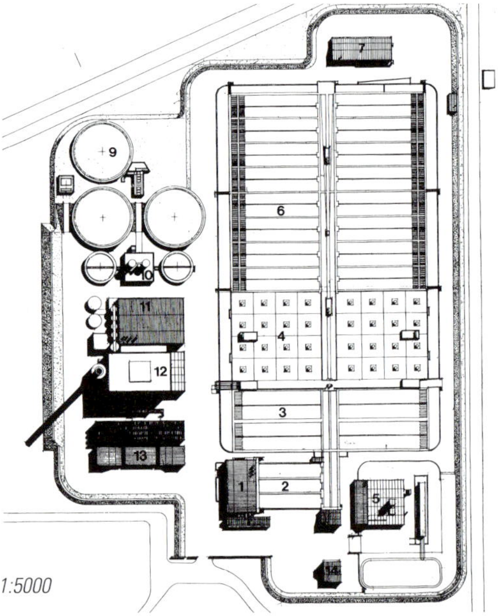

1:5000

The Press Building * **F229**

Skindergade 5, Indre By
1974

Client: The Danish Press' Co-operative Purchasing Society
Architect: Juul Møller & Erik Korshagen

This narrow, street building is a supplement to the neighboring Skindergade 7, where the client has offices. No. 5 houses meeting rooms and a canteen, to which there is access from the neighboring building through the stairwell. On the street level, the building covers the entire site, while the upper stories are smaller in area, and the courtyard facade is stepped-back. The non-bearing facades are of painted steel sections and dark, coated thermal glass. The street facade has finely tuned proportions in relation to its older neighbor. In addition to this, it displays a clear sense of its time and despite the sharp contrasts in color and material, it respects the most important features of the area's architecture.
Bibliography: Arkitektur DK 1976, 59

The Foreign Ministry **F232**

Asiatisk Plads, Christianshavn
1977-80

Client: Ministry of Housing
Architect: Halldor Gunlögsson & Jørn Nielsen
Landscape architect: Jørgen Vesterholt

The buildings primarily contain offices as the Foreign Ministry's ceremonial rooms are in the Eigtved's Warehouse and in the Asiatisk Kompagni's buildings on Strandgade street. This was the reason for the buildings' uniform transverse module, which is based on the depth of an office space. This module is combined in different building sections with single or double corridors and varying heights. The section is terminated by a low hipped roof over the stepped-back top floor, and forms the gable motif toward the harbor, which refers to the old warehouse gable walls. Despite this adaption, the large monolithic buildings have a more reserved monumentality than the older buildings in the area.
Bibliography: Arkitektur DK 1983, 22

F233

Housing restoration

Rigensgade, Olfert Fischers Gade, Fredericiagade, Ny København
1981-82

Client: Urban Renewal and Redevelop Company Copenhagen
Architect: Erik Møllers Tegnestue A/S

*New housing.
Architect: KBI*

The buildings described here lie in the western end of the city block between Rigensgade and Kronprinsessegade streets. They were built during the later part of the seventeenth century and survived the great fire of 1728. They are thus among the oldest remaining buildings in Copenhagen. Their age is also a major reason for their renovation. For many years, they had been neglected due to expansion plans for the Danish Technical College, which was then located on a neighboring site. When these plans were abandoned, the mood had changed to a positive one for the preservation of these buildings, including the most dilapidated, as long as they were old. The row of houses along Fredericiagade street is now protected and here one can find some of the original decorations. Due to the poor condition of many of these buildings, the restoration has in some cases involved a reconstruction, and characteristic features such as the extremely low ceilings, have been preserved. The facades facing Fredericiagade illustrate a pristine, slightly embellished, picture of Copenhagen about 1700, while the two courtyards are literally idylls with their picturesque and well-preserved building remnants, although far from original. This housing environment is now one of the best within the old city area.
Bibliography: Arkitektur DK 1983, 39

Østerport Station *, renovation, and Østerport shopping arcade F234

Oslo Plads, Østerbro
1984, 1990-91

Client: The Danish State Railways (DSB) and Højgaard & Schultz A/S
Architect: DSB Building department and KHR A/S Arkitekter
Landscape architect: Susanne Struch

The station building is from 1884-97 and was designed by architect Heinrich Wenck. The decorative and rural, arts and crafts style illustrates its function as the end station for the Kystbane coastal line. This ambience is maintained in the renovation, where the building contributes to the complexity of the heavily trafficked and open Oslo Plads square. A similar contribution to the area can be found in the new Østerport shopping arcade. With building fragments consisting of a fractured portal, a curved arcade, a crooked glass pyramid and spidery neon lettering, it attempts to maintain the chaotic mixture of roaring traffic and dramatically different buildings such as Den Frie Udstilling exhibition building and Hotel Østerport. Toward Oslo Plads, the shopping arcade forms a stage set for today's fleeting cosmopolitan life. Toward the railway area, the station's motif with the stepped roofs leading to the platform is repeated in the new building, and a similar adaption to tradition can be found in the facade facing Folke Bernadottes Allé.

Bibliography: Arkitektur DK 1986, 122 and 1991, 386

F254

Gammelholm, district renewal

Six city blocks in the Gammelholm district, Indre By
1975-85

Client: SBS Byfornyelse
Architect: Anders and Lars Hegelund

For almost 350 years, most of the Gammelholm district was owned by the naval shipyards, until it was moved to Nyholm in 1859. The ensuing building work in this area was based on a plan by Ferdinand Meldahl, and continued until the middle of the 1870's. The plan was organized according to a Parisian pattern with wide streets and elegantly decorated facades. The State had charged a handsome price for the property, so it had to be heavily exploited. From the beginning, there were many small, dark courtyards behind the fine facades. The renewal project thus aimed at opening the middle of these blocks and bringing the apartments up to a modern standard. The process involved a collaboration with the existing tenants, and despite radical alterations, there were no dramatic confrontations between the residents and the authorities as was the case with the concurrent Nørrebro renewal project.
Bibliography: A. and L. Hegelund: Gammeholm fornyes. 1986

Courtyard renovation on Havnegade **F255**

Havnegade, Cort Adelers Gade, Herluf Trolles Gade
1989-1990

Client: SBS Byfornyelse
Landscape architect: Charlotte Skibsted

The 2000 sqm garden was established in conjunction with the Gammelholm urban renewal project. A finely trimmed beech hedge winds across a central, gentle hilly lawn. This forms a number of small garden areas for recreational purposes and Birgit Krogh's ceramic sculpture. Along the facades there are different kinds of seating areas. The courtyard appears both harmonious and lush, due to the many creepers, which climb the facade trellises to form green walls.
Bibliography: Landskab 1994, 62

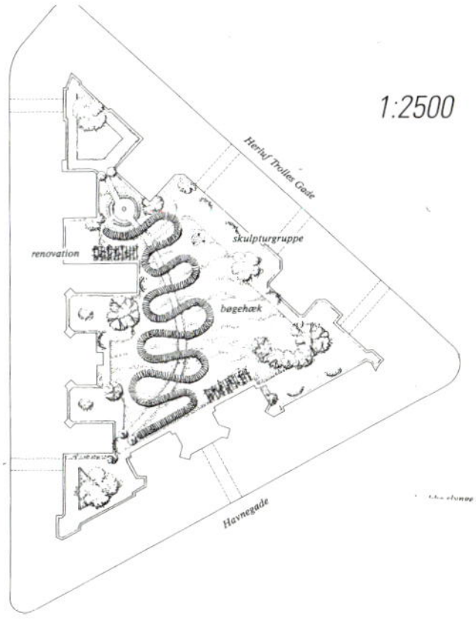

1:2500

F256

Blegdamsvej court yard renovation

Blegdamsvej, Helgesensgade, Ryesgade, Trepkasgade, Østerbro
1977-81

Client: SBS Byfornyelse
Landscape architect: Gerd Wiboe, A. Muusfeldt & I. Ravn

In the center of the courtyard and opposite a solid building – a former home for retired artisans – lies a common green. This 5000 sqm courtyard area is characterized by lively trees such as bird cherries and rowans as well as vigorous twining plants along the wooden cabins and on the fences.
Bibliography: Landskab 1986, 110

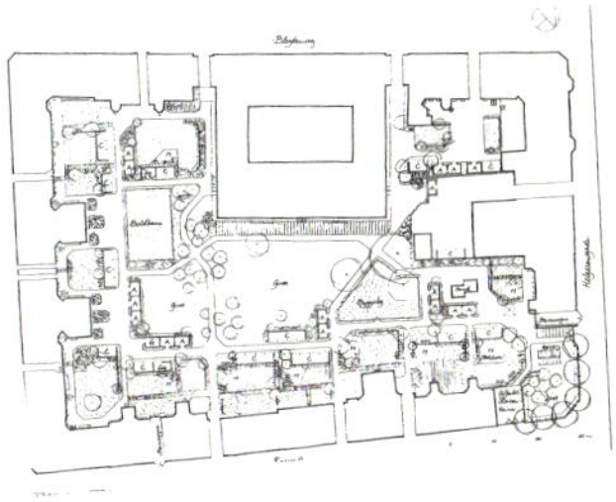

F270

Strøget, walking streets and side streets

Indre By
1962-95

Client: Copenhagen Municipality
Architect: The municipal architect's department, the municipal engineer's department

Strøget is a common name for a number of streets and connected squares in the inner city running from Kongens Nytorv square to Rådhusplads square. The area was designated as a pedestrian street in the early sixties and the squares at Magasin Torv, Nikolaj Church and Gråbrødre Torv were the first to be renovated. In the 1990's, the neighboring parallel Kompagnistræde street was designated as a "filter street", and Vimmelskaftet, Amager Torv, Gammel Torv and Nytorv squares were renovated. At the time of this writing, Højbro Plads square and the Rådhusplads city hall square are being renovated. Sculptor Bjørn Nørgaard created a new paving with an exuberant pattern of granite pentagons in five different colors: rose, yellow, black and two shades of grey. Gammel Torv and Nytorv squares have become large granite surfaces, where the number of benches, lighting fixtures and other equipment has been reduced to a minimum and carefully situated. The plan trace of the former town hall is marked with long granite pavers.

ROYAL COPENHAGEN
CRYSTAL

F284

BT building

Kristen Bernikows Gade, Grønnegade, Indre By
1994

Client: BT daily newspaper
Architect: Henning Larsens Tegnestue

On a modest corner site, this six-story office building gives a new scope to Copenhagen's renewal. The building connects the newspaper's two older properties, which each face a separate street. There is only one room on each floor of the new building, with the reception on the ground floor, editorial offices on the upper floors and a meeting room and roof terrace on the top floor, which is topped by a thin, flat roof. Two concrete slabs rise over the roof as fire walls and form a precisely defined space for this building. Both facades are of clear glass. The facade facing Grønnegade street is exposed so that the life within can be viewed from without, especially at night. Toward Kr. Bernikowsgade street, the glass is covered by a screen of perforated steel panels, with open joints that form a delicate facade grid. From here one can see into the rooms as though through a halftone screen. At the joints of the grid, there are small low-voltage lamps, a subdued illumination, just like the refined, red neon signs. There are literally and figuratively several layers in this newspaper building, which both day and night, renders its pulse through its architecture's discrete poetry.

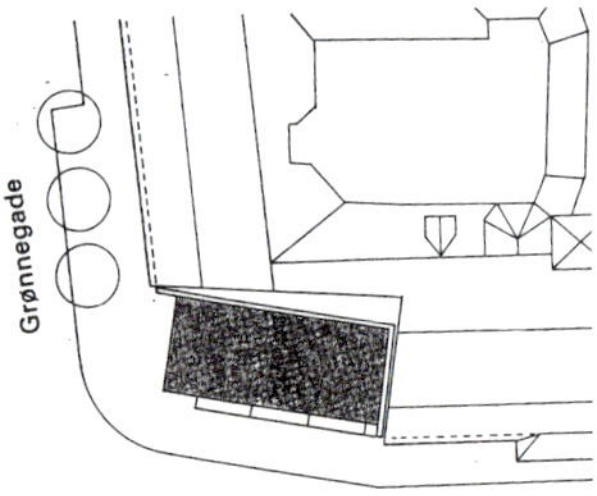

Company House F288

Midtermolen, Søndre Frihavn
1994

Client: Østasiatisk Kompagni (ØK)
Architect: PLH Arkitekter A/S
Landscape architect: Svend Kierkegaard

With its perimeter solidly founded in the water, this complex represents an exclusive housing and commercial scheme on the center pier in the old free port area. The six-story building toward west continues the line of the other commercial buildings. The curved 12-story block toward east surrounds a large atrium, with a glass roof borne by a fan-shaped steel structure. This area houses the common facilities for the businesses that have leased space as the building is not entirely a domicile for ØK. With its predominant location and the coolly reserved architecture, the Company House is a symbol for the current development in the old harbor area.

The Architects' Building F296

Strandgade 27, Christianshavn
1995-96

Client: Arkitekternes Pensionskasse
Architect: Nielsen, Nielsen & Nielsen
Landscape architect: Jeppe Aagaard Andersen

An open competition in 1994 for an Architects' Building was won by architects Nielsen, Nielsen & Nielsen from Århus. The project will be completed in August 1996. Toward Strandgade street, the upper three floors, like a closed modernistic block, float above the open lower floor. These upper floors are reserved for the neighboring Foreign Ministry, while the architect organizations have the lower floor and the area facing the harbor. On this side, the facade is all glass, screened by interior wooden louvers. In the middle of the building there is a panoptical space with a freestanding stairway and ramps. The space opens downwards toward the harbor with a stairway to the bottom of the old dry dock, which was filled up in 1918. This stepped space will be used for exhibitions and meetings.
Bibliography: Arkitekten 1994, 602

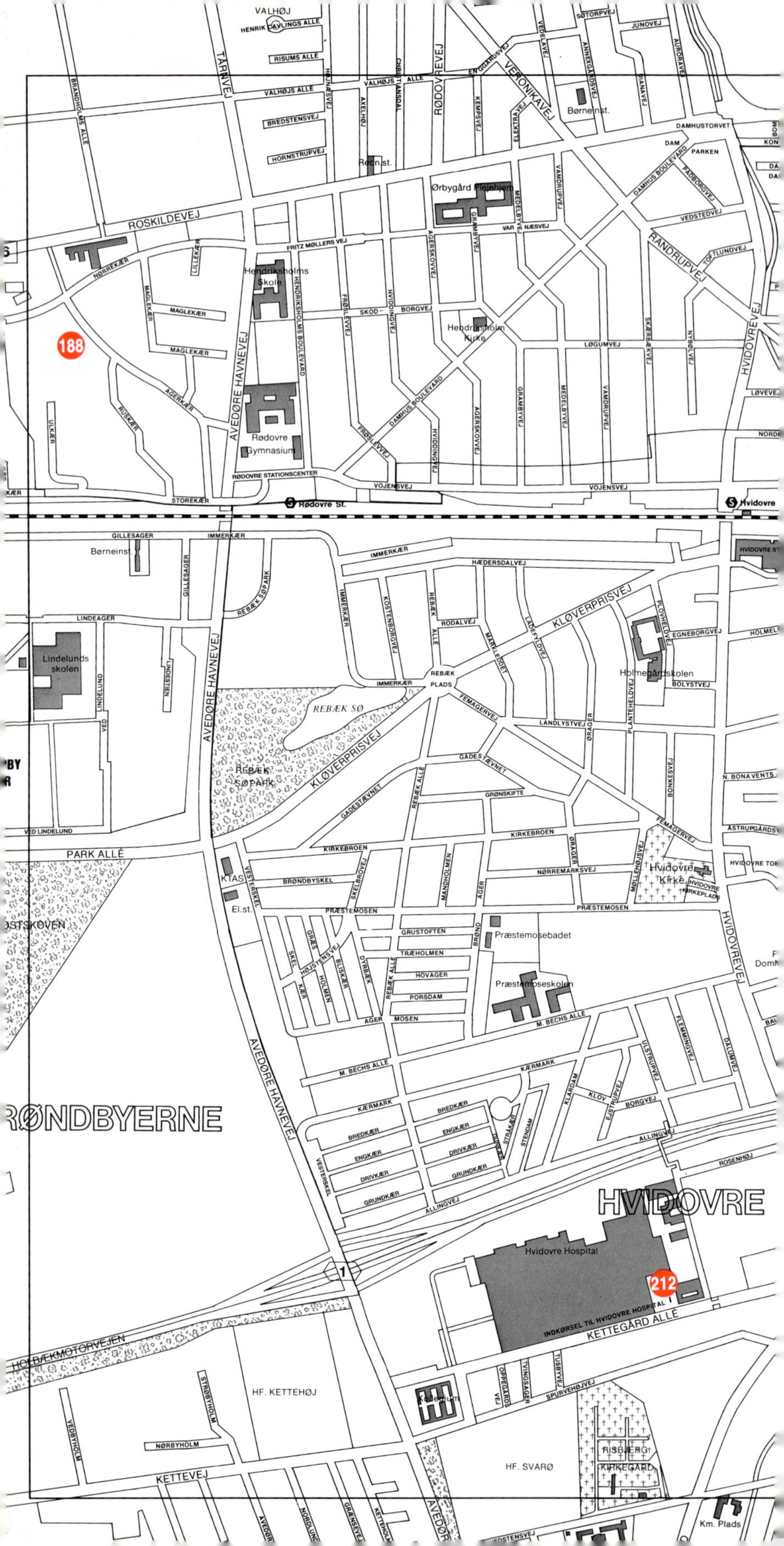

VALHØJ
HENRIK DAVLINGS ALLÉ
RISUMS ALLÉ
VALHØJS ALLÉ
BREDSTENSVEJ
HORNSTRUPVEJ
TÅRNVEJ
BRANDHOLMS ALLÉ
HØJNÆSVEJ
AXELHØJ
CHRISTIANSDAL
RØDOVREVEJ
ENGGÅRDSVEJ
KEMPSVEJ
ELEKTRAVEJ
VERONIKAVEJ
VEDELSVEJ
ANNEXGÅRDSVEJ
SØTORPVEJ
JUNOVEJ
DIANAVEJ
AURORAVEJ
Børneinst.
DAMHUSTORVET
DAM
PARKEN
DAMHUS BOULEVARD
PADBORGVEJ
VEDSTEDVEJ
RANDRUPVEJ
TOFTLUNDVEJ
Rødn.st.
Ørbygård Plejehjem
ROSKILDEVEJ
GRAMBYVEJ
MEDELBYVEJ
VAMDRUPVEJ
VARNÆSVEJ
FRITZ MØLLERS VEJ
AGERSKOVVEJ
LILLEKÆR
NØRREKÆR
Hendriksholms Skole
HENDRIKSHOLMS BOULEVARD
FRØSLEVVEJ
HVIDINGVEJ
SKOD-BORGVEJ
Hendriksholm Kirke
LØGUMVEJ
SKÆRBÆKVEJ
NYBØLVEJ
HVIDOVREVEJ
LØVEVEJ
NORDØ
MAGLEKÆR
188
AGERKÆR
RUSKÆR
ULKÆR
AVEDØRE HAVNEVEJ
Rødovre Gymnasium
DAMHUS BOULEVARD
RØDOVRE STATIONSCENTER
VOJENSVEJ
STOREKÆR
Rødovre St.
Hvidovre
GILLESAGER
IMMERKÆR
Børneinst.
REBÆK SØPARK
HÆDERSDALVEJ
HVIDOVRE ST
LINDEAGER
KOSTENBORGVEJ
REBÆK ALLÉ
RODALVEJ
MARKLEDDET
LADEFYLDVEJ
KLØVERPRISVEJ
PLOVHELDVEJ
EGNEBORGVEJ
HOLMEL
Lindelunds skolen
LINDESTIEN
LINDELUND
VED
REBÆK PLADS
Holmegårdsskolen
BOLYSTVEJ
REBÆK SØ
FEMAGERVEJ
LANDLYSTVEJ
ØRAGER
PLANTEHELDVEJ
REBÆK SØPARK
GADESTÆVNET
BONKESVEJ
N. BONAVENTS
GRØNSKIFTE
ASTRUPGÅRDSV
VED LINDELUND
PARK ALLÉ
KIRKEBROEN
MØLLEHØJSVEJ
Hvidovre Kirke
HVIDOVRE KIRKEPLADS
HVIDOVRE TOR
KTAS
El.st.
VESTERSKEL
BRØNDBYSKEL
SKELBROVEJ
MANDHOLMEN
AGER
NØRREMARKSVEJ
PRÆSTEMOSEN
OSTSKOVEN
GRÆS
HØJSTENSVEJ
SKEL
KÆR
HOLMEN
BLISKÆR
DYRBÆK
GRUSTOFTEN
TRÆHOLMEN
HOVAGER
PORSDAM
AGER MOSEN
BRØND
Præstemosebadet
Præstemoseskolen
M. BECHS ALLÉ
FLEMMINGVEJ
DALUMVEJ
ULSTRUPVEJ
KÆRMARK
KLARDAM
KLOV
BORGVEJ
EJSTRUPVEJ
BRØNDBYERNE
BREDKÆR
ENGKÆR
DRIVKÆR
GRUNDKÆR
ALLINGVEJ
STRÅKÆR
STENDAM
ROSENHØJ
HVIDOVRE
Hvidovre Hospital
212
1
INDKØRSEL TIL HVIDOVRE HOSPITAL
KETTEGÅRD ALLÉ
HOLBÆKMOTORVEJEN
HF. KETTEHØJ
STRØBYHOLM
NØRBYHOLM
VEDBYHOLM
KETTEVEJ
OPPEGÅRDS VEJ
TVINGSAGER
TUSBYVEJ
SPURVEHØJVEJ
HF. SVARØ
RISBJERG KIRKEGÅRD
Km. Plads
NORDLUND
GRÆNSEVEJ
AVEDØRE

G
156
ROSKILDEVEJ
ÅLHOLM PLADS
Ålholm Kirke
BRAMSLYKKEVEJ
VALBY LANGGADE
BIRKEBAKKEN
LINDEBUGTEN
VESTERVANG
ÅLHOLMVEJ
VIGERSLEVVEJ
HØJDE DRAGET
HØJDEDRAGET
HARRESTRUPVANG
PARKBO
HAVEBO
LÆSTEDET
SOLSKRÆNTEN
MELLEMLEDDET
HANSSTEDVEJ
Hanssted Skole
Brandst.
NAKSKOVVEJ
NYSTEDVEJ
MARIBOVEJ
BANDHOLMVEJ
RØDBYVEJ
KNUTHENBORGVEJ
HARDENBERGVEJ
Idrætshal
SÆBYHOLMVEJ
HOLMVEJ
LANGVADDAM
SAXHØJVEJ
HERSTRUPVEJ
ULRIKSDALVEJ
JOHANNES V. JENSENS ALLÉ
LÆRKESKELLET
EGESKELLET
TJØRNESKELLET
AHORNSKELLET
POPPELSKELLET
PILESKELLET
ASKESKELLET
LINDESKELLET
BØGESKELLET
BIRKESKELLET
PLATANSKELLET
BETTY NANSENS ALLÉ
HJØRNELODDEN
Ålholm Skole
VIBEHOLMEN
NORDENS PLADS
RÅDMAND STEINS ALLÉ
HELGE RODES ALLÉ
Skole
Busanlæg
291
109
187
O2
NORDRE ALLÉ
SØNDRE ALLÉ
VESTRE ALLÉ
FRILANDS ALLÉ
NYBOVEJ
MONRADS ALLÉ
AMALIE SKRAMS ALLÉ
OVERBYS ALLÉ
TRAPS ALLÉ
J. P. E. HARTMANNS ALLÉ
ANSGARS ALLÉ
HERNINGS ALLÉ
DRONNING DAGMARS ALLÉ
CHRISTENBERGS ALLÉ
Timotheus Kirke
Langgade St.
HERMAN BANGS PLADS
HARALD KIDDES VEJ
HJALMAR BERGSTRØMS VEJ
VILH. TOPSØES VEJ
NØRREOFTE ALLÉ
BORGMESTER FISCHERS VEJ
MAGNOLI
CÆCILIAVEJ
LUKRETIAVEJ
BEATEVEJ
BLANKAVEJ
VALBORG ALLÉ
SELVEJE ALLÉ
GASEBÆKSVEJ
GLAHNS ALLÉ
GENERALVEJ
DALGAS BOULEVARD
BAHNSONS VEJ
JYLLANDSVEJ
HOFFMEYERSVEJ
CAMILLA NIELSENS VEJ
HIELYSTVEJ
Vigerslev Godsst.
VIGERSLEV GODSVEJ
KAMHUSENE
HUSVEJ
DAMSBO VÆNGE
SKYTTEGÅRDVEJ
LANGAGERVEJ
VIGERSLEVSTRÆDE
SKYGGELUNDSVEJ
HØJBOVEJ
HF. BROHAVEN
HF. HARRESTRUP
HF. DAN
HF. DANSHØJ
HF. VIGERSLEV
DANSHØJVEJ
LUNDSFRYDVEJ
HØJSAGER PLADS
HØJSAGERVEJ
Lykkebo Skole
LØNBORG ALLÉ
ROSENHOLMS VEJ
PRISHOLMVEJ
FLIDSAGERVEJ
LUNDSFRYDVEJ
GLADBOVEJ
VIGERSLEV ALLÉ
El.st.
LYKKEBOVEJ
Vigerslev Kirke
KÆRSKIFTEVEJ
Plejehjemmet Vigerslev
VANGS ALLÉ
HELDBOVEJ
BAVNAGERVEJ
VIGERSLEV VÆNGE
KULBANEVEJ
HORNEMANNS VÆNGE
VIGERSLEV
GÅRDSTEDET
VIGERSLEVPARKEN
CENTERPARKEN
KONGSHAVEN
SØNDERVANGS ALLÉ
OLE BORCHS VEJ
CARL LANGES VEJ
STEENBERGSVEJ
PANUMSVEJ
STADFELDTSVEJ
CASTBERGSVEJ
ESCHRICHTSVEJ
MANSASVEJ
STEINS PLADS
STEINSVEJ
FENGERSVEJ
SAXTORPHSVEJ
Børneinst.
Vigerslev Allés Skole
Solgavehjemmet
VILH. THOMSENS ALLÉ
AUGUST WIMMERS VEJ
HØFFDINGSVEJ
GASVÆRKSARB. HF.
RETORTVEJ
FRUGTMARKEDET
GRØNTORVET
LINDEHAVEN
Tekn.Sk.
VÆRKSTEDVEJ
BEKKERSGÅRD VÆNGE
122
21
NÆSBORGVEJ
VIGERSLEV ALLÉ
I.G. SMITHS ALLÉ
ULRIKSBORG VEJ
ELSBORG VEJ
SØNDERKÆR
KROG
STENS ALLÉ
ELME ALLÉ
BIRKE ALLÉ
SYDKÆRSVEJ
HUMLEHAVEN
NØDDEHAVEN
ROSENHAVEN
ÆBLEHAVEN
RØNHAVEN
HESTEHAVEN
FOLEHAVEN
HF. TREKANTEN
URTEHAVEN
BORGHAVEN
DANHAVEN
ÅHAVEN
FRUGTHAVEN
Kirsebærhavens Plejehjem
Margrethe Kirken
Margrethehjemmet Plejehjem
KIRSEBÆRHAVEN
Kirsebærhavens Skole
BLOMMESTIEN
VINHAVEN
DRUEHAVEN
151
VESTKÆRS ALLÉ
KARISE ALLÉ
TORSTENS VEJ
RØDVIG ALLÉ
EJBY ALLÉ
Krogstenshave Plejehjem
KROGSTENS ALLÉ
POPPEL ALLÉ
EGE ALLÉ
MØRUPS ALLÉ
BJEVERSKOV ALLÉ
GREVE ALLÉ
RISBJERGGÅRDS ALLÉ
TORS ALLÉ
BLOMMEHAVEN
ØSTERGÅRDS ALLÉ
HARRESTRUP ALLÉ
GRØNNEHAVE ALLÉ
BÆRHAVEN
STAKHAVEN
STAKLEDET
LODDEN
ENG
VIGERSLEVVEJ
Kl. pumpest.
VIGERSLEVPARKEN
SØNDERVEJ
BEND

G109

Vigerslev Haveforstad

Both sides of Vigerslevvej, Vigerslev
1914

Client: Den la Courske Koncern, Copenhagen Municipality
Architect: Charles I. Schou

At the beginning of this century town planning, as well as the planning of large contained areas, was just beginning. The Vigerslev Haveforstad housing area was an early example and part of an even larger plan for the areas south and west of Damhussø lake. Charles I. Schou's plan differed from this in that he only worked with a few straight, through roads. The villas were organized along short dead end streets, winding local roads and small squares. In the middle of the area was a large common. The turning spaces, intersections and changes in road direction were marked by the location of the villas. This concept was inspired by the English town planning theorist, Ebenezer Howard and the Letchworth garden city, which was planned in 1903 according to Howard's ideas by architects Raymond Unwin and Barry Parker. Vigerslev Haveforstad was one of Charles I. Schou's first town planning efforts. He was co-founder of the Danish Town Planning Laboratory in 1921, and participated in the planning of the Grundtvig Church area. (B 115).

Vigerslev Park

G122

Vigerslev
1929, 1941-44, 1980's

Client: Copenhagen Municipality
Landscape architect: Jacob Bergmann, Copenhagen Municipal Park Department

The almost four kilometer long Vigerslev Park lies as a narrow strip in a hollow along Harrestrup Å stream. This creates an almost uninterrupted connection between Damhussø lake and Valby Park. The park is quite open and in some places there are wide vistas along the slight, bowl-formed grassy fields with groups of oaks and larches and shrubbery thickets. There are also a number of ball fields and playgrounds. During the 1980's, north of Vigerslevvej road, three separate flower gardens were established as sensing gardens for the blind and visually impaired. They are planted with fragrant flowers and leaves: lavender, roses, thyme, etc. The sensing gardens are marked by special paving and white posts.

1:6000

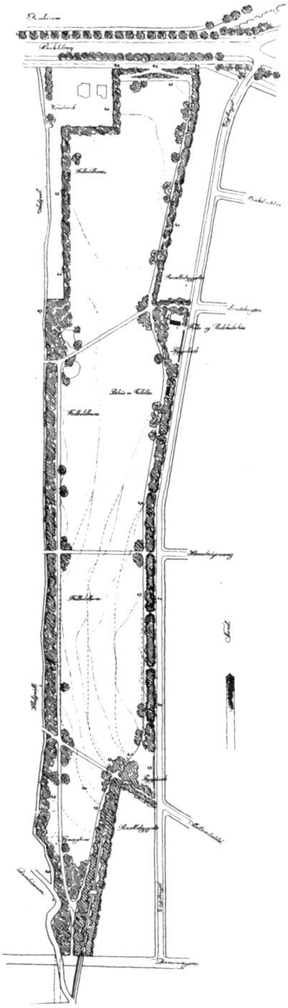

G187

Hanssted school

Rødbyvej 2, Vigerslev
1955-58

Client: Copenhagen Municipality
Architect: Municipal architect F.C. Lund and Hans Chr. Hansen
Landscape architect: Copenhagen Municipal Park Department

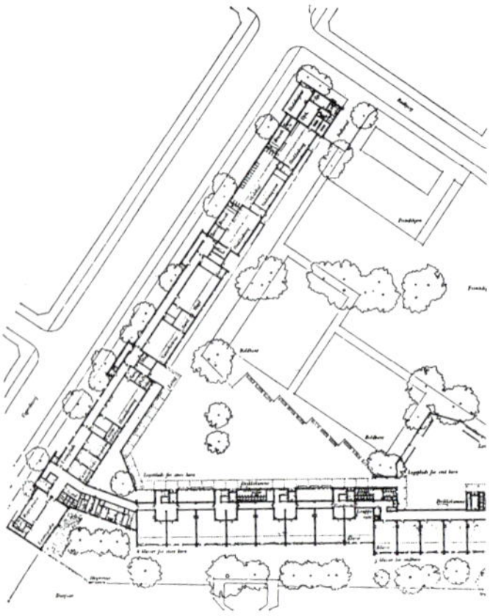

1:3000

The building scheme forms a sharp angle that surrounds the playgrounds and sports areas. The two-story wing along Vigerslevvej houses the special-subject rooms and is connected to the neighboring building to the south. The other wing, with both one and two floors houses the classrooms for the youngest and oldest students respectively. The facades are an interplay between the strip sided grey fiber cement siding on the main buildings and the yellow brick work on the stairwells, which with their steep roofs gives the scheme a fixed rhythm. The choice of materials and design contribute to the informal, easy tone, which is struck in the main disposition and so graciously accommodates the relatively large complex in the surrounding housing area.
Bibliography: Arkitektur DK 1960, 97

The Milestedet housing scheme **G188**

Nykær, Nørrekær, Storekær and others, Brøndbyøster
1953-58

Client: Four public housing associations
Architect: Kay Fisker, Svend Høgsbro, Svenn Eske Kristensen, Gunnar Milthers, Erik Møller
Landscape architect: C.Th. Sørensen

When entering Copenhagen along Roskildevej road, the Milestedet high-rise blocks signal that one is in a major city. The building scheme has 2,500 living units in both high- and low-rise buildings in a pattern of blocks and angles separated by large open areas. These quite different buildings were designed by architects Kay Fisker, Svend Høgsbro, S. Eske Kristensen, Gunnar Milthers and Erik Møller. Milestedet's radical modernistic urban building style gave rise to an energetic professional criticism when they were built. Several of the buildings have been renovated in recent years with major changes in appearance, such as artistic decorations on the end walls. However, this has not taken the sting out of the original criticism.

Surplus earth from the building projects was piled in large flat berms along the railway and Roskildevej road. These are landscaped with oak, which has formed heavy thickets that today counteract the large scale of the buildings.
At the nearby Vestbad there is a complex of curved ponds with sculpture by I.P. Junggreen Have.

G212 **Hvidovre Municipal Hospital**

1968-75

Kettegård Allé 30, Hvidovre

Client: Copenhagen Municipality

Architect: Architect office Krohn & Hartvig Rasmussen represented by Gunnar Gundersen and Bent Nielsen

Landscape architect: Morten Klint and Knud Lund-Sørensen

In the Nordic hospital competition in 1962, E. Hartvig Rasmussen's winning proposal was one of the few without a high-rise patient building. The flat structure of his proposal with a ground area of ca 25 acres, is the exact opposite of the county hospital in Herlev, which was built at the same time. The concept is based on four small hospitals gathered in a common framework. Running across the 500 meter long lobby lie five, two-story patient buildings. The treatment units are located on the floor below the lobby. The enormous low building mass cannot be distinguished as a whole. It is perceived as rows of isolated functions and building sections, which despite the uniform expression has its strength in the clear, local layout, thoughtful design and convenient access to the many small gardens.

Bibliography: Arkitektur DK 1973, 307, Landskab 1984, 121

The building complex has ca 70,000 sqm of gardens on the concrete decks, either as roof gardens or atriums. The gardens have a varied of landscaping with delicately leaved trees like locust, staghorn sumac and rowan planted in a green bed with scattered flowering perennials and bushes. The gardens are now being renovated by Copenhagen Municipal Park Department.

1:6000

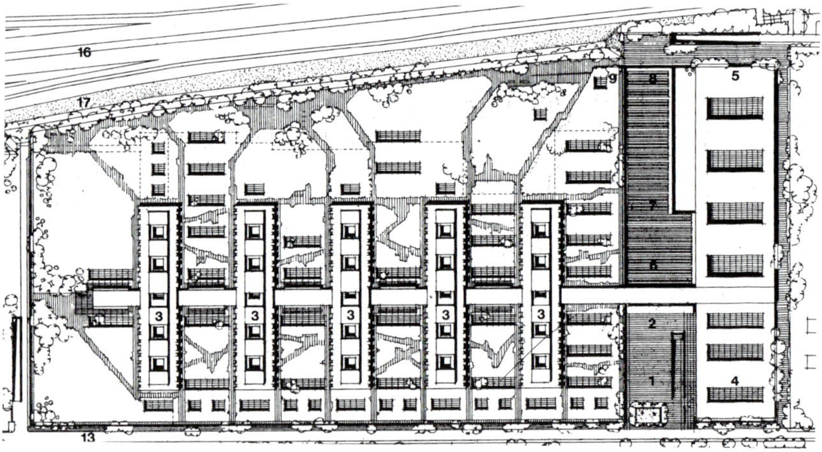

The Akacieparken housing scheme ——— **G291**

Carl Th. Dreyersvej 1-324 (at Skellet and Valby Langgade), Valby
1995

Client: Lejerbo Housing Association
Architect: Hvidt & Mølgaard A/S
Landscape architect: Knud Lund-Sørensen

This area of Valby was originally a mixture of large street blocks of housing and older, building society houses. It is this structure that determined the Akaciapark housing plan with 5-story blocks toward east and 2-story row houses facing west. The plan subdivides the large building mass in a clear and taut pattern. The high-rise blocks contain a wide variety of 300, primarily 3-room units, while the 94 row houses have identical 4-room units. Both building forms are dense and the general impression has a strong urban character. The compressed mixture of familiar housing forms expresses both the special character of the place and the current status of the public housing sector.

SOLBJERG KIRKEGÅRD
ZOOLOGISK HAVE
132
FREDERIKSBERG
Haveselskabets Have
Idrætsanlæg
Kirke
Frederiksberg Slot
Lakagården
Tennishal
19
ROSKILDEVEJ
ROSKILDEVEJ
JACOBYS ALLE
ASMUS
VESTERBROG
SØNDERMARKEN KIRKEGÅRD
123
AZALEA VEJ
NORMAS VEJ
PELARGONIEVEJ
SØNDRE FASANVEJ
ZOOLOGISK HAVE
SØNDERMARKEN
PILE ALLE
BAKKEGÅRDS ALLE
HALLS ALLE
RAHBEKS ALLE
Børneinst.
Bakkehuset
KAMMAS
MAGNOLIAVEJ
MAGNOLIAVEJ
AURIKELVEJ
SKELMOSEVEJ
CECILIAVEJ
LAURAVEJ
LUKRETIAVEJ
BEATEVEJ
HORSEKILDEVEJ
GADEKÆRVEJ
BYMOSEVEJ
MOSEDALVEJ
MOSESTYKKET
BLANKAVEJ
VALBORG ALLE
SYLVIAVEJ
SMEDESTRÆDE
BRØNDKÆRVEJ
BAG SØNDERMARKEN
BYKILDEVEJ
KIRSTINEDALSVEJ
VALBY LANGGADE
NY CARLSBERG
63
GAMLE CARLSBERG VEJ
Carlsberg Bryggeri
ANNEXSTRÆDE
SKOLEGADE
Valby Skole
TINGSTED
VALBY
LILLE GADE
RUGHAVEVEJ
TOFTEGÅRDS ALLE
MØLLE ALLE
79
Jesus Kirke
VALBY KIRKEVEJ
VESTBANEVEJ
JERNBANEVEJ
GAMMEL
SKOVBOGÅRDS ALLE
SØNDERMARKSVEJ
TOINETTEVEJ
BJERREGÅRDSVEJ
BJERREGÅRDS SIDEVEJ
VÆNGET
BANEVOLDEN
TOFTEVEJ
Valby St.
CARLSBERG VIADUKTEN
192
Otto Mønsteds Kollegium
Rektorparken
VESTRE KIRKEGÅRD
LYSHØJGÅRDSVEJ
LYSHØJGÅRDSVEJ
Børneinst.
JAKOB KNUDSENS VEJ
JOHAN KROHNS VEJ
SCHARLINGSVEJ
THYREGODSVEJ
PEDER HJORTS VEJ
LYSHØJ ALLE
BRED AHLSVEJ
OVERSKOUSVEJ
AARESTRUPSVEJ
RASMUS RASKS VEJ
SIBBERNSVEJ
TOFTEGÅRDS PLADS
MOLBECHVEJ
KJELDSGÅRDSVEJ
VIGERSLEV ALLE
VIGERSLEV ALLE
Vigerslev Alles Skole
185
VALBY
Medborgerhus
Politist.
HT
Transf.
BRYGGERIVEJ
Johs. Døbers Kirke
Ottiliahus
OTTILIAVEJ
KRUMTAPPEN
Købmandsskolen
GERDASGADE
GERDASGADE
OTTILIAVEJ
KLØVER
TREKRONERGADE
STRINDBERGSVEJ
CARL TORPS VEJ
BJØRNSONSVEJ
VALBYGÅRDSVEJ
SJÆLØR BOULEVARD
Nordre Kapel
71
VESTRE
KIRKEGÅRD
Søndre Kapel
Bavnehøj Kirke
TRANEHAV
MOSAISK KIRKEG.
KATOLSK KIRKEGÅRD
KARENSGADE
Sankt Annæ Gymnasium
Vestre Borgerdydskole
JULIUS LASSENS VEJ
STRINDBERGSVEJ
BJØRNSONSVEJ
Dronning Ingrids Hjem
BLADSGADE
CARL JACOBSENS VEJ
Østre Kapel
ALLE
RAMSINGSVEJ
TORVEKANTEN
TORVEPORTEN
IDRÆTSANLÆG
GAMMEL KØGE LANDEVEJ
FØLAGER
Dyre Hospital
POPPELSTYKKET
CARL JACOBSENS VEJ
HF. STIEN
Sjælør St.
ERNST KAPERS VEJ
Frederiksholm Børneinst.
P. KNUDSENS
HØRDUMSGADE
Ellebjerg Skole
Frederiksholm Kirke
HF. FR
TREKRONERGADE
Km.pl.
ELLESTYKKET
PILESTYKKET
STRØMMEN
ELLEBJERGVEJ
Ellebjerg St.
HAYDNSVEJ
BORGMESTER CHRISTIANSENS GADE
HANDELSVEJ
STUBMØLLEVEJ
GRØNRISVEJ
SJÆLØR BOULEVARD
OFFENBACHSVEJ
STRAUSS VEJ
ENGHOLMEN
MOZARTS PLADS
MOZARTSVEJ
SCHUBERTS VEJ
BEETHOVENSVEJ
WAGNERSVEJ
51
BLUSHØJVEJ
JULIUS ANDERSENS VEJ
Valby Hallen
VALBY IDRÆTSPARK
Børneinst.
HANDELSVEJ
RUBINSTEINSVEJ
HF. NY ROSENHØJ
HF. NY KGS ENGHAVE
SPONTINISVEJ
DAMAGERVEJ
HAMMELSTRUPVEJ
WAGNERSVEJ
ROSSINISVEJ
STRADELLAS
TARTINISVEJ
GLINKASVEJ
VERDISVEJ
Sjælør Kirke
Børneinst.
PUMPEHUSVEJ
Strandpark-skolen
HF. FREDERIKSH
HF. SOL SKRÆN TEN
HAMMELSTRUPVEJ
147
Særdeles legeplads
HF. FREDERIKSHOLM
Kl.pumpest.
HF. KALVEBOD
Gasbeholder
HF. SUNDBO
VALBYPARKEN

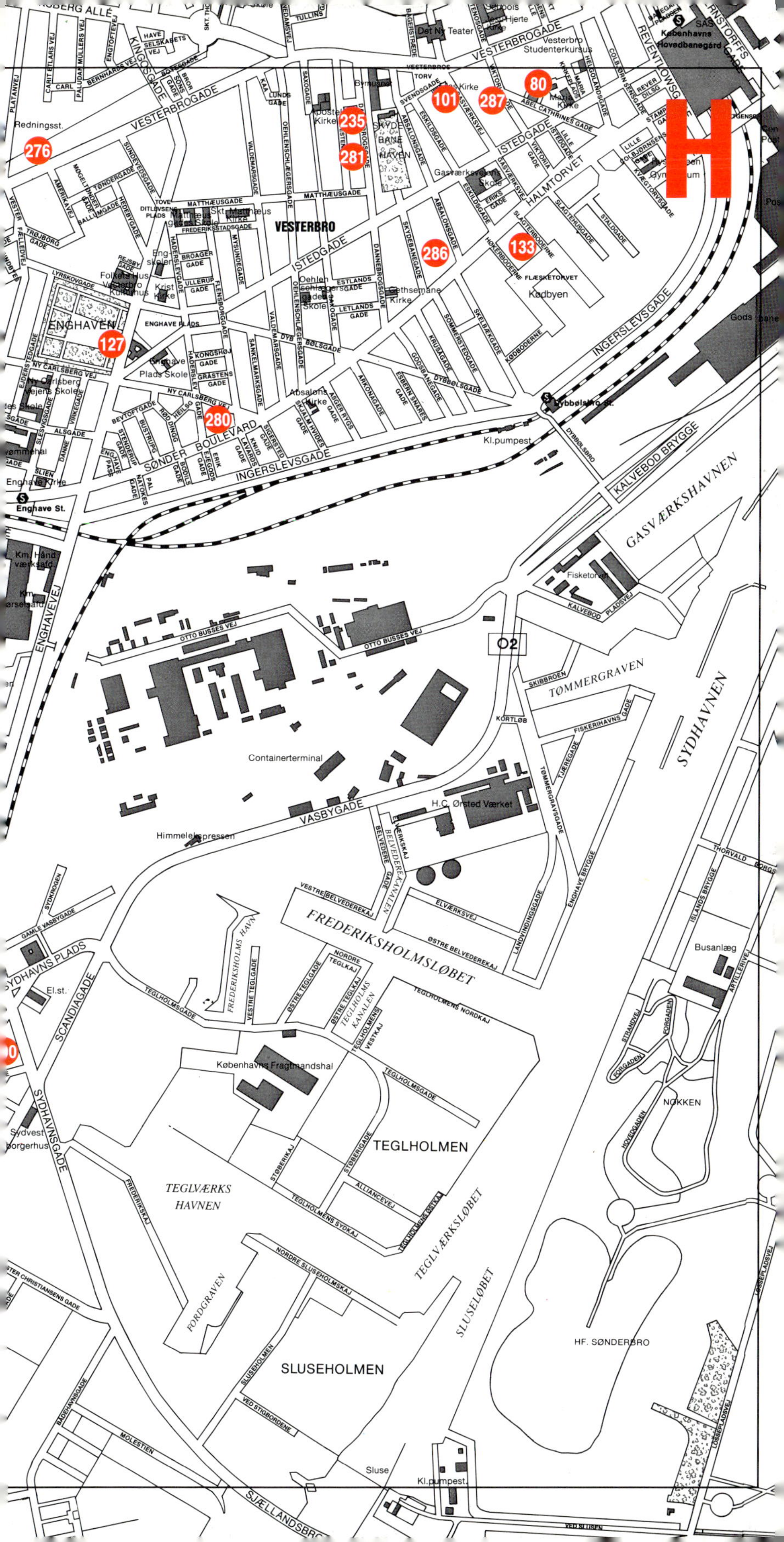

VESTERBROGADE
Det Ny Teater
Vesterbro Studenterkursus
København Hovedbanegård
SAS
REVENTLOWSGADE
H
Redningsst.
276
235
281
101
287
80
286
133
127
280
Bymuseet
Apostel Kirke
SKYDEBANE HAVEN
Mariæ Kirke
ABEL CATHRINES GADE
STEDGADE
HALMTORVET
Gasværksvejens Skole
VESTERBRO
ISTEDGADE
MATTHÆUSGADE
Skt. Matthæus Kirke
Matthæus gades Skole
FREDERIKSSTADSGADE
Folkets Hus Vesterbro Kulturhus
Krist Kirke
ENGHAVEN
ENGHAVE PLADS
Enghave Plads Skole
NY CARLSBERG VEJ
Ny Carlsberg Mejeris Skole
Gethsemane Kirke
Oehlenschlægersgades Skole
Absalons Kirke
FLÆSKETORVET
Kødbyen
INGERSLEVSGADE
Dybbølsbro St.
Kl.pumpest
SØNDER BOULEVARD
Enghave Kirke
Enghave St.
KALVEBOD BRYGGE
GASVÆRKSHAVNEN
Fisketorvet
ENGHAVEVEJ
OTTO BUSSES VEJ
O2
TØMMERGRAVEN
Containerterminal
VASBYGADE
H.C. Ørsted Værket
Himmelekspressen
FREDERIKSHOLMSLØBET
SYDHAVNEN
SYDHAVNS PLADS
SCANDIAGADE
El.st.
Busanlæg
FREDERIKSHOLMS HAVN
TEGLHOLMENS NORDKAJ
Københavns Fragtmandshal
NOKKEN
SYDHAVNSGADE
Sydvest borgerhus
TEGLHOLMEN
TEGLVÆRKS HAVNEN
TEGLVÆRKSLØBET
FORDGRAVEN
SLUSELØBET
HF. SØNDERBRO
SLUSEHOLMEN
Sluse
Kl.pumpest.
SJÆLLANDSBRO
VED SLUSEN

H19

Frederiksberg Palace *

Roskildevej 28, Frederiksberg
1699-1738

Client: The national government
Architect: Ernst Brandenburger et al.
Landscape architect: H.H. Scheel et al.

The oldest part of the palace is the center wing facing north. It was built in 1699-1703 for Frederik IV as a large Italian inspired villa with Ernst Brandenburger as architect. Up until 1711, wings had been added toward east and west by architects J.C. Ernst and W.F. von Platen. In the east wing, a luxuriously equipped palace chapel was built and the now H-shaped complex also housed expensive furnishings and decorations. The curved buildings that surround the palace court toward east and west were completed in 1738 from drawings by J.C. Ernst, L. de Thurah and E.D. Häusser. Several of the original interiors have been preserved including the great hall. This was completed in 1711 by C.F. Harsdorff who also designed the marble bath in the basement with a recessed bath tub and a mirrored coffer ceiling. The palace had its grandest period as a royal residence during the reign of Frederik VI (1808-39). He often sailed with his family along the canals in the park, which was a favorite Copenhagener excursion spot. Since 1869, the palace has served as headquarters for the Military Officers School. The exterior restoration is scheduled for completion in 1996. As part of the park's rearrangement according to the Romantic garden style, a colorful and imaginative Chinese summerhouse was built in 1799-1800 on an island between the canals. A bridge with a similar Chinese expression crosses the canal to the island. Both of these structures were designed by Court Architect Andreas Kirkerup. In a similar spirit, the "Apis Temple" was built in 1802-04 according to drawings by painter Nicolai Abildgaard and architect C.B. Hornbech. The temple served solely as an evocative "morning temple". The name comes from the Apis bull depicted in a relief on the pediment.

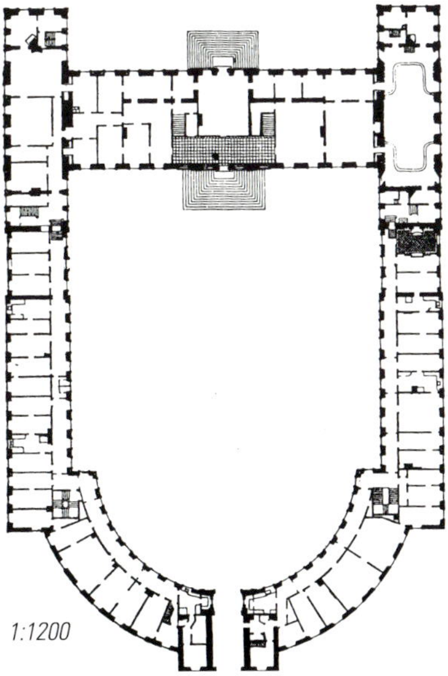
1:1200

H19

Frederiksberg Garden and Søndermarken *

1700, 1800

Client: Frederik IV, Frederik VI
Landscape architect: Hans Hendrick Scheel, Johan Cornelius Krieger, Peter Petersen, The Royal Palaces and Gardens

Frederiksberg Allé has a beautiful longitudinal section that terminates at the Frederiksberg Runddel circus, the main entrance to the Frederiksberg Garden. As crown prince, Frederik IV received an estate, "Prinsens gård", and the gardens were the basis for Frederiksberg Garden. At the same time the palace on Valby Bakke hilltop was built, a baroque garden was established, presumably designed by engineer officer Hans Hendrick Scheel. He was influenced by a never realized plan, by the Swede, Nicodemus Tessin the younger in 1697. Scheel's garden was based on a system of alleys around eight identical, square and star-shaped shrubs. The main emphasis was placed on the palace's cross axis, but the main axis was accentuated by four oval pools and an island surrounded by canals.

In Søndermark field across the Roskildevej road, alleys were planted in 1708 in a goosefoot pattern, i. e. the three alleys radiate from the same spot in front of the palace entrance facade. On the axis, there was a long pool that was to serve as a reservoir for the cascades. A large circular pool was recently built here.

The change in grade leading up to the palace plateau was used by Johan Cornelius Krieger in the 1720's to form a cascade on the center axis framed by terraces planted with linden trees.

Plan of Kriegers cascade from the 1720's

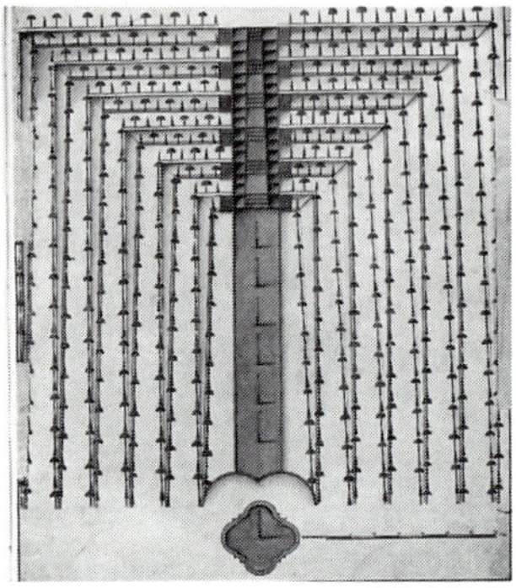

Hans Hendrick Scheel's plan from 1697

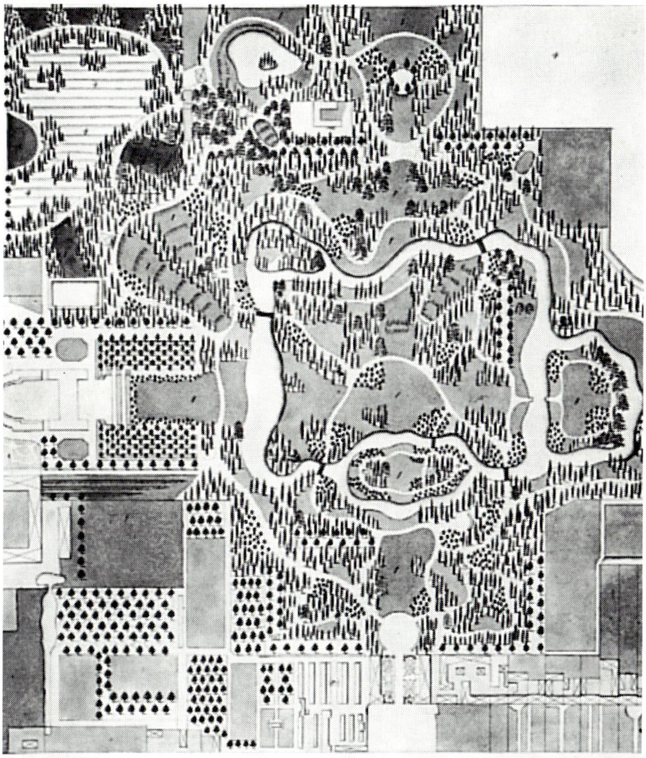

Plan from the late 1700's

H19

In 1744 at "Prinsens Gård" at Frederiksberg circus, Nicolai Eigtved converted the south wing to an orangery. When the center building burned in 1753, Lauritz de Thurah designed an entrance to the Garden and the iron gate still exists. The sandstone vases came from Hirschholm Palace. Frederiksberg Garden changed very little for many years after. There were large royal parties with dining in the garden, music and fireworks, such as Queen Juliane Marie's birthday in 1772. The park was open to the public earlier than 1750, while Søndermarken fields first opened a century later.

About 1780, a proposal was made to redo Frederiksberg Garden and Søndermarken in the English style. Work was started in 1800, though the terraces by the palace were preserved, the perspective on the cross axis was kept clear, and part of the alleys were saved. Under the supervision of palace gardener Peter Petersen, winding canals were established. Some of the excavated earth was placed on Andebakken, the island where the Chinese summerhouse was built in 1800. The water was dammed to form a lake. In addition grottos, bridges, pavilions and summerhouses were built.

In front of the palace, the cascades, lower ramps and the linden trees on the horizontal terraces were removed. The preserved trees have been rejuvenated several times by extensive pruning.

Bibliography: Landskab 1993, 118

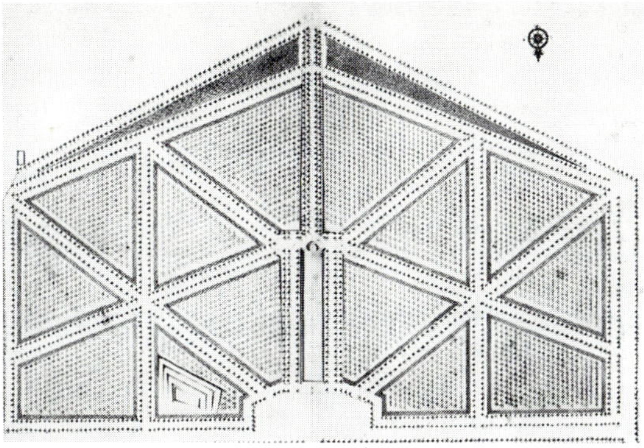

Søndermarken

The island with the Chinese summer house was renovated in 1990

H63

The Carlsberg Breweries

Valby Langgade 1, (Carlsberg Museum) and Ny Carlsberg Vej, Valby
1846-1969

Client: Carlsberg Breweries
Architect: H.C. Stilling, N.S. Nebelong, Vilhelm Dahlerup, Hack Kampmann, Vilhelm Klein, Svenn Eske Kristensen

J.C. Jacobsen received the king's permission in 1846 to move his brewery outside the city limits. The first buildings were built according to his own sketches in collaboration with architect H.C. Stilling and others. J.C. Jacobsen's own home was built in 1852-54, also from his sketches, with N.S. Nebelong as architect. The villa's architecture is an Italian inspired late classicism with decorations by the leading artists of the time. After his son, Carl Jacobsen's death in 1914, the villa was converted to an honorary residence for notables such as physicist Niels Bohr who lived there between 1931-62. Carl Jacobsen commissioned architect V. Dahlerup to design the tower building and twin-portal "Dipylon" built in 1892. In 1901, he built the main building with the luxuriously equipped hall designed by Hack Kampmann. Today the building houses Carlsberg's quality control department. Dahlerup also designed the fantastic Elephant Tower from 1901 that stands like a port over Ny Carlsberg Vej road. A brewing hall was built the same year from drawings by Vilhelm Klein in Florentine style as a finely tooled background for the enormous copper vats. The bottling hall facade toward the honorary residence's garden is another example of the favorable conditions architecture was given at Carlsberg. The brewery designed in 1969 by S. Eske Kristensen let the facade's many curved brick shells form a terraced garden. Carl Jacobsen's large art collection is now at the Ny Carlsberg Glyptotek (F 84).
Bibliography: D. Zanker-von Meyer: Die Bauten von I.C. und Carl Jacobsen. 1982

CARL & OTTILIA JACOBSEN
30

H71

Vestre Kirkegård

Vestre Kirkegårds Allé, Copenhagen SV
1870, 1894, 1929

Client: Copenhagen Municipality
Architect: H.J. Holm
Landscape architect: Edvard Glæsel, I.P. Andersen

The Vestre Kirkegård cemetery, with its ca. 125 acres, is Denmark's largest. It lies high on the site and is marked toward Sjælør Boulevard by a magnificent row of poplar trees. Edvard Glæsel, who also designed Bispebjerg and Frederiksberg cemeteries, designed the uniformly organized plan in collaboration with architect H.J. Holm. The interior of the cemetery is characterized by handsome, monumental alleys, mostly with elm trees that separate the various quarters where the traditional burial plots originally were the central feature. The fine, recessed urn garden and pool were designed by I.P. Andersen about 1930.

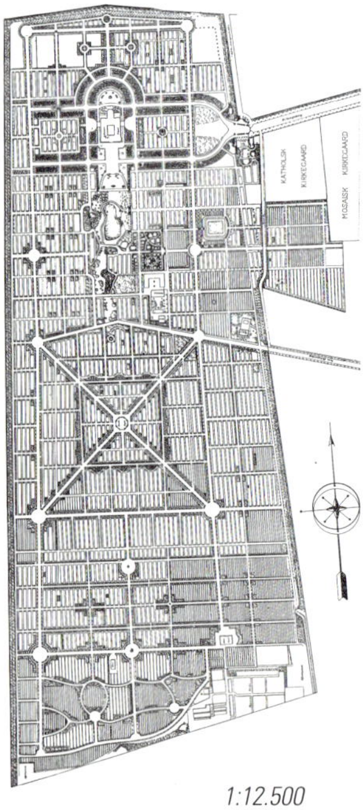

1:12.500

Jesus Church H79

Kirkevænget, Valby
1884-91

Client: Brewer Carl Jacobsen
Architect: Vilhelm Dahlerup

The church is a crypt church and a monument for the Jacobsen family, who founded the Carlsberg Brewery. In this light, it is reminiscent of the renaissance monuments for the great Italian patrons of the arts. It is a basilica inspired in part by the cathedral at Poiters, and its architecture includes ancient Christian, Byzantine and Romanesque elements. The 12-sided nave has a domed ceiling. Below the nave floor is a circular crypt. The church is magnificently decorated inside and out by various artists. The campanile has patterned brickwork with the swastika symbol, which was also Carlsberg's symbol (before its use in Germany) and the Church's entrance facade is dominated by an enormous round window with a clock – a symbol of respectability.
Bibliography: D. Zanker-von Meyer: Die Bauten von I.C. und Carl Jacobsen. 1982

Abel Cathrines Stiftelse * H80

Abel Cathrines Gade 13, Vesterbro
1885-86

Client: Abel Cathrines Hospital
Architect: Herman Baagø Storck

The institution was named after Abel Cathrine, whose testament in 1675 founded this place for the "sick, wretched and bedridden poor". It contained 39, one-room units with kitchens. The rooms were oriented toward the surroundings, while the corridor surrounded the courtyard formed by the four-wing scheme. There was also a church toward northeast. The exterior has a castlelike appearance, and the interior is like a quiet refuge. The architecture has a baroque character with fine details in the heavy red brick walls. It thereby differed from the popular international elegance of the time and marked the beginning of the Danish and Nordic versions of national romanticism.

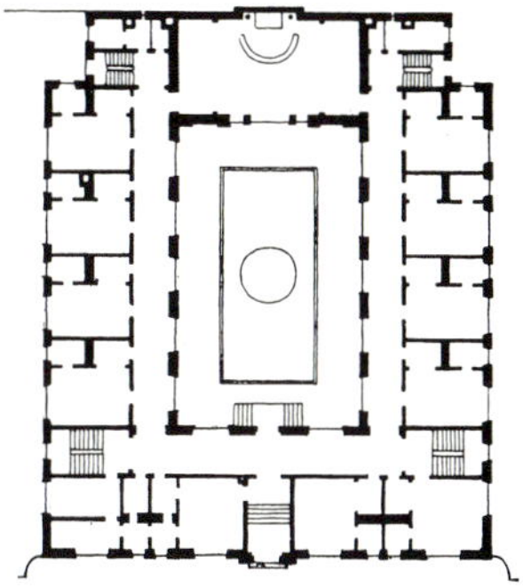

1:750

H101

Elias Church

Vesterbro Torv, Vesterbro
1905-08

Client: The Copenhagen Church Building Fund
Architect: Martin Nyrop

The church respects the urban context with its slightly protruding facade facing the square. It is extremely symmetrical with Romanesque features. This is emphasized by the two towers, which were inspired by the Romanesque churches in Fjenneslev and Tveje Merløse, although the rustic surface of the facade's split Neksø sandstone has a certain Italian renaissance character. A tall, wide, freestanding stairway leads up to the main entrance and distances the church from the local street life. The interior is formed like a basilica with a main aisle and two side aisles. Daylight enters alone from a prismatic skylight and two side windows in the nave barrel vault. The semicircular arches in the interior give a heavy Romanesque atmosphere.

Søndermark Krematorium

Roskildevej 59, Valby
1927-30

Client: Frederiksberg Municipality
Architect: Fritz Schlegel and Edvard Thomsen

The 1926 competition for a chapel crematory at the new Søndermark cemetery was won with a proposal, which after revision, was the basis for the new building. There existed no formal tradition for the chapel crematory. This gave the architects the freedom of employing a modernistic form idiom for the first time in Danish sacral architecture. The main plan is classically symmetric and the materials were traditionally Danish red brick and copper roofing, while the niches on the entrance facade, the large angel relief by Einar Utzon-Frank, and especially the large chapel interior were new features. The hall building has a cubistic character as does the chapel and choir niche, which are dimly lit from high windows and skylights. The space is decorated with only a few symbolic ornaments and has a bare and somber character, which reflected the modern, secular relationship to the church as an institution that characterized the period it was built.

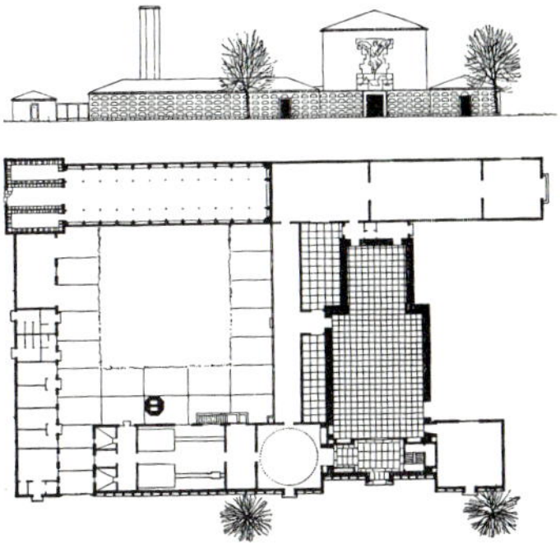

1:1500

H127

Enghave Park *

Enghave Plads Vesterbro
1929

Client: Copenhagen Municipality
Architect: Poul Holsøe
Landscape architect: Valdemar Fabricius Hansen, Copenhagen Municipal Park Department

Enghave park is one of the few parks in the Vesterbro quarter and it satisfies a great need in the densely populated area. The park is a beautiful example of neoclassicistic landscape gardening. It is 200 x 200 meters in size and the almost square area is subdivided by a simple series of alleys originally lined with elm trees. The alleys are clearly defined outwardly as a wall of leaves, and from within they create six spaces, each with a special function: water garden, perennial garden, rose garden, assembly area with a bandstand, ball park and a playground. The wading pool on the main axis was established in the late forties. Near the entrance is Kai Nielsen's sculpture "Eva with child" standing in the middle of a fine, graveled space that gathers visitors and filters them in and out of the park.
The water areas in the park offer possibilities for play as well as contemplation, and are especially refreshing in an urban area with much paving and far from the beach and sea.
The perennial garden is formally organized with long, wide borders and lush with plants like phlox, black-eyed Susans and monkshood.

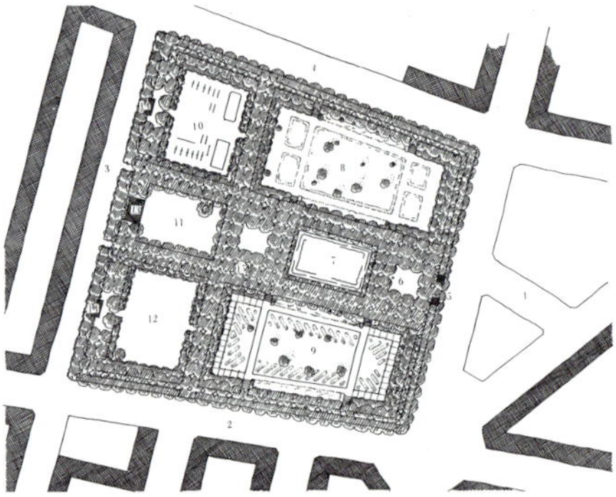

1:6000

Zoological Gardens

Roskildevej 32, Frederiksberg
1859, 1930's, 1980's

Client: Zoological Gardens
Architect: Fritz Schlegel, Edvard Thomsen, Dall & Lindhardtsen
Landscape architect: G.N. Brandt, Andreas Bruun

The Zoological Gardens were founded in 1859. During the 1930's, G.N. Brandt and architect Edvard Thomsen did a comprehensive plan for the area and a number of projects were carried out. This included a large bird pond with two islands behind the tower, an oval observation island and a square green island with butterbur. On the west bank of the bird pond, a large green was made and a flamingo complex with shallow pools and thatched roof houses for the birds. In the 1980's, Andreas Bruun designed several areas where the animals can be seen in more natural surroundings. This included the lion pit, penguin pool, rhinoceros yard, monkey jungle and a butterfly building. The entire area was renovated and the gardenlike character was strengthened, including a new flower bed in the central garden. The architect office of Dall & Lindhardtsen designed the new buildings for the apes, rhinoceros, antilopes and the children's zoo during this period.
Bibliography: Arkitektur DK 1991, 50, Landskab 1984, 169

H133

The brown * and the white Kødby

Halmtorvet, Vesterbro
Øksnehallen: 1901, The white Kødby: 1931-34

Client: Copenhagen Municipality
Architect: The Øksnehal: Ludvig Peter Fenger, The white Kødby: Municipal architect Poul F. Holsøe

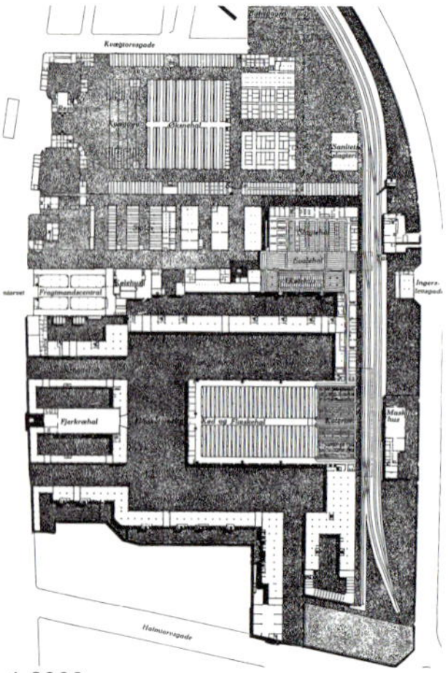

1:9000

Copenhagen's cattle market was established in 1874-79 and was in function until 1962. The market was a slaughterhouse area and is also called "The brown Kødby" or central meat yard. Among its reddish-brown brick buildings is the "Øksnehal" or the oxen hall, where cattle were traded. It is a large and finely detailed structure of cast iron and timber. It was recently renovated and now functions as an urban ecological center. To the southwest is "the white Kødby", which assumed most of the functions previously carried out at "the brown", and still houses meat product companies. Its clear, white cubistic form idiom signals functionalism's message of health and hygiene. It represented a rare agreement between form and content, and is thus one of the most genuine examples of a functionalistic industrial building.

Valby Park *

Hammelstrupvej, Valby
1937-1950, 1964, 1995-97

Client: Copenhagen Municipality
Landscape architect: Jacob Bergmann, Copenhagen Municipal Park Department

In the southwestern area of Copenhagen, at the end of the thirties, work was started on a large continuous park complex on low-lying areas filled with refuse from the city. Work on the park has been in progress for several decades as the original park areas were ransacked by coke scavengers during the fuel shortages. The border hedges frame large grassy areas, and the park contains ball fields, playgrounds, tract gardens as well as perennial gardens and a large circular rose bed from 1964. The outer circle has a seven meter wide border of wild roses followed by polyantha roses. In the center, within a low hornbeam hedge, there are low roses and creeping roses. There are a total of 12,000 different types of roses here. Valby Park is now undergoing an extensive renovation. A kilometer long diagonal alley of Lombardy poplars radiates from the entrance plaza at Hammelstrupvej road, touches the rose garden and the 17 new theme gardens and terminates at Kalvebod Strand.
Bibliography: Havekunst 1940, 122

1:5000

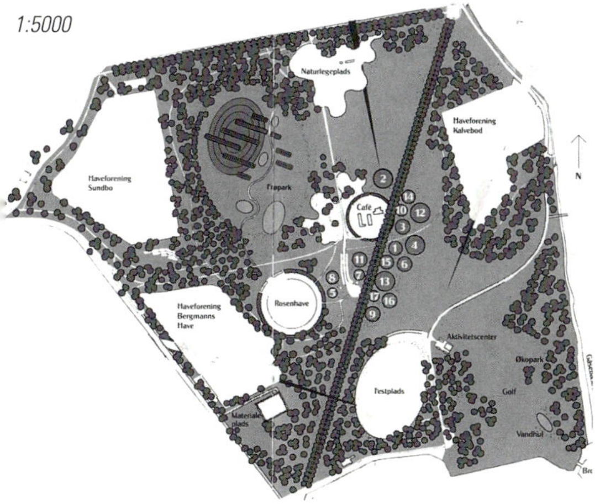

H185 **F.L. Smidth & Co. headquarters**

Vigerslev Allé 77, Valby
1952-57

Client: F.L. Smidth & Co.
Architect: Palle Suenson
Landscape architect: C.Th. Sørensen

While modernism dominated the light facade expression in steel and glass, this building was designed as a deliberate contrast. The dark red brickwork of specially made Flensborg brick stands direct and fast on the site, and the closely spaced, narrow brick columns form a powerful vertical effect. The columns also have a sun screening effect in combination with the recessed bronze windows. The eight-story building houses drafting rooms, the four-story building has offices and the two-story building contains the administrative offices. The latter two have recessed top floors with thin, flat copper roofs, which reinforce the impeccable elegance of the scheme.
Bibliography: Arkitektur DK 1958, 37

1:3000

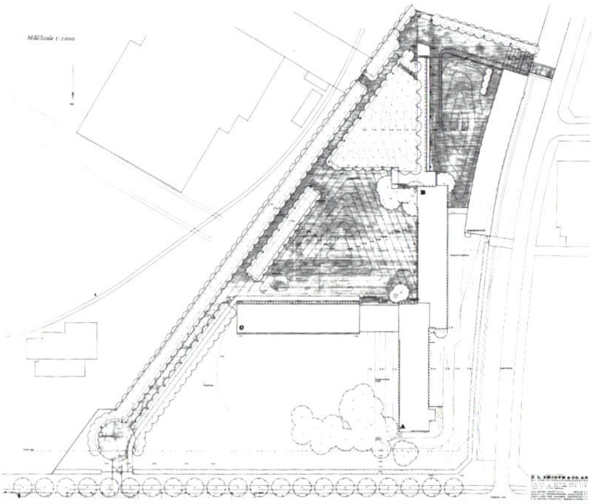

The Solbakken student residence hall **H192**

Rektorparken 12-24, Copenhagen SV
1954-56

Client: Private institution administered by the Society of Social Housing, FSB
Architect: Ole Buhl and Harald Petersen

The two architects worked at the same time with this student residence building and the high-rise housing towers at Bellahøj, which were considered to be Denmark's first skyscrapers. Apart from the height, the two projects are quite different. The Bellahøj housing consists of tower blocks, while the student residence building is a wing. What both schemes have in common is the large unbuilt areas for recreative purposes, in this case, the Rektor Park, which was originally part of the gardens surrounding Otto Mønsted's villa. The residence hall has an architecturally pronounced structuralistic, skeletonlike appearance due to the many small protruding balconies and the freestanding elevator towers. The twelve-story building has 140 units, primarily two-rooms, and there are several child care institutions.

H235

Garvergården, Vesterbro

The block formed by Saxogade, Matthæusgade, Dannebrogsgade; Vesterbro
1976-77

Client: The Society of Social Housing, FSB
Architect: Hauge & Kornerup-Bang represented by Gunnar Sørensen and Carsten Juel-Christiansen
Landscape architect: Agnete Muusfeldt

The scheme lies on the so-called Hudegrund property, which is about as wide as the long, narrow city blocks in this area of Vesterbro. The shape of the site has generated a different and spacious housing block form, which satisfies the scheme's varied usage: housing for the elderly, day center, nursing home, day-care centers, youth clubs, a social center and youth pension. The building provides a setting for a large and complex social work activity in the neighborhood, and this complexity is reflected in the architecture. The scheme is divided in smaller street buildings, which have different appearances due to the varied facade patterns, and different, clear colors. The facades facing the courtyard are even more varied with protruding bays and terraces. The building demonstrated a new direction for a socially and form conscious urban renewal.

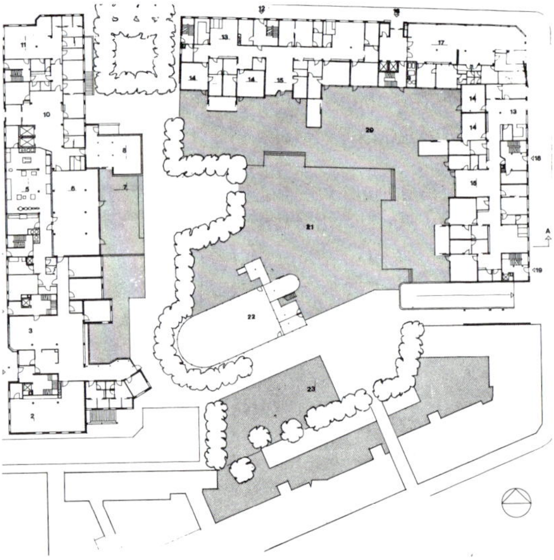

1:1500

Porthuset housing block H276

Vesterbrogade 126-132, Vesterbro
1991

Client: Copenhagen Social Housing Association KSB
Architect: Ib and Jørgen Rasmussen

A fire left a gaping hole in the city block, and the new infill housing replaced four former buildings. Thus the new building is longer than the normal width in the local urban pattern, but the vertical effect produced by the balconies on the street facade, and the large portal, counteract the sense of length. An adaption to the place was achieved by giving the 36 units direct access from the street instead of the courtyard, as is often the case in new housing schemes. Another feature is the orientation of the living rooms to the street. Noise problems were reduced with specially designed windows and doors. The building is a qualified solution for a large infill housing project.

Vesterbro Urban Renewal H280

The block formed by Sønder Boulevard, Ny Carlsberg Vej, Haderslevgade, Vesterbro
1993

Client: Copenhagen Municipality and the Copenhagen Urban Renewal Association
Architect: Box 25 Arkitekter

This urban renewal project involved the three municipal housing properties on the site, but the concept employed can be used with the remaining buildings. The renovated buildings contain units of varying size, which is reflected by the new additions toward the courtyard. The new towerlike buildings have primarily glass facades and contain new bathrooms, balconies and an elevator to the units for the elderly. The variations in the size and form of the additions give a life and sculptural effect to the facades facing the courtyard, which will be renovated in connection with the establishment of the ground floor common areas.
Bibliography: Arkitektur DK 1993, 369

H281

A housing renovation

Dannebrogsgade 18, Vesterbro
1992

Client: Copenhagen Urban Renewal Association
Architect: Boje Lundgaard and Lene Tranberg

This renovated building is part of a renewal scheme for the entire block between Dannebrogsgade street and Westend. The street facade toward east has been renovated so that the original appearance was maintained. However, the west facade was radically altered and completely sided with glass. The new climate shield is an independent structure, which has enlarged the units behind and also serves as a passive solar collector. The entire western roof surface is covered with solar collectors that supplement the building and its neighbor's hot water supply. Through the glass facade, one can sense the proportions of the building's heavy brickwork that now serves as a heat sink for accumulated solar energy. The new facade is built of thin, graphite-grey-painted steel sections, and this color matches the color of the glass in daylight. The fine proportioning and refined details give the new facade an elegant lightness, which offers an architectural lift for urban renewal in Vesterbro.
Bibliography: Arkitektur DK 1993, 264

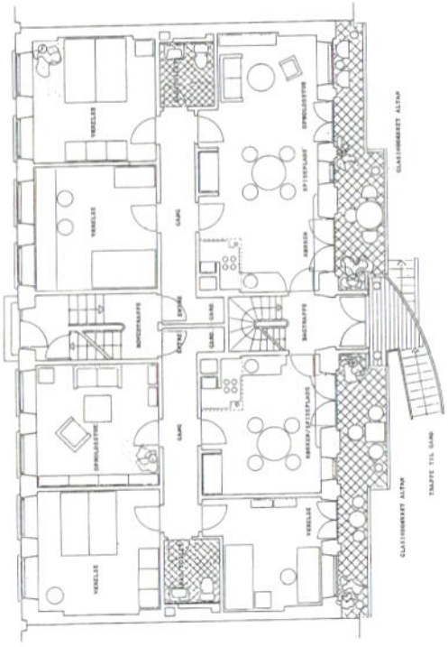

1:400

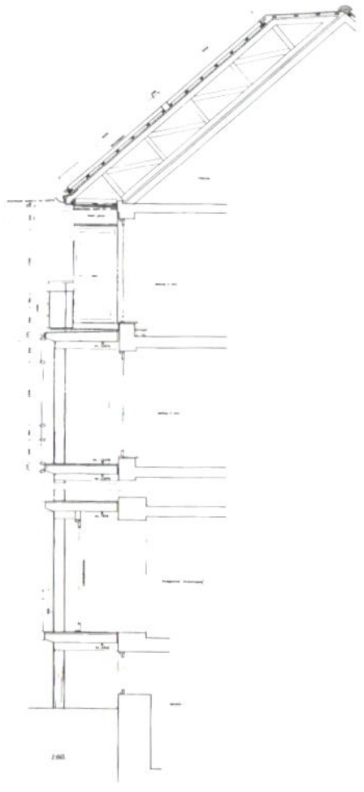

1:200

Skydebanegade renovation — H286

Skydebanegade, Vesterbro
1891-93, renovation 1994-96

Client: original building: Contractor Victor Jensen. Renovation: AB Skydebanen and the Copenhagen Urban Renewal Association
Architect: original building: Oscar Kramp. Renovation: O. Abildhauge A/S

The right-angled building rows along Skydebanegade street are an exuberant urban housing form with a curious abundance of decorations. The facades and roofs bulge with details in the brickwork, stucco and zinc, which are all executed with great care. This richness in detailing is also present in the main features of the buildings such as the outward corners, which are marked by elaborate towers. The street facade could be an illustration in Herman Bang's novel of the period, "Stucco". The renovation of the buildings on the east side of the street raises the 165 units and 15 commercial properties to a contemporary standard, while many of the exterior details have been restored to their original form and color.

Typical Vesterbro apartment house — H287

Gasværksvej 31, Vesterbro
1867-68 (urban renewal 1995)

Client: Master carpenter C.A. Kyhn
Architect: Unknown

This building is a typical example of the high-quality housing that is characteristic of most of the Vesterbro quarter's older buildings. The stuccoed basement and ground floor facades, together with the smooth, and in this case yellow brick, upper facades are a familiar motif on many streets in Vesterbro. The building is well-proportioned with simple, classical details such as the protruding end bays and the molded cornices. However, the more recent shop signage mars the ground floor facade. The typical Danish 4-framed windows round off the impression of a building that was built in accord with the solid building tradition of the time and the prevailing classic and historical form ideals. Buildings like this are considered worthy of preservation in Vesterbro's urban renewal plans.
Bibliography: Copenhagen Municipality: Bygningsregistrant Vesterbro

H290

Housing improvements, Kgs. Enghave

The block formed by Borgbjergvej, Peter Sabroesgade, Sydhavnsgade; Copenhagen SV
1994

Client: The Workers Cooperative Building Association, AKB and the Copenhagen Urban Renewal Association
Architect: Tegnestuen Domus Aps
Landscape architect: Domus

The triangular housing block consists of buildings built in the 1920's. The project for their renewal won first prize in the 1990, Housing Ministry's competition "Future Urban Renewal". On the courtyard facade, 12 towers were built in front of the rear stairs on the four upper floors. This has given the two- and three-room units new bathrooms and a new balcony/greenhouse in front of the modernized kitchens. The renovation also includes several ecological measures like solar collectors on the new roofs, water saving fixtures and rainwater purification in the gardens. The column supported towers are clearly separated from the old facades by a sober design in which the joints between the prefabricated concrete elements have a decorative effect.
Bibliography: Arkitektur DK 1995, 160

1:200

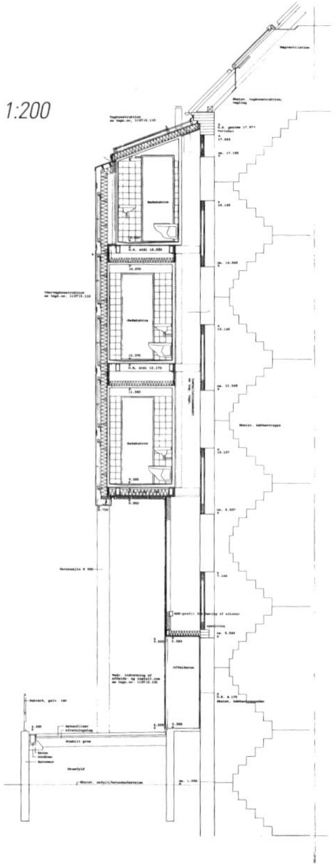

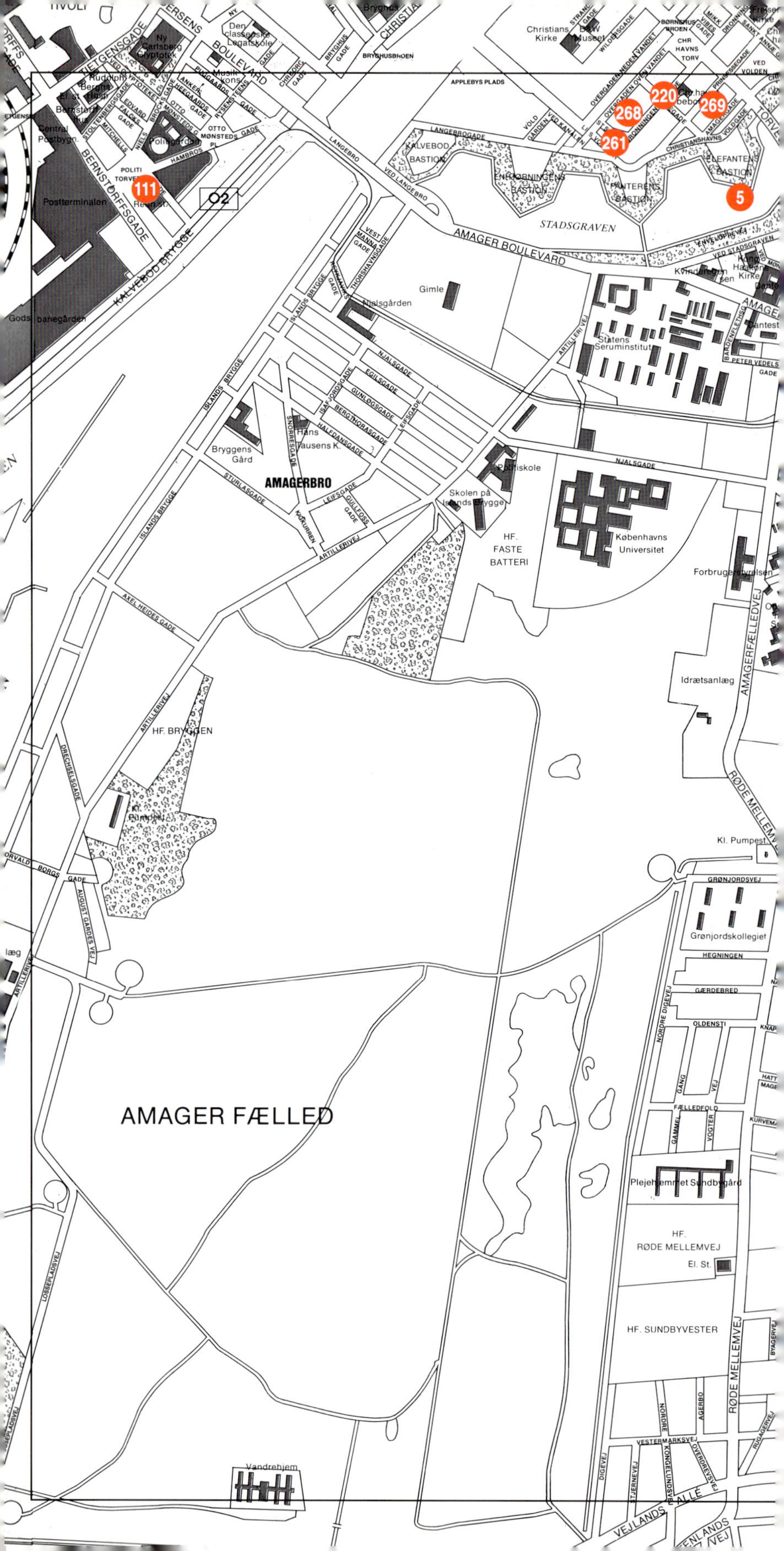

AMAGER FÆLLED
AMAGERBRO
AMAGER BOULEVARD
STADSGRAVEN
KALVEBOD BASTION
ENHJØRNINGENS BASTION
PANTERENS BASTION
ELEFANTENS BASTION
LANGEBRO
LANGEBROGADE
VED LANGEBRO
APPLEBYS PLADS
BRYGHUSBROEN
Christians Kirke
B&W Museet
Ny Carlsberg Glyptotek
Politigården
POLITI TORVET
Postterminalen
Central Postbygn.
Godsbanegården
KALVEBOD BRYGGE
BERNSTORFFSGADE
HAMBROS GADE
Gimle
Njalsgården
NJALSGADE
EGILSGADE
GUNLØGSGADE
BERGTHORASGADE
HALFDANSGADE
LEIFSGADE
ISLANDS BRYGGE
STURLASGADE
SNORRESGADE
Bryggens Gård
Hans Tausens K.
Politiskole
Skolen på Islands Brygge
HF. FASTE BATTERI
Københavns Universitet
Statens Seruminstitut
ARTILLERIVEJ
AXEL HEIDES GADE
Forbrugerstyrelsen
Idrætsanlæg
AMAGERFÆLLEDVEJ
RØDE MELLEMVEJ
Kl. Pumpest.
HF. BRYGGEN
Kl. Pumpest.
DRECHSELSGADE
AUGUST GARDES VEJ
GRØNJORDSVEJ
Grønjordskollegiet
HEGNINGEN
GÆRDEBRED
OLDENSTI
NØRRE DIGEVEJ
FÆLLEDFOLD
Plejehjemmet Sundbygård
HF. RØDE MELLEMVEJ
El. St.
HF. SUNDBYVESTER
VESTERMARKSVEJ
DIGEVEJ
STJERNEVEJ
VEJLANDS ALLÉ
LOSSEPLADSVEJ
Vandrehjem
O2
111
220
261
268
269
5

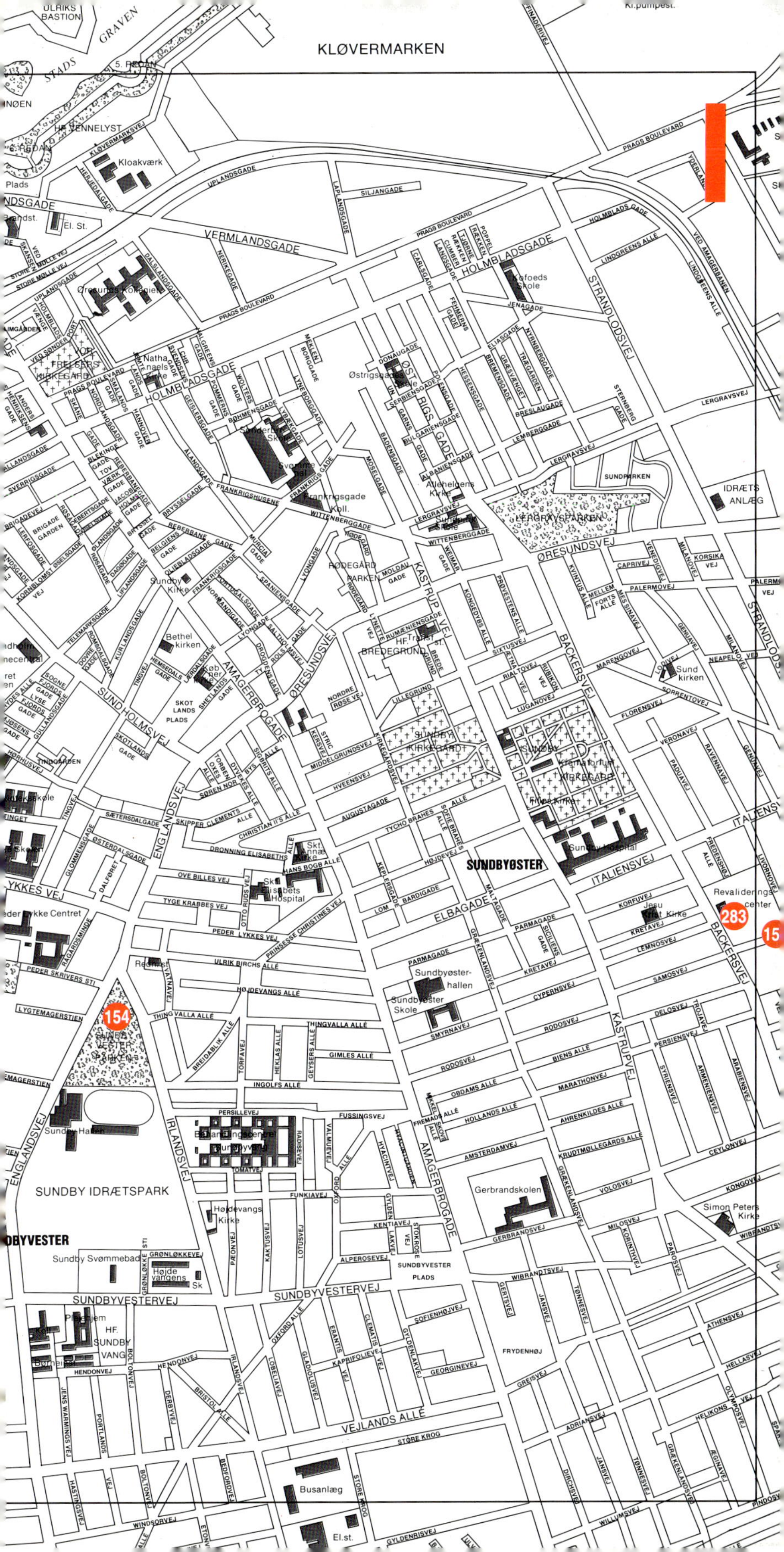

KLØVERMARKEN
ULRIKS BASTION
STADS GRAVEN
5. REDAN
HF. VENNELYST
Kloakværk
KLØVERMARKSVEJ
UPLANDSGADE
LAPLANDSGADE
SILJANGADE
PRAGS BOULEVARD
VERMLANDSGADE
HOLMBLADSGADE
LINDGREENS ALLÉ
STRANDLODSVEJ
VED AMAGERBANEN
Øresunds Kollegiet
Kofoeds Skole
JENAGADE
VOR FRELSERS KIRKEGÅRD
Østrigsgades Skole
LERGRAVSVEJ
SUNDPARKEN
IDRÆTS ANLÆG
LERGRAVSPARKEN
Sønderbro Skole
Frankrigsgade Koll.
WITTENBERGGADE
Allehelgens Kirke
ØRESUNDSVEJ
RØDEGÅRD PARKEN
KASTRUP VEJ
BACKERSVEJ
Sundby Kirke
Bethel kirken
AMAGERBROGADE
HF. BREDEGRUND
Sund kirken
SUNDHOLMSVEJ
SKOT LANDS PLADS
SUNDBY KIRKEGÅRD
Krematorium KIRKEGÅRD
Sundby Hospital
ITALIENSVEJ
SUNDBYØSTER
ELBAGADE
Skt. Annæ Kirke
Skt. Elisabets Hospital
Peder Lykke Centret
PEDER LYKKES VEJ
ENGLANDSVEJ
Revaliderings center
Jesu Krist Kirke
283
15
Sundbyøster-hallen
Sundbyøster Skole
154
SUNDBY VESTER PARKEN
Sundby Hallen
IRLANDSVEJ
Behandlingscentret Sundbyvang
SUNDBY IDRÆTSPARK
Gerbrandskolen
Simon Peters Kirke
Højdevangs Kirke
SUNDBYVESTER
Sundby Svømmebad
SUNDBYVESTERVEJ
SUNDBYVESTER PLADS
HF. SUNDBY VANG
FRYDENHØJ
VEJLANDS ALLÉ
STORE KROG
Busanlæg
El.st.

The Christianshavn embankments * I5

Christianshavn
1618-25, 1915-30

Client: Christian IV
Landscape architect: Christian IV, Valdemar E. Erstad-Jørgensen, Copenhagen Municipal Park Department

The Christianshavn embankments run from Langebro along the City Moat out to the Øresund Strait. Originally there were ten distinctive bastions on the Christianshavn side and six smaller ones on the Amager side. The embankment complex was established by Christian IV. In the beginning it was shorter, lower and less extensive. During the 1660's and 1720's it was enlarged to its present form. At the end of the last century, various areas of the embankments were dismantled as they no longer had a military significance. In the years that followed, the complex lay in a state of neglect. After an initiative in 1913 by the Society for Copenhagen's Improvement, and the establishment of the Committee for the Preservation of the Copenhagen Embankments in 1916, Copenhagen Municipality took over the care and renovation of a major part of the Christianshavn embankments. During the 1930's, the area on the Amager side was regulated and gradually opened to the public. Directly adjacent to this area lies the Vennelyst Tract Garden Society with its small garden plots and picturesque summerhouses.

I111

The Police Main Headquarters *

Polititorvet, Indre By
1918-24

Client: Copenhagen Municipality
Architect: Hack Kampmann, Hans Jørgen Kampmann, Aage Rafn and Holger Jacobsen

Gloomy solemnity and geometric formality pervade this large building complex, from the whole down to the smallest detail, and express the building's function while representing a concentrate of the formal and pathetic in neoclassicism. However the Police Headquarters is still an exciting work of architecture because the artistic consistency and care, especially in the interior, transforms the gloom to a masterly play of forms, color and refined details. The 45-meter diameter circular courtyard has a visual force as a light-giving atrium in the massive building form, and the powerful facade cornices emphasize the horizontality. In the smaller, square court opposite the main entrance, verticality is emphasized by eight enormous columns that support a coffered ceiling with an opening for a faint daylighting on the high niche with Einar Utzon-Frank's sculpture "The Serpent Killer". Contrasts and pathos are the major effects in this muscular architectural work, which is a monument to the most theatrical features of neoclassicism.

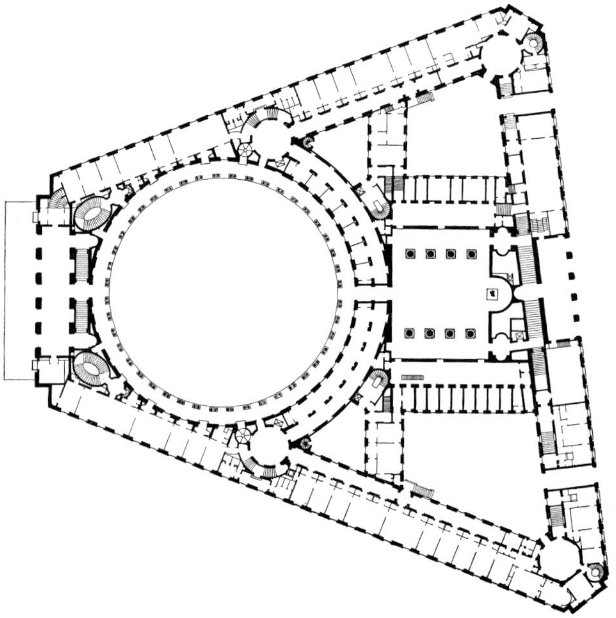

1:1500

I150 **Skolen ved Sundet, school** *

Samosvej 50, Amager
1938

Client: Copenhagen Municipality
Architect: Kaj Gottlob

Functionalism's gospel of air and light as a source of health gave rise in the beginning to schools that lacked significant spatial qualities. At the Skolen ved Sundet school the gospel was freely interpreted and supplemented with decorations and forms other than quadratic. The central aula has a rectangular plan with elliptical balustrades and lantern. In addition, the linoleum floor in the aula depicts a map of Copenhagen, and the ceiling is decorated with a large compass card. At the neighboring school for delicate children, the classrooms are octagonal and their large windows form a continuous sculptural glass facade with the windows in the sleeping hall opposite. The scheme was an emancipated attempt to create festive school atmosphere.

1:1500

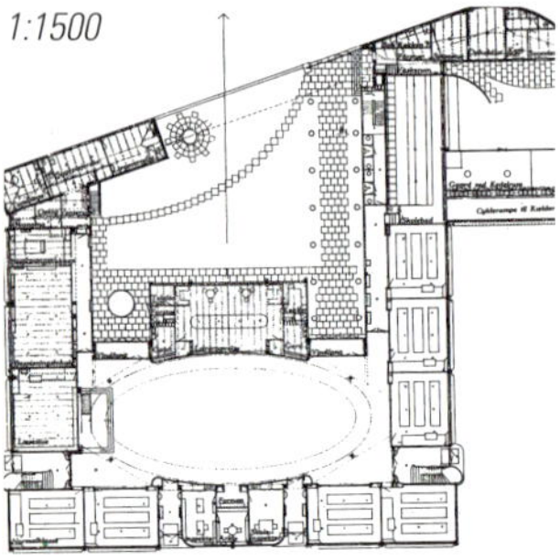

Sundbyvester Park * I154

1938-1940

Client: Copenhagen Municipality
Landscape architect: Jacob Bergmann, Copenhagen Municipal Park Department

This fine, unassuming park is designed primarily to satisfy the need for recreation, play and games. It is a result of the same park program employed at Bispeparken and Damhusengen. At the southern end of the triangular park there is a small playground with a wading and sailing pool as well as a shelter. Povl Søndergaard's granite sculpture, "the Sports Girl", is also located here. The lawn in the center is surrounded by a lush woodslike landscaping of birch, Scotch pine and larch with a border of yew and mountain currant. The surrounding roads are edged by distinctive rows of trees and Sundby Sports Center lies directly to the south.
Bibliography: Havekunst 1940, 109

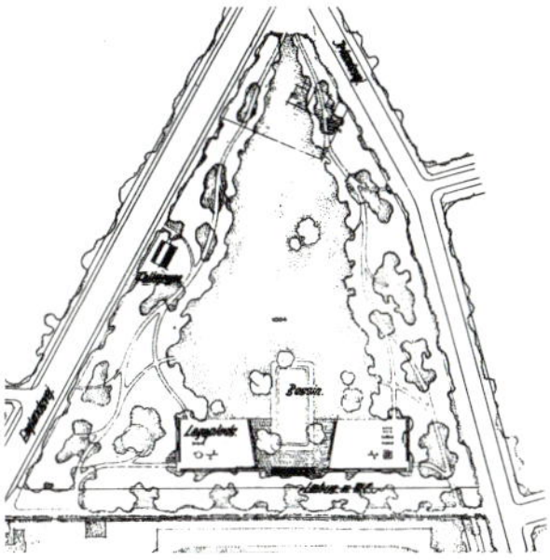

1:7500

Sofiegården I220

Sofiegade 1-7, Dronningensgade 43-49, Overgaden oven Vandet 32, Christianshavn
1970-72

Client: The Sofiegården private foundation
Architect: Box 25

For some years before this scheme was built, the buildings on the site were occupied by young housing activists. The clearing of the area in 1969 led to a dramatic confrontation between the local authorities and the activists. In hopes of achieving a physical and social integration in the quarter, the building was based on a matrix inspired by architecture theorist Christoffer Alexander. The courtyard with playgrounds on a raised plateau is connected to the surrounding streets by portals. The colorful facades with their animated window rhythm maintain the original structure of the neighborhood due to their size and proportions. Sofiegården has 144 units, most of them small, but supplemented with many common facilities and a day-care center.
Bibliography: Arkitekten 1973, 477

1261 **Courtyard renovation at Overgaden oven Vandet**
Overgaden oven Vandet, St. Søndervoldstræde, Dronningensgade, Sofiegade, Christianshavn
1980

Client: Copenhagen Municipality, A69
Landscape architect: Ginman, Harboe and Borup

The courtyard has a large, unifying center lawn with spread trees, and private zones with a gardenlike character adjacent to the housing units. The buildings have a variety of facade expressions and architectural qualities. The plan inspired many of the courtyard projects that followed. The "Blue Corner" was built later in the southern area of the site.
Bibliography: Landskab 1992, 178

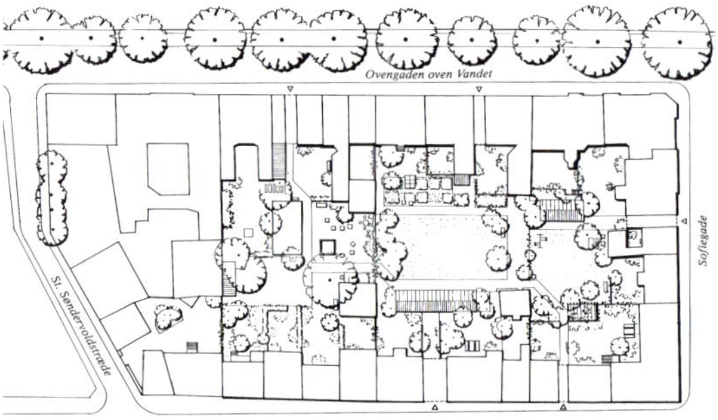

1:1000

1268 **The Blue Corner housing scheme**
1989
Dronningensgade, Store Søndervoldstræde, Christianshavn

Client: The Social Housing Society (FSB)
Architect: Tegnestuen Vandkunsten
Landscape architect: Tegnestuen Vandkunsten

This modest scheme offered a dynamic contribution, both in an architectural and housing political sense, to the local urban renewal debate. The two angular and separate buildings with their steep shed roofs, and white brickwork combined with bright blue metal siding, stand out in every way from the neighboring buildings. Regardless of this, with their scale and cheerfulness, they possess a special "Christianshavn character". The minimal free areas are a result of the large common courtyard behind the neighboring building on Dronningensgade street. The 420 sqm scheme has only six apartments, and it represented a new tendency for housing associations to support small projects. The urban renewal details had now become a subject for public housing.
Bibliography: Arkitektur DK 1994, 236

The Prinsessegade courtyard scheme I269
Prinsessegade, Sofiegade, Amagergade, Torvegade,
Christianshavn
1991

Client: SBS Byfornyelse
Landscape architect: J. Palle Schmidt and Gerd Wiboe

The scheme is an example of a courtyard renovation, which is varied with small, individual gardens and a large common recreational area, while still maintaining a unified, relaxed architectural expression. Through the skillful use of trees, creepers on light fences, flowering bushes and perennials, a high degree of diversity and lushness was achieved.

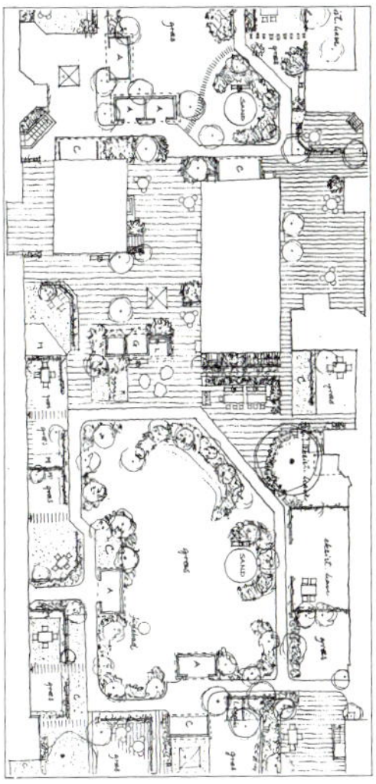

Livornoparken housing for the elderly I283
Livornovej 10-128, Amager
1991-92

Client: The Federation of Housing Associations SAB
Architect: Bornebusch Tegnestue A/S
Landscape architect: Ginman, Harboe and Borup

The perimeter buildings along the streets consist of 31 single-story row houses. The three, two-story blocks in the center of the scheme have 48 units. All the apartments have two rooms, and the units in the upper floor of the blocks are reached from elevators and balcony corridors. These two familiar housing types are combined in a lively, visual whole, in which the facades sided with panels and vertical trellises give the buildings a light and summerish expression. In the courtyards formed by the blocks there is a more consistent lush atmosphere. The scheme has common facilities and a home nursing center adjacent to the main entrance.

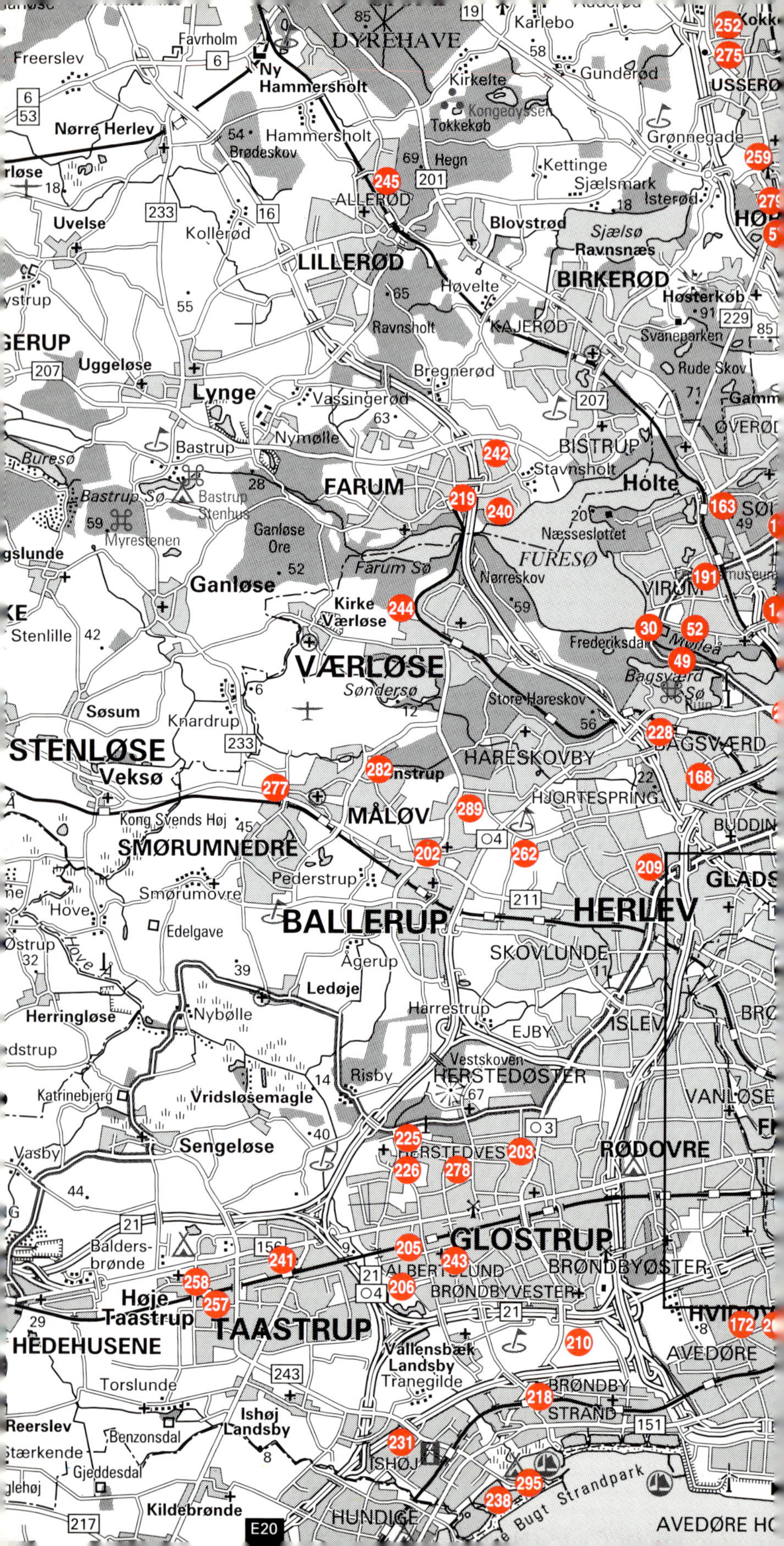
Favrholm
Freerslev
DYREHAVE
Karlebo
Ny Hammersholt
Kirkelte
Kongedyssen
Gunderød
USSERØ
Nørre Herlev
Hammersholt
Brødeskov
Tokkekøb
Hegn
Grønnegade
Kettinge
Sjælsmark
Isterød
ALLERØD
Uvelse
Kollerød
Blovstrød
Sjælsø
Ravnsnæs
LILLERØD
Høvelte
BIRKERØD
Høsterkøb
Ravnsholt
KAJERØD
Svaneparken
Rude Skov
Uggeløse
Bregnerød
Lynge
Vassingerød
ØVERØD
Nymølle
Bastrup
BISTRUP
Stavnsholt
Buresø
FARUM
Holte
Bastrup Sø
Bastrup Stenhus
Myrestenen
Ganløse Ore
Næsseslottet
FURESØ
Farum Sø
Nørreskov
Ganløse
VIRUM
Kirke Værløse
Stenlille
Frederiksdal
Mølleå
VÆRLØSE
Søndersø
Bagsværd Sø
Søsum
Knardrup
Store Hareskov
STENLØSE
Veksø
HARESKOVBY
MÅLØV
HJORTESPRING
Kong Svends Høj
SMØRUMNEDRE
BUDDIN
Pederstrup
GLADS
Smørumovre
Hove
Edelgave
BALLERUP
HERLEV
SKOVLUNDE
Østrup
Ågerup
Ledøje
Nybølle
Harrestrup
EJBY
ISLEV
Herringløse
Vestskoven
HERSTEDØSTER
Risby
VANLØSE
Katrinebjerg
Vridsløsemagle
Sengeløse
RØDOVRE
HERSTEDVESTER
Vasby
GLOSTRUP
Balders-brønde
ALBERTSLUND
BRØNDBYØSTER
Høje Taastrup
BRØNDBYVESTER
TAASTRUP
HEDEHUSENE
Vallensbæk Landsby
Tranegilde
AVEDØRE
Torslunde
BRØNDBY STRAND
Reerslev
Ishøj Landsby
Benzonsdal
Stærkende
Gjeddesdal
ISHØJ
Kildebrønde
HUNDIGE
Køge Bugt Strandpark
AVEDØRE HO
E20

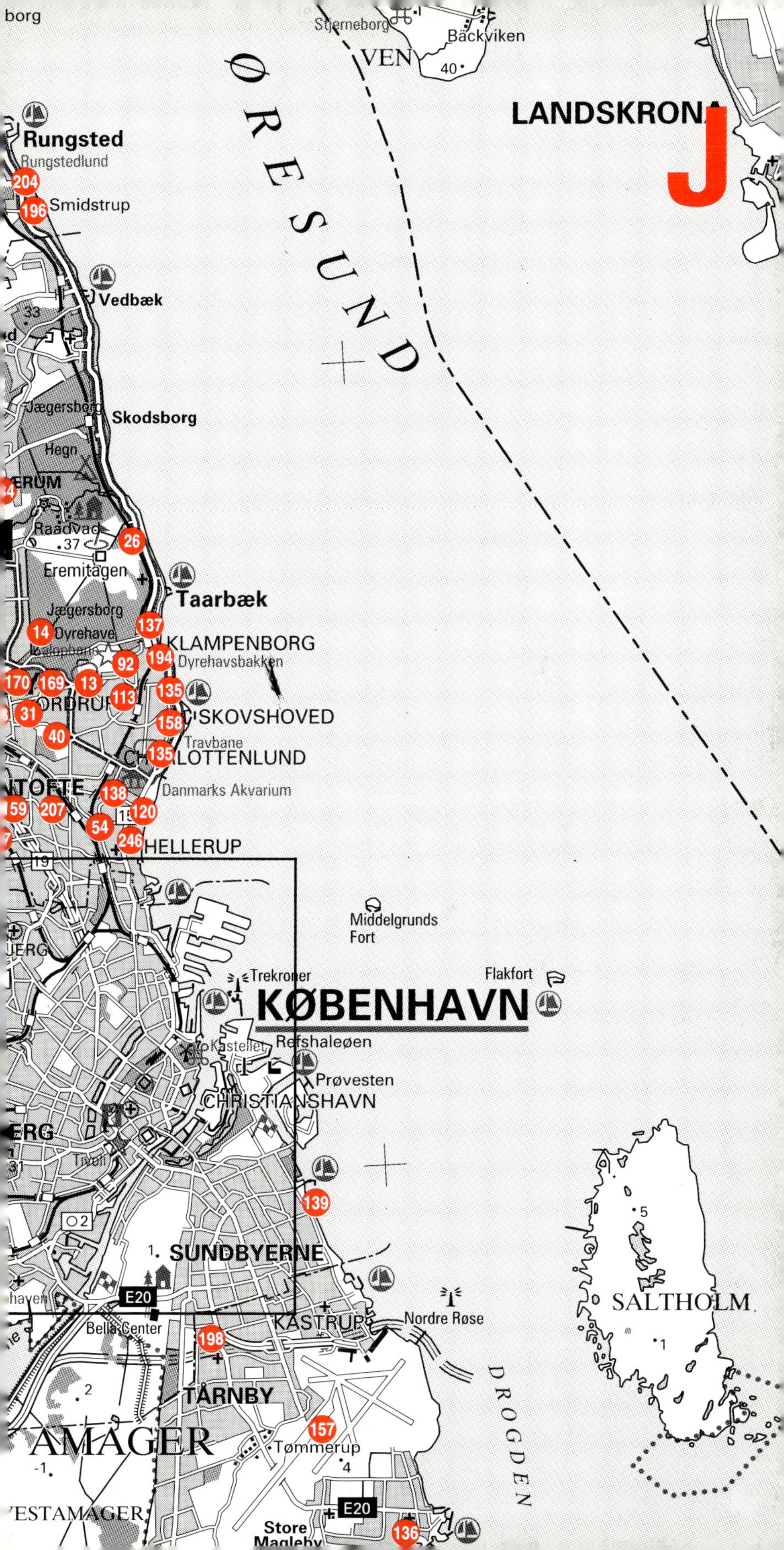

Stjerneborg
Bäckviken
VEN
40
LANDSKRONA
J
ØRESUND
Rungsted
Rungstedlund
204
196
Smidstrup
Vedbæk
33
Jægersborg
Skodsborg
Hegn
ERUM
Raadvad
.37
26
Eremitagen
Taarbæk
Jægersborg
14
Dyrehave
137
KLAMPENBORG
92
194
Dyrehavsbakken
170
169
13
113
135
SKOVSHOVED
31
158
40
Travbane
135
CHARLOTTENLUND
TOFTE
138
Danmarks Akvarium
159
207
120
54
246
HELLERUP
19
Middelgrunds
Fort
Trekroner
Flakfort
KØBENHAVN
Kastellet
Refshaleøen
Prøvesten
CHRISTIANSHAVN
ERG
Tivoli
139
O2
5
1
SUNDBYERNE
E20
SALTHOLM
Bella Center
KASTRUP
Nordre Røse
198
1
2
TÅRNBY
DROGDEN
AMAGER
157
Tømmerup
-1
4
VESTAMAGER
E20
Store
Magleby
136

J12

Frilandsmuseet, open-air museum

Kongevejen 100, Lyngby
1650-1850, 1960-62, 1901-

Client: The National Museum
Landscape architect: C.Th. Sørensen with Ole Nørgård and I.P. Junggreen Have

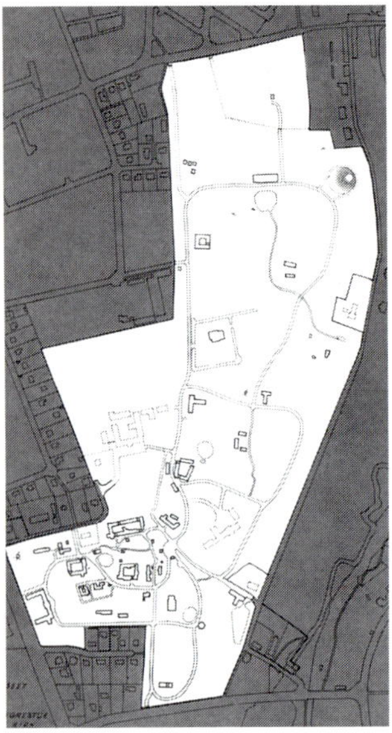

The purpose of the museum is to illustrate historical rural life. This is done by exhibiting old buildings and their furnishings, which relate life in the past in different regions and different social classes. The museum's 90 acres now include 40 buildings from both Denmark, The Faroe Islands, south Slesvig and southern Sweden. The museum was started in 1901 on private initiative, and in 1920 became a department of the National Museum. The old rural buildings have been relocated from the areas they were originally built and meticulously reconstructed with the original materials. Attempts have also been made to recreate the special character of the home region in the way the buildings are placed in the landscape. Therefore, the museum is an important archive for old Danish building methods from the mid 1600's to the mid 1800's. The old utensils and furniture in many of the buildings offer an insight into the rural living culture during the period when Denmark was primarily an agricultural nation. The Frilands museum also attempts to recreate the older cultural landscape by implying the field divisions with various kinds of fences and walls such as wattle. With the mid- and west Jutland buildings there are heather meadows. The roads are also historical with road change stones, bordered with the roadside flora. The landscape gardening of the various periods, with respect for the peasant class conditions, is represented by occasional small farm gardens with mignonette, lavender, boxwood and hops. An amphitheater was built during the 1960's for meetings and folk dance displays.

J14

Jægersborg Dyrehave park *, Ermelund

From Klampenborg and c. 6 km north along the Øresund coast
1670

Client: Frederik III, Christian V

Dyrehaven park is an area of more than 2500 acres with red deer, fallow deer and sika deer. There is access through 13 red gates for pedestrians, bicyclists and horseback riders. The park is fenced in due to the animals. It was Frederik III, who in 1670 established the area as a hunting ground for his son Christian V, who later enlarged it. Dyrehaven consists of open fields and dense groups of oak, beech and hawthorn. A characteristic feature is that the bottoms of the tree crowns are all horizontally trimmed by the deer feeding on their leaves. The German forester, Johann G. von Lange, who came to Denmark in the 1760's, introduced new mixtures of trees and new methods of management, and many of Dyrehaven's old, beautiful trees still reflect his efforts. Architect Johs. Magdahl Nielsen, first during this century, created the many beautiful feeding stations for the game, and several of Dyrehaven's gamekeeper houses, such as that at Raadvad and the rebuilding of Peter Lieps Hus forest restaurant. Dyrehaven also contains the Bakken amusement park from 1830, as well as a golf course.
Ermelunden park, which borders on the southern edge of Dyrehaven, is an old grazing area for the king's horses and cattle. Today it is still an open grazing landscape for horses.

J26

Eremitage manor *

Dyrehaven, Eremitagesletten
1734-36

Client: The national government
Architect: Lauritz de Thurah

This small hunting manor was built at the same time as Christiansborg palace in Copenhagen, and in contrast to that larger project, Thurah created an atmosphere of secluded, majestic tranquillity. The building's location at the top of the sloping Eremitage plain makes it well suited as a landmark in the scenic landscape. From the large windows on the piano nobile, there is a fantastic view across the plain to the Øresund strait. The facades have a German baroque character, richly decorated with ornaments and figures including a relief bust of Christian VI. The interiors were furnished in the greatest baroque splendor, which is evident in the well-preserved dining room with its imitation marble columns, gilded stucco and inlaid mirrors on the walls and ceiling. Originally there was a so-called "taffel machine" here – a dumbwaiter with a silver tray that could be raised up through a hole in the dining table from the basement kitchen. Thus the guests could dine and party free of inquisitive servants. In French this is known as an eremitage – hence the manor's name. An extensive renovation was completed in 1991.

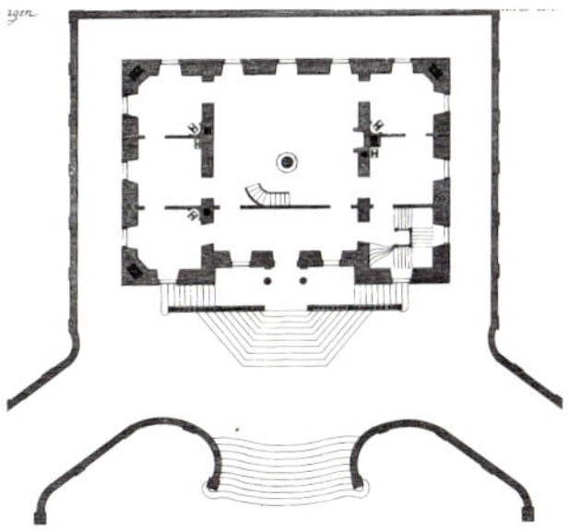

1:750

J30

Frederiksdal *

Hummeltoftevej 181-189, Virum
1744-45

Client: Count Johan Sigismund Schulin
Architect: Nicolai Eigtved and J.G. Rosenberg

The original building on the site was a hunting manor from the 1600's, which Christian VI gave to count Schulin in 1739. The count had the now-existing Frederiksdal built as a "maison de plaisir" or a country estate from drawings by Eigtved. He furnished the one-story building with his characteristic roof type: the cocked hip roof with balustrades. In this form, the manor was a fine example of French inspired, Danish rococo. In 1752-53, after Eigtved's death, J.G. Rosenberg rebuilt the manor with a mansard roof, which destroyed much of its original beauty.

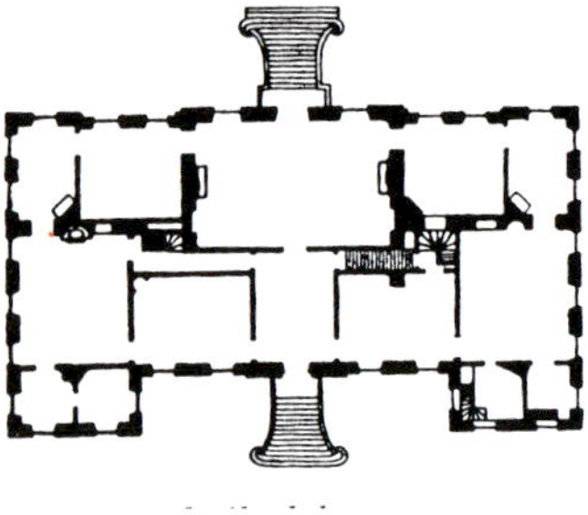

1:800

Schæffergården * J31

Ermelundsvej 105, Jægersborg
1747, several additions and changes, latest 1986-87

Client: The Danish-Norwegian Foundation and the Danish School of Administration
Architect: Diderich Schæffer, Kaare Klint, Palle Suenson, Wilhelm Wohlert, Skaarup & Jespersen
Landscape architect: Torben Michelsen

There was originally a cavalry stable for Jægersborg Manor on the site. A rebuilding project about 1755 by the owner, Court carpenter Diderich Schäffer gave it late baroque character. In 1920, Kaare Klint restored it to its original appearance. When the Danish Norwegian Foundation took over the building in 1949, the side wings were given an extra floor by architect Palle Suenson. An addition in 1972 toward east by Vilhelm Wohlert included a dining room. The latest rebuilding and addition projects were by Skaarup & Jespersen and include a new seminar wing and two new accommodation wings. The seminar center's extensive building complex offers glimpses of two centuries of architectural trends. Its white facades and red tile roof provide a typical Danish interplay with the park.
Bibliography: Arkitektur DK 1988, 172

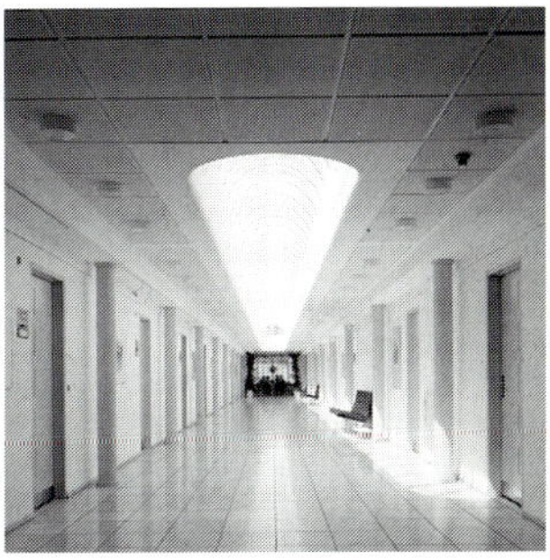

Addition by Skaarup & Jespersen, 1986-87

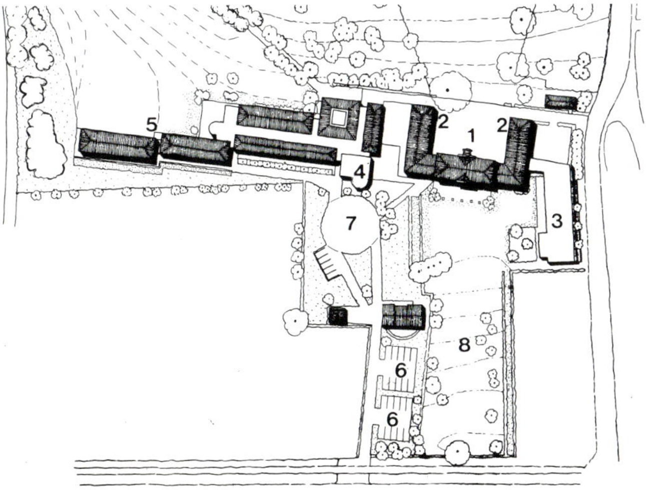

1:3000

Main building, 1747

J39

Gl. Holtegård *

Attemosevej 170, Søllerød
1756-57

Client: Lauritz de Thurah
Architect: Lauritz de Thurah

The white facades and black glazed tile, hipped roof give a graceful and light unity to this summer residence that architect Thurah built for himself. The formal baroque symmetry is consistently maintained throughout the scheme including the dormers and chimneys. However the low buildings give the scheme its rural simplicity in a fine interplay with the surrounding park. The property was purchased in 1900 by the wealthy merchant, H.N. Andersen who commissioned architect Gottfred Tvede to build a new farm building. The frontispiece facing the garden was added in this century. The entire scheme was renovated in 1979-82 and converted to an archives and exhibition building for Søllerød municipality by architect Jørgen Ott.

"Vedbæk find". Skeletons from the early stone age are the basis for the permanent exhibition
Exhibition architect: Inger Sogenfrei

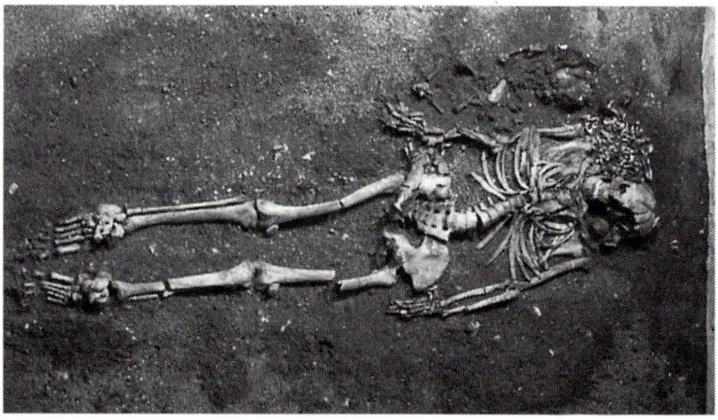

Bernstorff Manor * J40

Jægersborg Allé 91-101, Gentofte
1760-67

Client: Foreign Minister J.H.E. Bernstorff
Architect: Nicolas Henri-Jardin

The client only lived ten years in the palace and after his death in 1772 his nephew A.P. Bernstorff inherited the property. They both introduced reforms here that later inspired the grand agricultural reforms of the 1780's. The manor was one of N.H. Jardin's first works in Denmark in which rococo was replaced by a French inspired classicism. The clear, simple buildings are symmetrical in facade and plan, and the semicircular bay with its cupola roof facing the garden is a distinctive classicistic motif. In the early 1800's a mezzanine level was added under the cupola and the original roof balustrade was removed. The manor is now used by the civil defence. The park planned by A.P. Bernstorff is almost totally preserved.

The two original main-facades

J49 **Sophienholm ***

Nybrovej 401, Lyngby
1802-05, 1963-67, 1993

Client: Merchant Constantin Brun, Lyngby-Taarbæk Municipality
Architect: Joseph-Jacques Ramée
Landscape architect: Th. Holmskiold, Joseph Ramée, Sven-Ingvar Andersson

1:5000

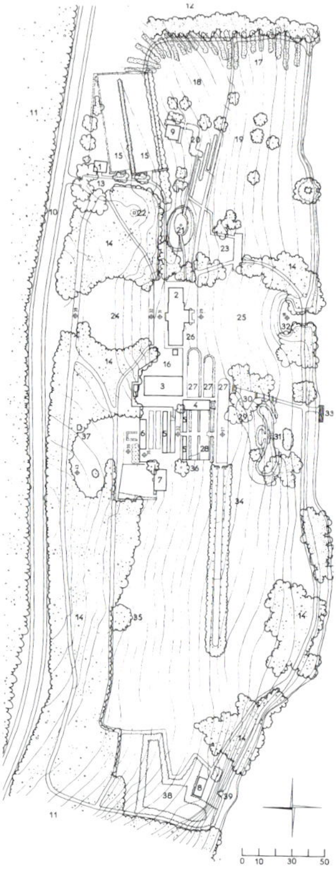

Sophienholm is the most imposing estate in the Bagsværd Sø lake area. During the period from 1807-35, merchant Brun's wife, Frederike held literary salons here with among others, Adam Oehlenschläger, Jens Baggesen and the Rahbeks. The main building has a formal, almost cubistic classicism with a low pitched roof. The symmetrical layout of the low guest and servant wings on either side of the tall main building is characteristic of Ramée. He was also responsible for the layout of the park with grottos, greenhouses and a Chinese summerhouse.

When Lyngby-Taarbæk municipality took over Sophienholm in 1963, Sven-Ingvar Andersson was commissioned to renovate the park in collaboration with the Park Director, S.A. Hansen, and to create a public park. The area is now used for exhibitions, concerts, park entertainment, and the municipal park department maintains an almost manor estate-like upkeep with fine flower beds, hotbeds, greenhouses and vegetable gardens.

Sophienholm Park lies on a 25 meter high south slope on Bagsværd Sø lake. The site is divided in three long areas. The location of the main building on the site is marked behind the building by a clearing in the beech forest. As a counterpart to this, there is a bowl shaped depression in front of the building with groups of trees.

A renovation during the 1960's added three new elements as "gardens" within the park, namely the terraces between the main building and the parade house, the yew area, and the parking lot. The yew formation surrounds a large sandstone urn, near the path of trimmed copper beeches. Other elements are the setpieces of hazel bushes along the path to the lake, the long perennial beds down the grassy slope, and the circular beds on the plateau. The exotic tree groups were supplemented with a group of tulip trees on the hill by the spring.

Near the "Norwegian House" on the edge of the lake, sculptor Hein Heinsen and landscape architect Torben Schønherr created the stair sculpture "The Mountain Climber" in 1993.

Bibliography: Steen Høyer, Annemarie Lund and Susanne Møldrup (ed.): Tilegnet Sven-Ingvar Andersson, Landskab 1992, 166

J52

Villa Spurveskjul *
Spurveskjul 4, Virum
1805

Client: Nicolai Abildgaard
Architect: Nicolai Abildgaard

Abildgaard was both painter and architect. For its time, this modest rural home with its thatched roof and trellis-work on the stuccoed walls was distinctive due to its fine proportions. The rural materials and details on a building that had classicistic features and proportions can seem unusual, but a typical feature of the classicism of this period was a passion for the primal ideals. C.F. Hansen worked with several projects for rural homes and cottages with thatched roofs. In the beginning of this century, Villa Spurveskjul inspired a number of neoclassicistic and functionalistic garden houses, with similar modest dimensions and simple architecture.

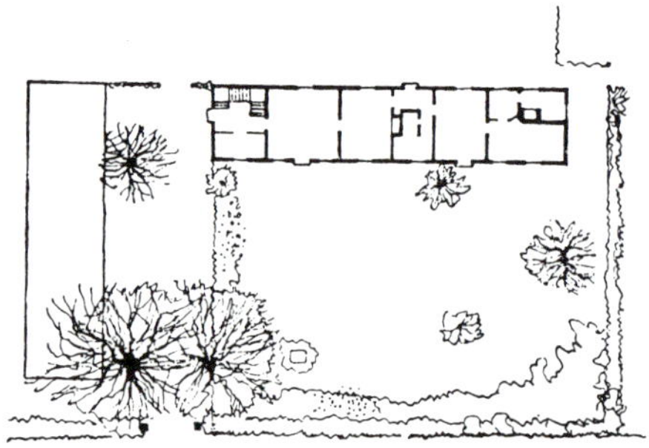

1:750

Øregård * **J54**

Ørehøj Allé 2, Hellerup
1806

Client: Merchant Johannes Søbøtker
Architect: Joseph-Jacques Ramée

This country house was characteristic of Ramée with its tall main building and lower side wings. The classicistic features, with the triangular pediment, window shutters and roofed veranda have a less formal expression than at Sophienholm, which was built several years earlier according to Ramée's drawings. The trees along Øregårds Allé and Ørehøj Allé are protected, and across from Øregårds Park in the direction of the Øresund strait vista, the building's main axis is marked by the trees along Hambro's Allé. The property was acquired by Gentofte municipality in 1917 and was restored in 1952 by architect Poul Gøtzsche. It now houses the Øregård Museum with Gentofte municipality's historic-topographical collection.

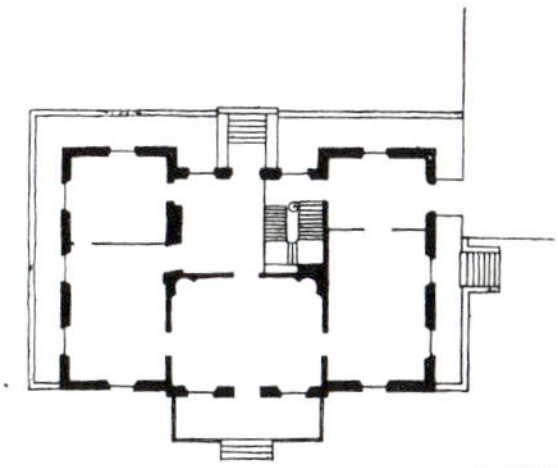

1:750

The romantic scenic garden is noteworthy for its large, old trees and lawns with great beds of spring bulbs established by G.N. Brandt in the 1920's.

J57

Hørsholm Church

Kirke Allé, Hørsholm
1820-24

Client: The national government
Architect: Christian Frederik Hansen

Hirschholm Palace was torn down in 1810-12 together with the palace chapel that had served as a parish church. A new church was built here to replace the old chapel. For financial reasons, there was less ornamentation than the architect wanted, but it was still one of this favorite buildings. The lack of a tower was not just the result of the modest budget, but also because C.F. Hansen did not approve of towers. The small bell frame above the entrance is a characteristic motif, which can be seen on some of his other churches. Just as Vor Frue Church, Hørsholm Church's entrance is in the end wall, and the light effects are similar in both churches. Hørsholm Church was restored in 1987-88 by Vilhelm Wohlert's Tegnestue.
Bibliography: A.L. Thygesen and H. Lund: C.F. Hansen. 1995

J. Fr. W. Schrøter's gardens from the 1720's and J.C. Krieger's project from the 1730's are still evident in the symmetrical, axial baroque complex: a uniform lake with two islets, straight linden alleys and slopes with a forestlike landscaping. The amphitheater is still evident in the shape of the terrain at the southern end of the garden.

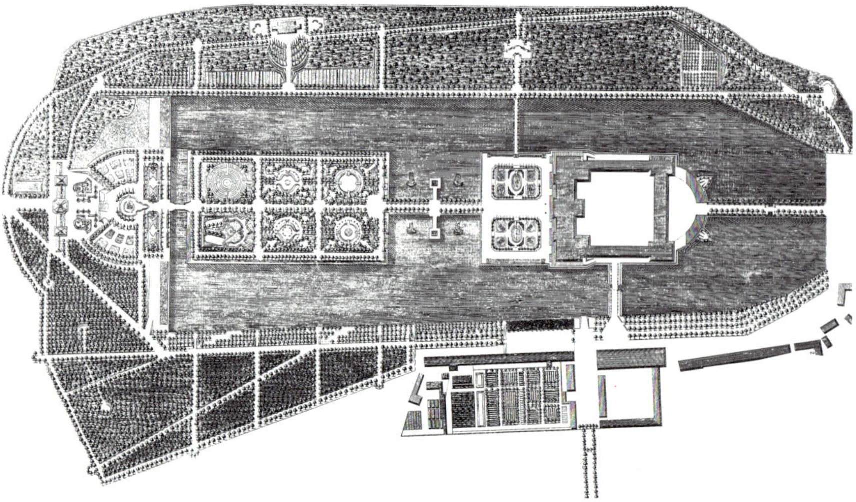

The English row houses *

Christiansholms Tværvej et al, Klampenborg
1901-03

Client: An English consortium
Architect: Rasmus Jensen

The English client influenced both the site plan, the plans and the neobaroque facades. Despite their row house character, the buildings are individual, attached homes, and with their courtyards as common areas they represent a pattern that first became common in Denmark many years later. The units range in size from 200 to 400 sqm and have high basements. In the English fashion, there is service access to the basements from the courtyard, while the main entrance has a stairway from the street. The site was originally part of Copenhagen's fortification terrain, and in case of war the houses were to be blown up. The "explosion clause" was lifted in 1921 and the scheme is now an exclusive, desirable housing area.

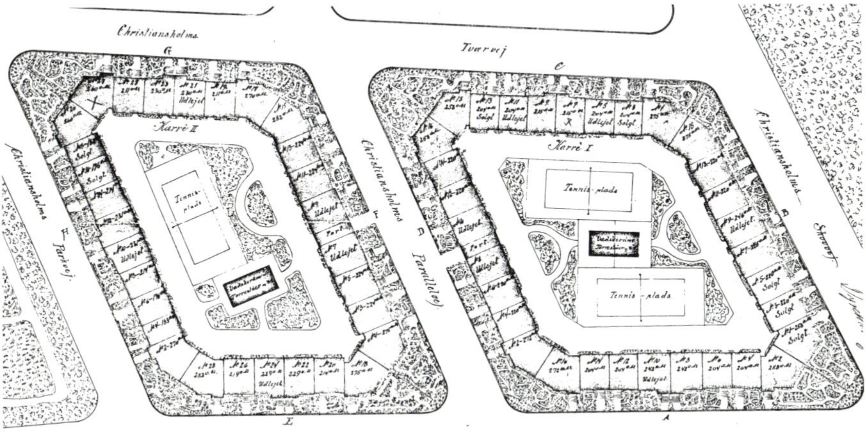

J113

Ordrup cemetery and G.N. Brandts Garden

Ørnekulsvej 3, Ellensvej, Ordrup
1914, 1920-30

Client: Gentofte Municipality
Architect: Edvard Thomsen (chapel)
Landscape architect: G.N. Brandt

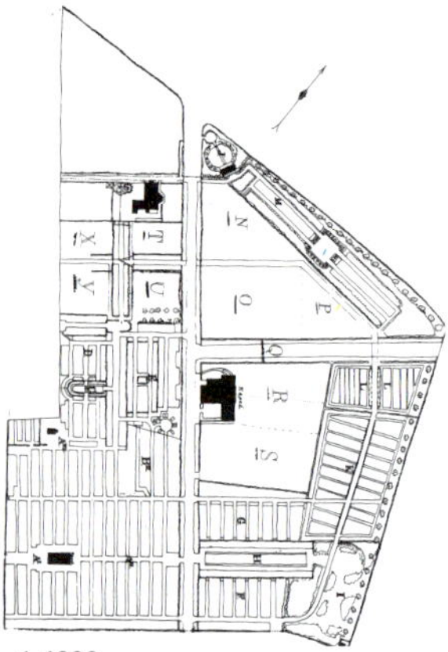

ca. 1:4000

The oldest area of Ordrup cemetery is from 1892. This was enlarged by Brandt as cemetery gardener in the 1920's, previous to the Mariebjerg cemetery. The characteristic and identifying features are the through road with the twisted locust trees on a wide grass shoulder, a Japanese cherry tree alley, and a square with trimmed horse chestnuts. The forest cemetery concept was tried for the first time in the northern corner, with pines and dark yews. An exceptional feature is the long, wide grass paths leading to the common grave area. The grass on the center of the path is closely cut, while along the slightly sloping edges, the grass is higher with spread bushes and spring bulbs. Brandt's garden was established in 1914. It is surrounded by the cemetery grounds and is now a public area. It has a neoclassicistic character with a sequence of five, well-defined spaces in which Brandt employed elements from the cultured landscape. The villa, which was torn down in the 1960's, was in the first space. Thereafter is a small grove of fruit trees by a thatched-roof hut. A rock wall resolves the change in grade to the flower garden hollow with water and marsh plants. To the rear is a wooded area with birch and beech groves and wild flora. The fifth space is long and narrow with a grass path running the length of the garden.
Bibliography: Arkitektur DK 1990,166, Landskab 1985, 34

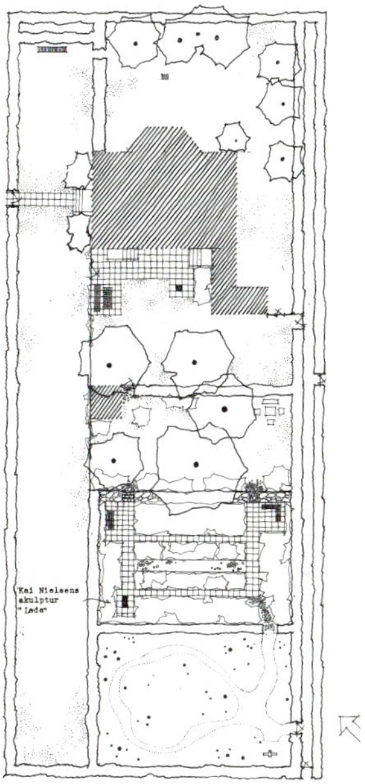

1:800

Sundvænget Row houses **J120**

Sundvænget, both sides, Charlottenlund
1925-26

Client: Merchant C.J. Lund
Architect: Thorkild Henningsen

The exclusive location on the Øresund strait, and the form intended for a sheltered private life were in keeping with the well-to-do fashion of the times. They were large, attached individual units. They were oriented toward the sun giving the street a new, asymmetrical section, and a new row house access pattern. The south sides are flanked by garages and sheds, and the north sides by gardens that give access to the houses. On the south facade there are small, one-story bays to screen the terrace from the neighbors'. The plan of the units is also based on a reduction of noise from the neighboring units. The row house had become fashionable, but the houses on Sundvænget are still characterized by the impeccable, provincial traditions from the Better Building Methods movement.

J135

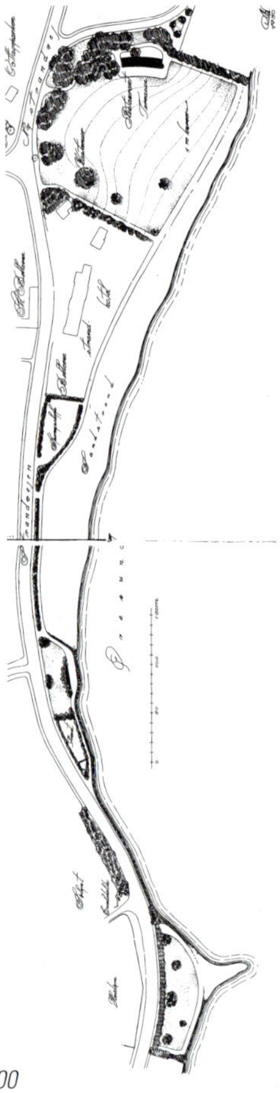

1:10.000

Strand parks at Hvidøre, Klampenborg and Charlottenlund

The Øresund strait coast from Charlottenlund to Klampenborg
1930-1935

Client: The national government, Gentofte municipality
Architect: Povl Baumann
Landscape architect: C.Th. Sørensen, Aksel Andersen

In the 1920's and 1930's, the public regained access to the Øresund strait coast at Charlottenlund and Klampenborg due to efforts by the Danish Conservation Society and artist Erik Struckmann. To the south lies Hvidøre Strand Park, which later lost contact with the strait due to the establishment of the Vandstrandvej coastal road. An extensive green still exists here with a few trees, and separated from the old coastal road by a long curved wall with a pergola designed by Povl Baumann. From here and 600 meters north to Bellevue Strandbad, a beach was created by pumping sand in from the strait. At the northern end is Klampenborg Strand Park also called Stauning's Plain, where the bluff was excavated to create a gradual sloping plain with freestanding trees.Several kilometers south lies Charlottenlund Fort, which was established in 1886-88 as part of the Copenhagen coastal defenses. The fort was discontinued as a defence complex in 1932 and converted to a public area, Charlottenlund Strand Park. Besides the embankments and moats there is also a large lawn with groups of enormous trees and Charlottenlund Søbadeanstalt public swimming facility designed by Andersen & Juul Møller v. Dan B. Hasløv in 1985.
Bibliography: Havekunst 1931, 13

Staunings Plain

Dragør, urban preservation ________________________________ **J136**

Dragør, Amager

The town had its origins as a harbor and market during the 12th century herring industry on the Øresund strait. During the 17th century, it was the home for many of Amager's Dutch immigrants. The houses in the old quarter, form a unique, homogeneous unity, and are primarily from the period around 1800, when Dragør flourished as a maritime town. Many of the houses are protected today, and many of these can be attributed to master builder J.H. Blichmann (1739-1815). The town plan is unusual with a system of east/west streets and north/south lanes. Preservation efforts in Dragør began in the 1930's on the initiative of the local residents, and have since been extended to include the surrounding areas especially the beaches. Dragør is one of the country's few concentrated, old town unities, which is preserved and still functions as a town.

Bibliography: Miljøministeriet: Dragørs bevaring. 1988

J137

Bellevue *

Bellevuebadet, Bellevista housing scheme, Strandvejen 419-33, Bellevue Theater, Strandvejen 451, Klampenborg 1932-37

Client: Gentofte Municipality and a private consortium
Architect: Arne Jacobsen

The building scheme lies in the fashionable Klampenborg beach area and is an outstanding example of Arne Jacobsen's personal version of international functionalism. The simple service building and the round life guard towers at the Bellevuebadet from 1932 illustrate the modern unrestrained life of the time, and they still serve their original purpose. Bellavista from 1934 still radiates an elegant Mediterranean modernity and is one of the most distinct examples of the so-called white functionalism, even though the structure is not concrete, but stuccoed brick. The three-winged scheme opens toward the view of the strait, which the apartments on the side wings also can enjoy due to the staggered balconies. At Bellavista, the balconies are an integral architectural element as opposed to the other buildings of the time in which the balconies were attached to the facades. Bellevue Theater was built in 1937 as a setting for summer revues. The exterior also signals a sommerish levity, which is further underscored by the operable roof over the seating, which can be opened in favorable weather, creating the ambience of an outdoor theater. Today the building still functions as theater. The former restaurant south of the theater has been converted to housing.
Bibliography: Huse i Gentofte, 1984, 168 and 172

1:1000

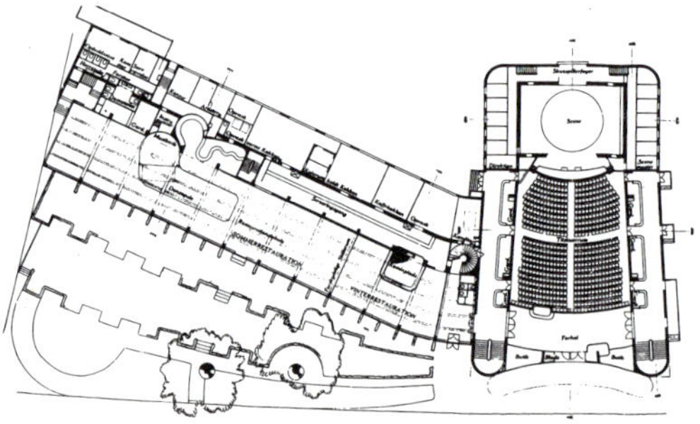

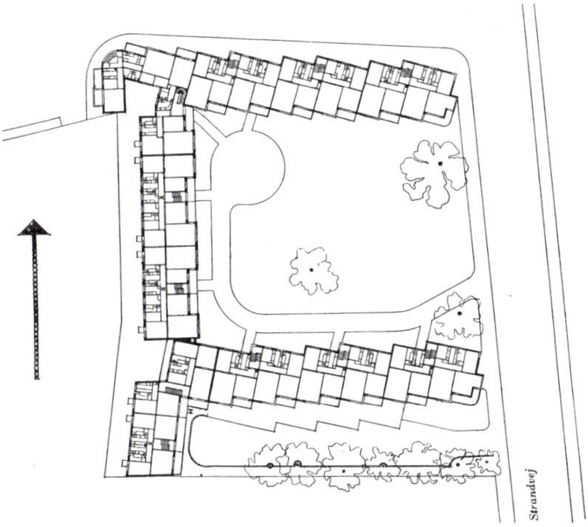

1:1500

J138

The Blidah Park housing scheme
at Phistersvej, Hellerup
1933-34

Client: Consortium represented by attorney Rasmus Nielsen
Architect: Edvard Heiberg, Karl Larsen, Ivar Bentsen, Vagn Kaastrup and Ole Buhl et al of Kooperative Arkitekter
Landscape architect: C.Th. Sørensen

Ivar Bentsen, Jørgen U. Berg and Acton Bjørn were responsible for the first blocks in the Blidah Park scheme, while the others were designed by the "Kooperative Arkitekter" group, which was formed in 1934 and consisted of Edvard Heiberg, Karl Larsen, Ivar Bentsen, Vagn Kaastrup and Ole Buhl among others. This joint collaboration of architects was one of functionalism's new statements, and several of the members were active on the political left wing, inspired by the Bauhaus school's coop-session. The sun oriented block scheme had been tried several years earlier at Ryparken (B 131), but at Blidah Park, the new building form was more carefully treated, such as with the staggered alignment of the blocks and a more varied design of balconies and end walls. This is most evident in the northern blocks, designed by A. Skjøt-Pedersen. The landscaping of the areas between the blocks was greatly emphasized and Blidah Park is one of the best results of the early block and park schemes in Denmark.

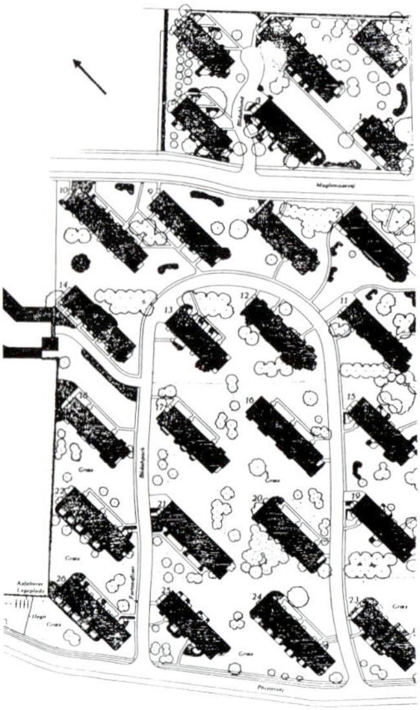

1:4000

Amager Strand Park and Kastrup Fort *

Amager Strandvej, Amager
1933-37, 1949

Client: Copenhagen Municipality
Landscape architect: Jakob Bergmann, Copenhagen Municipal Park Department

During the 1930's the coast north and south of Copenhagen was opened to the public. From the public swimming complex at Helgoland in the north to the shallows along Amager's east coast, several kilometers of bathing beaches were established by pumping in sand from the strait, thus moving the coast line further out. During the 1940's, the public recreational area was enlarged toward south to Kastrup fort by the establishment of an immense common green with large groups of grey poplars. Kastrup fort was converted to a public park in 1933 and the area culminates toward south with Kastrup Strand Park. In connection with the building of the Øresund strait crossing, there are plans for further land reclamation to create a new "riviera"
Bibliography: Havekunst 1940, 122

J145

Mariebjerg cemetery and crematorium

Mariebjergvej, Gentofte
1936

Client: Gentofte Municipality
Architect: Fritz Schlegel
Landscape architect: Gudmund Nyeland Brandt,
Sven Hansen, Morten Falmer Nielsen

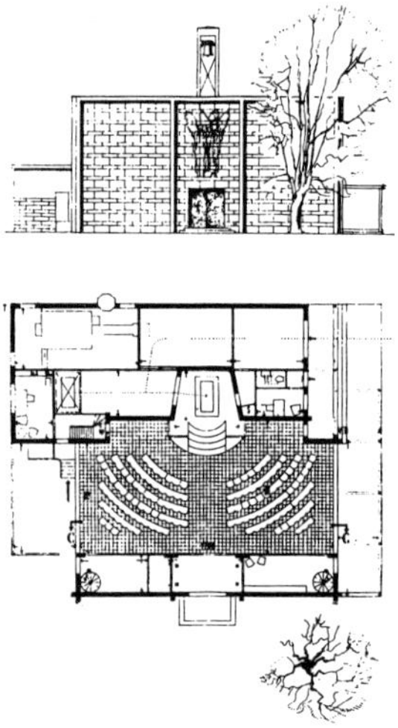

1:750

The crematorium represented modernism's decisive breakthrough in Danish sacral architecture. This is evident in the form idiom, the materials and the details. The main form is purely cubistic with the square as the main proportional element visible on the facades and in the chapel hall. The slender structural framework is of reinforced concrete, filled out with hollow concrete block, a combination, which together with the simple pergolas gives the whole an abstract lightness. The main facade is decorated with cruciform openings that admit a finely filtered light into the chapel hall. Besides being a result of the construction they are also a Christian symbol. At the time of its completion, the crematorium represented a modern, respectfully distant expression of the building's sacral function. The 68-acre cemetery project was a large commission for G.N. Brandt in 1926. In 1929, landscaping began with a checkerboard of yew hedges and the distinctive outer, inner and traverse alleys, each planted with a different type of tree. The mixed tree landscaping of the outer edges, burial sections and urn area could be cleared when needed. The plan is uniform and quite formal. About fifty rectangular burial areas are framed by wide borders of yew. These burial areas are subordinate to the distinctive alleys, which ease orientation and give the plan its structure. There are two rectangular systems of alleys, a small one with alleys formerly of column elm and now of column hornbeam within a larger system with rows of Scotch pine. Both rectangles are intersected by wide alleys of white willow and formerly four rows of elm in the largest alley, which were replaced with Norway maple in 1995. The roads in the outer rectangle have the character of forest roads formed by Scotch pine, ferns and ivy. The individual burial areas have been developed over many years partly during G.N. Brandt's period as cemetery gardener and later in the 1970's by Sven Hansen, and Morten Falmer Nielsen since the 1960's. The burial areas have widely different character and each with a distinct set of grave easements. Thus, there are burial areas for children with simple stone markers laid in the grass and surrounded by a simple lilac hedge, spaces with groups of spread deciduous trees like oak or locust, more traditional spaces with trimmed hedges surrounding the individual plots, and a forestlike space with hemlock and pine. A more pantheistic area is arranged as a grassy valley, a former gravel pit, with hewn fieldstones marking the urn graves. As a whole, the complex has a high quality, a distinguished Danish counterpart to the early forest cemeteries in Stockholm and Hamburg.

Bibliography: Arkitektur DK 1990,170, Havekunst 1948, 33, Landskab 1985, 35

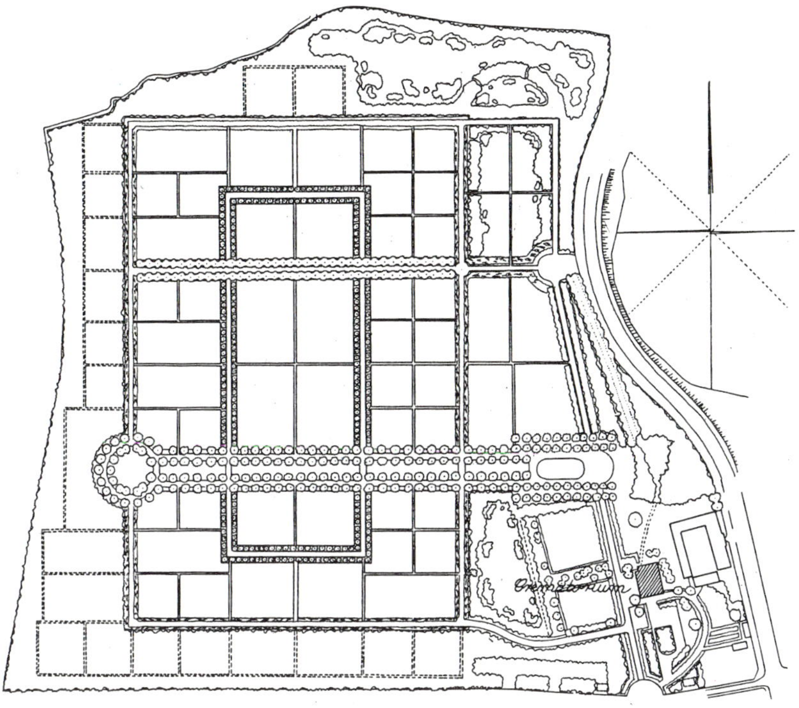

ca. 1:7000

1:1000

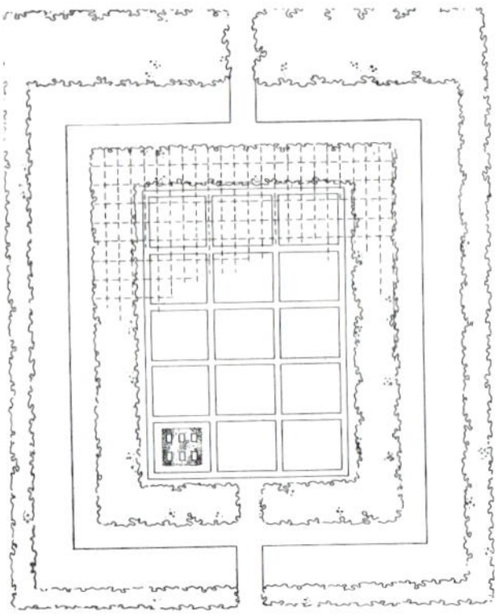

Copenhagen Airport J157

Kastrup
1939-95

Client: Københavns Lufthavn A/S
Architect: Vilhelm Lauritzen et al
Landscape architect: Ginman, Harboe and Borup, Susanne Struch,

Air traffic at Kastrup Airport began in 1925. In 1936, a competition arranged for a large building complex was won by Vilhelm Lauritzen. The main building was both architecturally and technically a new expression for this new building type, and it became a major work in Danish functionalism. Today, the terminal can barely be distinguished in the tangle of additions and new buildings. A new terminal building, also designed by Vilhelm Lauritzen and completed in 1960, still forms the basis for the international terminal, which has proved its durability through countless additions and rebuilding works. However, with the new Finger B, from 1986, the cool, functionalistic architecture was replaced by a more expressive character inspired by aviation's form idiom and materials. KHR AS Arkitekter were responsible for this new direction, which also inspired the domestic terminal from 1988-89 by the same architects. With the new Finger A from 1994-95, Holm & Grut Arkitekter developed the airplane inspired design to a freer composition of curved roof surfaces supported by branching columns. The airport's secondary facilities have been given their own treatment as with the parking garages by the foreign and domestic terminals from 1988-89 and 1990-91 respectively, by KHR AS Arkitekter. In connection with the Øresund strait crossing project, a new subway is being built from Copenhagen with a station at the new terminal building designed by Lauritzens Tegnestue.
Bibliography: Arkitektur DK 1987, 285, 1991, 354, 1995, 182

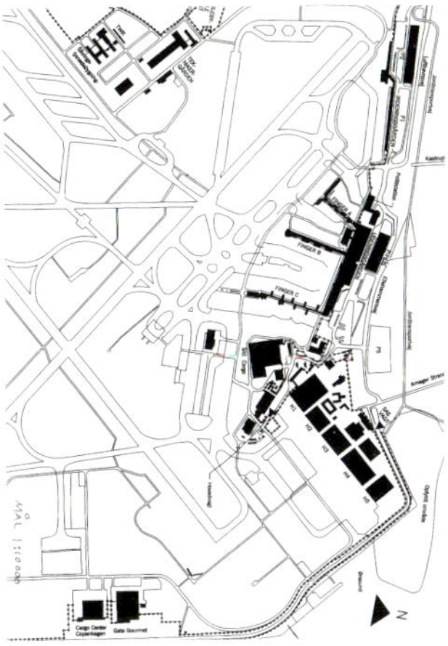

1:50.000

J158

Filling station *

Kystvejen 24, Skovshoved
1938

Client: Texaco
Architect: Arne Jacobsen

The growth in automobile production and traffic during the 1930's created a need for a new series of service facilities such as the filling station. There were a number of examples of how this function was adapted to the classical architectural ideals. However Arne Jacobsen employed functionalism's cool and formal form idiom at this filling station, which was designed as a standard type for Texaco oil company. The white tile siding on the building signals order and cleanliness, and the form of the oval canopy offers a sign effect – also at night when it is lit from below. The unity of the building and canopy, and its simplicity, represent a distinct archetype.

J159

Linked houses

Ellebækvej 21-29 and 22-36, Vangede
1939-43

Client: A/S Gentofte Rækkehuse
Architect: Arne Jacobsen

This staggered row house type offers a number of advantages. It eases the adaption of the buildings to the terrain, it allows optimal solar orientation and it creates screened outdoor spaces adjacent to the houses. The units north of the road have access from a path on their north side, thus the gardens are undisturbed by traffic. The houses have a half basement; living room, dining room and kitchen on the ground floor; and two rooms and a bath on the top floor. There is nothing especially innovative about this scheme and the building form is traditionally Danish, however the proportions and details have a discreet and refined special quality, which is evident in the scheme's austere postwar character.
Bibliography: Arkitekten M 1945, 40

Lyngby town hall

Lyngby Torv, Lyngby
1938-41

Client: Lyngby-Taarbæk Municipality
Architect: Ib Martin Jensen & Hans Erling Langkilde
Landscape architect: Lyngby-Taarbæk Municipality

The design was the result of a competition in 1938, which was won with a proposal for a concentrated office building with five stories and a copper covered penthouse. The structure is reinforced concrete and the facade siding is Greenland marble. The concave entrance facade has a supple grip on the triangular arrival plaza, and the uniform facade pattern is broken by the asymmetrical entrance and the two-story windows in the town council hall. The building harmonizes with the special local situation and is an example of the functionalistic town halls that were build in that period and caused a fierce debate for and against traditional monumentality.

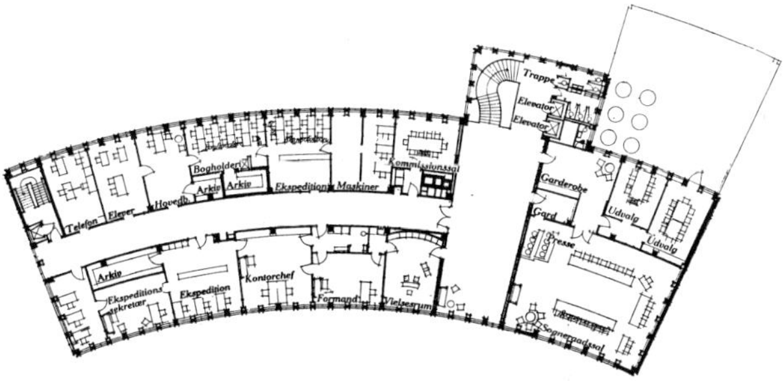

1:750

J163

Søllerød town hall *

Øverødvej 2, Søllerød
1940-42

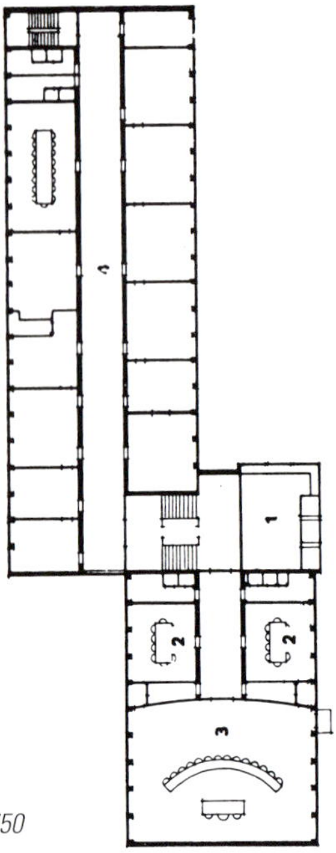

1:750

Client: Søllerød Municipality
Architect: Arne Jacobsen and Flemming Lassen
Landscape architect: Arne Jacobsen

The interplay between the two building masses, one with the ceremonial spaces and the other with offices, is a simple motif that won the 1939 town hall competition. The structure is a reinforced concrete frame. The facades are sided with Porsgrund marble and the roofing is copper. The few architectural effects employed here are refined to the utmost in the masterly facade composition, in details like the small carillon on the north wall, and in the interiors where the architects designed all the details and furnishings, a quality that makes this the most pristine of Denmark's functionalistic town halls. An annex toward east (not shown) was added in 1967 by the same architects.

Tract gardens in Nærum * **J166**

Nærumgårdsvej, Nærum
1948-49

Client: Søllerød Municipality
Landscape architect: C.Th. Sørensen

The oval tract gardens in Nærum, Haveforeningen Wesselsminde, are considered one of C.Th. Sørensen's major works. On a wavy grass plain, he placed a dynamic sequence of forty oval tract gardens, each ca 25 x 15 meters. The area between serves as a common green. The gardens are surrounded by hedges with small sheds, with a variety of placements yet still subordinate to the whole. The hedges were originally planned as trimmed and untrimmed, optional plants such as hornbeam, hawthorn or privet, but today they are primarily privet and hawthorn trimmed in different heights and forms. Bibliography: Steen Høyer and Sven-Ingvar Andersson: C.Th. Sørensen – en havekunstner. 1993

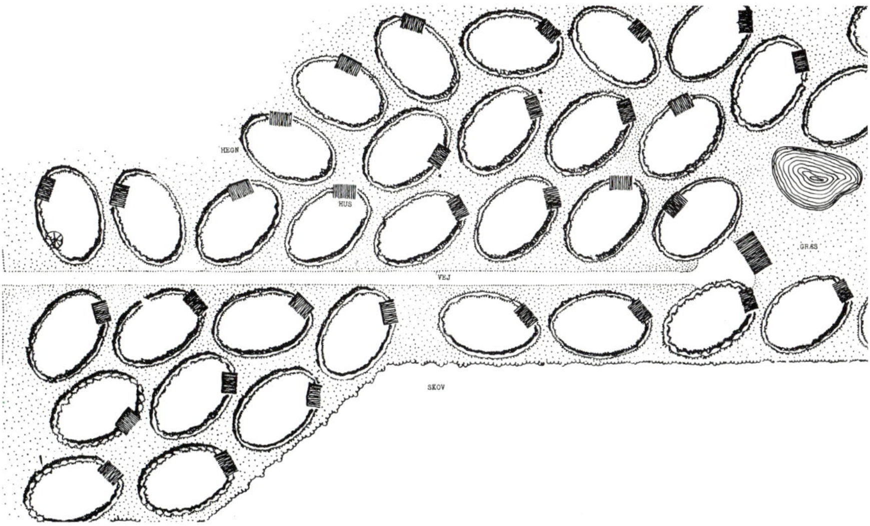

J167

Munkegårdsskolen

Vangedevej 178, Vangede
1948-57

Client: Gentofte Municipality
Architect: Arne Jacobsen
Landscape architect: Arne Jacobsen

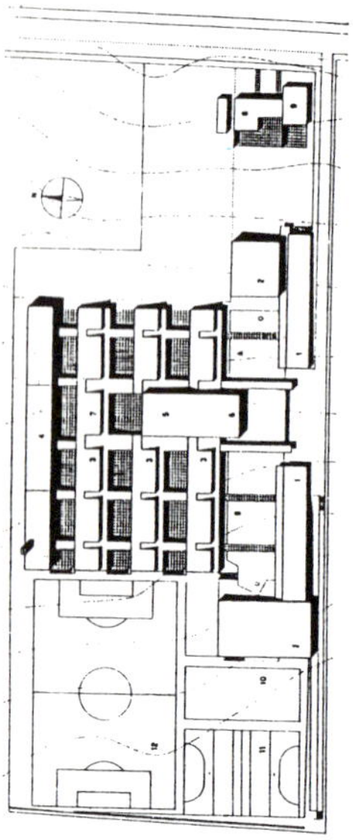

Arne Jacobsen designed the refined garden himself. Perpendicular to Vangedevej road, a series of parallel beech hedges, under trimmed plane trees, marks the school's location. The small courts were all given an individual character with varied paving, choice landscaping and copies of ancient sculpture as wall reliefs or freestanding elements.

This building scheme represented a new type of school in which the atrium courts were part of the classrooms. The one-story classroom buildings are connected by glass corridors to form a network with the landscaped courts as the mesh. The special subject classes are located in two-story buildings on the edges of the net. The assembly hall, teachers' rooms etc. are also in a two-story building by the main entrances. This school type is simple and easy to grasp even here with ca 1000 pupils. The scheme lies on one level on a sloping site with stairs leading down to the playing fields. The typical classroom section was innovative at the time, with supplementary daylight from high roof windows to light the rear of the space. The school's light and humane atmosphere owes much to the careful proportioning of the building masses and shapes as well as the meticulous detailing. As in many of Arne Jacobsen's buildings, a characteristic feature is the way he could develop a formal system to produce a living building.

Bibliography: Arkitektur DK 1957, 1

The Søndergårdspark housing scheme J168

Ibsvej et al, Bagsværd
1949-50

Client: The Danish Public Housing Association, DAB
Architect: Poul Ernst Hoff & Bennet Windinge
Landscape architect: Aksel Andersen

1:10.000

As a low-rise park scheme, Søndergårdspark was a bold innovation in the area of public housing, which until then had been dominated by large multistory schemes. The open character of the scheme was attractive to families with children, and the units had new features such as dining alcoves and dining entries. These overlapping functions were new, space-saving initiatives, but as a whole, the scheme had a high-quality, generous character. Especially the small private gardens and large common areas were a new and radical gesture, perhaps too radical as the large green did not have the intended social rallying effect. About 1950, DAB was responsible for several progressive housing schemes, and Søndergårdspark was presented as a "cottage scheme". This implied an English inspiration, and the main plan with the large central green and the mixture of freestanding and attached houses is also suggestive of the English garden cities from the beginning of the century. The homogeneous yellow brick architecture and the concise forms were nevertheless Danish. The scheme clearly belongs to the functionalistic tradition, and its design, materials and landscape treatment are in keeping with the movement's greatest effort: Århus University, from the early 1930's. In a similar spirit, Søndergårdspark is a major work in the history of Danish housing.

Bibliography: Arkitekten 1967, 389

The units all have small gardens, edged by tongue-shaped hedges. At the ends of the house rows, large groups of poplar trees resolve the transition to the large green.

J169

Skovgårds school

Skovgårdsvej 56, Ordrup
1949-51

Client: Gentofte Municipality
Architect: Hans Erling Langkilde & Ib Martin Jensen
Landscape architect: Aksel Andersen

The school property was originally part of a country estate, therefore the buildings are surrounded by large old trees that create a forestlike character. The informal plan is organized around two courtyards, one for older children and one for the youngest. Next to each courtyard there are special subject rooms for the two age groups. The one- and two-story buildings have yellow brick, mortar-brushed facades and large hipped roofs with red tile. The form idiom is traditional but the relaxed organization and the low, intimate character of the buildings was a new element in school building at the time. As a whole, the scheme harmonizes with the landscape and the neighboring, well-kept villa quarter.
Bibliography: Arkitekten M 1951, 137

1:2000

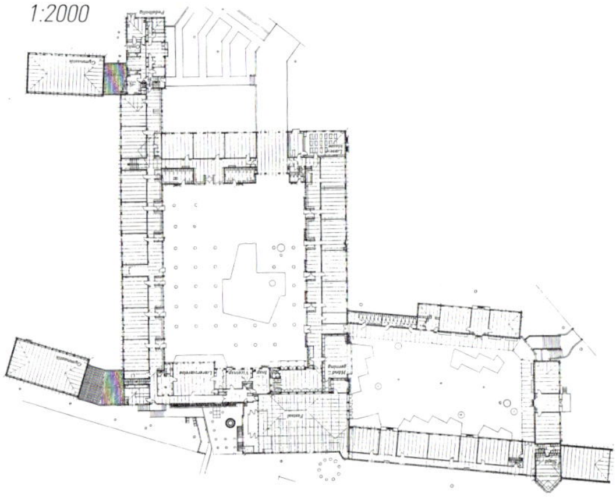

The Ermelundshuse housing scheme **J170**

Ved Ermelunden 2-34 and Ibstrupvej 44-66, 55-69, Jægersborg
1949

Client: Private consortium
Architect: Viggo Møller-Jensen og Mogens Black-Petersen
Landscape architect: Aksel Andersen

The short groups of row houses follow the sloping site, which is primarily organized in common areas. The private gardens are thus quite small, but with the narrow street spaces and the dense landscaping, they form an intimate and lush milieu. The yellow brick facades and red tile roofs are typically Danish, and the white facade bands that mark the floors give these homogeneous houses an unobtrusive yet refined character. Architecturally, the Ermelundshuse scheme belongs to the functionalistic tradition, but in its main disposition it represents a forerunner to the dense/low housing movement introduced twenty years later.

J172

The Bredalsparken housing scheme

Neergårds Allé and others, Hvidøvre
1949-55

Client: The Danish Public Housing Association, DAB
Architect: Svenn Eske Kristensen, Emil Hansen, Hans Frederiksen, Niels J. Holm
Landscape architect: Aksel Andersen, Ingwer Ingwersen, J. Palle Schmidt

Based on the freestanding block housing type from the 1930's, Bredalsparken is a mild Danish version of orthodox functionalism. The somewhat short blocks lie parallel to each other according to solar orientation, but staggered to harmonize with the terrain. Bredalsparken was one of the first schemes to be designed with standard ceiling heights and with prefabricated elements, yet these exercises in industrialized building did not hamper a thorough architectural treatment, which is clearly evident. In general, the architecture is of the functionalistic tradition, but there are also modernistic features such as the balconies that break through the roof, and there are neoclassicistic features in the symmetrical end walls. The scheme is especially noteworthy for its high quality design, the craftsmanship evident in the apartments and buildings, and the nonpretentious, refined interplay between the site plan, the park space and the landscaping. It is well-designed from detail to the whole. The row of shops along Neergårds Allé are typical of the period and well preserved.
Bibliography: Landskap 1977, 160

The buildings are well-sited in the slightly hilly terrain. Dense, dark green thickets nestle together as soft forms away from the buildings while groups of locust trees, pines, etc. stand close to the facades. Between the short, spread blocks toward east and the long building toward the western border of the site, there is a large green for play and ball games. Here the terrain is further modelled and planted with groups of large poplars and wide, space defining borders of hawthorn, oak, etc. The buildings have a rare beauty and seem to lie in a large park.

Today the scheme is terminated by a huge winding building.

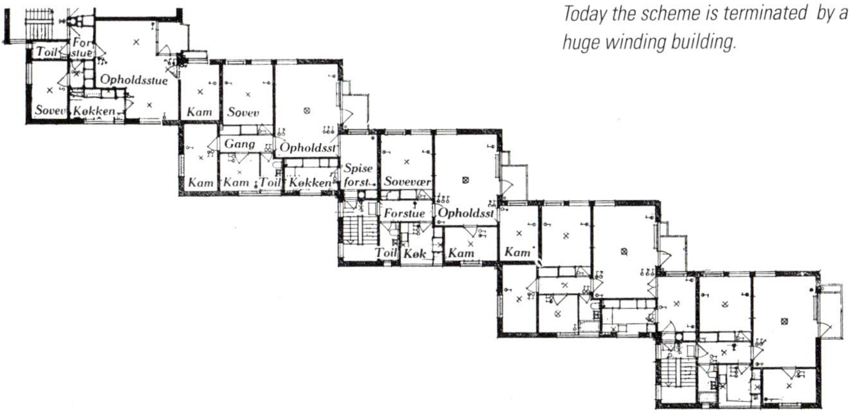

Older plan, 1959.

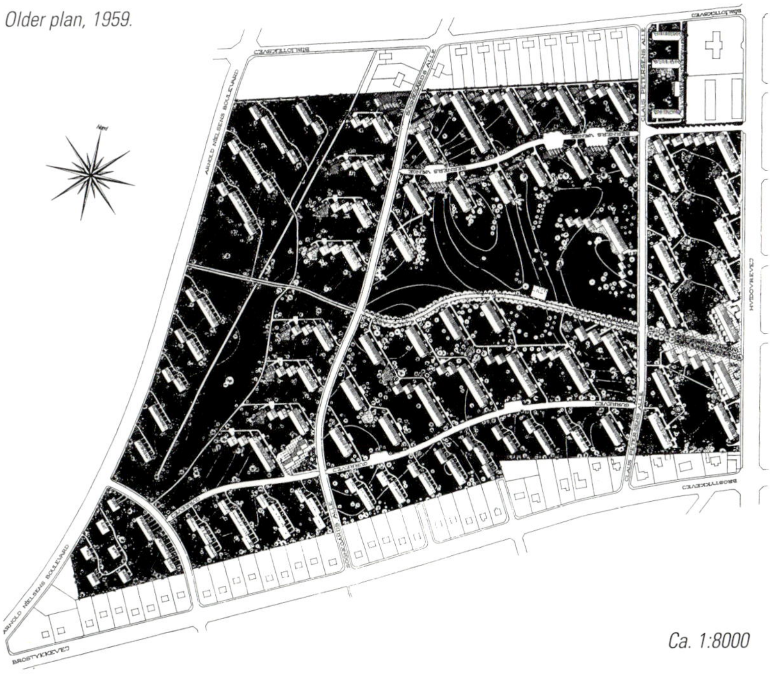

Ca. 1:8000

J173

The Høje Søborg collective housing scheme

Søborg Torv 2-12, Søborg
1949-51

Client: The Danish Public Housing Association, DAB
Architect: Poul Ernst Hoff & Bennet Windinge
Landscape architect: Aksel Andersen, J. Palle Schmidt

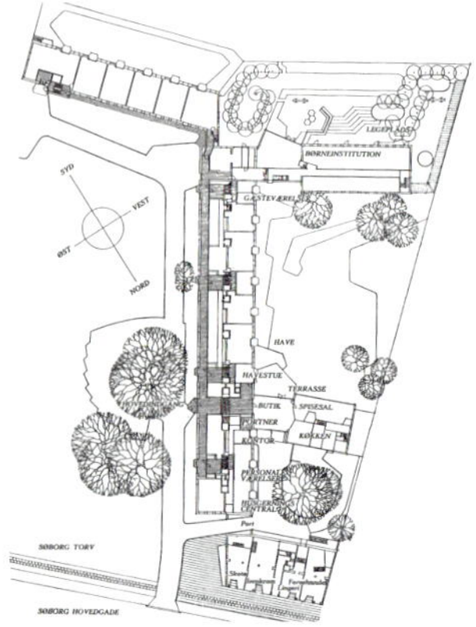

1:2500

Among DAB's experiments at the time, was this collective housing scheme for families with working wives and single mothers. The program can be credited to the strong social engagement of DAB's director of that time, Erling Knudsen. The small apartments were supplemented with common service facilities such as kitchen and dining hall, shop, kindergarten, janitor, cleaning service, etc., and the scheme still functions as originally planned. The two regular housing wings mark the urban location as borders to the square, but the common rooms on the ground floor and the small group of shops are gathered around the west oriented garden. The informal plan on this level represents a freedom in keeping with the function of the scheme. A similar accordance between form and content is implied in the red brick facades, white balconies and the balcony-corridors' white railings, which signal both Danish tradition and international functionalism.

1:600

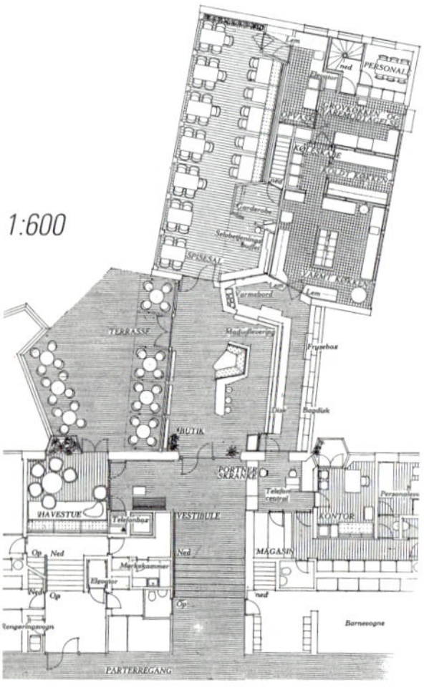

The Alléhuse housing scheme

Jægersborg Allé 185-229, Jægersborg
1949-53

Client: Private consortium
Architect: Arne Jacobsen

The five, parallel housing blocks are staggered and oriented to the sun in a typical early functionalistic fashion. The individual blocks are staggered in keeping with the park housing schemes of the period. However, all other associations with that time or the past ended here. The exterior of the building blocks and the plans were completely new, despite similarities to the nearby Jacobsen scheme, Ibstruppark from the early 1940's. The solar oriented facades are of continuous yellow brick, while the vertical shift in the large openings, and the different roof slopes create an intense movement like pistons on a crankshaft. As opposed to this, the entrance facades have a static appearance with their tall triangular towers. The interior, cylindrical stairways produced lopsided and complicated apartment plans, which could seem to be inspirational sources for what is going on today. This scheme differs from most of Arne Jacobsen's housing projects due to its free sculpturality.

Bibliography: Arkitekten U 1953, 285

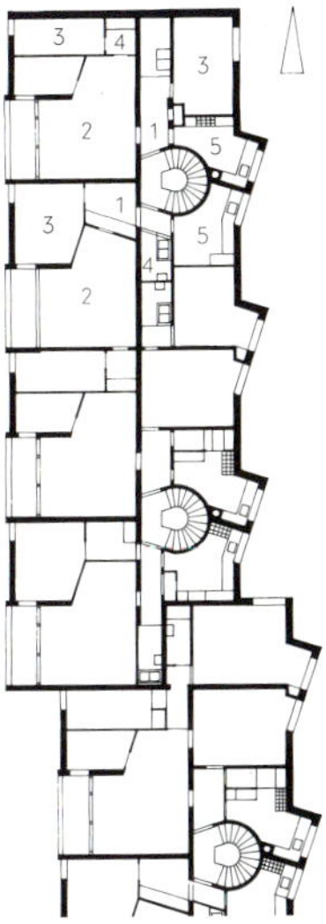

1:800

J184

The Nærumvænge housing scheme

Nærumvænge and Fyrrevejen, Nærum
1949-61

Client: Søllerød Public Housing Association
Architect: Palle Suenson
Landscape architect: C.Th. Sørensen

From a distance, the effect of the red hipped roofs of the Nærumvænge scheme is unusually homogeneous and signals the Danish building tradition in the scale of a small provincial town. As part of this tradition, the planted stone berms form a precise border to the landscape to the west. The scheme includes 159 units in the multistory blocks and 181 row houses. These two housing types constitute an urban whole, which is also homogeneous in the interior design. The building methods employed with the yellow brickwork are also traditional, but for financial reasons many of the details were standardized. The high lying buildings surrounding the square lie at the northern end of the scheme and have the same form idiom as the housing. The form idiom and materials were inspired by the old Nivå brickworks, but Nærumvænge continues the functional tradition with a slight tinge of romanticism.
Bibliography: J. Casper Crone and Peter Hancke: Palle Suenson. 1987

The Nærumvænge scheme also includes a 300 meter wide, open area between the buildings and the highway. This large green is landscaped to give it an extensive wild appearance, with large grassy fields, marshes, birch groves and a varied wild flora, etc. Other smaller areas have been laid out as playing fields.

Virum Apotek **J191**

Frederiksdalsvej 73, Virum
1951

Client: Pharmacist C.C. Frederiksen
Architect: Erik Christian Sørensen and Mogens Boertman

The ground floor of the building and a small garden fill the entire site. Originally the garden was a for cultivating medicinal herbs. The two upper floors float as a separate box over the lower level, and the space between admits a clerestory light into the pharmacy's airy sales area. The emphasized skeletal structure and the filling out of the upper facades with glass and enameled steel panels were inspired by the American architectural trends of the time, such as the works of Mies van der Rohe and Richard Neutra. One senses a reflective minimalism, which due to the classical proportions and human scale, resulted in a sensitive architectural presentation. A number of alterations have been made in the exterior detailing and the pharmacy interior.
Bibliography: Skala 1994, 70

J194

The Søholm row houses *

Bellevuekrogen 1-26 and Strandvejen 413, Klampenborg
1951-54

Client: E. Steffensen
Architect: Arne Jacobsen

The three different housing types in this scheme demonstrate the architect's masterful ability to work with attached, exclusive housing, with consideration for interior and exterior privacy. The five apartments toward south, built in 1951, have living rooms on the first floor balcony over the dining area below. This context is illustrated on the exterior by the staggered roofs. Arne Jacobsen lived in one of these apartments and the garden still bears witness to his exceptional talent, also as a landscape architect. In 1952, nine row houses were built toward west with angled, sculptural roof cut-offs. In 1954, the scheme was completed with the four, one-story linked houses toward north. The strong modelling of the individual building elements is a motif that appeared earlier in the Alléhuse scheme from 1952 (J 183) The landmarking of Arne Jacobsen's housing scheme at Bellevue also includes the Ved Bellevue Bugt houses at Strandvejen 415A-417F.

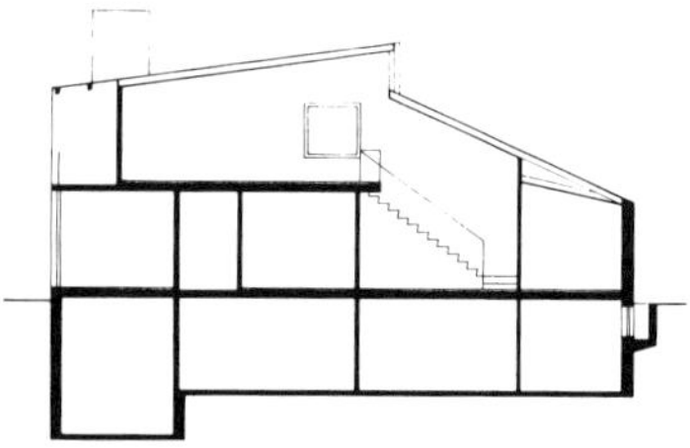

1:400

The Søllerød Park housing scheme

Søllerød Park, Søllerød
1955

Client: Jørgen G. Andersen
Architect: Eva & Nils Koppel
Landscape architect: Knud Preisler og Axel Thomsen

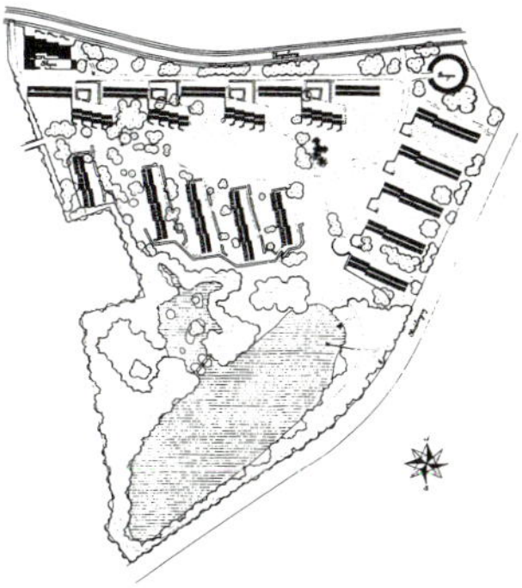

White end walls, red tile roofs, and dark wood and concrete facades are the primary elements in this scheme, which was built in an old park area. The accentuation of the building components expresses the building system with the supporting cross walls and the staggered building blocks that eased adaption to the terrain and existing landscape. The 350 units consist of one-story apartments on the ground floor and two-story units above with access from balcony corridors. The parallel staggered blocks, their form, and the different unit types all place Søllerød Park between the traditional park housing of the period and the coming dense/low-rise housing type. Despite the size of the units and the scheme, these characteristics produced an intimate and amiable total effect.

J196

Christiansgave

Strandvejen 24-56, Rungsted Kyst
1954

Client: Jean Fehmerling
Architect: Jean Fehmerling

The neoclassicistic villa with its 12 acre park was built in 1918 with Carl Brummer as architect. After Jean Fehmerling took over the property, he subdivided it and designed the housing scheme with 28 atrium houses and 21 long houses, all with modest private gardens. The units had common facilities in the old villa, which was later divided into condominiums. The new housing scheme consists of low, cubistic buildings with subdued colors, carefully grouped around the villa to retain the parklike character of the site, which slopes down to the Øresund strait. The scheme is an early example of the dense/low-rise housing form, with a sensitive balance of nature and architecture.

J197

Row houses

Ørnegårdsvej 22-50, Sløjfen 22-48, Lyngby
1957

Client: A. Jespersen & Søn
Architect: Arne Jacobsen

The three blocks of row houses have almost identical front and rear facades, built as non-bearing curtain walls. The light wood construction is well proportioned with frames for panels of glass and colored fiber cement, yet these very subdued facades give the scheme a cold institutional character. The two-story units have a correspondingly clear and simple plan. On the ground floor there is an entry, family kitchen and a living room that spans from facade to facade. The first floor plan is symmetrical about the long axis with two large and two small bedrooms as well as a bath. Perhaps the design of these row houses was influenced by Jacobsen's concurrent work with Rødovre town hall.
Bibliography: Arkitekten U 1955, 93

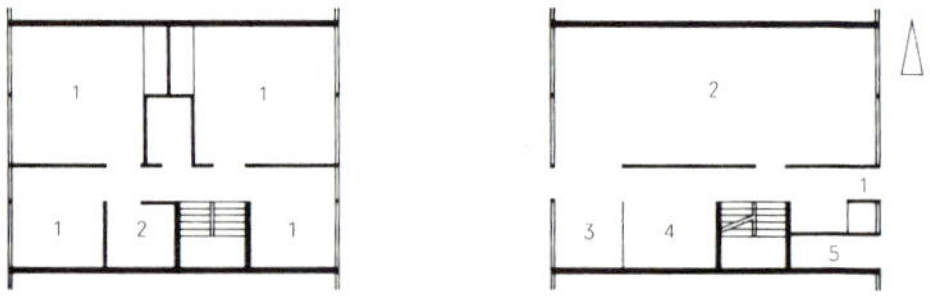

Tårnby town hall * J198

Amager Landevej 76, Tårnby
1957-59

Client: Tårnby Municipality
Architect: Halldor Gunlögsson & Jørn Nielsen
Landscape architect: Edith and Ole Nørgård

The town hall is the result of a competition in 1953. A nondirectional modular grid was the basis for the plan's two, staggered rectangles. This grid is also visible in the facade's narrow, identical windows. The two-story, atrium scheme surrounds two courtyards, one of which is the town hall ceremonial space, lit from a band of windows just under the floating roof. The other atrium is an open water garden. The arrival plaza's emphasis of the entrance axis, the Norwegian marble siding and the exclusive detailing give the building its gravity and dignity. Thus, without traditional effects, the architecture provides a degree of monumentality expected in a town hall building.
Bibliography: Arkitektur DK 1960, 121

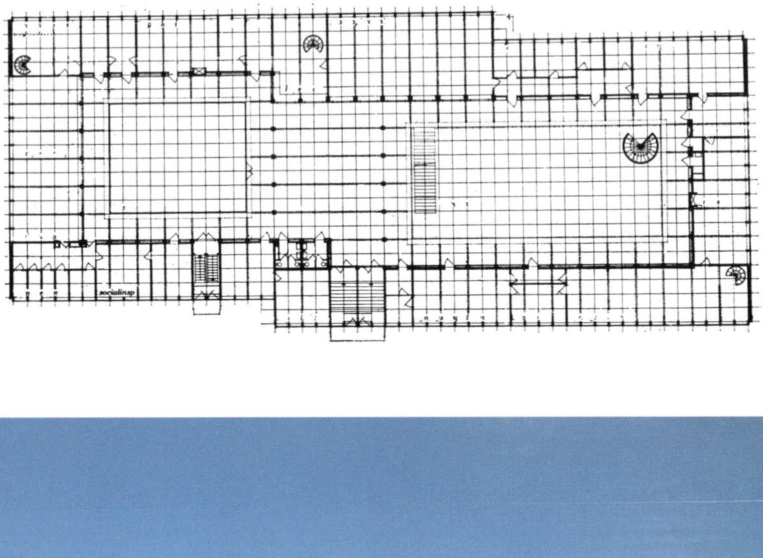

1:750

J199

Denmark's Technical University (DTU)

Anker Engelunds Vej, Lyngby
1959-74

Today, DTU lies surrounded by a large oak forest. The building complex has many different, beautifully designed courtyard gardens.

Client: Ministry of Education'
Architect: Eva & Nils Koppel (after 1967: KKET)
Landscape architect: Edith and Ole Nørgård

The building scheme was a replacement for the original Polyteknisk Læreanstalt on Østre Voldgade in Copenhagen. The new, expansive complex expresses the four separate branches: civil engineering, chemical engineering, electrical engineering and mechanical engineering. Danmarks Ingeniør Akademi was added later. The campus concept employed in the site plan seems immense in terms of the functions and compared to more recent university centers. Due to the large distance between the outermost buildings and the common center, a number of local common facilities were spread throughout the scheme. The architecture is a formal and cold structuralism, which underscores the institution's spacious character.
Bibliography: Arkitektur DK 1974, 205

1:5000

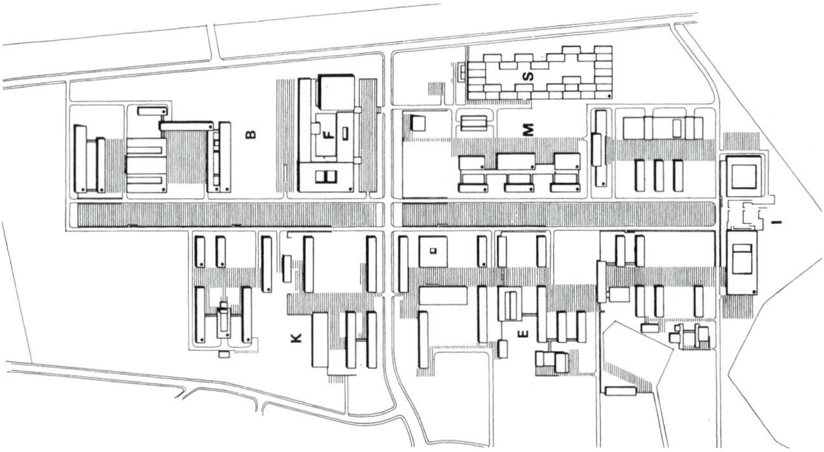

Sankt Nikolaj Church

Strøbyvej 2, Hvidovre
1960

Client: The Danish Catholic Church
Architect: Johan Otto von Spreckelsen
Landscape architect: Ole Nørgård

In a similar manner as Spreckelsen's Sankt Nikolaj Catholic church in Esbjerg from 1969, the church in Hvidovre is characterized by an austere geometric formality. In addition to the church building, the complex includes two separate priest quarters, which are part of the firm and simple facade composition toward both Strøjbyvej and Hvidovrevej roads. The yellow brick facades appear as unbroken surfaces. The plan of the main church space is a distorted square, which results in a tapered entrance and vestibule as well as the fissures in the west facade that admit daylight onto the altar. The distortion of the plan is reflected in the double-curved concrete roof, which is covered on the interior with pine boarding in square panels. The diagonal disposition of the space with the black granite altar in the highest corner is strong and simply reinforced by the building's main form and the eminent treatment of daylight.
Bibliography: Arkitektur DK 1960, 179 and 1990, 14

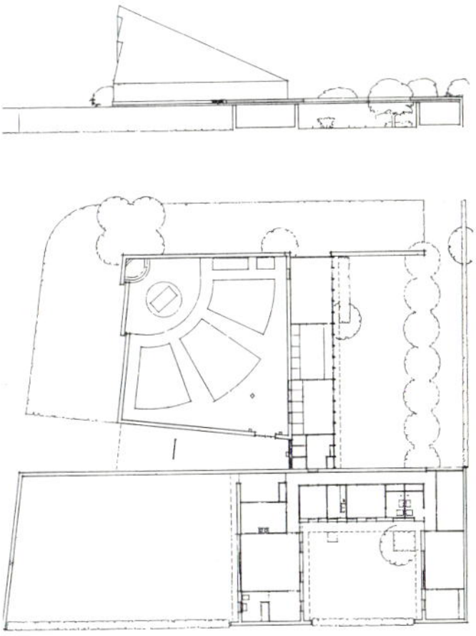

1:1000

J202

Toms Factory

Ballerup Byvej, Ballerup
1960-62

Client: Toms fabrikker A/S
Architect: Arne Jacobsen
Landscape architect: Arne Jacobsen

The factory's production of chocolate and other confectionery items is spread out in an enormous, one-story hall with a great ceiling height. Glassed-in footbridges run above the machinery and are primarily used by the factory's many guests. The concrete element facades are covered with white ceramic tile, which emphasizes the strong simplicity of the large, well-proportion building volumes. As such, the scheme represents a prototype for the flat, extensive industrial complex, and the white facades also signal a hygienic production. In 1995, a guest lobby and video theater were built in the adjoining office building by Dissing + Weitling, arkitektfirma A/S.
Bibliography: Arkitektur DK 1962, 217

Nordre Kirkegård cemetery J203

Gl. Landevej 1, Glostrup
1961

Client: Glostrup Parish Council
Architect: Gehrdt Bornebusch, Max Brüel, Jørgen Selchau and Henning Larsen
Landscape architect: Sven Hansen

The cemetery is a fine example of a modern burial ground from the 1960's, similar to Hillerød Kirkegård and typical of Sven Hansen with its simple, clarified form. It is located on a large, flat grassy field, bordered by a low stone berm planted with a hawthorn hedge. A diagonal cobblestone path runs up to the crematorium chapel. On each side of this path there are four burial spaces, both square and rectangular, surrounded by a precisely formed beech hedge. The formal hedged-in spaces offer a contrast to the spread groves of Scotch pine.

Piniehøj housing group J204

Piniehøj 1-8, Rungsted Kyst
1961-62

Client: Contractor H. Nissen et al
Architect: Jørgen Bo & Vilhelm Wohlert

The interplay with nature is a determining feature in this group of seven single-family homes. The white-painted brick walls and the slim brown eaves represent an extreme simplification of the buildings' outer surface, and together with the large window areas create a flowing transition between architecture and nature. At the same time, the houses are closed off toward the road and the neighbors. The form idiom was inspired by the American architecture of the period, and had been tried earlier by the architects at their Louisiana art museum in Humlebæk, however the simplification went even further here.
Bibliography: Arkitektur DK 1963, 168

J205

The Albertslund Syd new town

Kongsholm Allé et al, Albertslund
1963-68

Client: Two local public housing associations; administrator: KAB and Arbejderbo
Architect: Town plan: Knud Svensson; housing: Fællestegnestuen and Dominia's architect department
Landscape architect Edith and Ole Nørgård.

The placement of almost 2200 housing units within one area was Denmark's largest town building project, and was carried out according to a concept by professor Peter Bredsdorff et al. Both the town plan, housing and building technology represented a major experiment with totally new methods. The differentiation of pedestrian and vehicular traffic was known only from abroad. The atrium houses were only known from the southern countries and Jørn Utzon's Kingo houses from a few years earlier. A stipulation for public subsidies required the scheme to be built with "nontraditional building methods", in other words industrialized building with prefabricated concrete elements. The predominantly low-rise town represented a weighty contribution to the ongoing debate about high-rise contra low-rise housing brought on by the concurrent construction of the Høje Gladsaxe housing scheme (A 214). The division of the Albertslund new town in low atrium houses within a periphery of row houses, and the multistory blocks in the central town band along the canal was a clear but also schematic concept. However there are many visual qualities in the individual houses and housing groups, and the housing type is both spacious and well planned. At the end of the 1970's, extensive building damage was discovered in most of the houses and the resulting renovation has altered their appearance. The atrium houses no longer have flat roofs, and the facades are now sided with wood. The "roof litigation" in Albertslund resulted in a completely new legislation for the repair of building damages.
Bibliography: Arkitektur DK 1969, 1, Landskap 1969, 21

The program for the recreational areas in the Albertslund new town involved a hierarchial structure ranging from the individual atrium courts, the housing group squares, the canal street and quarter parks out to the expansive surrounding landscape, Kongsholm Park and St. Vejleådalen dale, which continue in the Vestskov forest in one direction and to Køge Bugt Strandpark in the other. A clear and pronounced border was established between Albertslund Syd and the river dale. The town ends abruptly with a precise border to the impressive grassy plain.
The area around the town hall lake and the canal was renovated in 1987-90 with new paving, paths, bridges and gardens by Ginman, Harboe and Borup.

1:20.000

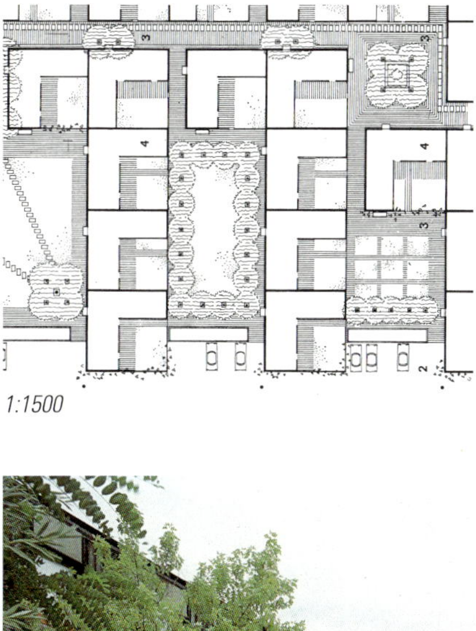

1:1500

J206

Store Vejlådalen with Kongsholmsparken, Vallensbæk Mose, and Herstedvester Badesø

Albertslund
1968-79

Client: Albertslund, Høje Taastrup, Vallensbæk and Ishøj municipalities, I/S Vallensbæk Mose
Town Plan: Peter Bredsdorff, Knud Svensson, Ole Nørgård and municipal engineer Chr. Høegh
Landscape architect: Edith and Ole Nørgård with the Store Vejleå committee (Store Vejleådal), Nørgård, Ginman and Harboe with engineer Ole Mortensen, sculptor Knud Brogård and Albertslund municipal engineering department (Kongsholmparken, Vallensbæk Mose)

Along the Store Vejle Å stream, a continuous landscape belt runs from Herstedvester to the Køge Bugt bay, and buildings, highways and other technical facilities have been erased by landscape screens. When the highly concentrated Albertslund Syd new town was built, Albertslund Municipality acquired a number of large areas, some of which were zoned as recreational areas. A number of grand scenic features were established with surplus earth, building activity, rainwater, agricultural grass and small forestry plants. A long depression in the terrain, the Store Vejleådal dale, is the basis for this project. The dale is covered with expansive grassy meadows and ponds. The wooded areas, primarily mixed oak forests, lie at the top of the dale slopes and visually accent the gentle bowl shape. In some areas, wooded wedges project into the area forming pockets for playing fields, scout cabins, riding schools, etc.
At Kongsholm Park, the surplus earth was used to form a thirty meter high hill in the shape of a truncated cone marked by precise belts of pine. Rainwater from the housing area is collected in delay ponds and led from the town hall pond by a 1500 meter long and 8 meter wide canal through terraced pools at the end, on to two large ponds. Store Vejleådal's water system has two, 35 acre delaying ponds. They are located on each side of the southern highway. The pond on the north is formed with a number of small coves and points for dinghies and fishing. The other pond is deeper and used for waterskiing.
The forest wedges north of Roskildevej road have circular clearings with playing fields and a large swimming pond with slightly sloping edges to form a beach.
At Vallensbæk Mose marsh, south of Kongsholm Park and the highway interchange, a low dam and a geometrical group of hills separate the pond from the low meadows toward south. The landscaping is varied, with a natural character consisting of oak, sloe, hawthorn, willows and poplar.
Bibliography: Landskap 1969, 21 and 1976, 121, Landskab 1992, 172

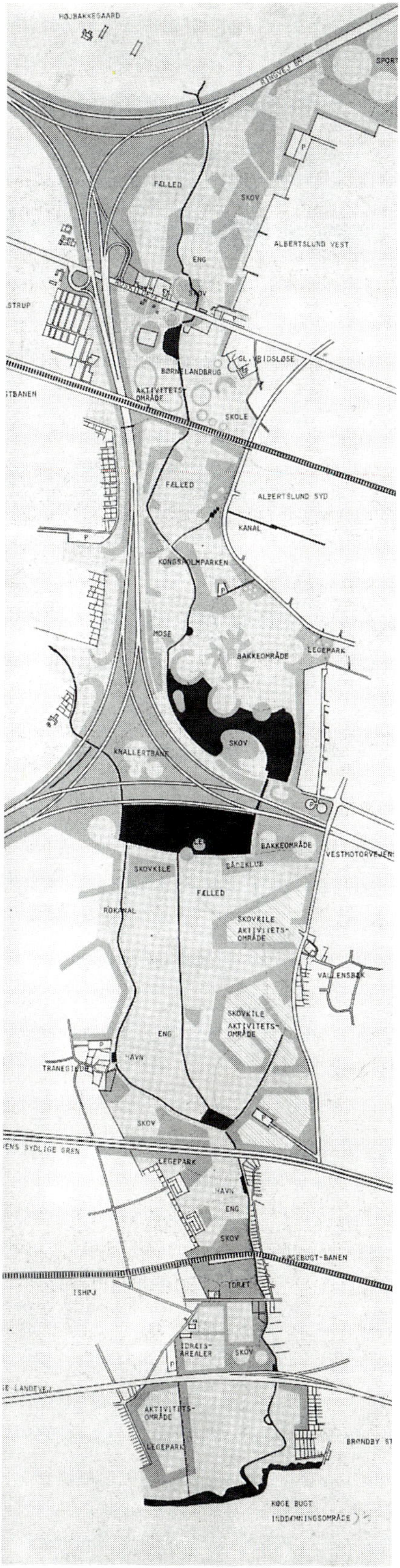
HØJBAKKEGAARD
SPORT
RINGVEJ B4
FÆLLED
SKOV
ALBERTSLUND VEST
ENG
SKOV
STRUP
GL. HEDSLØSE
BØRNELANDBRUG
AKTIVITETS-OMRÅDE
TBANEN
SKOLE
FÆLLED
ALBERTSLUND SYD
KANAL
KONGSHOLMPARKEN
MOSE
BAKKEOMRÅDE
LEGEPARK
SKOV
KNALLERTBANE
BAKKEOMRÅDE
VESTMOTORVEJEN
SKOVKILE
BÅDEKLUB
FÆLLED
ROKANAL
SKOVKILE
AKTIVITETS-OMRÅDE
VALLENSBÆK
SKOVKILE
AKTIVITETS-OMRÅDE
ENG
HAVN
TRANEGILDE
SKOV
ENS SYDLIGE GREN
LEGEPARK
HAVN
ENG
SKOV
KØGEBUGT-BANEN
ISHØJ
IDRÆT
IDRÆTS-AREALER
SKOV
E LANDEVEJ
AKTIVITETS-OMRÅDE
LEGEPARK
BRØNDBY ST
KØGE BUGT
INDDÆMNINGSOMRÅDE

J207 **Kildeskovshal**

Adolphsvej 25, Gentofte
1966-72

Client: Gentofte Municipality
Architect: Karen & Ebbe Clemmensen and Jarl Heger
Engineer: Chr. Ostenfeld & W. Hønsson
Landscape architect: Agnete Muusfeldt

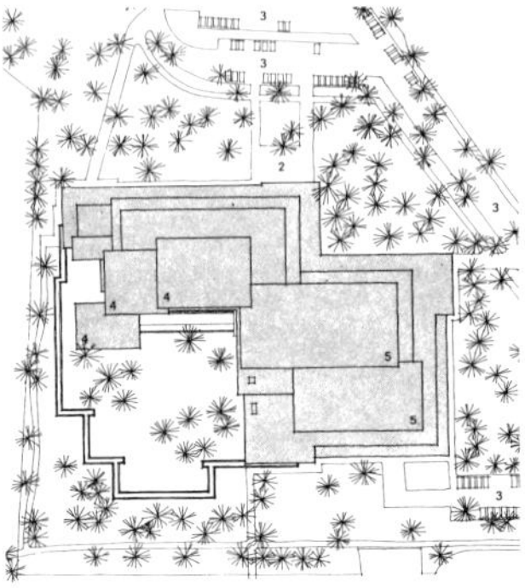

1:5000

The architecture expresses a building complex dedicated to recreation and exercise rather than ardent sport. The location on the wooded site gives the relaxed atmosphere of a picnic pavilion – an expression that is reinforced and developed by the transparent, rhythmic charm. The slim steel columns and the roof's filigree space frame grow out of the heavy brown brickwork in the lower buildings and garden walls. It is a light and poetic metaphor of forest floors, tree trunks and crowns. The scheme is divided in different size cubes with heights according to function: the swimming hall with three pools, and the two sports halls. In this way, the large building volume is reduced to manageable elements with a clarified spatial interplay with the surrounding nature. In keeping with the exquisite location, the quality materials and fine detailing give the scheme an exclusive touch.
Bibliography: Arkitektur DK 1970, 169

1:1000

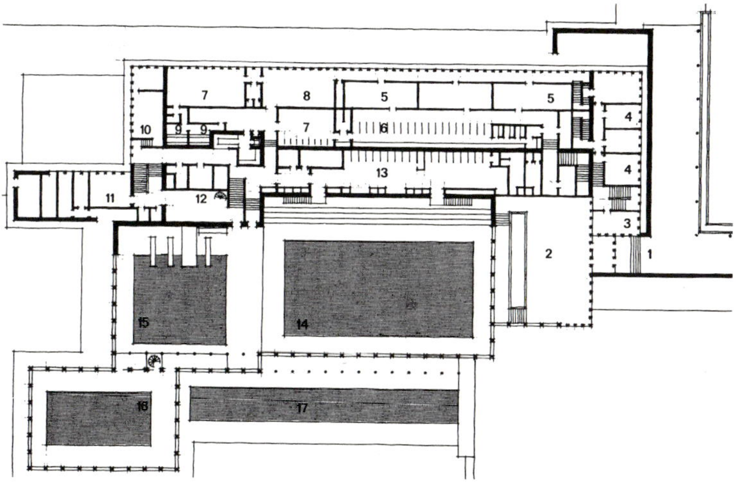

J209

Copenhagen County Hospital in Herlev

Herlev Ringvej, Herlev
1966-76

Client: Copenhagen County
Architect: Gehrdt Bornebusch, Max Brüel, Jørgen Selchau
Landscape architect: Sven Hansen

It is tempting to compare this scheme with the towering gothic cathedrals. A society tries with all its might to express its deep respect and great ambitions by creating grand monuments. The respect here grew out of the sickness of the 1960's, and the political-technical ambitions were to utilize all available resources in visualizing this war against sickness. Architecturally this monument is a success. Despite its vast expanse and skyscraper height, the spatial composition is both formal and organic, structural and living. The interiors have an antiauthoritarian atmosphere, which is underscored by Poul Gernes' decorative color scheme. The structure of the hospital is a three-dimensional system of coordinates. Patient treatment takes place along the horizontal axes in the low, expansive building, and the patients stay in the vertical axis, the "bed tower". The treatment building is organized according to a formal grid like an American city, with treatment streets in one direction and distribution streets in the other. The bed tower has 48 beds and service facilities on each floor. A 120-meter high elevator tower runs up along side the bed tower. At its base there is an auditorium building formed like huge trumpeting organ pipes. The monument has a symbolic effect as well as great sculptural power.
Bibliography: Arkitektur DK 1977, 169

1:1500

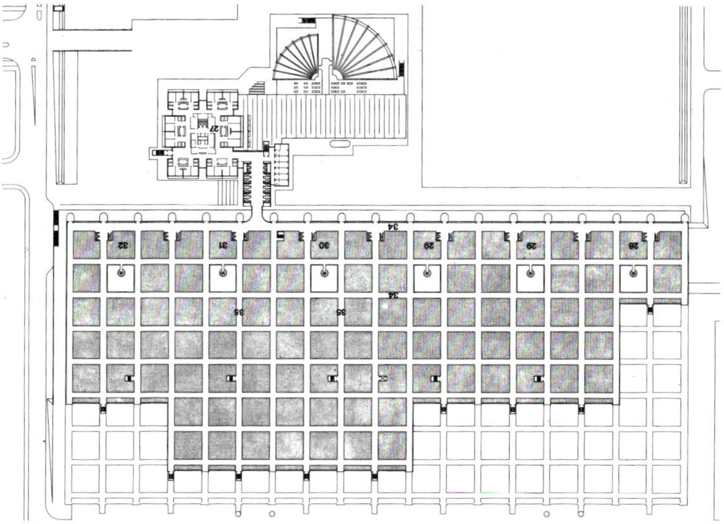

1:4000

J210

Brøndbyernes Haveby, garden city

Mosebjergvej, Brøndby
1964

Client: The national government
Landscape architect: Erik Mygind

The plan of the garden city resembles two clusters of grapes. On the flat fields on both sides of Søndre Ringvej road, 20 circular quarters were established, each with 20 to 30 gardens. Toward the common green, the gardens are edged by sculptured hawthorn hedges. Inside the circles, the ground gradually slopes down toward the center and the round parking area. From here there is access to the individual gardens, which are formed like cake wedges.
Bibliography: Havekunst 1963, 127

J218

The Brøndby Strand housing scheme

Strandesplanaden, Brøndby Strand
1969-73

Client: Four public housing associations
Architect: Svend Høgsbro and Thorvald Dreyer
Landscape architect: Morten Klint and Knud Lund-Sørensen

The ca. 3000 units are distributed in row houses and 4 to 16-story, multistory blocks. The scheme is divided in four identical sections. As part of a comprehensive traffic differentiation plan the high-rise blocks are placed on a raised concrete deck that augments the hard urban atmosphere. However in the 4-story blocks, experiments were made with variations of concrete elements, which has resulted in a studied and varied facade expression. This expression was altered in the 1991-93 renovation by Tegnestue Vandkunsten. Brøndby Strand represented the height of concrete building technology, but as a housing milieu it was criticized for its lack of human scale.

The Farum Midtpunkt housing scheme **J219**

Frederiksborgvej, Midtpunktstien et al, Farum
1970-74

Client: Farum Housing Association and Copenhagen Public Housing Association (KAB)
Architect: Fællestegnestuen
Landscape architect: Ole Nørgård, Måns Ginman and Søren Harboe

The 3- and 4- story terraced housing lies in a formal parallel pattern forming a dense urban quarter. The units are raised above grade with a parking garage under the entire building scheme. The ca. 1650 apartments are primarily for large families. All the units have large terraces and the apartments on the upper level are in two stories. In the center of the wide, lower housing level there is an internal street that offers access to all the units. The facades are concrete, sided with Cor-ten steel as a deliberate, rust-red contrast to the green plants on the terraces. Some of the siding has now been removed. The scheme is a blend of functionalism's consistent solar oriented blocks and the atrium house, introduced a few years earlier at Albertslund Syd (J 205). The masterful treatment of materials and color gave Farum Midpunkt an air of unconventional fashionability. The scheme was planned with consideration for an active tenant participatory democracy, which from the start primarily involved the young and well-to-do. In 1986-89 an extensive renovation was carried out by several offices including A5 Tegnestuen.

Bibliography: Arkitektur DK 1976, 1

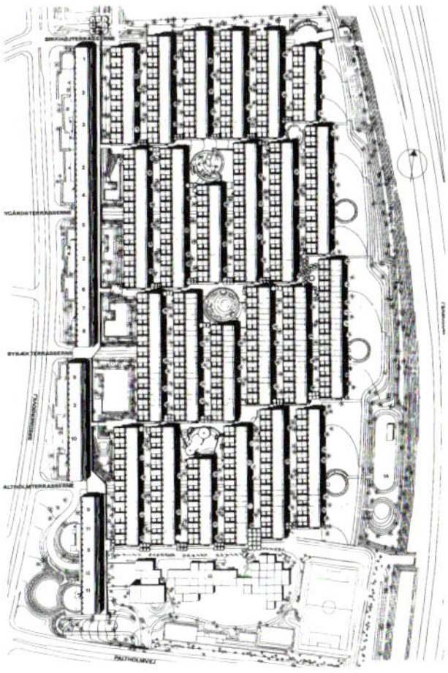

1:12.000

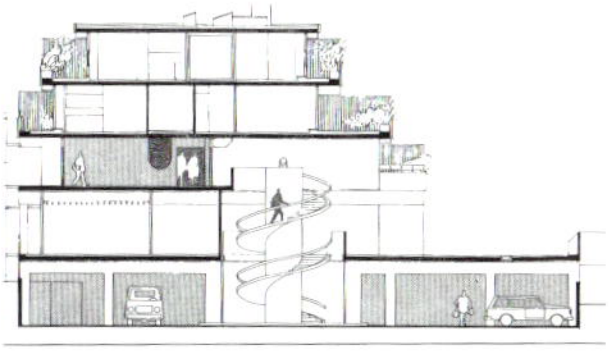

1:800

J222

The Gassehaven housing scheme

Gassehaven, Gl. Holte
1972

Client: A/S V.M. Brockhuus
Architect: Palle Suensons Tegnestue
Landscape architect: Edith and Ole Nørgård

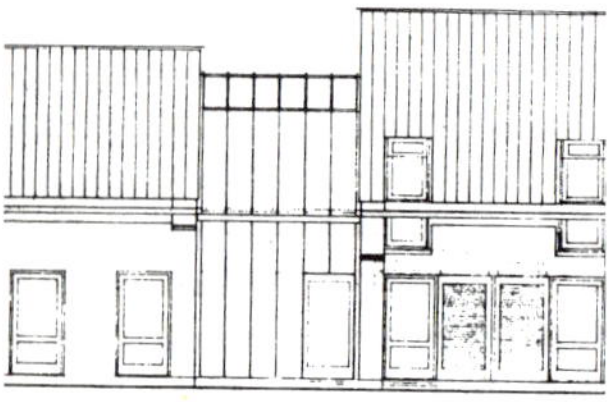

1:300

The interplay between buildings and nature is the main motif of this scheme. This is underscored by the protected landscape toward west, which is drawn in between the two areas of the scheme. Vertical and horizontal shifts help to adapt the row house groups to the nature of the hilly site. The yellow brick architecture is equally reserved – a late offshoot of the functional tradition – but the greenhouses connecting the brick blocks were a new feature at that time. The greenhouses contain a family room and conservatory in two stories, a so-called climate space and a motif that inspired many housing schemes that followed. The 110 units have about 150 sqm in two types.
Bibliography: Arkitektur DK 1973, 1

1:4000

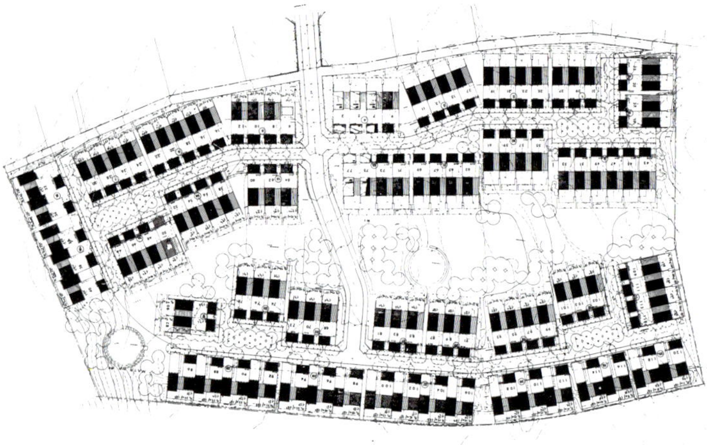

The Galgebakken housing scheme

Gamle Landevej, Albertslund Nord
1973-74

Client: Vridsløselille cooperative housing association (VA)
Architect: Jens Peter Storgaard, Jørn Ørum-Nielsen, Hanne Marcussen and Anne Ørum-Nielsen
Landscape architect: Jørgen Vesterholt

This housing scheme is the result of a 1968 competition. It was a reaction to the dense, high-rise housing of the time and was based on experience gained with the Albertslund Syd scheme. This dense, low scheme was designed with special consideration for the tenants' social contact outside the units, and there is a flowing transition in the hierarchy of private and common outdoor spaces. The ca. 570 units are in one-story atrium houses and two-story row houses. The atrium houses are gathered in a cross pattern, which offers a variety of neighbor contact between the units. The row houses have a split-level section with a kitchen and dining area on the middle level facing the path between the houses. The construction system was prefabricated concrete elements, but the wooden facade areas and the landscaping along the paths and private terraces are the dominant visual features. Galgebakken was a pioneering effort in the dense/low-rise housing movement that followed.
Bibliography: Arkitektur DK 1974, 81

1:15.000

There is a fine system of differentiated outdoor spaces with small peaceful gardens on one side of the row houses and between the atrium houses, and more outward-oriented front areas facing the access paths. These pleasant paths, which in some areas are covered by pergolas with creeping plants, lead to the large common areas for play and ball games. The idea was that play activity should take place throughout the scheme and not just on special playgrounds. The entire complex is surrounded by a wide, lush wooded area.

J226

The Hyldespjældet housing scheme

Damgårdsvej, Kærmosevej, Albertslund Nord
1974-76

Client: Vridsløselille Housing Association
Architect: Ole Asbjørn Birch
Landscape architect: Andreas Bruun

1:10.000

Compared to the standards of the time, Hyldespjældet with its 304 units was a modest project, but the apartments were widely varied in plan and there were ten different types in one and three-story buildings. The internal path system divides the scheme in three sections, each with right-angled housing groups. By rotating these formations, a variety of street and square patterns was created, which together with the different building heights and facade colors gives the scheme a Mediterranean character. Hyldespjældet demonstrates that a totally industrialized building project with room-size concrete elements can also result in a living and almost exotic housing milieu.
Bibliography: Arkitektur DK 1977, 314

Vangede Church

Vangedevej 50, Vangede
1974

Client: Vangede parish council
Architect: Johan Otto von Spreckelsen
Landscape architect: Edith and Ole Nørgård

All of Spreckelsen's four churches (three in Copenhagen and one in Esbjerg) are based on the square and the cube. At Vangede Church, the plan of the church space is a square, as are the diagonally adjoining spaces. The organ case front is of steel sections divided up in squares. The suspended square ceiling is rotated diagonally in relation to the space thus illuminating the corners with a diffused daylight from above. In one of these corners is the organ, while the altar is in the center.
The church complex also includes a meeting room, offices and living quarters for the verger in two separate buildings. The outer red brick surface appears like a crystalline formation, and the church space is a refined interplay of geometry and softly modelled daylight.
Bibliography: Arkitektur DK 1990, 15

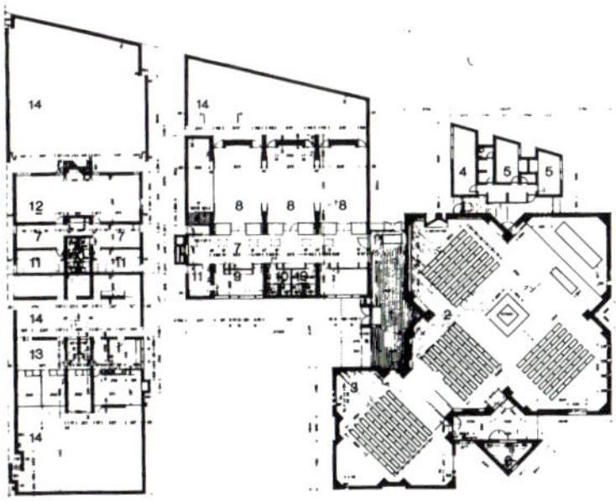

1:1500

J228 **Bagsværd Church**
Taxvej 16, Bagsværd
1974-76

Client: Bagsværd parish council
Architect: Jørn Utzon

This church exhibits a dramatic tension between in and out. The exterior has an industrial, prefabricated character that does not say "church", but there are still discreet, refined facade details. The interior is magnificent, not because of expensive materials but due to a flowing interplay of soft and sharp forms and a profusion of finely varied daylight. The outer roof construction's free and moving span between the narrow, stepped down side buildings is simple and structural, while the undulating concrete ceiling in the church offers a strong and poetic cloud metaphor, which was the architect's greatest inspiration. Just as the ceiling is spatially diffuse, the walls in the church are dissolved. The space runs partially out into the side buildings from where a strong, reflected daylight enters, and the altar wall consists only of a fine net of thin, white ceramic tiles. While both formal and organic, the church is a very personal work without any clear architectural paradigm. It has contributed new dimensions to Danish church building, which have no religious reference, but are universal.
Bibliography: Arkitektur DK 1983, 82

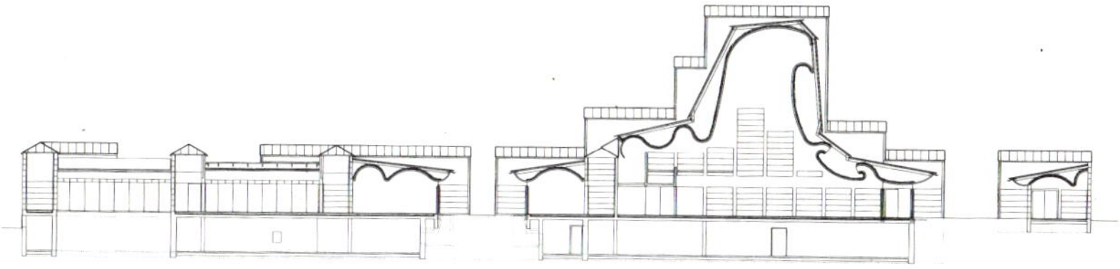

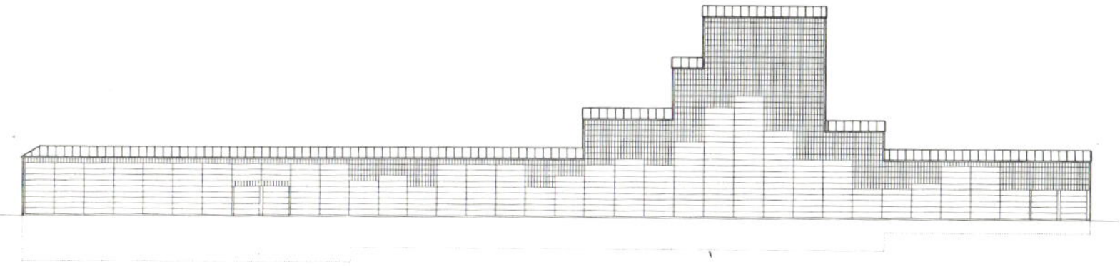

1:800

J231 — **The Gadekæret housing scheme**

Ishøj Boulevard and Ishøj Parkvej, Ishøj
1975-79

Client: Vridsløselille Public Housing Association
Architect: Kooperativ Byggeindustri A/S (KBI)
Landscape architect: KBI together with Andreas Bruun, Peter Samuelsen and Henrik Ulfstedt

The Gadekær scheme was a reaction to the uniform character of the large multistory projects. Here the architects sought inspiration in the old Danish village motif while still employing prefabricated industrialized concrete element methods. There are visual qualities in the winding streets and crooked squares, and the small pond that gives the scheme its name, contributes to the feeling of provincial idyll. However the imitation of the old villagescape emphasizes the lack of old village functions, and Gadekæret has more the character of a stage set than other similar schemes. The 560 units have access to common facilities.
Bibliography: Arkitektur DK 1977, 324

J237 — **Sophus Lund's flowergarden**

Toftegårdsvej 3A and 3B. Lyngby
1978-81

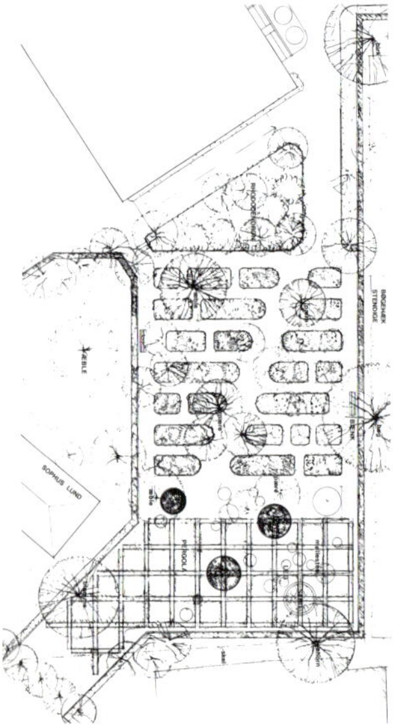

Client: Lyngby-Taarbæk Municipality
Landscape architect: Box 25 Arkitekter and the municipal park director's department

The closed and lush garden consists of two quite different areas. An airy, arched pergola structure of aluminum sections is covered with wisteria in one area. The other, colorful and luxuriant flower garden consists of cat's tongue shaped beds planted with a fine composition of perennials below flowering bushes. A fieldstone berm with a wide beech hedge marks the border toward the cemetery and the buildings.
Bibliography: Landskab 1981, 101

Køge Bugt Strandpark **J238**

1977-80

Client: Køge Bugt Strandpark I/S
Architect: Ib Andersen and Elith Juul Møller, Peter L. Stephensen
Landscape architect: Svend Algren

Køge Bugt Strandpark, together with the green wedge between Køge Bugt banen and Roskildebanen, and Vestskoven is an important part of the recreational areas in Copenhagen's western district. Much of the building activity in the greater Copenhagen area during the sixties and seventies took place in the western district. According to the comprehensive plans, more than 40,000 housing units were to be built as well as facilities for a well-functioning urban community. On the coastal stretch from Avedøre Holme to Greve, a massive land reclamation project resulted in a 1250-acre recreational area. An eightkilometer stretch of coastline was moved further out into Køge Bugt bay. The project goal was to create a new recreational area that harmonized with the existing landscape features. The sand islands have been reinforced and a long range of dunes planted with beach grass to created expansive new areas of sand bathing beaches. Behind the rows of dunes are large areas with lakes divided by tongues of land with docks, well suited for sailing dinghies and windsurfing. In addition, there are four pleasure boat harbors built according to the "island harbor principle", where the harbors can be expanded in well-arranged divisions. The beach houses, club houses, life guard towers, signage and other equipment have a rustic and sober expression in keeping with the dunes and the surrounding landscape.

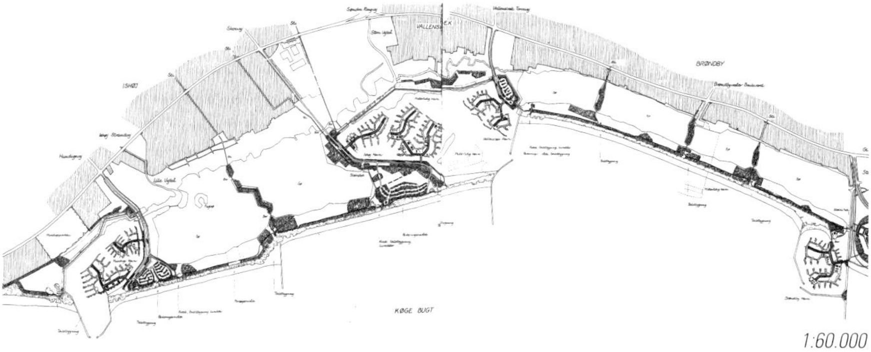

1:60.000

J240

Stavnsholt Church

Stavnsholtvej 25, Farum
1979-81

Client: Farum parish council
Architect: Johan Otto von Spreckelsen
Landscape architect: Edith Nørgård

The site plan is base on two squares with aligned diagonals. One of the squares is the church and the other is a courtyard surrounded by offices and meeting rooms. The church is a cube with facades divided in large areas of yellow brick. The outer walls slope at the base for structural as well as acoustical reasons. This detail is emphasized by the reveal in the low windows that exposes the thick, sloping brickwork. Seen from the exterior, the complex is an intricate sculpture of closed, cubistic forms. The finely proportioned geometry in the homogeneous, pale materials in the church and courtyard offer a sensitive setting for contemplation.
Bibliography: Arkitektur DK 1990, 18

1:1000

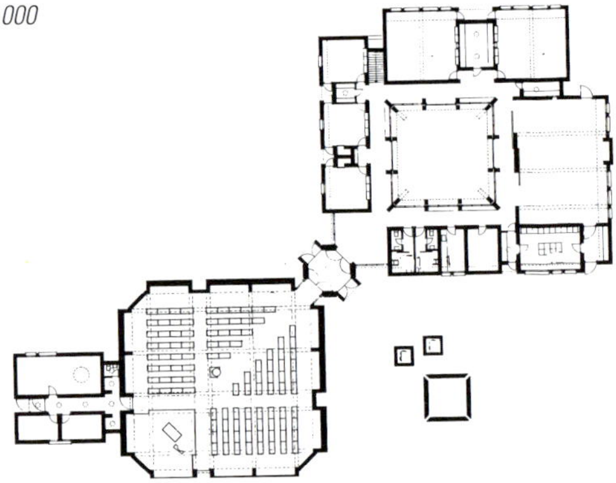

Høje Taastrup county high school **J241**

Frøgård Allé 2, Høje Taastrup
1980-81

Client: Copenhagen County
Architect: Henning Larsens Tegnestue
Landscape architect: Regitze Johnsen and Malene Hauxner

During the 1970's it was quite common to build special subject high schools without homerooms for the pupils. In the 1978 competition for this high school, won by Henning Larsen, the client wanted the school to be divided in smaller units called home areas. The scheme consists of three of these areas, each with its own common area, and a fourth that contained special subject classes, the teachers' facilities and the administrative offices. The four, two-story units are grouped around a courtyard, which is the center of the scheme. The school's large central interior space, with the canteen and library has large areas of glass opening onto the courtyard. In a similar way, the architecture opens to the countryside with a cheerful, summery attitude due to its blue and white striped awninglike roofs – a discreet postmodernistic gesture. From the surrounding park landscape, the school appears as a sober formation of white blocks akin to early functionalistic buildings. In this way the scheme circles elegantly around modernism.
Bibliography: Arkitektur DK 1982, 274

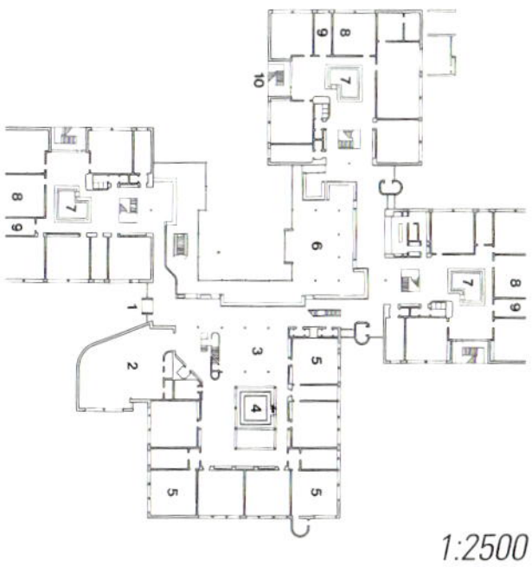

1:2500

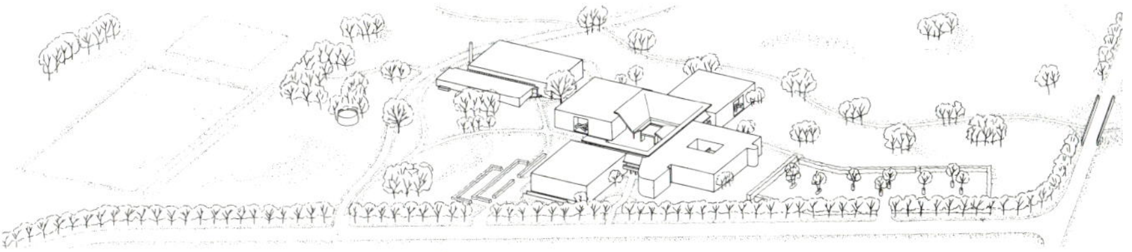

J242

Stenvad School and the Fuglsang Park housing scheme

Borgmester Jespersens Vej, Farum
1979-81 and 1981-83

Client: Farum Municipality and Boligfonden Bikuben, The Medical Society's Housing Building Association
Architect: A5 Tegnestuen and Tegnestuen Vandkunsten
Landscape architect: A5 Tegnestuen and Tegnestuen Vandkunsten

The integration of schools, recreational areas, housing and ecology was the theme for the 1979 competition won by these two offices. They created an almost organic, natural structure for the housing and its surroundings, which made the plan one of the most complete and expressive in the post war years. The Stenvad School is built like a small town with streets and a square. It is divided according to function so that the special subject classes are in the south, angled wing, while the homerooms are in the four, freestanding sections toward north. The roofs are of grey fiber cement corrugated sheeting and the facades are mortar-brushed brick with panelling of wood and steel, painted in bright colors. The housing scheme consists of 137 public housing units and 52 cooperative units as well as a common house in the western end of the area. The plan pattern created a mixture of town and gardenhouses, as the units on one side face the small streets and on the other side open to the common greens in the middle of the complex. In this way there is a hierarchy of private, semi-private and public outdoor spaces, running from the units all the way out to the school. The sloping sequence of building heights along the streets facing the large green underscores the plan concept. Although the construction employed standardized industrial building methods, there are many visually pleasant surprises akin to the architecture of Stenvad School.
Bibliography: Arkitektur DK 1982, 224 and 1985, 198

1:6000

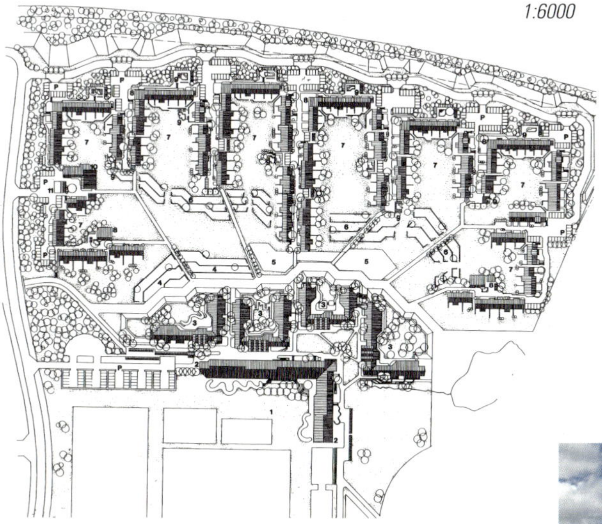

J243

Opstandelses Church

Gymnasievej 2, Albertslund
1982-84

Client: Herstedvester parish council
Architect: Inger and Johannes Exner
Landscape architect: Edith and Ole Nørgård

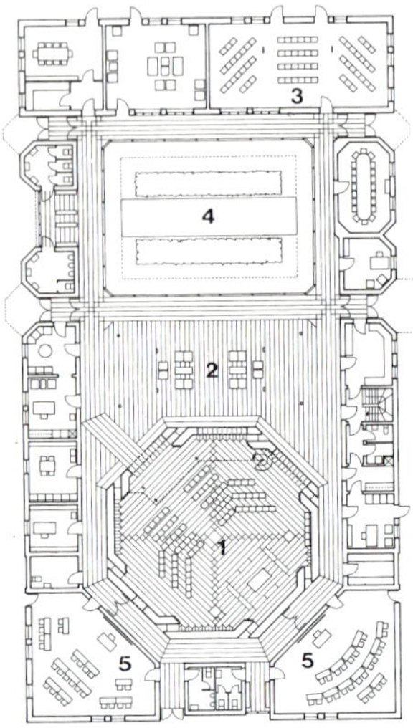

1:800

The church lies in an urban context in the new town, Albertslund. Therefore, it was formed as a compact rectangular complex of low buildings surrounding the main church building and a courtyard. The flower-shaped bell tower is the only element outside the complex. Its unfolded petal forms are repeated in the church building's brick surfaces and indicate an upwardness throughout the scheme. The main form has several sources of inspiration: Octagonal Byzantine churches, the apse gallery at Roskilde Cathedral, and the German eighteenth century central room churches. Church history and the liturgy played an important role in the design of the church. The octagonal church space with the light slots, which like a sundial register the changing light during the day, despite its geometrical clarity, also has a tone of mannerism and mysticism due to the organic rose-colored wall ornamentation. Irrationality is also present in the exterior, which exhibits a deliberately planned decay. The peeling facade stucco symbolizes the world's entropy – a motif used by the architects in previous schemes. (F 10)
Bibliography: Arkitektur DK 1988, 114

The Hesselbo housing scheme and Nørgård's estate J244

Sækkedamsvej 4-146 and 5-177, Værløse
1983-84

Client: Værløse Public Housing Association, administration DAB
Architect: Tegnestuen Vandkunsten
Landscape architect: Tegnestuen Vandkunsten

The housing association built 121 units in this scheme, while a cooperative housing association built 24. The latter were larger as were their common facilities. This difference is a result of housing legislation, however the site plan and architecture gather the scheme together in a masterful whole. A characteristic feature is the outer side of the perimeter buildings' angled form, where the large yellow tile roof surfaces offer a lively color contrast to the green lawns and wooded areas. The units in these buildings have two and three stories toward the street, and the living rooms toward the open areas have sloping ceilings that follow the roof. The so-called estate houses, that lie perpendicular to the perimeter buildings are one-story, split-level, which results in covered entrances and terraces. This unit type also has sloping ceilings in the large spaces.
Bibliography: Arkitektur DK 1985, 206

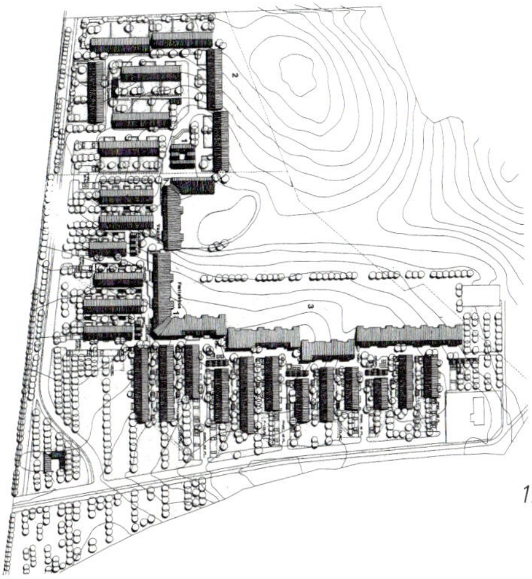

1:6000

J245

Crimpgården

Solvang 30, Allerød
1984-85

Client: Crimp A/S: Kjeld Schouboe
Architect: Tegnestuen Vandkunsten
Landscape architect: Tegnestuen Vandkunsten

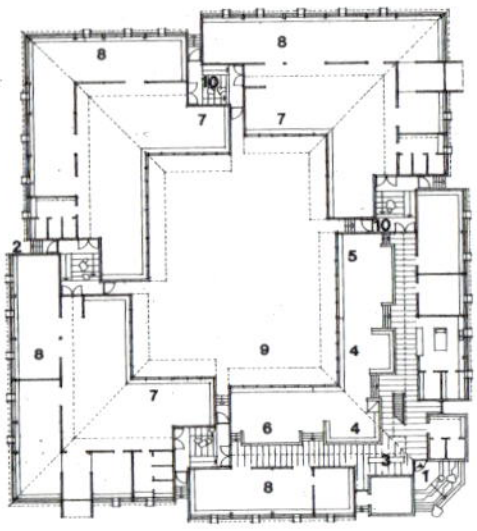

1:1500

This electronics company building is a radical departure from the many commercial buildings in this quite ordinary industrial zone. The fortresslike exterior seems forbidding from the distance, but on closer inspection it grows friendlier due to the unorthodox details, and inside there is the relaxed, cozy atmosphere of a country lodge. The scheme consists of four identical corner buildings, with two stories on the outer edge and one story facing the courtyard. The offices and meeting rooms are on the upper floor. The lower floor is in concept a continuous sequence of spaces with the canteen, lounge and demonstration department surrounding the courtyard. Crimpgården is a clear architectural expression of a democratic attitude, which is evident in the main disposition and details, with a good portion of humor.
Bibliography: Arkitektur DK 1985, 252 og 1994, 208

Gentofte main library

Ahlmanns Allé 6, Gentofte
1984-85

Client: Gentofte Municipality
Architect: Henning Larsens Tegnestue A/S
Lanscape architect: Knud W.Ø . Larsen

This building scheme is the result of a closed competition in 1978. It consists of a two-story perimeter building surrounding a two-story library hall. There are two entrances, and the area between them, which contains the lobby, circulation desk and newspaper reading room, serves as a public walk and separates the library hall from the building section with the exhibition facilities and meeting room. The perimeter building houses offices, carrels and reading rooms. The interior is white and sculptural with large variations in light intensity, spatial form and size, and in the shift between sharp and smooth forms. The exterior expression has functionalistic references. The plastic treatment of the building and the free form expression that characterize this scheme also can be associated with the contemporary works of Richard Meier and the "New York Five". The marble floors, the rounded white concrete structure and the perfectionistic detailing give the building an exclusive character not seen since the library and archive buildings of the nineteenth century.

Bibliography: Arkitektur DK 1985, 318

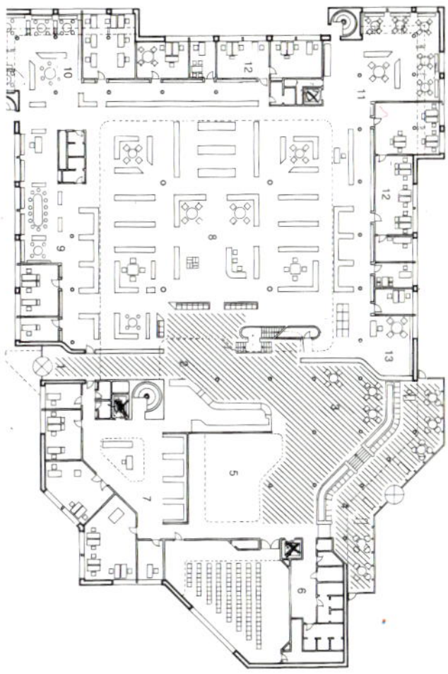

1:1200

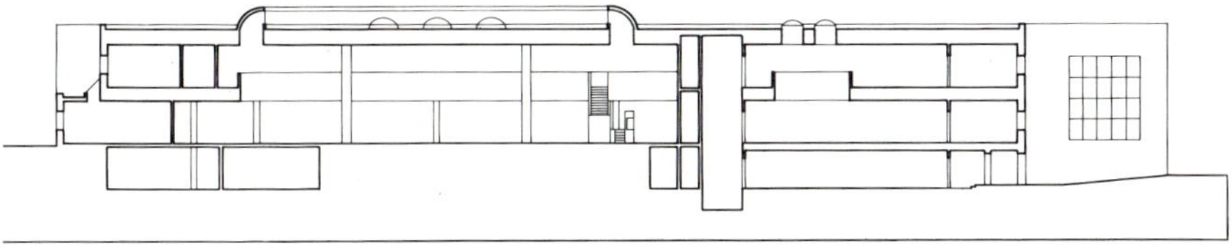

J247

The Hulsø Ege housing group
Knudsvej 1-7, Rungsted Kyst
1983-86

Client: Peter Suhr and Jørgen Smidt
Architect: Tage Lyneborg

The four atrium houses lie on a square site surrounded by a stepped wall. The houses are individually formed within this clear demarcation. In this way, the one-story housing form is related to Jørn Utzon's atrium houses in Helsingør and Fredensborg. The scheme is discreetly recessed in the sloping site, and the grey brickwork and white woodwork underscore the architecture's restraint on this idyllic scenic site. The houses form a small square and an alley that leads down to the marsh and pond, and the dense landscaping forms a lush background for this architectural chamber recital.
Bibliography: Arkitektur DK 1991, 66

J252

The Egedalsvænge housing scheme and renovation
Egedalsvej, Kokkedal
1971-73, renovated 1986

Client: KBI/ FB-the Trade Union Housing Association
Architect: Hoff & Windinge, Tegnestuen Møllen ApS (renovation)
Landscape architect: Tegnestuen Møllen ApS

This building scheme went through a vicious circle of social and technical problems, which led to a radical renovation that totally changed the appearance. The original flat roof was altered to a saddle roof with broad eaves. The facades were given a new siding and insulation, as well as small shed roofs over the doors and windows, and the balconies were enclosed with sliding windows converting them to small greenhouses. The largest of the ca. 500 apartments were subdivided into smaller units making them easier to let. The scheme also contains 166 youth units and several day-care centers. Egedalsvænge now has a bright and living appearance, which is a radical contrast to its former state.
Bibliography: Arkitektur DK 1988, 28

Avedøre district power and heating plant J253

Hammerholmen 50, Avedøre Holme
1985-91

Client: Elkraft A.m.b.a.
Architect: Arkitektfirmaet Claus Bjarrum A/S and Jørgen Hauxner
Landscape architect: Henrik Ulfstedt, Malene Hauxner

The project is the result of a closed competition in 1983. The site is a flat, reclaimed coastal area, which reinforces the enormous scale of the scheme. The tallest building is the boiler and generator hall and the lower building house the smoke cleaning system. The outer shell is a steel structure sided with coated aluminum. Both buildings have low pitched, 1:4 roofs, which together with the two aligned roofs surfaces gather the enormous volumes in a clear, prismatic structure visible from a great distance. In a similar fashion as these large simplified forms, the detailing is especially meticulous, making the building a major work of postwar industrial architecture.
Bibliography: Arkitektur DK 1991, 209

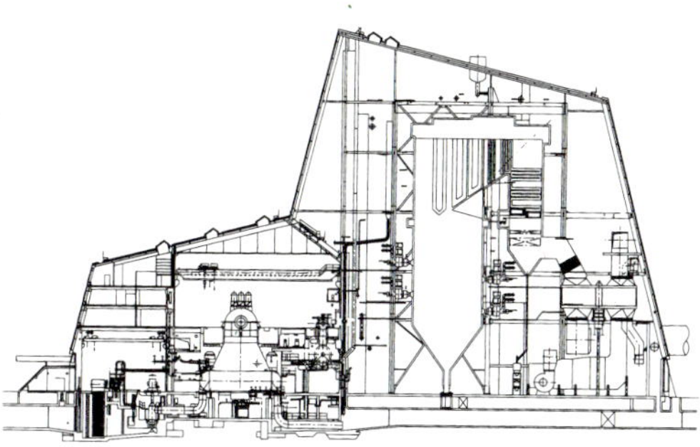

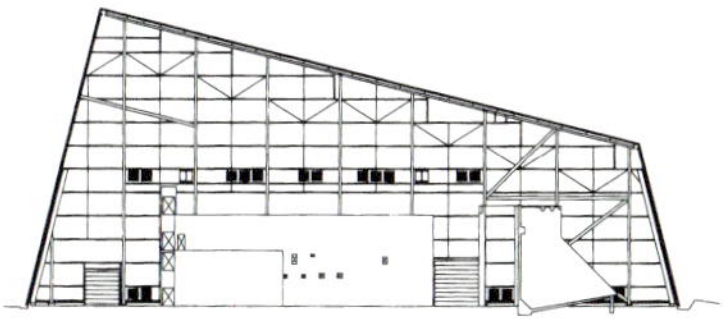

1:2000

J257

Høje Taastrup new town

Høje Taastrup
1978-

Client: The national government and Høje Taastrup Municipality
Architect: Jacob Blegvad Arkitektkontor
Landscape architect: Paul le Fevre Jacobsen

The winning proposal in the 1978 closed competition for a new town in Høje Taastrup was a surprise. City planning in the previous decade had dealt with small, comfortable garden towns with picturesque dense/low-rise housing. In sharp contrast to this, the plan for the new town Høje Taastrup was neoclassicistic with axes, symmetry and formal, identical building inspired by the Luxembourg architects, the Krier brothers' classical urban visions. The plan anticipated housing development of the 1980's with the increased interest in classicism such as Dalgas Have from the close of the decade (E 265). Despite a number of compromises during realization, Høje Taastrup is the largest and most consistent effort with classic urban planning, which also included an integration of housing and commercial spaces. The plan has two main axes: one running across the railway line where the new station is located (J 258), and another to the south. The junction of these two axes is the town's central square, which is accented by a monumental sculpture. The classic scenery continues in the buildings, which according to a fixed set of standards have classical fragments in the facades and details. The contemporary character of the town's life and the building technology emphasizes the pastiche in the town plan and architecture.
Bibliography: Arkitektur DK 1988, 294

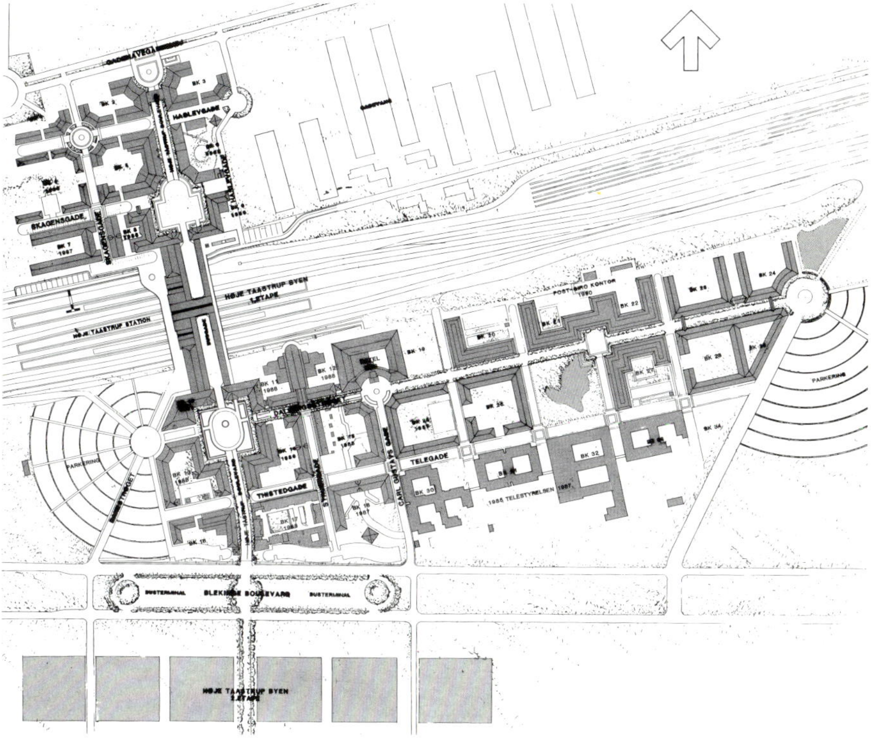
BK 3
BK 2
HASLEVGADE
SKAGENSGADE
SKAGENSGADE
BK 7
1987
HØJE TAASTRUP BYEN
1.ETAPE
HØJE TAASTRUP STATION
BK 19
BK 12
1988
BK 11
1988
TELEGADE
THISTEDGADE
CARL GUSTAVS GADE
BK 30
BK 18
1987
BK 17
BK 15
PARKERING
POST- BIRO KONTOR
1990
BK 22
BK 24
BK 21
BK 20
BK 28
BK 27
BK 32
BK 34
1985 TELESTYRELSEN 1987
BUSTERMINAL
BUSTERMINAL

1:8000

J258 **Høje Taastrup Station**
Høje Taastrup Boulevard, Høje Taastrup
1986

Client: DSB, Høje Taastrup Municipality and the Greater Copenhagen Council
Architect: DSB building department and Jacob Blegvad A/S Arkitektkontor
Landscape architect: Poul le Fevre Jacobsen, DSB, Roskilde forestry department

The station spans the railway line creating a connecting link between Høje Taastrup's two town quarters. The center, barrel-vaulted roof reaches out over the bus street along the station, which is further marked by portals. The large expanse of the station hall and the vast amount of daylight streaming in through the end-wall windows give a visual flow that is fitting for a railway station. The classical formal roof form and the furnishings reinforce the cold countenance. This architectural attitude and that of Høje Taastrup new town are part of the same neorationalistic town plan from 1978. The simple forms used in the station have such a strong symbolic value that Høje Taastrup is officially called "the town of arches".
Bibliography: Arkitektur DK 1988, 314

1:4000

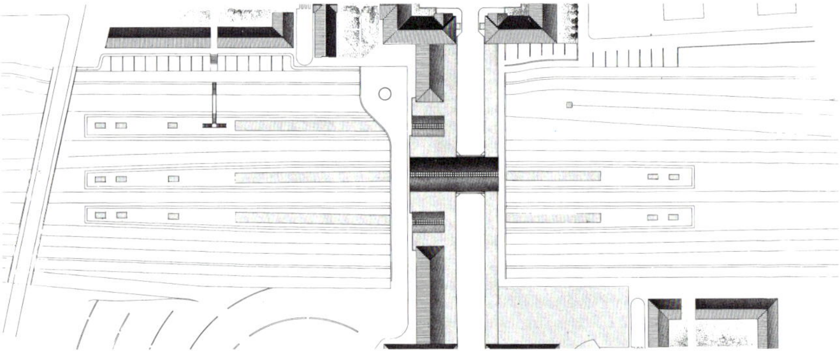

Culture and commercial center, Trommen

Hovedgaden 55, Hørsholm
1986-88

Client: Hafnia Ejendomme
Architect: Knud Munk

The scheme, which is the result of a 1985 competition, consists of three functions, each with its own building idiom. A straight pedestrian walk connects these functions: a commercial center with shops and offices; the polygonal culture center, which houses a large library with balconies; and a cylindrical shaped theater called Trommen (the drum). The three functions are marked with different patterns of glazed brick on the yellow brick facades. The commercial building has horizontal bands, the library has diagonal, crossing lines and the theater has zigzag stripes. These super graphics have their roots in the decorated architecture of the nineteenth century, and are characteristic of the architect. Together with the clarified forms they give the place a distinct identity.
Bibliography: Arkitektur DK 1991, 186

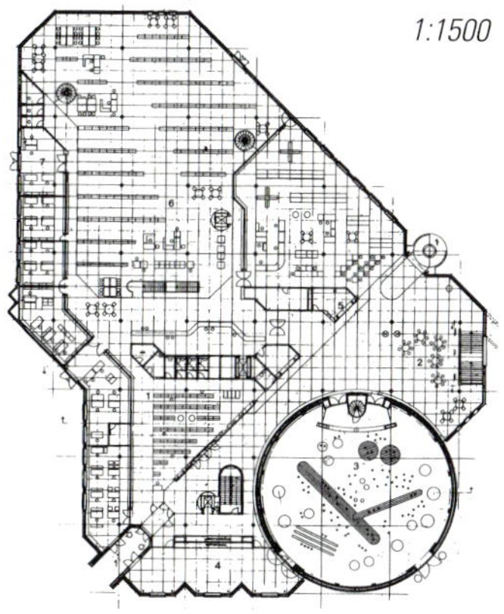

1:1500

J262

The Baltica office complex

Klausdalsbrovej 601, Ballerup
1987-89

Client: Assurance-Compagniet Baltica, life insurance company
Architect: Dall & Lindhardtsen A/S
Landscape architect: Peter Thorsen

This enormous office complex, the size of a small provincial town, borders on a park area. The green surroundings form a contrast to the low, compact building mass and the dark red brick facades. Besides the central building that houses the canteen with large windows facing the park, the scheme consists of two building types. One is formed like a city block and is primarily for small offices. The other has a glass-roofed central corridor and is for large offices. In contrast to the dark facades, the interior is white and the internal traffic paths are like sunlit Mediterranean streets. As a setting for an insurance company, the scheme has an appropriate atmosphere of seriousness and familiar contrasts.
Bibliography: Arkitektur DK 1991, 26

1:5000

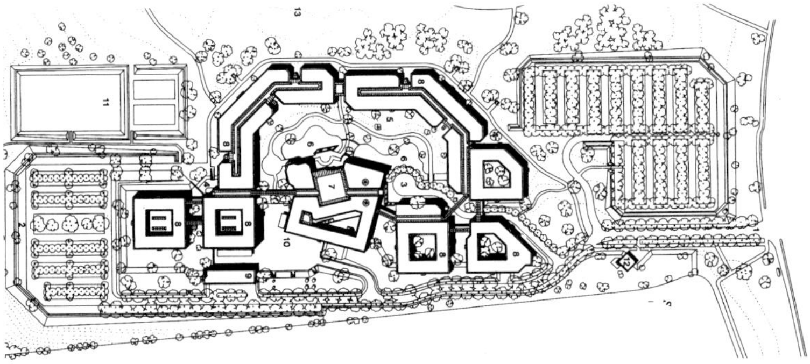

J275

Egedal Church

Egedalsvej 3, Kokkedal
1990

Client: Karlebo Municipality
Architect: Fogh & Følner Arkitektfirma ApS
Landscape architect: Nørgaard & Holscher

The client wanted the building to look like a church. This wish was fulfilled without the use of traditional church building forms, but the traditional cloister complex served as a model for the main disposition. The small courtyard that opens onto the "town hall green" is thus the center of the scheme. This is a logical consequence of the scheme's dual function as both parish community center and church, even though it makes access to the church more ambiguous. The church is one of several similar buildings and the simplicity of the interior is almost puritanical. The white, brick walls are discreetly broken by courses of white glazed brick, the pale wood strip ceiling waves slightly to one side and daylight streams in from tall slots along the side toward the altar. The traditional procession form of the room and the austere, lyrical appearance clearly signals that it is a church. From outside, the roof surfaces all slope toward the courtyard, creating a concentrated introverted impression. Together with the fixed blocks of orange brick with white horizontal stripes as a scale giving element, these features create a living arrangement with the timeless character of a place of worship.
Bibliography: Arkitektur DK 1994, 170

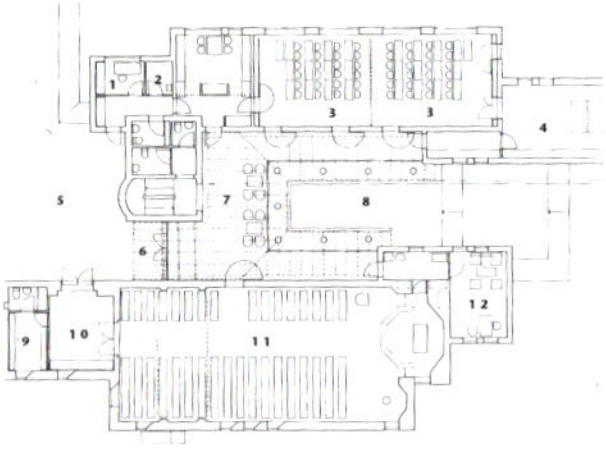

1:1000

Novo Nordisk Park J277

Novo Nordisk Park, Måløv
1991

Client: Novo Nordisk A/S
Architect: Dissing + Weitling
Landscape architect: Dissing + Weitling

As a pharmaceutical research center the scheme consists primarily of laboratories. These lie in buildings that radiate from the main building's semicircular plan. This assures that most of the workplaces in the center have a fine view of the landscape toward north. A two-story lobby space runs the entire length of the curved main building and gives access to all the facilities. The main form of the scheme as a half wheel with spokes, has a formal, urban character toward the arrival side, and a soft flexibility toward the landscape. In a similar way, the architecture is both logically formal in its principle features, and sensitive in materials and details. The existing buildings are only part of a comprehensive plan, which besides research facilities also includes production.
Bibliography: Arkitektur DK 1992, 236

The Morbærhaven youth housing scheme, renovation J278

Morbærhaven, Albertslund Nord
1991-93

Client: DIS Bygge- og Ejendomsadministration
Architect: Tegnestuen Domus ApS
Landscape architect: Tegnestuen Domus ApS

Morbærhaven consists of ca. 1100 youth housing units and four center buildings. It was built in 1971 as an extremely rationalized buildings scheme that soon proved to have a limited durability. This was the reason for the radical renovation that totally altered the architectural expression. The flat roofs on the housing wings were replaced with saddle roofs, which in some cases have given an extra floor. The many small units were thus supplemented with a number of two-room units. The center buildings have also been given an extra floor under the new saddle roofs, and new stairways of glass and steel at the end walls. The new architecture is a pleasant but firm response to the problematic past.
Bibliography: Arkitektur DK 1995, 150

J279

The Dianas Have housing scheme

Dianas Have 11-77 and Søndre Jagtvej 5 A-C, Hørsholm
1992

Client: Magistrenes Pensionskasse
Architect: Tegnestuen Vandkunsten
Landscape architect: Tegnestuen Vandkunsten

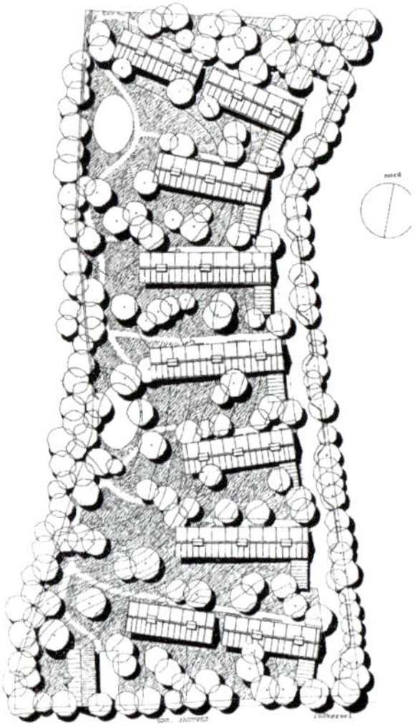

The site was on a choice piece of north Zealand landscape, covered with large old trees and adjacent to a lake with Hørsholm Church and protected buildings on its edge. The scheme lives up to its unique location with a refined interplay of architecture and nature. The roof surfaces on the individual buildings lie on the same horizontal level, while the building forms follow the sloping terrain. This is both a supple and self-aware consideration for the surroundings and is characteristic of the entire scheme. The long buildings, which run from two to three stories, are penetrated by openings for transverse paths that weave the buildings tightly together with the terrain. The black and grey horizontal facade bands signal an elegant lightness, which is reinforced by the yellow, unstained pine windows, and the thin roofs with broad eaves hold these moving building forms together. The sheds and carports lie along the access roads between the buildings and in a simple fashion, mark the border between the semi-public and private common areas. There are 41 units of very differing size and form, in one to three stories. The office employed the same building type in a concurrent project in Borås Sweden and later in Skejby near Århus. At Dianas Have, the theme is played with extreme virtuosity. Among the large, nondescript private housing schemes of the period, Dianas Have stands out as an elegant and relaxed exception.
Bibliography: Arkitektur DK 1994, 256

The Jonstruphusene housing scheme

Chr. Hauchs Allé 11 and Jonstrupvej, Jonstrup
1993-94

Client: Hareskov-Værløse cooperative housing association
Architect: Boje Lundgaard & Lene Tranberg
Landscape architect: Svend Kierkegaard ApS

The site plan is both formal and living with axes running through portals and an implied symmetry around the common areas. In a similar fashion, the tall building section and the high facades are a formal expression underscored by trim details, but balanced by the human scale. The architecture is finely balanced between freedom and formality, and the personal design is given an extra accent in the newly developed facade bricks. The scheme contains 50 units of varying size in one and two stories, and a common house, which lies toward north. The project is the result of a closed competition in 1990.
Bibliography: Arkitektur DK 1993, 248

1:3000

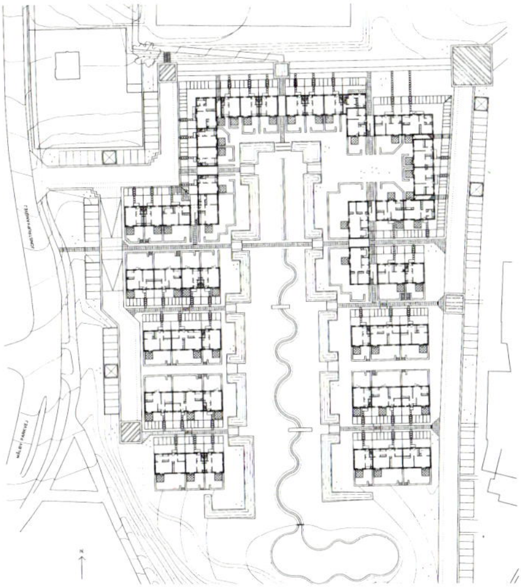

J285

E. Pihl & Søn office building

Nybrovej 116, Lyngby
1993-94

Client: E. Pihl & Søn A/S
Architect: KHR A/S Arkitekter
Landscape architect: Susanne Struch

In principle, the building consists of two parallel, three-story L-shaped blocks. The main entrance runs into the space between them. Almost all of the workplaces have access to the high ceilinged, brightly lit foyer, which lies at the angle of the two blocks. This underscores the feeling that the building is a unity, with a character evident in the smallest detail. All the furnishings were especially designed for the building in a stringent austere form idiom, making the interiors an example of well-detailed design. The spatial sequence is free of abrupt transitions, which expresses the firm's project oriented work method. The thin, specially designed steel window sections lie flush with the brickwork. The glass and brick surfaces thus become an abstract and weightless composition with associations to modernism's painters. The building is precisely and brilliantly tailored to its function and offers an inspiring innovation for architectural history.
Bibliography: Arkitektur DK 1994, 460

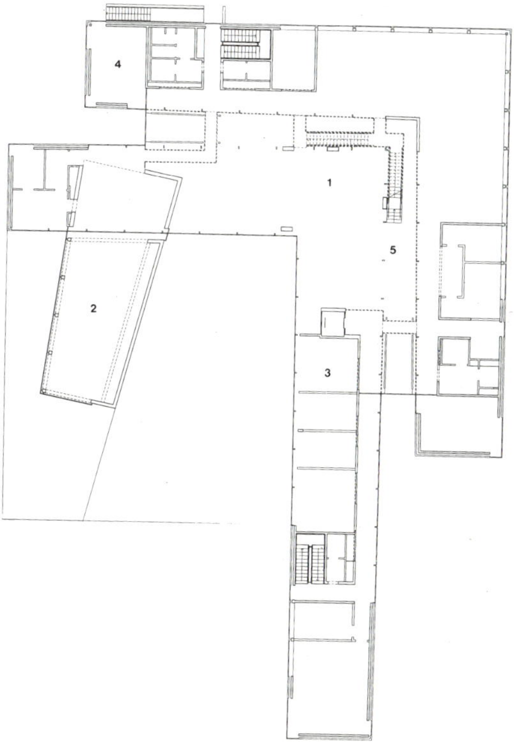

1:600

J289

The Egebjerggård quarter

Egebjerg Bygade et al, Ballerup
1985-96

Client: Ballerup Municipality
Architect: The municipal planning office in collaboration with city planners Dybbro & Haastrup, Angels Colom and Jan Gudmand-Høyer, Henning Larsens Tegnestue, Tegnestuen Vandkunsten et al

The code word for this new town quarter was integration: of function, traffic, forms of ownership, decisions and of different forms of architecture and art. A 1985 idea competition formed the basis for a time consuming planing process that included the neighbors and future clients, residents and users. The process was supervised by the municipal authorities in collaboration with the planning consultants, The State Building Research Institute and The Building Development Council. A project competition for the design of the first stage followed and was won by architects Angels Colom and Jan Gudmand-Høyer. After ten years of experimental town building, the result is a living and flexible urban structure with a wealth of architectural impressions, brought about by projects from many different architects. The integration of small businesses with the housing has proven difficult, but the structure is open and can be changed. As a planning type, Egebjerggård is a continuation of the 1970's ideals for informal and self-sown qualities, and is a reaction to the functionalistic division of the modernistic town. The wild architectural variations can appear chaotic, but this effect also makes the quarter both familiar and in keeping with the times.
Bibliography: Arkitektur DK 1991, 474 and 1990, 574

Angels Colom and
Jan Gudmand-Høyer

Tøndehvælvet. Tegnestuen Vandkunsten

Agernskrænten.
Henning Larsens Tegnestue

J293

Discount shopping center

Nybrovej 2, Gentofte
1995

Client: Ikea A/S
Architect: Tegnestuen Vandkunsten
Landscape architect: Tegnestuen Vandkunsten

The building facades form a sensible, subdued background for the giant advertising signs that signal the existence of the center's discount stores. The facades facing Lyngbyvej's highway traffic are closed with corrugated fiber cement and galvanized steel panels, and the large neon signs hang as signboards to be read while driving at high speeds. The facades facing the parking lot are less stringent, though there are no shopping windows. The sign posts form portals around the entrances and stairways. The exterior architecture reflects an area of the discount culture where thrift and quality can meet in a well-designed whole.

The Forest and Landscape Research Institute ____________ J294

Hørsholm Kongevej 11, Hørsholm
1995

Client: the Ministry of Environment and Energy
Architect: Bornebusch Tegnestue
Landscape architect: Jørgen Vesterholts Tegnestue

Two bent building wings with a spine consisting of a tall, thick wall, form a space in which the center's common functions are located. The offices and meeting rooms lie on the outer side of the wings, while the spinal wall contains secondary spaces such as rest rooms and archives. The one-sided corridor runs along the inner side of the scheme behind the steel and glass facade. The main plan is clear and informal, and the building is in harmony with the hilly wooded site, which offers a symbol of the center's area of research. This research area is further illustrated in the way the local flora grows into and up the buildings, and by the use of wood for the office facades, the structural members and the flooring.

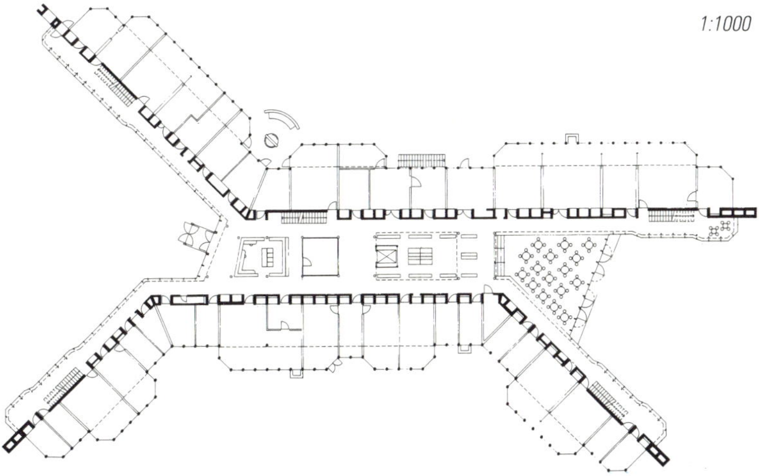

J295

Arken, Museum of Modern Art

Køge Bugt Strandpark,
Skovvej 100, Ishøj
1996

Client: Copenhagen County
Architect: Søren Robert Lund

Copenhagen County sponsored a competition in 1988 for the design of a new art museum, which was won by architecture student, Søren Robert Lund. His proposal placed the museum on the beach, which was in disagreement with the nature preservation regulations. Thus the siting was altered as was the museum's form, but the proposal's deconstructivistic concept was retained. A 150-meter long "art axis" is marked by a straight wall and a curved wall. Along the straight wall, there is a right-angled structure with exhibition spaces, while the curved wall runs against an arched structure with the lobby, multipurpose rooms, etc. The strong contrasts in the plan correspond to the great differences in ceiling and construction heights, and a choice of materials that indicates the various functions. The scheme has a dynamic, decomposed expression, which was inspired by architects like Frank Gehry, Zaha Hadid and Rem Kolhaas.
Bibliography: Arkitekten 1994, 138

1:2000

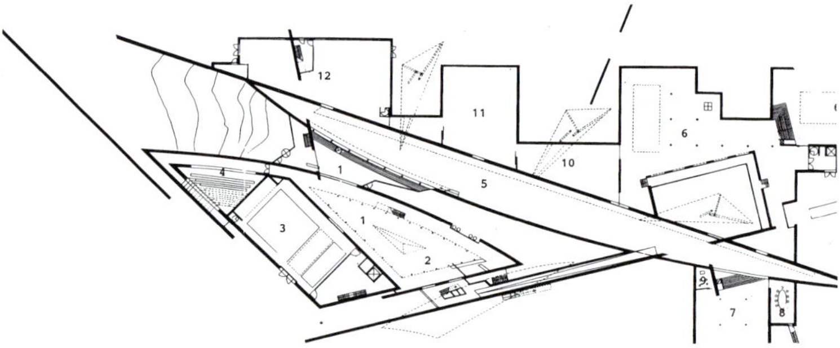

INDEX OF NAMES

Andersson, Sven-Ingvar and Steen Høyer: C.Th. Sørensen – en havekunstner. Arkitektens Forlag, 1993

Bidstrup, Knud: Ebenezers Disciple. Dansk Byplanlaboratorium, 1971

Bramsen, Bo (red.): København før og nu – og aldrig. Palle Fogtdal, 1987-90

Dirckinck-Holmfeld, Kim: Guide to Danish Architecture II. Arkitektens Forlag, 1995

Faber, Tobias: Dansk Arkitektur. Arkitektens Forlag, 1963 and 1977

Fisker, Steffen, Johan Fisker and Kim Dirckinck-Holmfeld (red.): Kay Fisker. Arkitektens Forlag, 1995

Gaardmand, Arne: Dansk Byplanlægning 1938-92. Arkitektens Forlag, 1993

Hauxner, Malene: Fantasiens Have. Arkitektens Forlag, 1993

Høyer, Steen, Annemarie Lund and Susanne Møldrup (ed.): Tilegnet Sven-Ingvar Andersson. Arkitektens Forlag, 1994

Jørgensen, Lisbet Balslev, Jørgen Sestoft and Morten Lund: Vilhelm Lauritzen. Bergiafonden. Aristo, 1994

Kunstakademiets Arkitektskole, Landskabslaboratoriet: Haver og Parker i København og omegn. Stencileret hæfte, 1979

Københavns parkmuligheder og deres udnyttelse. Stencileret skrift, udateret

Langberg, Harald: Danmarks Bygningskultur. Gyldendal, 1955

Langkilde, Hans Erling: Arkitekten Povl Baumann. Arkitektens Forlag, 1991

Lind, Olaf and Jonas Møller: Folkebolig – Boligfolk. Boligselskabernes Landsforening, 1994

Lund, Hakon (red.): Danmarks arkitektur. Nordisk Forlag, 1979

Lund, Hakon: De kongelige lysthaver. Gyldendal, 1977

Lund, Hakon and Anne Lise Thygesen: C.F. Hansen. Arkitektens Forlag, 1995

Lund, Nils-Ole: Nordisk Arkitektur. Arkitektens Forlag, 1991

Millech, Knud, Kay Fisker (red.): Danske arkitekturstrømninger 1850-1950. Østifternes Kreditforening, 1951

Pedersen, Johan: Arkitekten Arne Jacobsen. Arkitektens Forlag, 1954

Sestoft, Jørgen and Jørgen Hegner Christiansen: Guide to Danish Architecture I. Arkitektens Forlag, 1995
Rasmussen, Steen Eiler: København. G.E.C. Gads Forlag, 1969

Sørensen, C.Th.: Haver – tanker og arbejder. Chr. Ejlers' Forlag, 1975

Sørensen, C.Th.: Om haver. Emil Wienes Bogforlag, 1939

Trap Danmark, bind 2-5. G.E.C. Gads Forlag, 1959

Wassard, Erik: Ture i København. Politikens Forlag, 1994

There are also references to the following periodicals: Arkitekten, Arkitektur DK, Havekunst, Landskap and Landskab.

Olaf Lind, b. 1936, is the architectural critic for Morgenavisen Jyllands-Posten newspaper, and is a frequent contributor to periodicals ARKITEKTEN and ARKITEKTUR DK. He coauthored "Arkitekternes Årbog" together with Kim Dirckinck-Holmfeld and Leif Leer Sørensen. He wrote "Planen i Virkeligheden", and the large book on the development of Danish public housing, "Folkebolig - Boligfolk".
Olaf Lind is an architect and has practiced both as a building architect and city planner.

Annemarie Lund, b. 1948, is a landscape architect and since 1983 has been editor of the periodical, LANDSKAB. She has been a news writer for the periodical ARKITEKTEN since 1990. She coauthored "Havekunst i Danmark" (1990) with Sven-Ingvar Andersson, and contributed to the book "Tilegnet Sven-Ingvar Andersson" (1994). Annemarie Lund has been responsible for several exhibitions and catalogues about Danish landscape architecture. This included the travelling exhibition "Architecture Danois du Paysage Contemporain" (1991) and "Strejf i dansk havekunst" (1994).